基于《论语》英译的
中国典籍翻译传播创新研究

范 敏/著

图书在版编目(CIP)数据

基于《论语》英译的中国典籍翻译传播创新研究 / 范敏著. —上海：立信会计出版社，2023.7
（序伦财经文库）
ISBN 978-7-5429-7405-1

Ⅰ. ①基… Ⅱ. ①范… Ⅲ. ①《论语》-英语-翻译-研究 Ⅳ. ①H315.9②B222.25

中国国家版本馆 CIP 数据核字(2023)第 132762 号

责任编辑　　彭秋龙

基于《论语》英译的中国典籍翻译传播创新研究
JIYU LUNYU YINGYI DE ZHONGGUO DIANJI FANYI CHUANBO CHUANGXIN YANJIU

出版发行	立信会计出版社	
地　　址	上海市中山西路 2230 号　邮政编码　200235	
电　　话	(021)64411389　传　真　(021)64411325	
网　　址	www.lixinaph.com　电子邮箱　lixinaph2019@126.com	
网上书店	http://lixin.jd.com　http://lxkjcbs.tmall.com	
经　　销	各地新华书店	
印　　刷	江苏凤凰数码印务有限公司	
开　　本	710 毫米×1000 毫米　1/16	
印　　张	23.25	
字　　数	312 千字	
版　　次	2023 年 7 月第 1 版	
印　　次	2023 年 7 月第 1 次	
书　　号	ISBN 978-7-5429-7405-1/H	
定　　价	98.00 元	

如有印订差错，请与本社联系调换

基金项目:该专著系国家社科基金项目"《基于〈论语〉英译的中国典籍对外传播机制创新研究》(NO.17BYY063)"结题成果。

序　言

《基于〈论语〉英译的中国典籍翻译传播创新研究》是国家社科基金项目成果。从立项到结项，经过专家的多轮审核，本书的立论和价值得到众多专家的认可。

本书不仅要求作者具备深厚的传统文化功底，也要有翻译和英语表达准确与否的鉴别能力。这些对于外语研究者而言尚且具有较高的挑战性，但作者都做到了。本书语料丰富，分析过程扎实到位，匠心独运，研究结论令人信服。总体而言，本书学术价值相当高，值得出版。

本书结合定性与定量研究，深刻、系统、客观分析了《论语》英译概况、基于语料库的《论语》英译个案研究、《论语》英译传播与海外接受，并在此基础上探索具有一定理论价值而又能提升中华传统文化国际影响力的中国典籍翻译传播机制创新策略。

本书着重探讨了《论语》翻译传播过程中的文本内外制约因素，分析了译者风格、语篇特征、文化特征、修辞特征、翻译传播环境、翻译传播模式与翻译传播路径在《论语》翻译传播与海外接受过程中的重要作用，指出了中国典籍翻译传播机制的创新应主要围绕翻译传播主体、翻译传播路径与翻译传播人才培养三方面进行。

本书由《论语》英译的本体研究上升到中国典籍翻译传播机制的创新研究。当前中国典籍翻译传播要以全球化时代为契机，重视中华传统文化软实力与跨文化认同在中西文化交流中的重要作用，从时代、语境、文化、主体与受众等多维度思考中国典籍的翻译与传播，重构中国典籍对外传播话语体系及提高文化国际表达力，以进一步推动中西文化融通与国际文化交流。而其中关于中国典籍翻译传播机制的创新研究，对于中国典籍翻译传播和文化"走出去"传播战略都有着深远的指导意义。

总之，本书对于促进中国典籍翻译传播研究发展，推动中国典籍对外传播实践，促进中西文化对话与文明互鉴，建构中西融通话语体系，以及提升中国在世界的形象等都具有重要的学理意义与现实意义。

上海外国语大学博士生导师　冯庆华

2023 年 7 月

目　　录

第一章　绪论 …………………………………………………… 1
　一、本书的重要意义 ………………………………………… 1
　二、国内外研究现状 ………………………………………… 5
　三、研究思路与研究方法 …………………………………… 8
　四、小结 ……………………………………………………… 11

第二章　《论语》英译概况 …………………………………… 12
　一、《论语》简介 …………………………………………… 12
　二、《论语》节译本 ………………………………………… 15
　三、《论语》编译本 ………………………………………… 16
　四、《论语》全译本 ………………………………………… 22
　五、小结 ……………………………………………………… 33

第三章　基于语料库的《论语》英译个案研究 ……………… 34
　一、《论语》翻译语料库的设计与应用 …………………… 34
　二、《论语》中的语篇特征及翻译 ………………………… 48
　三、《论语》中的文化特征及翻译 ………………………… 94
　四、《论语》中的修辞特征及翻译 ………………………… 129
　五、小结 ……………………………………………………… 156

第四章 《论语》英译传播与海外接受 ……………… 157
　　一、《论语》英译传播历程 ……………………………… 157
　　二、《论语》英译传播模式 ……………………………… 164
　　三、《论语》英译传播途径 ……………………………… 175
　　四、《论语》英译海外接受调查 ………………………… 184
　　五、小结 …………………………………………………… 189

第五章 中国典籍翻译传播机制创新探索 ……………… 190
　　一、中国典籍翻译传播现状 ……………………………… 190
　　二、中国典籍翻译传播主体多元化 ……………………… 196
　　三、中国典籍翻译传播路径创新 ………………………… 206
　　四、中国典籍翻译传播人才培养模式创新 ……………… 225
　　五、小结 …………………………………………………… 248

第六章 结论与展望 ……………………………………… 249
　　一、结论 …………………………………………………… 249
　　二、展望 …………………………………………………… 252

参考文献 ……………………………………………………… 254

附录 第三章例句英译分析示例 …………………………… 276

后记 …………………………………………………………… 361

第一章 绪 论

随着中国国力的日益增强以及中国地位的崛起,中华优秀传统文化典籍的翻译及其传播越来越受到关注。其中,中华优秀传统文化的主流思想儒家文化以修己治人、治国理政、教化民众为宗旨,对东西文明互鉴与发展产生了重要影响。因此,以儒家文化为代表的中国典籍《论语》的翻译传播也引起更多重视。本章主要从研究意义、国内外研究现状、研究思路与研究方法等方面进行论述。

一、本书的重要意义

《论语》在世界经典研究中不可缺失,是人类文明史中重要的儒家文化经典,对东西世界文明发展产生了重要作用。此外,当前国家语言文化战略非常重视以《论语》为代表的中华优秀传统文化的对外传播。因此,本书对于促进中西文化交流具有重要的社会意义、学理意义与现实意义。

(一) 社会意义

《论语》既具有民族特点,又具有世界普适性特点,其中所"蕴含的博大而深厚的思想是可以穿越时空的,时至今日仍然闪耀着智慧的光芒。现代社会出现的新问题,层出不穷的新思潮,都不能掩盖《论语》的光辉;相反,却一遍又一遍验证着它的普世与超越"(文若愚,2013)。从孔子时代至今,儒家文化一直是中华文化的主线,是中华传统文化的重要组成部分,也是中华民族生生不息、发展壮大的重要滋养。

在当前的国际形势大局中,国家实力的较量日益复杂。这不仅体现在政治、军事、社会、经济力量等方面,还体现在文化的生命力与影响力上。"文化只有在客观地反映人类对自然和人类自身活动的真理性认识的时候,才具有生命力,才能是各种文化思想推动整个社会不断向前发展的内驱力。而中国的传统文化博大精深、厚德载物,具有充分的精神底蕴和活力,所以中华民族才能在历史的发展中演变中不断壮大,虽经无数劫难而终能重新走向辉煌"(郑铁生,2016)。

在当前全球化语境下,人类面对的最大焦虑是自我身份认同与他者、异域、全球一体化等层面的冲突与张力所带来的困惑。塞缪尔·亨廷顿认为,冷战后的世界,冲突的基本根源是文化方面的差异(塞缪尔·亨廷顿,2010)。习近平总书记曾强调:思想文化是一个国家、一个民族的灵魂(习近平,2014)。2013年习近平指出,要用辩证唯物主义视角研究儒家思想,使其在新时代发挥积极作用(钟岳文,2014)。习近平还强调,中华优秀传统文化是国家文化的重要软实力,而"提高国家文化软实力,关系我国在世界文化格局中的定位,关系我国国际地位和国际影响力"(高永中,2014)。我们相信构建中华传统文化价值体系的要素可以在以《论语》为主导的儒家文化中溯源,并经过继承创新,对东西方文化产生深远影响。

当前,中国在践行优秀社会传统文化价值观的同时,也在大力推行"中国文化走出去"战略。在该文化战略影响下,更多的中华优秀传统文化将会传播到国外,这将进一步提升中华文化在国外的影响力与竞争力。安乐哲曾说,"儒学不是中国的儒学,而是世界的儒学"(卞俊峰,2019)。那么,在中西文化互动过程中,儒家的社会价值观能否激发出一套新的社会价值、伦理道德,帮助中国培育一种全球的责任意识,使之既利于自身,又利于社会呢?此外,以儒学为代表的中华传统文化及其海外传播是否会受到挑战,应该怎样解决中西文化融通发展?这些问题的思考使得本书更加具有重要的社会意义。

(二) 学理意义

本书具有一定的科学指导价值,可为中国典籍翻译传播提供理论参考与实践借鉴。目前学界多采用后殖民主义等西方翻译理论指导中国典籍翻译,这些理论多由西方国家提出,对中国文化语境考察不足。本书可以对这些翻译理论进行验证、修正和补充。本书基于图里(Toury,1995)的描述翻译理论,结合中国语境,注重客观思考,避免主观推断和规定性论述,重在分析以《论语》为个案的中国典籍翻译和传播策略,不仅重视中国典籍译本的翻译讨论,而且重视中国典籍对外传播路径在翻译传播过程中的重要作用。

本书所探讨的中国典籍翻译主要是指中国古代典籍翻译,尤其是指先秦典籍。中国先秦典籍内容以政治、军事、伦理以及自然哲学思想为主,篇幅短小,语言精练,加之汉字字体和意义变迁、意识形态的时代更替,以及誊写讹误,导致典籍内容对后人而言字义晦涩、句读不一,原文意义不定,有较大的阐释空间(刘骥翔,2019)。相较于其他文学(古代小说、戏剧和诗歌)翻译,中国先秦哲学类典籍翻译会在译本内附有大量副文本,如序言、前言、注释、评论、附录等,而且由于缺失语境,文本解读更具有抽象性、思辨性与哲理性。由此可见,根据文体特征不同,中国典籍各类文本的翻译和诠释存在一定差异,但其翻译传播主体研究、翻译传播受众研究、翻译传播路径研究以及翻译传播人才培养研究等方面也有很多共性特点,值得进一步思考与探讨。

本书还可为中国典籍翻译传播理论提供有力支撑。现在国家认识到在全球建构文化软实力可以提高中华文化影响力,但当前我国对提高中华传统文化软实力的对外传播研究不足。本书结合文化学、语言学、翻译学与传播学等理论,分析了《论语》的英译传播历程、《论语》英译传播模式与传播途径,以及《论语》英译海外接受调查中出现的问题,并基于《论语》英译传播研究探讨了中国典籍翻译传播的机制创新等,形成了属于中国典籍的翻译传播创新理论,有助于丰富并完善现有传播理论研究。

此外,本书有助于我们在当前社会语境对外传播中华优秀文化价值观,促进中外话语融通体系构建,提高中国文化国际影响力,有利于建设富有创新力的国际话语理论体系。本书还探讨了跨文化传播与社会意识形态问题,可以推进相关学科如翻译学、传播学与社会学研究的发展,有利于进一步推动中西文化沟通与交流。

(三)现实意义

本书注重理论联系实际,结合个案与实证研究,探讨基于《论语》翻译与传播的中国典籍翻译传播路径等,有助于人们更深入思考以《论语》为代表的中国典籍翻译传播过程中的社会互动,有助于我们共同解决世界语言、文化与信仰等问题,增强国外受众对中华传统文化的理解与接受,提高儒学的世界意义。

本书注重中国典籍翻译传播过程中提升中国文化形象的问题。一个国家的文化形象往往能反映该国家的文化传统、文化软实力与文化创造力,也在某种程度上影响该国家的国际话语权与影响力。因此,注重形象可以使外部事物产生内在变化,消除彼此之间的距离感,从而更加有助于加强国际交流与对话。译介内容的选择将在很大程度上影响其在异域国家所塑造的国家形象。因此,本书注重中国典籍的译介内容,并注重从文化战略高度提高译文国际表达力,用外国受众较易接受的方式和语言传播中华优秀传统文化,增进外国受众对中华文化的了解,从而有助于构建有效的中国典籍翻译传播模式,并为翻译批评、翻译实践、翻译教学以及翻译传播人才培养提供参考。

总之,本书探讨中国典籍的翻译传播主体如何超越时空、跨越国度,将中华优秀传统文化得体、有效、系统地传达给西方,并为西方所认可,有助于我们在复杂的国际环境中增强文化软实力,弘扬传统文化,传播和谐世界理念,解决世界语言、文化与信仰等国际冲突问题。在世界越发关注中国,而中华文化时常被误读的情况下,本书更加具有社会意义、学理意义和现实意义。

二、国内外研究现状

《论语》的英译研究始于20世纪90年代，主要集中在翻译领域。学者最初从语言层面开展研究，后来随着文化研究的转向，逐渐过渡到《论语》文化研究及其翻译传播研究。

《论语》英译的国内研究自20世纪90年代逐渐实现零的突破，研究焦点多限于翻译感悟，如汪福祥(1996)、刘重德(1996)、李天辰(1999)。21世纪《论语》英译研究随着语言学理论与文化研究发展进入跨学科研究时期。《论语》英译研究逐渐转向文化研究与语言学研究，表现为"三多三少"的特点。

三多：一是多为语言层面的个别核心哲学词语诠释，如杨平(2008)对核心概念"仁"的英译分析。二是多为单个译者评述，如钟明国(2009)、陈国兴(2010)与王东波(2011)分别探讨了辜鸿铭与安乐哲的翻译思想。三是多为译者策略的概括比较，如儒风(2008)的译者研究。李伟荣(2009)指出早期《论语》翻译传播过程中基督化倾向是最突出的诠释精神，后来逐渐体现怀疑精神和求实精神。杨平(2012)比较了西方汉学家与海内外华人的《论语》翻译文化传播与利用现象。金学琴(2015)探讨了理雅各和森舸澜译本的注疏与"学术型翻译"翻译策略。

三少：一是宏观研究少，从国家战略高度对《论语》对外传播研究有待增强。二是跨学科研究少，如黄国文(2006,2011)、孟健(2012)、陈旸(2012)、黄勇(2012)分别从语篇语言学、文化顺应论、功能语言学、语料库语言学视角探讨《论语》翻译，但跨学科研究仍待增强。三是定量与定性研究结合少，如张升君、文军(2008)基于语料库探讨了刘殿爵和Arthur Waley两个译本，孟怡村(2011)运用语料库探讨了哲学词"仁义礼智信"的翻译策略，周小玲(2011)基于语料库探讨了理雅各译者文体研究，黄勇(2012)基于语料库对韦利译本进行定量与定性分析。但是,这些研究仅限在某几个译本的某个层面进行,定量与定性分析结合不足,因此未能对《论语》文化内容、译者风格及其受众接受的影响因素等进行深入分析。

2013年习近平总书记强调,要继承与弘扬中华优秀传统文化。周明伟也多次呼吁,中华文化能否"走出去"很大程度上依赖于翻译质量与国际输出能力建设。国家文化战略与国际文化交流的需求也促使更多学者越来越关注《论语》《尚书》《中庸》《道德经》等中国典籍的翻译传播。这在一定程度上促使中西方学者对中华文化和儒家思想进行深入研究。在中华优秀传统文化崛起环境下,《论语》翻译传播研究也由边缘走向中心,进入主流研究时期,更多关注《论语》翻译的外围研究,强调与翻译工作相关的间接因素对文化传播战略的实现具有重要作用。

这一阶段的研究内容主要包括:儒家文化英译、国家形象建构与影响力、译者身份与话语权、儒家文化传播等。例如,金学勤(2015)、赵巍(2015)、张政(2015)、范敏(2015,2016,2017,2019,2021)、李伟荣(2015)、鞠玉梅(2016)、张晓雪(2018)、陶友兰(2018)、谷慧娟(2019)、刘立胜(2020)等学者分别探讨了《论语》"学术型"典籍翻译、《论语》中国中心主义、《论语》术语文化内涵、《论语》文化翻译策略及传播路径与方法、《论语》文化传播外部路径、《论语》修辞与话语权威、《论语》英译本海外传播现状与对策探讨、《论语》英译海外传播多元化策略、《论语》英译与中华文化"走出去"以及金安平《论语》英译与海外传播等问题。

还有很多学者对中国典籍的翻译、传播与出版等作出探索。例如,陈梅与文军(2011)、罗选民与杨文地(2012)、王宏(2012)、许多与许钧(2015)、李宁(2015)、裘禾敏(2016)、杨柳(2016)、李伟荣(2016)等学者分别从国外阅读市场、文化自觉与中国典籍、中国典籍译介情况与对策、《大中华文库》评价与思考、《大中华文库》国人英译本海外接受调查、中华传统文化海外传播策略、中国典籍英译趋势、中国典籍出版等维度对中国典籍翻译传播进行探索。

此外,有些学者在其著作中探讨了基于个案的中国典籍在英语世界的翻译与传播。例如,谭晓丽(2012)探讨了安乐哲儒学典籍英译研究,王琰(2013)探讨了汉学视域中的英译研究,王鹏飞(2014)探讨了《红楼梦》在英语世界的译介与研究,赵征军(2015)探讨了《牡丹亭》的译介,赵长江(2017)探讨了19世纪中国文化典籍英译史,郭晓春(2018)探讨了《楚辞》在英语世界的译介与研究,魏倩倩(2018)探讨了《孙子兵法》在英语世界的英译与传播,张德福(2018)探讨了19世纪60年代以来汉学家的《论语》英译研究,陈向红(2019)探讨了杨宪益作品在英语世界的翻译、传播与接受研究,李海军等(2019)探讨了《聊斋志异》的英语译介研究(1842—1948年),范祥涛(2020)探讨了哲学、历史、诗词歌赋、小说、戏剧和中医药等不同文体的中华典籍外译研究,并提出选题建议。

另外,有很多中国学者和国外学者在国外重要刊物发表相关文章,推动了中华优秀传统文化的翻译与传播。他们主要从社会学、意识形态与中西哲学比较等视角阐述中国典籍翻译的思想内容。研究内容主要涉及中国典籍思想介绍、解读、译本述评、关键词翻译、翻译策略及文化传播等问题。例如,Arthur F. Wright(1960)、Daniel K. Gardner(2003)、Pertti Nikkilä(1992)、Yao Xinzhong(2000)、Chang Chiyun 和 Orient Lee(2012)、Fan Min(2015,2021)、Peimin Ni(2017)等阐释了儒学的核心概念内涵、儒学思想的意义、儒家文化的现代解读、中华传统文化的生命力及其创新等问题,并结合现当代语境探讨了西方学者对中华传统文化关键词的理解、领悟与接受等问题。又如,Fan Min(2007)、Yang Huiling(2011)、Cui Ying(2016)、Qian Menghan(2017)、Wang Jinbo(2020)等分别探讨了《红楼梦》中的习语翻译、理雅各的中国典籍翻译及其政治含义、中国典籍翻译的理论与实践、企鹅出版经典以及中国典籍的回译等,对中国典籍的翻译策略、文化传播、译文出版与海外接受等进行探索。

综上所述,《论语》等中国典籍翻译研究的动态趋势表现为:研究地位由边缘走向主流,研究内容趋向多元化,研究方法由关注语言过渡到关注文化,由单一译本评价研究过渡到多个译本比较评价研究,由单一理论应用过渡到跨学科研究,由定性研究过渡到定量与定性结合研究。上述研究成果奠定了良好的基础。但就全局而言,国内外研究零散研究多,系统研究少,未能深入系统探讨中国典籍翻译传播;关注语言对比多,关注文化语境少,未能从宏观层面多方位把握考量;单一理论研究多,跨学科理论研究少;研究方法比较单一,定性与定量分析结合不够,实证研究与案例分析有待加强。目前深入系统探究提高中华文化国际影响力的中国典籍的翻译传播研究有待进一步探索。

　　由此可见,中国典籍的翻译传播研究空间很大,广度与深度仍待扩展。我们可以在上述研究的基础上,进一步深入探讨《论语》在英语世界的翻译与传播研究,并基于《论语》的英译传播研究对中国典籍文化传播机制的创新研究进行实践探索。因此,本书基于国内外文献,结合定量与定性研究,通过讨论《论语》五译本的语篇特征、文化特征、修辞特征及其翻译,试图全面揭示译文调整现象以及译者为此提出某些有规律性翻译策略的原因。此外,通过讨论《论语》的英译概况、传播历程、传播模式、传播途径与海外接受,尝试对中华传统文化在海外的传播与接受提出建设性建议,并结合当前形势对中国典籍文化传播的创新机制进行探讨,以期为中国的典籍文化英译与翻译传播研究提供启示,为提升中国经典文化国际影响力作出理论贡献,并总结出较为有效的以《论语》为代表的中国典籍翻译传播的创新路径。

三、研究思路与研究方法

　　本书借助语料库与文化翻译理论、篇章语言学与接受美学等理论对《论语》五个英译本(理雅各、辜鸿铭、刘殿爵、安乐哲与罗思文、森舸澜)的翻译传播进行研究,并基于该个案研究系统诠释中国典籍的翻译传播与海外接受的创新机制问题。

（一）研究思路

首先，本书根据篇章语言学与话语分析理论、文化翻译理论与接受美学建构研究框架，注重"内部"与"外部"研究相结合。人们可按"内在理路"和"外在理路"评析学术事件："内在理路"是指学术自身的传承、对话与流变如何影响学术的发展，"外在理路"则关注具体的历史社会因素如何形塑了一个时代的学术旨趣和特性（乔纳森·波特、玛格丽特·韦斯雷尔，2006）。因此，本书的内部研究侧重语篇的形式转换、意义转换、翻译技巧等内容，外部研究侧重各种外部制约因素如意识形态、文化态度、语言规范、历史环境等对翻译传播过程的影响，探讨在中西文化交流的不同时期，《论语》英译策略、翻译传播模式、翻译传播途径等对《论语》海外接受的影响程度及存在的问题。

其次，本书借鉴国际汉学研究，采用比较方法与实证研究方法，注重《论语》文化英译的历时思考。在比较译本时，本书注重选择不同时期有重要影响的《论语》译本，并梳理比较《论语》五译本。本书通过探讨《论语》英译概况、基于语料库的《论语》英译个案研究、《论语》英译传播与海外接受，阐释《论语》向世界译介传播的轨迹和方式、中华传统文化在英语世界的容纳和接受以及英语国家在历史进程发展中在不同的政治、经济和文化条件中形成的"中国观念"，分析翻译传播主体与文化语境等在翻译传播过程的作用，并在此基础上进一步对中国典籍翻译传播的机制创新进行探索，指出为使外国受众理解和接受我国传统文化，翻译传播主体在语言文化战略、批评话语分析与跨文化传播视域下，探索中华传统文化翻译传播与受众接受的创新路径。

最后，本书注重理性研究，"理性尊重一切'有根据的、合逻辑的、可理解的'观点；探讨依据诠释学的进路，辨明'究竟说什么、想要说什么、能够说什么、应该说什么'"（傅佩荣，2018）。本书结合定量与定性分析，从微观、中观与宏观上进行探讨，思考这些核心价值词汇的不同翻译及其原因。在微观与中观上，本书试图揭示译文中出现的对于源语文本内容进行调整的原因以及译者为此提出某些有规律性翻译策略的动机及其影响因素,在研究过程中注意结合实证案例分析,探讨译者如何处理《论语》高频文化词,如何补偿上下文语境与社会语境,并根据译入语历史环境提高《论语》文化翻译传播。在宏观上,本书依据对《论语》英译比较分析的线索,梳理中华传统文化有效"走出去"以及提高中华文化国际影响力的相关问题,重点探讨外部环境等制约因素对《论语》文化翻译融通发展的影响以及《论语》文化对社会的形塑影响,在更广阔的学术视野下探讨以《论语》为代表的中国典籍的英译研究、翻译策略与传播方式。

总之,本书基于《论语》英译传播与海外接受,探讨为使西方受众真正理解并接受中华优秀文化,提升中华文化国际影响力,译者在传播学、翻译学与篇章语言学关照以及跨文化传播视域下,通过同西方学术话语与当代语境对接,探索中国典籍翻译传播与接受的创新方式与创新路径。本书还探讨了中国典籍翻译人才的创新培养理念及其路径,为中国典籍翻译事业的发展提供有力支撑。

(二) 研究方法

(1) 比较分析法。本书从微观与宏观上比较五译本的词、句、语篇、修辞与文化翻译,探讨《论语》译者风格与翻译策略;还通过比较不同历史阶段的《论语》翻译,探讨儒家文化在不同社会语境下的接受情况。

(2) 跨学科研究法。本书融合翻译学、语言学、传播学与接受美学等学科理论知识,借助辩证法与系统论,客观、系统、全面地分析《论语》的文化思想(如文化隐喻、文化典故与文化概念)的英译、传播与接受。

(3) 描述性研究法。本书基于图里的描述翻译理论,把翻译当作文化事实,将文本语境化,以描述、解释以及预测该研究现象为主要目标,重在找到影响翻译行为背后的社会文化规范,并客观揭示翻译行为背后的各种原因。

（4）归纳与演绎结合法。本书依据典籍《论语》五译本译介比较分析线索，归纳出《论语》翻译规律、传播模式和传播途径，再借助相关理论，通过演绎法将该结论应用到中国典籍翻译中检验所得结论，以此循环往复，修正、补充所得结论。

（5）定性与定量结合法。本书利用语料库软件对《论语》五个英译本进行统计分析，通过词频、关键值等比较，分析《论语》原文、译文以及国内外文化环境、不同国家政策与读者层次等的异同。本书通过对五译本标准化类符/形符比、句长与特色词以及读者评价等比较，运用翻译学与批评话语分析等理论，分析影响儒家文化接受的各种因素。

（6）历时与共时研究。本书不仅注重不同时期《论语》及其英译的翻译传播与读者接受情况，而且关注某一时期《论语》翻译在跨文化传播中的接受情况及其原因。

四、小结

本书基于相关文献研究，借助个案研究、定性与定量结合等研究方法，结合文化理论、翻译理论与语言学理论探讨五译本在语言风格与翻译策略上的异同以及《论语》英译的海外传播与接受。在此基础上，本书进一步探讨基于《论语》英译传播的中国典籍的翻译传播与接受。本书对于提高《论语》等中国典籍在国外的传播接受，增强中华传统文化软实力、提升中华文化影响力都具有重要的指导意义，还有助于我们在复杂的国际环境中增强国际传播能力，促进中外文化交流与互鉴。

第二章 《论语》英译概况

《论语》英译迄今已有 300 余年历史。目前,《论语》的原创译本主要包括全译、节译、编译、译注、改译等各种形态的翻译。本书主要从《论语》简介以及《论语》英译的三种主要变译本(节译本、编译本、全译本)等方面论述。

一、《论语》简介

《论语》是中国最早的语录体著作,集中体现了孔子的政治主张、思想道德与教育理念。《论语》约成于战国初年。经秦传到西汉有三种《论语》:(1)《鲁论》,20 篇;(2)《齐论》,22 篇,比前者多《问王》《知道》2 篇;(3)《古论语》,出于孔壁,21 篇,有《子张》2 篇,篇次亦与《鲁论》《齐论》不同。汉成帝时,张禹授《鲁论》,并讲《齐论》,称《张侯论》。东汉末,郑玄以《鲁论》为基础,参考《齐论》和《古论语》,为之作注,成为后世的流传本(中国孔子基金会,1997)。

《论语》全书结构具有逻辑性特征,内容与结构浑然一体。《论语》各篇章之间看似没有逻辑,还有很多重复章节,甚至有些字句完全相同,但是整体上看,《论语》的篇章结构是经过深思熟虑进行设计的。例如,"博学于文",先见于《论语·雍也》,又见于《论语·颜渊》;"巧言令色,鲜矣仁",先见于《论语·学而》,又见于《论语·阳货》。表面上看,"结构在研究成果的形式上,似乎是一种'硬件',但它是一种'会思想的硬件'。思想可以通过结构,进行模式化的放大;结构可以通过思想,进行生命化的演绎"(杨义,2016)。

杨朝明也指出,"当我们回看《论语》时,发现它其实有内在的严密逻辑。《论语》首篇围绕做人这一个中心问题展开,以下各篇分别谈为政以德、守礼明礼、择仁处仁等,层层剥离,依次展开"(杨朝明,2013)。例如,孔子在《论语·尧曰》(即《论语》的最后一章)中提出人要"三知",即"知命""知礼""知言"。"子曰:'不知命,无以为君子也。不知礼,无以立也。不知言,无以知人也'。"其意思是说:"不懂得命运,就不可能成为君子。不懂得礼,就没有办法立足于社会。不懂得分辨人家的言语,便不能了解别人。"孔子认为,命运具有客观性与不可预知性,君子需要学会安身立命,熟悉礼制的内容与形式,并深谙人性,只有这样才可以在社会真正立足。全部《论语》以此终篇,与第一章相呼应,从自觉努力学习开始到获取知命、知礼、知言的能力,是人生的全部内容,是生命的真正意义与价值。由此可见,全书的结构、形式与内容浑然一体。

《论语》共分 20 篇,分别为《学而》篇、《为政》篇、《八佾》篇、《里仁》篇、《公冶长》篇、《雍也》篇、《述而》篇、《泰伯》篇、《子罕》篇、《乡党》篇、《先进》篇、《颜渊》篇、《子路》篇、《宪问》篇、《卫灵公》篇、《季氏》篇、《阳货》篇、《微子》篇、《子张》篇与《尧曰》篇。

- 《学而》篇第一,主要讲"务本"的道理,重点探讨学习、自省、和为贵以及仁、孝、信等道德范畴。
- 《为政》篇第二,主要涉及孔子治理国家的道理和方法、学习与思考的关系以及对孝、悌等的进一步阐述。
- 《八佾》篇第三,主要涉及礼制、礼节的种种规定,强调"君使臣以礼,臣事君以忠"的政治道德主张。
- 《里仁》篇第四,主要涉及义与利的关系、个人仁德修养、孝敬父母以及君子与小人的区别等内容。
- 《公冶长》篇第五,主要以仁德为主线探讨仁德特征,如"听其言而观其行""敏而好学,不耻下问""其行己也恭,其事上也敬,其养民也惠,其使民也义""三思而后行"等。

- 《雍也》篇第六,主要记录孔子和弟子们的言行,讨论君子与为政者的美德修行,强调"仁"且"智"并"中庸"才是美德。
- 《述而》篇第七,探讨了孔子的教育思想和"三人行,必有我师"的学习态度以及对仁德等道德范畴的进一步阐释。
- 《泰伯》篇第八,主要涉及孔子的道德思想以及曾子在若干问题上的见解、孔子教学方法和教育思想的进一步发挥,如"鸟之将死,其鸣也哀;人之将死,其言也善""士不可以不弘毅,任重而道远"等。
- 《子罕》篇第九,主要涉及孔子的道德教育思想,重在孔子的行事风格与主张等,如"知者不惑,仁者不忧,勇者不惧""逝者如斯夫,不舍昼夜"等。
- 《乡党》篇第十,主要涉及孔子的言谈举止、衣食住行和生活习惯,称赞孔子的行为举止都符合"礼"的君子风范。
- 《先进》篇第十一,主要记录孔子的教育言论、中庸思想、学习知识与做官的关系以及孔子对待鬼神、生死问题的态度。
- 《颜渊》篇第十二,主要涉及孔子的教育思想、如何实行仁德、为政以及遵守礼仪的处世态度。
- 《子路》篇第十三,主要记录孔子论述为人和为政的教育思想与政治主张,如"居处恭、执事敬、与人忠""名不正则言不顺,言不顺则事不成"等。
- 《宪问》篇第十四,主要记录为政之人、退隐之士以及为政之德等内容,探讨君子品德、孔子对当时社会评论以及"见利思义"的义利观等,如"不在其位,不谋其政""仁者不忧,知者不惑,勇者不惧"等。
- 《卫灵公》篇第十五,主要记录孔子及其弟子在周游列国时关于仁德治国、教育思想等的言论,如"人能弘道,非道弘人""人无远虑,必有近忧"等。
- 《季氏》篇第十六,主要记录孔子论君子修身以及如何用礼法治国,内容涉及孔子的政治思想、教育思想、天命思想、道德修养等。

- 《阳货》篇第十七,主要记录孔子论述仁德、礼乐治国之道与孔子为实现政治抱负和理想的处世权变思想。
- 《微子》篇第十八,主要记录孔子及其弟子周游列国中的言行及周游途中世人对于乱世的看法,如"往者不可谏,来者犹可追"等。
- 《子张》篇第十九,主要记录孔子和弟子们探讨求学为道的言论以及弟子对孔子的敬仰,如"百工居肆以成其事,君子学以致其道""博学而笃志,切问而近思,仁在其中矣"等。
- 《尧曰》篇第二十,主要记录古代圣贤言论和孔子对于为政的论述,如"君子惠而不费,劳而不怨,欲而不贪,泰而不骄,威而不猛""不知命,无以为君子也""宽则得众,信则民任"等。

由上所述,《论语》中的思想寓意深刻,意义深远。其中,"仁爱""德政""礼治"等思想对于指导世人为人处世与治国理政都具有重要价值。如果将《论语》中的文化思想成功译介到国外,也必定对西方文明产生重要影响。因此,根据英语世界读者的个性特点与接受情况,译者可以采用各种变译策略对《论语》中的文化内容进行变通、翻译与传播,满足他们的不同需求,有力推动中华传统文化走向世界,并有力促进世界文明的交流与互鉴。

二、《论语》节译本

《论语》节译本主要是指译者选取《论语》中的部分章节按照先后顺序进行翻译出版的译本。《论语》节译本以1809年的马士曼的英译本最为典型。

马士曼作为一位传教士,他翻译《论语》的目的就是要向西方人展现汉语的形式与特征,使这种语言不再神秘,从而引领他们深入研究中国文学与典籍著作,最终达到向中国人介绍西方的科学发现,尤其是向中国人介绍至纯至善的《圣经》以帮助他们开辟道路的目的(Marshman,1809)。

1809年,传教士马士曼在印度出版了他翻译的《孔子著作》第一卷。这是《论语》英译的最早版本,也是节译本。马士曼"不仅是一位传教士和教育家,同时还是一位颇有造诣的学者、语言学家、神学家和翻译家"(高志强,2016)。马希曼虽然没有到过中国,但他凭借对语言的造诣并在华人的帮助下学习中文,完成了《论语》第一章至第九章的翻译。

马士曼的《论语》译本结构如下:(1) 浸信会秘书C. E. Wilson写给Fletcher Moorshead的信;(2) 封皮页;(3) 书的全名页;(4) 献辞;(5) 勘误表;(6) 附录;(7) 论汉语的文字和读音,附有基本字和单音节字的表(包括论文全名页、内容大概、勘误表);(8) 孔子生平(包括根据《史记·孔子世家》翻译的孔子生平、"五经四书"介绍、《论语》各篇大意、中国简明上古史和马士曼翻译原则);(9)《论语》前十篇的翻译。

为了让英国学者尽快掌握汉语知识,马士曼尽量采用字字对译的方式,给每一个汉字和对应的英文单词编号。

虽然马士曼后来并没有完成《论语》剩余部分的翻译,但是已出版译本对于中国儒家思想的对外传播起到了重要作用。例如,1836年,当美国著名学者爱默生读到马士曼翻译的《孔子著作》时,开始对孔子思想产生兴趣,并在1843年4月他主编的《日晷》(*Dial*)杂志上选登了孔子的21段语录,题为《孔子语录》(崔玉军,2010)。

三、《论语》编译本

《论语》编译本主要是指译者为了满足读者需求,对《论语》中的文化内容有目的地进行选择翻译并出版的译本。典型的《论语》编译本有林语堂(1938)、丁往道(2008)、蔡志忠(2018)等译本。

（一）林语堂译本

林语堂的《论语》编译本 The Wisdom of Confucius 出版于1938年。林语堂译本对于促进中西文化交流对话以及中国典籍翻译具有重要的启示意义。林语堂的编译思想主要体现在以下两个方面。

1. 对儒家思想普世价值的主题提炼

在导论中，林语堂把孔子思想影响主要归结于三个方面：一是源自孔子学说的严谨和明确。孔子不是超验主义者，也从不干涉超世俗的事情。孔子思想是朴实的，全部涉及生命中的各种普通关系。孔子相信美德是建立在知识的基础上，是建立在对自己心灵的了解和对人类的认知之上的。二是因为当时的环境。当时的封建制度是百姓痛苦的主要原因。而孔子学说的伟大之处就是教导皇帝如何在其无限专制统治中正确使用自己的权力。但是皇帝只是所有当权者的典型——封建公爵、法官和家族之父。每个人只有服从孔子所规定的道德规范，才能正确地履行自己的职责。中国的统治者在儒家学说中找到了王权最坚强的基础，因此支持其思想的传播。三是《论语》包含了孔子学说的要旨，值得研究。这些思想、行为和准则形成了一种以简洁、平实著称的代码。我们不得不佩服其中所蕴含的人格力量、实践智慧和对人类需求的洞察，这也使得孔子能够在不要求任何神授的情况下广泛传播其思想与主张。

2. 林语堂所采用的编译策略

林语堂在翻译时具有强烈的读者意识。为了让普通读者容易理解儒家思想，林语堂没有按照传统的《论语》章节顺序进行翻译，而是从形式编排到内容处理再到语言表达都采用了独具特色的编译策略。

在导论部分，林语堂介绍了孔子思想的特性、孔子的品格、本书的取材、计划以及翻译方法，为英语读者了解孔子及其思想打开了一扇窗。在正文部分，林语堂整合了儒家经典《大学》《中庸》《论语》和《孟子》与《礼记》的主要内容，通过精心摘选编译，阐述了儒家思想体系的核心价值观,涵盖了孔子生平、中庸思想、道德与政治、理想社会、以六艺施教、礼乐与人性等内容,提高了英语世界《论语》译文的可读性,增强了英语读者对儒家思想的理解与接受。

在正文中,《论语》题目意译为 The Wisdom of Confucius。林语堂在翻译中注重译文可读性,围绕章节主题选取孔子与弟子语录进行翻译并注重译文的衔接与连贯。此外,还对一些具有中国特色的儒家概念(如灶神、奥神与天)的翻译与历史人名(如周公)的翻译作出注释。该类译文虽然不利于读者从原文对照角度进行学术意义的比较研究,但更容易拉近其与英语读者的距离。

以"子曰:'甚矣,吾衰也!久矣,吾不复梦见周公。'"(《论语·述而》)为例,林语堂翻译为"Confucius said, 'My, how old I have grown! For a long time I have not dreamed of Duke Chou again.'"。其中,林语堂把"周公"翻译为"Duke Chou",并在注释中补充文化背景知识:"Duke Chou was the symbol of the moral ruler and founder of the government system of the Chou Dynasty which Confucius was trying to restore."囿于所处时代、社会环境和个人经历,林语堂的翻译不免有历史的局限,如当时无拼音方案,专有名词都使用威妥玛拼音音译等。但是,补充的文化背景知识让我们了解到,孔子说自己很久没有梦到周公了,并不是说他失去了自己的梦想,只是生不逢时。虽然孔子发现自己进入迟暮之年,但是他复兴周公之道的梦想依然强烈。也正是因为怀着这样的梦想,他才会对生活、整理典籍以及教导弟子充满热情。林语堂用优美的英文、口语化的文体和生活化的语言向世界介绍中国人和历史文化,使之更加符合大众的口味。

综上所述,林语堂采取编译的策略将《论语》这一中国儒家经典形象通俗化地译介到西方,对于提升中华文化经典的通俗化、促进中华传统文化的海外传播以及增强中西文化交流都起到了重要的启示作用。

(二) 丁往道译本

丁往道的译本《论语(精选)》(*Sayings of Confucius*)于2008年由中国对外翻译出版有限公司出版。该译本主要包括前言、孔子和《论语》以及《论语》精选语录。

在前言中,编译者通过总结《论语》思想,指出了《论语》中育人治国的思想要义,并指出孔子地位的重要性,"孔子是中国思想史上第一个把道德作为做人和治国的首要条件和最高标准提出来的哲人。道德的核心是仁"(丁往道,2008)。

在正文部分,该译本针对初级学者,精选了《论语》中100条经常被引用的语录,如"克己复礼为仁""君子博学于文""三人行,必有我师"等。为了便于读者阅读,编译者给每段语录都加上了标题,按内容分为12组,主题包括"论仁""论礼""论孝悌""论政""论知行""论教与学"等12个。该译本将孔子对道德、教育、修身、齐家、治国的思想系统地体现出来。语录本文和篇章序号都以杨伯峻先生的《论语译注》(中华书局1980年版)为根据。

每篇除了英汉对照,还附有白话文翻译和必要的注释,供读者参考。编译者在翻译过程中力求忠实于原文,并努力保持原文的简练风格。对于一些争议的问题,编译者在注释中也作了说明。

丁往道采用编译孔子及其弟子语录的方式,通过增加注释等帮助读者理解原文,这对学习英语的初级读者和对中华文化感兴趣的英语读者想进一步了解《论语》的核心内容和精华思想具有重要的指导意义,同时也对《论语》文化内容的普及及其译介的通俗化具有重要的启示意义。

(三) 蔡志忠译本

台湾著名漫画家蔡志忠插图译本 *The Analects: An Illustrated Edition* 于2018年6月由 Princeton University Press 出版。合作译者

为美国学者Brian Bruya。该译本出版后,由于采用卡通漫画的表现形式,又采用编译策略,主题突出,因此受到很多媒体的关注。

该译本以传统文化为主题的插图故事内容和中英文对照的语言,形象生动地表现了孔子的一言一行以及孔子与其弟子的对话场景,使《论语》变得鲜活、通俗易懂而且容易接受。目录主题包括孔子时代的中国地图插图、前言、导论、孔子生平、《论语》正文、孔子去世后、孔子弟子、专有名词发音索引等。

在前言中,哈佛大学东亚语言与文化系中国历史方向教授Michael Puett指出,"《论语》的确是一部真正伟大的哲学著作。但它不是我们通常所说的哲学文本。《论语》中的哲学是通过孔子与其弟子的一系列对话来表达的。它把孔子描绘成一个努力向善、试图教育弟子,并期望能创造一个更美好世界的人。《论语》中的哲学是以生活艺术为中心的"(Tsai,2018)。而蔡志忠则以图文并茂的形式,把孔子在生活中如何教育弟子、如何建言献策、如何身体力行栩栩如生地表现出来,同时也生动地展现了《论语》中所蕴含的幽默感。此外,Brian Bruya的译文不仅语言优美、用词贴切,而且提供了语境知识以方便英语读者理解孔子的思想内涵,进一步推动了《论语》在海外的大众传播。

在导论中,美国夏威夷大学比较哲学博士学位、中国早期哲学研究领域的专家Brian Bruya指出,"孔子思想的两种基本观念——文化与等级制度,是理解本书思想的前提条件"(Tsai,2018),并进一步分析了"文化"中的"礼"在维护社会安定和谐中的重要作用,以及"等级制度"中的"精英领导体制"和"孝""忠""义"等在儒家制度中的重要作用。

《论语》的正文包括学习、教育、政治、道德、理想以及日常生活礼节等主题故事内容。儒家哲学思想通过通俗易懂的语言、丰富有趣的故事以及幽默清新的画风为英语读者提供了愉悦的阅读体验。本书以《论语·子罕》中"知者不惑,仁者不忧,勇者不惧"为例,进一步说明蔡志忠、Brian Bruya《论语》译本的编译策略,具体如图2-1所示。

图 2-1 蔡志忠、Brian Bruya《论语》译本的编译策略

如图 2-1 所示,蔡志忠用他独特而富有吸引力的画风将《论语》中的智慧带入生活,折射出孔子思想的光辉。第一幅画中乘船的智慧老人与飞翔的鸟呈现出尽在掌控之中的和谐画面,第二幅画中坐在石头上微笑的中年人与头顶的白云呈现出笑而不语的和谐画面,第三幅画中一位高大的战士与很多渺小的敌人作战呈现出强烈对比的作战不畏惧的画面。另外,结合比较哲学博士 Brian Bruya 的忠实、简练而且蕴含哲学道理的译文,让读者更容易、生动、形象地理解原文的哲学含义。

由上所述,该类译本主题鲜明、图文并茂,有助于实现原文语境的可视化,生动塑造孔子的形象以及吸引大量读者。这对于中国典籍的普及传播以及中西文化交流都有着重要的意义。

四、《论语》全译本

通过比较表2-1《论语》五译本的题目、首次出版时间、出版社、翻译原则、翻译策略以及表2-2《论语》五译本内副文本结构,我们发现,由于时代变迁与译者所处历史环境不同,以及译者翻译动机与翻译目的不同,《论语》的五译本特征存在着一定差异。

表2-1 五译本概况比较

五译本	参数			
	译著题目	首版时间	出版社	翻译原则
理雅各 James Legge	*Confucian Analects*	1861	Oxford: Clarendon Press	尽量忠实原文
辜鸿铭 Ku Hung-ming	*The Discourse and Sayings of Confucius: A new special translation, illustrated with quotations from Goethe and other writers*	1898	Shanghai: Kelly and Walsh, Ltd.	以读者为中心
刘殿爵 D. C. Lau	*Confucius: The Analects*	1979	Hong Kong: Chinese University Press	注重原典
安乐哲与罗思文 Ames & Rosemont	*The Analects of Confucius: a philosophical translation*	1998	New York: Ballantine	凸显哲学特征
森舸澜 Edward G. Slingerland	*Confucius Analects: with selections from traditional commentaries*	2003	Indianapolis: Hackett Publishing Company, Incorporated	再现原文背景

结合表2-1和表2-2,我们进一步分析《论语》五译本的英译概况及其内副文本特征,探讨译者翻译原则、社会文化背景、翻译目的与读者考量等因素对译作产生的影响。

表 2-2　五译本内副文本比较

译者	副文本	
	题目	译本内副文本结构
理雅各	Confucian Analects	1. 标题,2. 理雅各生平传记,3. 序言,4. 导论,5. 注疏,6. 索引,7. 参考文献
辜鸿铭	The Discourse and Sayings of Confucius: A new special translation, illustrated with quotations from Goethe and other writers	1. 标题,2. 序言,3. 注疏,4. 译后记,5. 参考文献
刘殿爵	Confucius: The Analects	1. 标题,2. 再版注解,3. 引言,4. 注疏,5. 附录,6. 参考文献,7. 专用名词索引
安乐哲与罗思文	The Analects of Confucius: a philosophical translation	1. 译者序言,2. 致谢,3. 引言,4. 注释,5. 附录,6. 参考文献
森舸澜	Confucius Analects: with selections from traditional commentaries	1. 副标题,2. 前言,3. 致谢,4. 惯例,5. 引言,6. 传统年表,7. 注疏,8. 罗马字体,9. 附录,10. 参考文献

(一) 理雅各译本

理雅各的《论语》译本 Confucian Analects 于1861年(1893年再版)由克拉伦登出版社出版。理雅各译本包括正文本与内副文本,如标题、理雅各生平传记(翻译动机、宗教信仰、教育环境、工作环境、作为汉学家和教育家等)、序言(翻译目的、翻译策略等)、导论(中国典籍的意义、内容与权威性,《论语》文本的生成、评论以及相关材料)、注疏、索引以及参考文献。

理雅各在正文本中尽量忠实于原文。理雅各"是第一个认识到中国典籍的地位以及将这些经典融入基督教知识的必要性的人之一"

(吉瑞德,2011)。理雅各的主要翻译目的是向来华的传教士认真传播中国的儒家哲学。这不仅表现在理雅各用基督教的思想诠释解读《论语》中的核心思想,也表现在他对融合于《论语》译著中的基督教思想的无形赞扬上。理雅各的这种翻译策略也促使英语读者用基督教的思想了解中华文化,达到了传教与文化传播的双重目的。正因如此,"在西方,《论语》最初可能是被当作近似基督伦理箴言的东西来阅读的,或者由于预示了基督教神学,孔子因此被发现是值得尊崇的"(崔玉军,2010)。但在某种程度上,理雅各的基督教思维也束缚了西方读者对《论语》中儒家文化的理解。

理雅各译本是理雅各翻译的《中国经典——译文,评论、训诂注释,绪论,及丰富的索引》(*The Chinese Classics: with a translation, critical and exegetical notes, prolegomena, and copious indexes*)的一部分,其他部分还包括《大学》(*The Great Learning*)与《中庸》(*The Doctrine of the Mean*)等。该书副标题隐含着理雅各对中国典籍的尊重,从侧面说明译文只是一小部分。评论、训诂注释,绪论及索引也是译文的重要补充。理雅各花费了几十年的心血翻译《中国经典》。在整个翻译过程中,理雅各注重考证,严谨治学,认真借鉴参考王韬等人的学术研究成果,避免主观臆断,为中国典籍翻译研究提供了丰富的素材。

在理雅各传记一章,Lindsay Ride 指出,理雅各作为一名基督教传教士来到东方,不仅具有基督教使命,而且明确知道自己想完成的事业。这是促成理雅各从事这样一项艰巨的非基督教文明典籍翻译事业的直接动因。当然,理雅各也兼具聪明才智、能力高超、学术造诣很高与勤奋努力等优点。理雅各在中国传教的过程中,认识到中国的儒教思想有助于西方人理解中国人的行为方式、思想信仰以及政府管理方式。那些想了解中国的西方人士必须先了解中国经典。因此,理雅各成功翻译了五卷本《中国经典》。理雅各(Legge,1991)指出:"我对中国学术所做的成功之研究,是二十五年多的辛勤劳作的结果。为了让世界真正了解中国这一伟大的帝国,尤其为了顺利开展我们在中国的传教事业并获得永久的成功,这样的学术研究是必不可少的。我认为,将孔子所有的著作(儒家经典)翻译并加上注释出版,会为未来的传教士们开展传教工作带来极大的便利"(金学勤,2015)。作为传教士,理雅各相信基督教是最好的宗教。同时,理雅各对中华传统文化无比热爱,认为"除非掌握了中国的典籍,并对中国圣人所掌握的整个思想领域有所研究,否则他就不能胜任其职位的职责。因此,他将先对自己的人民与种族传教,然后再把东方的学术翻译解释给西方的学者与传教士"(Ride,1991)。为了帮助后来的传教士理解中国儒教理念以及提供学习汉语与了解中国的教材,理雅各认为自己有责任掌握并翻译《中国经典》的任务(其中包括《论语》),把中国的儒家思想传播给西方受众。

在传记中,理雅各在中国香港和英国的工作环境、学习和写作经历以及他作为汉学家与教育家的经历也帮助我们对理雅各及其译作的翻译过程有了更全面的了解。理雅各的一生是由传教士走向汉学家的过程,也是由最初向东方宣扬基督教义转至向西方传播中华文化的过程。由此可见,理雅各向西方传播中国儒教与其他文化理念时是本着对中华文化所表现出的尊重态度来完成的。

理雅各在导论中主要阐述了《中国经典》中所涉及的一些书籍的介绍,如"四书"(《大学》《中庸》《论语》《孟子》)、"五经"(《诗经》《尚书》《礼记》《周易》《春秋》),《中国经典》的意义、内容及其最高权威性的考证,《论语》作为孔子及其弟子的语录体的文本生成过程、相关评论以及相关材料等。

理雅各的严谨治学态度与学术型翻译策略为读者理解原文提供了丰富的资料。我们不可否认,理雅各作为当时一名深受基督教熏陶的传教士,多采用西方基督教文化视角的思维来翻译。理雅各在翻译过程中有时会借助儒家的"道"宣扬基督教义的完美,把一些基督教的宗教思想融合在译文中,从而展现出新传教士以耶释儒的策略。例如,理雅各把孔子多翻译为 Master，是因为 Master 在西方世界是对上帝的别称。理雅各在译本正文中还对原文中不容易理解的文化概念作了注释。

理雅各译本的注疏特点是词条多，词语注解篇幅占比较大，并多对《论语》中的文化概念进行阐释。该译本中大量中国式、教科书式的注解，为读者带来了丰厚的历史文化语境认知。

此外，理雅各译本的注疏内容还主要包括各章主题、注疏考据、文化释义与背景介绍等。索引位于译本末尾，分为主题词索引、专有名词索引。这些对于读者查询了解书中内容以及相关资料起到了重要的作用。

（二）辜鸿铭译本

辜鸿铭的《论语》译本 The Discourse and Sayings of Confucius: A new special translation, illustrated with quotations from Goethe and other writers 于 1898 年出版。辜鸿铭译本包括译本正文本与内副文本，如标题、序言、注疏、译后记与参考文献。

从这一副标题可以看出，辜鸿铭引用了歌德和其他西方作家的话作注释，旨在帮助那些不熟悉中华文化的英语读者更好理解中国的儒家经典文化。

辜鸿铭在序言中指出了理雅各译本的弊端。此外，英国人阿查立爵士的多次劝说也起到了一定的间接作用。辜鸿铭认为，理雅各译本所体现的中国的道德智慧会让英语读者产生异样的感觉。这是"因为理雅各博士开始从事这项工作的时候，他的文学训练还很不足，完全缺乏评判能力和文学感知力。他自始至终都表明他只不过是个大汉学家，也就是说，只是一个对中国经书具有死知识的博学的权威而已"（王东波，2008）。

辜鸿铭对东西方文化有着自己独特的理解，他认为，对于一些具有哲学与文学灵感的研究者来说，能够洞察理雅各在译著中所展示的中国的道德文化,但是对于绝大多数英国读者来说则是感到难以理解(Ku,1898)。为了消除那些受过教育的英国人对中国人的现有成见,并且为了消除英语读者的陌生感,辜鸿铭在译文中把孔子翻译为Confucius。Confucius一词最初是拉丁文,"最早是由明清时期来华的耶稣会传教士翻译的,他们为把儒学介绍给西方人,把'孔夫子'译成拉丁'Confucius',后来在西方广为接受。辜鸿铭为使英语读者容易接受译文,多译'Confucius'"(范敏,2016)。

辜鸿铭引用了很多西方文学经典、哲学名家(如歌德、华兹华斯、卡莱尔、伏尔泰、丁尼生、席勒、爱默生)的话。例如,辜鸿铭引用华兹华斯的话,强调"文与质"不可分割性:"Speaking of style in literature, Worsworth says, 'To be sure, it was the manner, but then, you know, the matter always comes out of the manner'"—Emerson's "English Traits"。辜鸿铭还引用旧约中的《诗篇》等来帮助读者理解儒家文化与西方基督教文化的共通性。辜鸿铭把仲由比作孔子的福音使徒彼得(Peter),并在注疏中解释了彼得的特点——勇敢、无畏、鲁莽与侠义的性格。辜鸿铭把颜回比作孔子的福音使徒约翰(John),并在注释中解释了约翰的特点——简单、英雄、理想性格,主人喜欢。

由此可见,辜鸿铭在译文中注重《论语》儒家文化与西方文化的相通性,试图通过寻找中西文化的相似点进行诠释来沟通中西思想。因此,他试图按照英国人的思维表达方式来翻译《论语》中的儒家思想。

(三) 刘殿爵译本

刘殿爵的《论语》译本 *Confucius: The Analects* 于1979年出版。刘殿爵译本包括正文本与内副文本,如标题、再版注解、引言、注疏、附录(孔子生平、年表、《论语》中的孔子弟子、《论语》篇章内容补充)、参考文献与专用名词索引。

刘殿爵的翻译风格受到英国哲学家吉尔伯特·赖尔(Gilbert Ryle)的影响,所以翻译《论语》时,用字准确精练,言简意赅。刘殿爵以其深厚的哲学及语言学功底、严谨的治学态度翻译中国古籍。刘殿爵的《论语》译本严谨、准确、平易近人,对于一些晦涩难懂的哲学术语的翻译有时采用互参与注释来解释,所以有时会给人一种庄重典雅但冗长枯燥的感觉。

在《论语》译本的再版注解中,刘殿爵强调,该版是对第一版的修订,主要包括两部分:一是对原文诠释的个别修订,二是对译文个别内容的修订。刘殿爵指出,当译文准确性与优雅性发生冲突时,准确性永远为第一位。刘殿爵还对伦敦大学亚非学院 D. E. Pollard 教授的帮助表示感谢。

刘殿爵在《论语》译本引言中简要介绍了孔子所处的时代背景与历史背景,梳理了孔子思想的发展脉络,重点介绍了孔子的思想内涵,阐明了儒家所崇尚的道德理想。刘殿爵详细解释了《论语》中的一些重要思想概念,如道、德、圣人、君子、仁、孝、悌、礼、知、义、文、质、学等在儒家思想中所体现的意义。在翻译过程中,刘殿爵对于一些难懂的词会根据语境进行注释,如在孔子回答樊迟的"崇德"问题时,他在"先事后得,非崇德与"的译文中增加注解:"德(virtue)"与"得(get)"看起来是同源词,"德"是通过追求"道(way)"而得道,从而帮助读者理解原文"德(virtue)"与"得(get)"之间的关联意义以及如何"崇德"的问题。刘殿爵的很多注释还体现了互文的特点。例如:"子曰:'赐也,女以予为多学而识之者与?'对曰:'然。非与?'曰:'非也,予一以贯之。'"(《论语·卫灵公》)刘殿爵在译文后增加了参考注释: The Master said, "Ssu, do you think that I am the kind of man who learns widely and retains what he has learned in his mind?" "Yes, I do. Is it not so?" "No. I have a single thread binding it all together."①

刘殿爵在该译文中建议参考《论语》中《里仁》篇所强调的一以贯之的内容,强调要用联系的、发展的、辩证的方法看问题,要善于举一反

---

① 原文出自 CF. IV. 15。

三,融会贯通,以帮助英语读者理解孔子的学习、处世态度与忠恕之道。例如:"子曰:'参乎! 吾道一以贯之。'曾子曰:'唯。'子出,门人问曰:'何谓也?'曾子曰:'夫子之道,忠恕而已矣。'"类似的互参例子在刘殿爵的译文中有很多,这不仅可以帮助英语读者深刻理解原文内容,而且有助于英语读者对《论语》中的儒家思想作出全面思考。

在附录部分,刘殿爵介绍了孔子生活中的一些重要事件,如父辈、出生、成长、任职等相关活动经历。刘殿爵还对孔子的一些重要弟子进行分类,如认为曾子、子夏、子游、子张、有子五个弟子尤其值得关注。原因主要是,在《论语》中,相对其他弟子而言,这些弟子有独立的言论记录,而且对传播孔子的儒家思想起到了至关重要的作用。刘殿爵还在附录部分对《论语》的篇章结构及其主要内容作了梳理介绍,分析了《论语》成篇的可能原因。此外,其他部分如参考文献与设置索引也有助于读者进一步理解《论语》译文。

(四) 安乐哲与罗思文译本

安乐哲与罗思文的《论语》译本 *The Analects of Confucius: a philosophical translation* 于1998年出版。安乐哲与罗思文译本包括正文本与内副文本,如译者序言、致谢、引言(包括历史与文本背景、哲学与语言学背景、引言注释)、注释、附录(包括定州《论语》版本,关于语言、翻译与阐释的再评论)与参考文献。

安乐哲与罗思文考虑到中西语言哲学的不同以及不同地域读者的认知差异,从哲学的视角来翻译《论语》中的孔子哲学思想。安乐哲与罗思文不仅解读、翻译文本所蕴含的哲学思想,而且通过哲学的思维来建构译本的翻译话语体系。

在译者序言中,安乐哲与罗思文说明了翻译动机,认为阅读《论语》是通向儒道的途径。为了引导读者深入地理解学习"儒道",译者提供了很多历史背景介绍,并采用了哲学的视角与意象的手段去解读儒家思想,由此可以帮助英语读者透过这扇窗户看到一个有别于西方的世界。他们在书中感谢了那些帮助他们完成这部译作,并使这部译作变得更加专业的所有同仁。

在译本引言中,安乐哲与罗思文介绍了《论语》的历史与文本背景,包括孔子的生平、哲学成就、思想传播(包括儒教内涵以及给弟子传授六艺等)、弟子简介(如颜回、子路、子贡、曾子、子夏、子张等)、文本介绍(成书过程、编排原因,引用的相关经典文本如《春秋》《礼记》相关经典评论),关于语言的玄学(翻译动机、语言特点、儒学概念理解),关于玄学的语言(古汉语的特点在翻译过程中是否有效呈现)。

安乐哲与罗思文基于中华文化"一多不分"的世界观,从中国思想文化本身的框架出发,对儒家哲学思想概念作出新的阐释与解读。他们对《论语》中出现的儒道概念如道、天、仁、礼、义、信、知及智、心、和、德、善、文、孝等逐一作了阐释,并在引言注释中建议参考理雅各、刘殿爵等译者的译本,从而使读者对本译文采用的哲学视角有更深刻的认识。安乐哲与罗思文从哲学视角,采用了创造性阐释翻译策略诠释译文,注释没有放在正文中,而是统一置于文末。

安乐哲与罗思文在关于语言、翻译与诠释的再评论中指出,关于"翻译是艺术"的话题一直有争论,而从哲学的视角研究翻译则更高一筹。他们从古汉语的书写、语法以及哲学内容等维度思考《论语》翻译策略,指出古汉语可使中华文化的重要理念浓缩在汉字中的象形表义特征,一以贯之的"词法即句法"构词法、重视因果与时间关系的语序排列,以及汉语所蕴含的"一多不分"的哲学特征,由此可以让读者了解中国语言与思想的事件性、动态性与关系性特征。他们对《论语》中的许多例子作出分析,如对《论语·学而》中"父在观其志,父没观其行,三年无改于父之道,可谓孝矣"所体现的过程哲学的理解与翻译作出阐释。

在附录部分,安乐哲与罗思文解释了选择《论语》定州版本的原因,主要是以当代考古学和文献学的新发现为重要依据。作为目前发现最早的《论语》抄本——定州《论语》于1973年在河北定州出土。译者发现,如果考虑到异体字和语法词,定州《论语》与传世版《论语》差别极大。"《论语》定州版本的许多文本特征能让我们对不同修订本的差异的本质有一个更清晰的认识,给我们提供了一个新的视角,可以帮助我们预测随后传世本的编辑与修订过程"(Ames and Rosemont, 1998)。

因此,安乐哲与罗思文在翻译过程中通过语境阐释让中国儒家哲学呈现其完整性,强调全球化语境中文化间的真正比较是要平等对话与相互提升,助力英语世界对儒家思想的正确认识与解读,从而展现儒家思想的文化价值,加强中西哲学深层次对话,使中国哲学在世界具有一定地位。

(五) 森舸澜译本

森舸澜的《论语》译本 *Confucius Analects: with selections from traditional commentaries* 于2003年出版。森舸澜译本包括正文本与内副文本,如包括标题、前言、致谢、惯例、引言、传统年表、注疏、罗马字体、附录(术语表、孔子弟子、历史人物、引用中国传统评论者、古汉语文本等)及参考文献。

森舸澜为加拿大英属哥伦比亚大学亚洲研究教授,精通中国先秦时期各种哲学思想,在古汉语研究、中西方宗教哲学思想比较与认知科学等领域都有很高造诣。森舸澜认为,中国古代哲学思想尤其是先秦时期的诸子百家思想和中国先秦之后流行的佛教与西方的基督教都有着本质不同。这些思想在现代西方哲学思想中是找不到的,有着自己独特的价值与指导意义。因此,森舸澜有时会在译文中采用拼音翻译原文哲学术语与专有名词,并采用了大量的文外注释,增加了很多的历史文化背景知识,从而帮助普通英语读者理解《论语》内容及与之相关的历史文化背景。

从森舸澜译本的副标题可以看出,森舸澜在译本中采用了很多注疏。在《论语》正文的每一篇的首段都有一个介绍主题思想的小结作为全篇的主旨内容,对于读者了解全篇内容起到了提纲挈领、画龙点睛的作用。此外,森舸澜在译文中采用了大量的注释与"丰厚翻译"策略,通过增加注释并伴有评解以实现文本意义的充分转换,从而"使文本存活于一个丰富的语言文化语境中"(Appiah,2000)。

  森舸澜在译本前言中叙述了《论语》的成书背景、遴选注疏的原则和标准、翻译动机与翻译策略等,尤其是围绕注疏进行讨论。森舸澜指出,《论语》具有深奥的哲学意义。森舸澜(Slingerland,2003)引用梅约翰(John Makeham)的话进一步强调说,"如果不给读者提供注疏语境,《论语》文本便是空空的骨架,没有一点肉,读起来常常让人觉得不过是偏狭训令与只言片语干瘪对话的杂糅,意义晦涩难懂。正是注疏赋予了《论语》活力,赋予其作为儒家经典的本质"(金学勤,2015)。从长远来看,这种翻译策略对于学术研究与文化发展有着积极的意义,能够为学术探索及中西文化交流与发展提供建议。

  在译本惯例中,森舸澜主要介绍了汉语拼音在译文中的应用,指出其主要是用于孔子弟子人名如 Zigong(子贡)、Zizhang(子张)、Zixia(子夏),以及一些文化负载词如 way(dao 道)、excellent person(shanren 善人)、propensity of circumstances(ming 命)等。

  在译本引言中,森舸澜简要介绍了《论语》的不同版本:《古论语》、《鲁论语》、《齐论语》、《张侯论》、郑玄《论语》版本、何晏等所撰《论语集解》、《朱熹集注》及程树德《论语集释》。程树德的《论语集释》成书于清末民初,堪称《论语》学的集大成之作,包含历代《论语》注疏,每一条注解都会历数其学术研究的焦点与考证(程树德,1990)。森舸澜指出,译本的读者群主要是英语普通读者,为进一步做学术研究的读者提供了在线网站 www.hackettpublishing.com,用以查询学术笔记、参考书目以及包含附注的参考文献等。

  译本附录部分包括文化术语概念(如君子、文质、道家)、孔子弟子(如曾子、有子、子路)、历史人物(如齐桓公、周公、管仲)、引用的中国传统评论者(如朱熹、范祖禹、王阳明)、中国传统文本(如《三国志》《春秋》《易经》)的介绍与诠释等,有助于英语读者进一步深入了解中国儒家文化思想。

综上所述,由于东西语言文化的差异,《论语》在翻译过程中会遇到较大程度的文化损失。文本的不确定性、阐释的模糊性与翻译语境的缺失性是《论语》文化英译的主要难点。就译文的通俗化而言,《论语》节译本与编译本可以帮助更多普通读者熟悉中国儒家文化思想。而就传递原文内容的完整性与学术性而言,相对于《论语》节译本与编译本,《论语》的全译本更能完整体现原文本的文化内容、译者翻译思想以及原文本所处的社会文化背景情况。

五、小结

总之,300多年来《论语》英译概况呈现多元化特点。由于社会文化背景、英语读者需求及译者翻译目的不同,《论语》英译本呈现节译本、编译本与全译本等多种译本情况。《论语》英译概况大体有两种情况:一种是翻译为通俗性著作,面向普通英语读者,采用节译、编译等策略译介中华传统文化与东方智慧。另一种是翻译为学术性著作,面向专业读者,注重考证原文的义理辞章,尽量忠实传达原文的哲学意义与文化内涵。因此,探讨《论语》英译概况对于中国典籍翻译传播主体借鉴语言文化翻译策略、传播中华优秀传统文化,进一步推进中国典籍翻译传播具有重要的指导意义。

第三章　基于语料库的《论语》英译个案研究

中华传统文化经典《论语》所蕴含的儒家思想丰富并滋养了中西文化传统与人类文明。因此,基于语料库的《论语》英译传播的个体研究具有一定代表性,对中国典籍的翻译传播及中西文化交流具有一定的借鉴意义和参考价值。本章主要探讨了以下内容:《论语》翻译语料库的设计与应用、《论语》中的语篇特征及翻译、《论语》中的文化特征及翻译、《论语》中的修辞特征及翻译等内容。

一、《论语》翻译语料库的设计与应用

(一) 文本选择

《论语》及其英译的个案研究对于中国典籍翻译传播有着重要意义。因此,在文本选择时应注意考虑各种因素,如历史背景、作者背景、时代特征、译者背景、译者态度、赞助人、出版社归属、作品本身可译性以及读者接受性等。

在本书中,《论语》中文本选自杨伯峻的《论语译注》(杨伯峻,2009),英译本选用理雅各、辜鸿铭、刘殿爵、安乐哲与罗思文以及森舸澜译本,主要有以下四个原因:

(1) 社会文化背景:某一特定历史时期社会、文化、政治等因素对译者的影响,导致译者有意或者无意地选择某些内容来翻译,以此回

应社会。

（2）译文可接受程度：译文是否能为译入语国家所接受，往往与翻译目的、译文风格、读者期望、翻译策略、时代背景以及译者背景与心理状态有关。

（3）对当前现代文化的影响：对各种不同译本的讨论反映了人们较为关注中华文化是否能够有效传播、接受并且能否促进中西文化融通等问题。

（4）个案研究意义：个案研究是了解某一特定个体、现象、主题的研究。梅里姆（Merriam）于1989年曾指出个案研究的特点：特殊性、描述性、启发性与渐进性。梅里姆认为个案研究着重于一种特定的情况、事件、节目或现象研究现实问题，最终结果是通过研究描述性报告帮助人们了解研究内容和得到新的观点，目的是依据归纳和推理过程，在大量资料检测中形成原理和普遍原则并发现新的联系（戴元光，2017）。

综上所述，《论语》五个英译本代表了不同的社会文化背景，而且在英语国家具有较高的可接受度。本书通过比较分析五个英译本，可以揭示译者在不同历史阶段儒学对外文化传播过程中所采用不同翻译策略的原因。此外，《论语》的儒家文化重构需要用现代性的理念去思考。而现代性是与历史密切关联的，是用开阔的、乐观的视野去看待的，是需要用理性去构造的（陈兼、陈之宏，2012；孔飞力，2013）。因此，在当前中华文化崛起环境下，《论语》五译本的英译传播研究对于中西文化融通交流具有重要作用，而且对于推动中国典籍的翻译传播具有重要的指导意义与启发意义。

（二）语料库软件应用与讨论

本书借助语料库软件 WordSmith，采用 WordSmith 默认的词作为参考标准，从《论语》中的标准化类符/形符比（standardised type/token ratio）、高频词、词长、句长分布等方面对《论语》五译本的用语特征进行讨论,结合翻译理论与定性研究,深入分析译者的不同翻译风格。需要说明的是,为了明确分析译者用词与翻译策略,论语的内副文本(如标题、序言、前言、注释、附录等)没有在语料库计算统计之内,但在译者风格分析以及《论语》中的语篇特征、文化特征与修辞特征的翻译讨论中起到了重要作用。

本书所探讨的是广义的译者风格研究。广义的译者风格研究可以分成两大类:狭义的译者风格(translator's style)与翻译风格(translation style)。前者主要考察译者特有的一些语言使用习惯(Saldanha,2011),后者则更关注译文针对原文本的反映方式。这两个概念既相互联系,又有所不同。一方面,两者相互依存、彼此体现;另一方面,翻译风格强调原作风格在译作中的体现,狭义的译者风格强调译者的个性特征及其翻译时显现的语言习惯和语言特点。

"Baker(2000)将译者风格定义为以一系列语言或非语言特征所表现出的有别于其他译者的个性特征,译者的翻译风格具体表现在文本类型和翻译策略的选择以及译者所运用的前言、后语、脚注、文内解释等方法。"(刘泽权,2011)译者的风格是由其世界观、创作天赋、艺术偏好决定的,并在翻译实践中形成和发展起来的,是"译者的人格倾向、选题倾向、文笔色彩以及译者所遵循的翻译标准、使用的翻译方法和译文语言运用技巧等特点的综合,尤其表现为语言运用的特点"(方梦之,2011)。

刘宓庆认为,翻译风格论"关注的中心是原语风格意义的所在,以及在对原语的风格意义进行分析的基础上获得译文风格对原语风格的'适应性'(adaptability),也可以说它研究的不仅是原语的风格表现手段,而且还包括如何使译文在与原语的对应中力求在风格表现上做到'恰如其分'(appropriateness)"(杨自俭和刘学云,1994)。刘宓庆指出,"表达法形式系统受制于思维和情感中最重要、最微妙的审美运作机制,双语转换不能回避审美情感问题,不能回避思维方式、思维特征和思维风格问题"(刘宓庆,2012)。

基于刘宓庆(2012)关于翻译风格的研究,根据《论语》的语录体特

点,译者在翻译《论语》时需要注意以下两点:

(1)《论语》作为先秦语录体文本,在语言文字以及文本的权威性上都有些特殊。由于时代变迁,原作的风格早已演变,有些古汉语的意思也发生了变化,而且由于语境的缺失,译者需要对原文进行重建式风格转化。译者在翻译时注重从交际功能出发,在保留原文对话的情况下,同时考虑当代读者的需求。

(2)语域、修辞、篇章、词句风格标记。由于时空差异、中西语言文化差异以及东西方思维方式、思维特征与思维风格的差异,目标语缺乏与原语相对应的风格符号系统,如音系标记、结构性变异的词语标记以及修辞标记等。因此,译者在翻译转化时需要注意译出语言的地道与可接受性特点。例如,用词的长度与难度就反映了译者的心理表征与翻译风格。

范敏(2016)利用语料库软件对《论语》五译本标准化类符/形符比、高频词、平均词长与平均句长进行分析。首先,在译文中,标准化类符/形符比的高低表明了译者所使用词汇量的高低与是否丰富。标准化类符/形符比越高就意味着译者使用的词汇数量大而且种类丰富;反之,则表示译者使用的词汇量越少。由表3-1可以看出,森舸澜译文的标准化类符/形符比最高,其他依次为安乐哲与罗思文译文、刘殿爵译文、理雅各译文与辜鸿铭译文。范敏通过分析表3-1指出,"从词汇数量来看,森舸澜译文的显化特征相对最为明显,理雅各译文最不明显。而在相同文字数量情况下,森舸澜译文使用的词汇类型最多、单词变化更丰富,而辜鸿铭译文在翻译过程中可能有意识地减轻类符数量,降低文本阅读难度"(范敏,2016)。

表3-1 五译本标准化类符/形符比、平均词长与平均句长比较

参数	原文	理雅各	辜鸿铭	刘殿爵	安乐哲与罗思文	森舸澜
库容	47 598	163 333	193 584	162 955	161 040	763 866
类符	3 096	3 081	3 234	3 493	3 718	8 835

(续表)

参数	原文	理雅各	辜鸿铭	刘殿爵	安乐哲与罗思文	森舸澜
形符	4 023	28 041	33 714	29 539	28 229	126 889
标准化类符/形符比	80.125	35.310 3	33.876 5	36.306 7	38.651 7	41.493 2
平均词长	3.989 8	4.125 7	4.282 8	3.993	4.196 0	4.455 8
平均句长	7.722	16.161 96	20.645 5	15.032 56	15.015 4	24.175 3

注：为使译文统计一致，在以上数据统计中，译文的前言、序言、附录与每章的大标题在统计时统统去掉，只留下正文作参考。

其次，高频词是指文本中使用频率比较高的词语。根据英语语料库(Bank of English)1998 年的统计，英语作为母语使用中频率最高的前五个词依次为 the、of、to、and 和 a (Hunston，2002)。而在英语翻译语料库中，前五个出现次数最多的词依次为 the、and、to、of、a (Olohan，2004)。由表 3-2 可以看出，五译本的高频词都包括 the、of、to、and、is，且都为虚词，排列顺序基本相同。范敏通过分析表 3-2 的虚词与共有人称代词发现，五译本"非常明显地具有语录体文体的特点。因为在《论语》中，孔子与弟子的对话并没有观念性的推理，而是通过指示性的陈述阐发思想观念，表达对事物的认识。而且 she/her 的缺失还体现了男性至上的儒家社会文化"(范敏，2016)。

表 3-2　五译本高频文化特色词比较研究(截取前 24 个最高频率词汇)

Term(s)	Freq.	File Co	TF-IDF	Ames	Ku H.M.	D.C.Lau	Legge	Slingerland
Size	310149			36549	41990	37361	36173	158076
Item(s)	258086			29780	35634	31034	30066	131572
	12512	5		3705	3263	3556	3219	9358
the	15650	5	-2835.1	1709	1827	2026	1947	8041
of	8391	5	-1529.86	876	1154	793	921	4660
to	7929	5	-1445.63	853	1341	998	938	3986
and	5985	5	-1091.19	660	719	515	683	3408
,	5693	5	-1037.96	803	932	792	862	2304
.	5535	5	-1009.15	807	931	751	755	2291
is	5065	5	-923.459	466	538	695	527	2839
in	4916	5	-896.293	503	808	585	467	2555
a	4907	5	-891.652	391	1071	537	469	2339
He	3144	5	-573.224	310	610	499	613	1112
not	3017	5	-550.064	437	395	420	514	1251
that	2582	5	-470.754	202	305	225	174	1676
his	2542	5	463.446	203	468	281	366	1224
Master	2453	5	-447.235	553	34	508	526	838
it	2406	5	-435.019	307	290	279	251	1239
said	2386	5		459	161	629	620	517
be	2382	5	-434.29	271	355	391	416	949
as	2107	5	-384.152	153	291	181	112	1370
I	1891	5	-344.77	303	391	383	337	477
Confucius	1800	5	-328.6	111	767	86	29	771
with	1779	5	-324.35	224	226	311	224	910
This	1562	5	-284.786	124	48	110	92	1188
are	1513	5	-275.863	253	221	143	212	684
you	1512	5	-275.67	255	324	219	177	537
was	1511	5	-275.488	145	239	190	182	755
for	1499	5	-273.3	168	207	210	121	793

此外，通过分析表 3-3 可知五译本高频文化词汇的翻译特点，相较

于理雅各与辜鸿铭的译文,刘殿爵、安乐哲与罗思文以及森舸澜译本的高频文化特色词翻译的显化特征更为明显。刘殿爵"译文的显化特征主要体现在使用(韦妥玛)拼音,如翻译 *Yi Chou shu*(《逸周书》),尽量忠实于原文语言特征。安乐哲与罗思文译文显化特征主要体现在从哲学的思维来理解与诠释术语,多采用增益或创造性翻译策略,如译 fraternal responsibility(xiaoti 孝悌),penal law(xing 刑),proper conduct(xing 行),fearful(zhanli 战栗)等。森舸澜译文显化特征主要体现在对术语的翻译则更多地采用拼音、汉字与注释相结合,如 xiangguan 相关(concern oneself with),xiepi 邪僻(irregular excess),xingming 性命(inborn destiny),yanjiao 言教[teaching through words(theoretical teaching)]与 yangqi 阳气(virile/healthy-vital essence)等的翻译"(范敏,2016)。

表3-3 五译本高频文化特色词比较(截取后28个最高频率词汇)

再次,平均词长反映了文本用词的复杂程度。一般文本的平均词长为4个字母左右,平均词长较长,说明用的长词较多,阅读难度越大。"就平均词长而言,森舸澜译文的稍高,刘殿爵译文稍低但接近于原文,理雅各译文、辜鸿铭译文、安乐哲与罗思文译文的相差甚微"(范敏,2016)。相对而言,森舸澜译文的书面语程度稍高,有一定阅读难度,而刘殿爵的译文则尽量传达原文的言简意赅的表达特点。整体而言,五译本译文的平均词长与原文的平均词长差别不大,都尽量使译语的语言尽量传达《论语》作为语录体的文体特征。

【例1】子贡问曰:"孔文子何以谓之'文'也?"子曰:"敏而好学,不耻下问,是以谓之'文'也。"(《论语·公冶长》)(英语译文参考附录)

原文是指,子贡问道:"孔文子为什么谥他'文'的称号呢?"孔子说:"他聪明勤勉,喜爱学习,不以向比自己地位低下的人请教为耻,所以给予他'文'的谥号。"孔文子是卫国大夫,姓孔名圉,"文"是谥号。

由译文比较看出,各译文显化特征都较为明显。森舸澜译文字数最多(205字),通过注释背景阐释原文内涵。相对于理雅各的用词如style,辜鸿铭的用词如add,刘殿爵、安乐哲与罗思文的用词如call等普通词汇,森舸澜使用了accord等难度稍大的词汇,不仅单词较长,而且增加了译文的阅读难度。

此外,关于"文"的翻译,安乐哲与罗思文翻译为refined(wen 文),森舸澜翻译为Cultured(wen 文),都采用了创造性的翻译策略。辜鸿铭采用西方文化中的Beau-clerc翻译。

理雅各翻译为Wan,接着在注疏中对"文"作了解释,认为其意义类似于成就(accomplished),用于追授子圉(魏国同姓官员,孔子同时代人)死后荣誉称号。虽然子贡质疑这一荣誉称号,但孔子认为,子圉具备那些使他被如此冠名的品质,而且中国有"对于死者,惟有称美"的传统。

刘殿爵翻译为wen,在注释中又解释为diligence in learning and seeking advice is called "wen",并对来源出处《逸周书》采用了韦妥玛Yi Chou shu拼写方式。注释如下:《逸周书》中关于死后题名的一章中,有这样一句话,"勤勉好学、乐于请教为'文'"(196页)。《逸周书》虽然传统上被认为比较早,但实际上很可能是把《论语》作为其来源之一。

森舸澜的注释显化策略如下:卫国大夫孔文子是孔圉的谥号。子贡对孔圉的追封感到不解,因为孔圉是一个相当不热心的人,以不忠和放荡著称。孔子的回应可能有双重目的。一方面,它是关于有教养的人应具有怎样的美德的陈述;另一方面,它告诉我们,圣人关注的是一个人的积极品质,而不是消极品质。这也说明了圣人之道的伟大和圣人美德的威严。如果仅仅依靠后人的叙述,就会使人认为孔圉是一个不值得讨论的人,从而错失了学习这种美德的机会。

综上所述,五译本译文采用了不同的显化策略,以注释为主。在解释原文的文化概念如"文"的翻译时,安乐哲与罗思文以及森舸澜都采用了创造性翻译。相对而言,在表现手法上,森舸澜的译文更加具有难度,辜鸿铭的译文相对符合西方的审美观点。理雅各与刘殿爵在译文正文中很少用到汉字拼写,但是偶尔也会在注释中出现原文中的汉字并作出解释。

最后,平均句长是指文本中句子的平均长度,可在某种程度反映句子的复杂程度。《论语》富有哲理,省略句与倒装句等特殊句式使得语句短小精悍。《论语》的平均句长约为 7.722 个单词,而森舸澜译本约为 24.18 个单词,辜鸿铭译本约为 20.65 个单词,理雅各译本、刘殿爵译本、安乐哲与罗思文译本依次为 16.16 个、15.03 个与 15.02 个单词。由于在译文中需要阐释原文的浓缩的含义,因此《论语》译文因语境的补充而产生的增益变化也合情合理。"Laviosa(1988)曾指出,翻译叙事文体译语文本的句子明显长于源语文本,其对英语译语及源语语料库平均句长的统计结果分别为 24.1 个和 15.6 个单词。可见,就句长而言,森舸澜译文、辜鸿铭译文最接近译语特点,而刘殿爵译文、安乐哲与罗思文译文则偏离最远。考虑到译语会明显地受到原文(句长 7.722)的影响,安乐哲与罗思文译文、刘殿爵译文、理雅各译文使用大量相对较短的句子体现了源语作为意合语言的特征,而森舸澜译文和辜鸿铭译文明显趋于易懂。"(范敏,2016)现在,我们就《论语》中一些常用的特殊句式对《论语》译本的句子层面作出分析。所谓特殊句式是指这些句子的结构与平常的句子结构存在不同,如省略句、倒装句、被动句、判断句等,这些句式在翻译过程中常根据语境变化与语义表达而作出相应调整。

(1) 省略句。省略句是指省去无用或可省略的语句的修辞手段,旨在避免重复,使语句更加简洁有力。文言文中的省略句可以根据上下文的具体情况同样译为省略句,也可以把省略的内容补出。需要说明的是,考虑到需对句长进行考量,因此本章各种句式类型的例句至少呈现一个。

【例2】子曰:"温故而知新,可以为师矣。"(《论语·学而》)(英语译文参考附录)

原文是指,孔子说:"在温习旧知识时,能有新体会、新发现,凭借这一点就可以做老师了。"其中,"以"后面省略代词"之"。现在,我们来比较"温故而知新"的五个译文。

比较五个译文发现,虽然原文省略了主语,但是各位译者在翻译过程中都增添了主语,而且都具有显化策略特征,使读者更容易理解原文的内容。相对于理雅各、辜鸿铭与刘殿爵的译文,安乐哲与罗思文、森舸澜的译文通过分别强调 such a person、someone able to do this 对省略的内容进行了补充说明。

此外,原文的"温故而知新"可作如下理解:一为"温故才知新",温习已闻之事,并且从中获得新的领悟(如理雅各、刘殿爵、安乐哲与罗思文译文);二为"温故又知新",一方面要温习典章故事,另一方面又努力撷取新的知识(如辜鸿铭、森舸澜译文)。理雅各在注释中对"温"的含义作出解释:旧的知识不断被掌握,并且不断地练习就是"温"。理雅各指出,现在有人认为新知识蕴含在旧知识里,意思可能是在吸收旧的知识中获取新的知识。而森舸澜对"温故知新"存在歧义的不同理解作为背景进行说明,是指"保持古代教义的生命力",或是指"将经典重释以便知道将来会发生什么",供读者思考辨析原义。由此进一步看出,译者的显化策略对于读者理解原文起到重要作用。

另外,从译文词长来看,相对于理雅各的 cherish、acquire 等词汇以及安乐哲与罗思文的 review、realize 等词汇而言,辜鸿铭的 go over、add 等词汇以及森舸澜的 keep、alive、understand 等词汇更加通俗易懂。从译文句长来看,整体而言,五个译文相差不大;相对而言,安乐哲与罗思文的译句最短,最能体现原文意合语言的特征。

【例3】子曰:"三人行,必有我师焉;择其善者而从之,其不善者而改之。"(《论语·述而》)(英语译文参考附录)

原文是指,孔子说:"三个人同行,其中必定有人可以作我的老师。要学习他们的优秀品德,把他们的缺点作为借鉴,改掉自己的缺点。"原文中"择其善者而从之"这句话,体现了孔子自觉修养、虚心好学的精神。它包含了两层意思:一是择其善者而从之,见人之善而学,是虚心好学的表现;二是择其不善者而改之,见人之不善就引以为戒,反省自己,是自觉修养的体现。这样,无论同行相处的人善与不善,都可以为师。原文中"择其善者而从之"省略了主语"我","其不善者而改之"省略了动词"择"。

通过译文比较发现,除了辜鸿铭译文使用第三人称 one、he,其他四个译文皆增加了主语 I。关于省略词语"择"的翻译,安乐哲与罗思文、森舸澜的译文对省略的动词"择"进行了补译,分别译为 identify 与 focus on。其他几位译者没有直接译出该词,但是其中的意思"有所选择"在译文中没有漏译。从译文句长来看,相对而言,理雅各的译句最短,最能体现原文意合语言的特征;森舸澜的译文因增加了补充词汇而使译文最长。相对而言,刘殿爵、安乐哲与罗思文的译文偏离译语特点最远,相对难懂,如两译文 in the company of 短语的使用,以及安乐哲与罗思文 stroll、accordingly 等词语的使用增加了译文的阅读难度。从显化翻译策略来看,森舸澜补充了注释如下:换言之,孔子或许是指同伴们具有的个性化的品质。他可以在任何人身上找到可以学习的优点以及可以避免的缺点。对孔子而言,道德教育的主要方法是效法榜样。这里的寓意是,教育的过程从来都没有完成,甚至孔子本人也有需要学习的地方。

(2)倒装句。语序对于汉语和英语而言是语言组织的重要手段。汉语中特意颠倒文法上的顺序称为倒装。运用倒装可改变文句常序,引起读者注意,使内容突出,表达鲜明。常位与殊位的差别不仅源于语法意义上的句法形式,而且从语用角度可以体现作者的不同意图,体现原文话语的不同主题意义,突出原文的信息的不同焦点。这些句式的翻译常常根据英语的习惯进行调整。

【例4】子曰:"巧言令色,鲜矣仁!"(《论语·学而》)(英语译文参考附录)

原文是指,孔子说:"花言巧语,伪装出一副和善的面孔,这种人很少是仁德的。"儒家学说的核心是"仁",如孝与悌。"仁"的对立面为"佞",表现为花言巧语,工于辞令。儒家崇尚质朴,反对花言巧语;主张说话谨慎,言行一致,反对说话办事随心所欲,言行不一。关于"仁"与"佞"的理解,森舸澜在译文注解中作出解释,并从古代发音的特点指出两者之间的联系。

原文中的"巧言令色,鲜矣仁!"属于主谓倒装句,正常语序应该是"巧言令色,仁鲜矣!"。五个译文都在句末翻译"仁"字。从句长来看,辜鸿铭与森舸澜的译文最短,而且译文相对容易理解,符合译语特征,如辜鸿铭 fine、found 等词的使用以及森舸澜 clever、fine 等词语的使用。刘殿爵译文因使用情感词语 indeed 并作为插入语,增强了原文的语气;而且短句的使用体现了原文作为意合语言的特征。安乐哲与罗思文使用拆字法翻译"仁"。根据《说文解字》,"仁"由"人""二"两字组成。在甲骨文中,"二"(☰)是"上"(☰)字的雏形,表明在"成仁"过程中的高下之分。孔子认为,"仁"的存在是需要人们相互辩证地去认识。因此,安乐哲与罗思文把"仁"翻译为 authoritative conduct(ren 仁),

汉字的出现使译语偏离了英语的语言特征。理雅各的译文句长适中,体现了原文言简意赅的特点。

【例5】定公问:"君使臣,臣事君,如之何?"孔子对曰:"君使臣以礼,臣事君以忠。"(《论语·八佾》)(英语译文参考附录)

在这里,孔子阐述了正确处理君臣关系的基本准则。孔子认为,君臣都应该遵从礼节,君主应当以礼待臣,臣子应当以忠事君,这样才能互相取得信任。君主身为强者,应在礼的方面率先垂范,才能令臣子受到感召,依礼依令而行。

原文中"君使臣以礼,臣事君以忠"为宾语前置句,正常语序应该是"君以礼使臣,臣以忠事君"。五个译文都用介宾结构把原文的语序以及意义表达出来。理雅各将其翻译为:"A prince should employ his minister according to the rules of propriety; ministers should serve their prince with faithfulness.";辜鸿铭将其翻译为:"Let the prince treat his public servant with honor. The public servant must serve the prince, his master, with loyalty.";刘殿爵将其翻译为:"The ruler should employ the services of his subjects in accordance with the rites. A subject should serve his ruler by doing his utmost.";安乐哲与罗思文将其翻译为:"Rulers should employ their ministers by observing ritual propriety (li 礼), and ministers should serve their lord by doing their utmost (zhong 忠).";森舸澜将其翻译为:"A lord should employ his ministers with ritual, and ministers should serve their lord with dutifulness."。

由此可见,在英汉翻译转换过程中,语序的调整和重组是常见的翻译手段。当译文语序与原文语序发生根本性冲突时,译者往往先关注哪种语序更加有利于原作者意图的表达、语用信息的传达、主题意义的体现和信息焦点的突出。我们知道,英汉语言在语序上的一个明显共同点是句子主干成分语序相似,即主语在谓语之前,宾语在动词之后。其中,虚词则对语序的调整起着重要的辅助作用。虚词主要与实词相对,是指缺少完整词汇意义而只有语法意义或功能意义的词。但是需要注意的是,相对而言,语序和虚词在英汉语言中的作用和地位存在着本质的差异。在以形态语言为根本特征的英语中,语序和虚词较之形态而言,始终是次要的。而在汉语中,形态标志的缺失使得汉语不得不在很大程度上依靠语序和虚词作为语言组织的重要手段,如古汉语倒装句中"于""之"等词的使用对于汉语语言组织来说是非常重要的,它是古汉语中常见而又复杂的语言现象。

就句长而言,理雅各与刘殿爵的句子最短,体现了原文的意合特点。安乐哲与罗思文的译文"礼"[ritual propriety(li 礼)]与"忠"[utmost(zhong 忠)]体现了中西文化差异,但使译文偏离了英语的语言特征。辜鸿铭把"定公"翻译为"鲁国君主",森舸澜在注解中对君臣礼仪之分的诠释,强调了仪式与美德的作用,如仪式是以前国王在考虑头衔和社会差别并以此消除混乱根源而使用的工具,从而增加了译文的可读性与易懂性。

(3)被动句。被动句是表示叙述句的主语和谓语属于被动式关系。一般有以下几种形式:用"为+动词""于""为所""为……所……"等表示被动。另外,古汉语中还有很多用"可""可谓"等表达主语被动语义的用法的意念被动句。

【例6】 子曰:"出则事公卿,入则事父兄,丧事不敢不勉,不为酒困,何有于我哉?"(《论语·子罕》)(英语译文参考附录)

原文是指,孔子说:"出外便服侍公卿,在家便服侍父兄,有丧事不敢不尽礼,不被酒所困扰,这些事我做到了哪些呢?"

原文中的"不为酒困"属于被动语态句式。现在分析五个译文的翻译,理雅各、辜鸿铭、刘殿爵、安乐哲与罗思文、森舸澜分别翻译为:not to be overcome of wine; in using wine, to be able to resist the temptation of taking it to excess; to be able to hold my drink; not to be overcome by drink; not allowing myself to be befuddled by wine。通过译文对比分析可以看出,辜鸿铭与刘殿爵的译文采用了主动语态,而其他三个译文则保留了原文的被动语态。

从句长来看,刘殿爵、理雅各的句长最短,而且使用很多短句,反映了原文的意合语言特征。辜鸿铭的用词如 do one's duty、be able to do 等词使译文相对易懂。森舸澜对原文的背景作出解释,指出这是对孔子同时代人中那些"虽谦卑却不愿意为高尚者服务,虽年轻却不愿意为年长者服务,而且在葬礼上敷衍了事、马虎草率、常常醉酒"的人的一种谴责。由此,英语读者可以清楚了解孔子的为人处世态度,即对自己严于律己,时时反省,并言传身教,以教导学生"学无止境",以此勉励他们从平凡小事学习修身、不懈努力,最终取得成就。

(4) 判断句。判断句是对客观事物表示肯定,构成判断与被判断关系的句子。判断句的谓语一般是对主语所指的人或事物进行分类,指出主语所指的人或事物属于哪一类情况。判断句通常由以下几种方式构成:以虚词配合一定的句式表示的判断句,如借用"者""也"等词构成,借助于"乃""是""为""则""悉""本"等词构成,或者省略"者""也",只用名词或名词性短语作谓语表示判断。

【例7】孔子于乡党,**恂恂如也,似不能言者**。其在宗庙朝廷,便便言,唯谨尔。(《论语·乡党》)(英语译文参考附录)

原文意思是指:"孔子在本乡显得十分温和恭敬,像是不会说话的样子。但他在宗庙里、朝廷上却很善于言辞,只是说话比较谨慎而已。"

原文中的"恂恂如也""似不能言者"都是判断句。对于"恂恂如也",理雅各、辜鸿铭、刘殿爵、安乐哲与罗思文、森舸澜分别翻译为 looked simple and sincere, was shy and diffident, was submissive, was most deferential, was respectful and circumspect;"似不能言者"分别翻译为 as if he were not able to speak, as if he were not a good speaker, seemed to be inarticulate, as though at a loss for words, seeming to be at a loss for words。这些皆为判断叙述句式。

从句长而言,刘殿爵句子最短。从使用短句来看,理雅各、刘殿爵、辜鸿铭都大量使用短句,与原文的言简意赅的特点相契合。安乐哲与罗思文把原文中具有明显对照意义的两句在译文中使用连词 and 与 yet 表达的一句话完成,把孔子的言谈举止对照以轻松的语气传达了出来。森舸澜在译文注解中解释了孔子的说话方式是随着社会环境的变化而变化的原因:孔子在乡间表现得很谦恭,避免通过展示自己的智慧而把自己置于他人之上。这是因为在乡间有很多孔子的长辈与先辈,他没有夸夸其谈的必要。而在宗庙里、朝廷上,孔子由于要遵守礼仪与处理公务,他说话的时候自然会很流畅清楚,同时又很注意分寸。他不仅表现了对尊长者应有的恭敬之意,还能不卑不亢、清晰明了地表达自己的观点。

结合语料库分析可以得出,《论语》译本的显化现象非常明显。通过对比《论语》五译本可以发现,在句子层面,理雅各与刘殿爵的译文语言简练,辜鸿铭的译文相对易懂,安乐哲与罗思文的译文采用了哲学诠释,森舸澜的译文增加了大量的文化诠释与评论。译本的显化现象对于我们了解译者翻译背景、理解译者翻译思想、熟悉译者翻译动机、解读译本生成机制、思考译者翻译风格成因都具有重要的指导意义。同时,译本的显化现象对中华传统文化对外传播,以及有助于英语读者了解、接受中国的儒家思想都具有重要的意义。

二、《论语》中的语篇特征及翻译

在语篇语言学领域,语篇通常被定义为一个交际事件。典型的交际语篇应具有七个语篇特征,即"衔接性、连贯性、意图性、可接受性、信息性、情境性与互文性"(de Beaugrande and Dressler, 1981)。其中,衔接性与连贯性关涉语篇的形式与意义问题,意图性与可接受性关涉语篇的主体与受众问题,信息性关涉语篇的内容问题,情境性关涉语篇的文化语境问题,互文性则关涉语篇文本之间及其与社会之间的关系问题。如果其中任意一项标准没有达到,语篇就失去了交际性。《论语》以语录体为主,叙事体为辅,是由若干篇章的叙事篇章组合而成,是具有交际价值的语篇。《论语》的语篇特征研究需要将其视作一个有机的整体进行系统研究。现在将从语篇的七个特征方面探讨《论语》的语篇特征及其翻译中的显化现象。

(一) 衔接性

语篇的衔接性与文本的表层成分有关(de Beaugrande and Dressler,1981)。衔接,"从语篇生成的过程来看是组句成篇必不可少的条件,从业已生成的语篇来看是语篇的重要特征之一"(李运兴,2001)。衔接性关注的是文本表层结构以一定语法规则顺序相互连接的方式,常常借助于语篇功能与衔接手段来实现。衔接是一种以语义网和逻辑关联性为依托的形式机制。衔接是形式,连贯是语义性的,是语篇的无形网络。衔接与连贯相辅相成,相得益彰。

刘宓庆指出,在翻译时需注重文本形式衔接与意义连贯的平衡问题,侧重文本内容的深层翻译(言下之意与言外之意)以及文本内在关系的动态表现。翻译过程中注意以下几点:(1)表层结构是意义的依据,但它只是形式载体,不是实体。(2)注重内在关系分析(句法的、语义的、语段的)及动态表现。(3)注重指称意义的把握和表现、意义与意向的理想整合。(4)整合的必然结果:① 注重语段机理重组;② 注重题材和体裁的特色和表现法;③ 十分重视目标语读者接受;④ 基本特点是"取善择优"及实现大体"等效"(刘宓庆,2001)。

【例8】有子曰:"信近于义,言可复也。恭近于礼,远耻辱也。因不失其亲,亦可宗也。"(《论语·学而》)(英语译文参考附录)

原文是指,有子说:"讲信用要符合于义,(符合于义的)话才能实行;恭敬要符合于礼,这样才能远离耻辱;依靠亲近自己的人才是可靠的。"

从词汇层面分析,有几个古汉语词汇需要注意理解:(1)近:接近、符合的意思。(2)义:儒家的伦理范畴,是指思想和行为符合一定标准的"礼"。(3)复:实践的意思。朱熹《论语集注》(2013)云:"复,践言也。"(4)远:使动用法,使之远离的意思,亦可以译为避免。(5)因:依靠、凭借。(6)宗:主、可靠。"可宗"即被认为是可靠的,属于意念被动。

从句子层面分析,原文使用了排比结构,没有使用条件句,这也符合古汉语的表达特点。通过译文比较可以发现,五个译文也基本使用了排比结构。理雅各与辜鸿铭还使用了条件句。由于英汉语言差异,为使英语译文清楚易懂,译者需要注重英语衔接的表达。衔接一般有四种途径:照应(reference),省略(ellipsis),替代(substitution),连接词语(conjunction)和词汇衔接(lexical cohesion)(Halliday,1985)。现在我们将从照应、替代、省略、连接与词汇衔接五个维度分析《论语》的五个译文。

(1)照应。照应在系统功能语法中是一种语法衔接手段。在语篇分析中,照应一般分为人称照应、指示照应、比较照应与分句照应。

人称照应是指用形容词性物主代词、名词性物主代词、反身代词、相互代词及名词所有格所表示的照应关系。通过上述人称手段形成的语言成分接应关系是语篇语义连贯的基础。英语人称手段比较丰富,有的还涉及性、数、格的变化。翻译时需要确立原文中人称和参照语之间的照应关系,必要时根据译入语习惯调整人称照应手段。例如,原文中有子说的话泛指任何人,译文中译者也相应地采用了 one、his、you 等泛指词汇。具体来说,理雅各使用了 one、a man、proper persons、he、them 等词汇,辜鸿铭使用了 you、your、friends、them 等词汇,刘殿爵使用了 one's、a man、his、he 等词汇,安乐哲与罗思文使用了 one's、one 等词汇,森舸澜使用了 your、you、them 等词汇。区别是第三人称比第二人称更客观,而第二人称在感情距离上更亲近一些。因此,与其他译文比较,辜鸿铭的译文在感情呼唤功能上更加贴近英语读者。

指示照应是指用指示代词、相应的限定词或冠词来表示语言成分之间某种限定说明关系的语义照应衔接手段,是通过指示代词建立语篇连贯性的衔接方法。当指示代词替代一个名词、短语、句子时,所替代的语言成分就是解释指示代词含义的参照点。根据 Halliday(1985)等的分类,英语指示照应的词语包括:起修饰限定功能的限定词(this/these、that/those、the)、具有附加语功能的副词(here、there、now、then)。根据陈安定(1998)的分类,汉语指示代词的作用有:指代人或事物,指代地点,指代时间,指代性质、状态及程度。在指示指称问题上,英语和汉语之间最明显的差异是定冠词。定冠词用作指称限定语是中性指称,即在所指的时间和空间概念方面没有远近之分,而 this、these、here、now 是指近,that、those、there、then 是指远。李运兴(2001)指出,"必须认识到,指代衔接是跨越句子界限的语篇特征,一个代词总是与上下文中的有关名词和其他代词铰接在一起,共同承担交际功能的。这就要求读者/译者要具有站在语篇层次上识别和理解指代关系的能力"。

通过比较原文与译文,我们可以看出,原文的指示照应蕴含在句子意义中,各译者在翻译过程中也对此进行了明晰化处理,添加了指代照应词。例如,理雅各使用了 the parties、proper persons、them、guides and masters 等词汇形成指代衔接链,辜鸿铭使用了 friends of those、them 等词汇形成指代衔接链,刘殿爵使用了 a man、his、the 等词汇形成指代衔接链,安乐哲与罗思文使用了 it、those、whom 等词汇形成指代衔接链,森舸澜则使用了 in that、it、these、that、this 等词汇形成指代衔接链。

比较照应是指通过比较两个事物之间相同或相似的关系得到解释。英语比较照应有两大类型:运用词汇和句法手段与通过改变形容词和副词的形态变化来表示总体比较意义。汉语没有形态变化,比较意义只有通过词汇手段表达。英汉语的比较照应衔接原理是一样的,即比较性语言成分的存在依赖比较对象,回指比较对象的过程就是语篇连贯的形成过程。如原文中的"近"与"远"形成对比,在译文中分别翻译如下:理雅各翻译为 is shown/keeps far from,辜鸿铭翻译为 confine … within/keep out of,刘殿爵翻译为 being observant of/stay clear of,安乐哲与罗思文翻译为 close to/keeps … at a distance,森舸澜翻译为 comes close to/to keep … at a distance。

分句照应主要是指前后各分句内容之间的相互关照。原文有三个意思:义、礼、不失其亲。现在我们分析五个译本,理雅各的译本采用了三个由 when 引导的条件句(when agreements are made, when respect is shown, when the parties upon whom a man leans are proper persons to be intimate with),辜鸿铭使用了三个以 if 引导的条件句(if you make promises/if you confine earnestness/if you make friends),刘殿爵使用了两个不定式结构(to be trustworthy/to be respectful)与一个条件句(if, in promoting good relationship with relatives by marriage),安乐哲与罗思文使用了三个主谓语结构[that making good on one's word(xin 信)gets one close to being appropriate(yi 义)/ that being deferential gets one close to observing ritual propriety(li 礼)/those who are accommodating and do not lose those with whom they],森舸澜使用了两个 in that 排比分句(in that your word can be counted upon/in that it allows you to keep shame and public disgrace at a distance)形成鲜明对比。

(2) 替代。替代是指用简短的替代词取代上文中某些词语的衔接手段。代词与被替代词有着相同的语法功能、相同的语义内容,所以替代与所代有同指和同结构的特征。要确定替代词的具体意义,必须到被替代项中去寻找具体含义。汉语倾向借助词汇复现手段来维持前后文的语义链,达到语义连贯的目的。英语为了避免重复通常采用替代手段来维系语义链,替代词的含义完全依赖被替代的语言单位。这种替代与被替代关系也是一种照应互文关系,可以称作替代照应关系。

替代一般可以分为名词性替代、动词性替代和分句性替代。名词性替代是指用替代词取代名词词组或名词词组中心词的现象。常用的替代词是 one/ones、the same、the kind、the sort、the former、the latter 等。动词性替代是指用替代词取代动词词组或动词词组中心词的衔接手段。这类替代词主要包括：代动词 do，复合代动词 do so、do it、do that、do this、do the same，替代句型如 so+do+主语、so+主语+do、so+be+主语、so+主语+be、so+will+主语、so+主语+will 等。小句性替代是指用替代词取代上文出现的名词性小句。例如，用替代词 so 或 not 取代 that 宾语从句，用 if so 或 if not 取代条件从句等。

在上例中名词性替代非常明显，动词性替代和小句性替代不明显。如在名词性替代中，理雅各翻译为 one/he，辜鸿铭翻译为 you/your，刘殿爵翻译为 a man/he，安乐哲与罗思文翻译为 one/they，森舸澜翻译为 you/your。

(3) 省略。省略是一种特殊的替代，被称作"零替代"，是用词项空缺的方式达到上下文衔接的目的。省略是"在简洁和清晰两者间的一种协调"(de Beaugrande and Dressler, 1981)。语篇分析中常把省略分为三类：名词性省略、动词性省略与分句性省略。李运兴(2001)指出，"汉译英中值得关注的省略现象，是汉语的零位主语的问题。汉语不是主语突出的语言，组词成句围绕主题，有时主语无须出现，而读者自明"。因此，汉译英时需要在译文中补充说明。

通过译本比较可以看出，原文中有子说的话是泛指，主语省略。而在译文中，五位译者都增加了相应的词汇如 one, you, a man 等以使词意清晰。此外，将汉语句群与英语句群相对照，可以看出英语译文是怎样补充主语及重建英语句型的。例如，理雅各使用被动句型(when agreements are made/what is spoken/when respect is shown)与条件句(when the parties upon whom a man leans are proper persons to be intimate with)，辜鸿铭使用了条件句(if you make promises/if you confine earnestness/if you make friends),刘殿爵使用了不定式结构(to be trustworthy/to be respectful)与条件句(if, in promoting good relationship with relatives by marriage),安乐哲与罗思文使用了结构主系表[that making good on one's word(xin 信)gets one close to being appropriate(yi 义)is because/that being deferential gets one close to observing ritual propriety(li 礼)is because],森舸澜使用了排比分句(in that your word can be counted upon/in that it allows you to keep shame and public disgrace at a distance)。

由此可见,在翻译转换过程中,译者对汉语中省略的主语添加了名词、代词等词汇补充手段以及用被动句、条件句等句法手段,以达到英语句法的要求。

(4)连接。作为衔接手段的连接是指通过连接词体现语篇中各种逻辑关系的衔接手段。语篇中常见的逻辑关系有时间、对照、递进、转折、举例和因果等关系。语篇中的逻辑关系包括显性(以连接词明示逻辑关系)和隐性(不使用连接词)两种情况。连接所涉及的翻译技巧是增词和减词译法:前者如源语的零连接为译入语的连接词所取代,后者如源语的连接词为译入语的零连接所取代。

如以上译例中的增词译法,理雅各在译文中使用了 when 引导的时间状语从句,辜鸿铭与刘殿爵使用了 if 引导的虚拟语气条件句,安乐哲与罗思文使用了因果连词 because 引导的状语从句突出原因,森舸澜使用了 in that 原因状语从句进行补充。

(5)词汇衔接。词汇衔接包括词汇重复、同义词、反义词、上下义词和搭配等。例如,理雅各使用了同义词 guides and masters,辜鸿铭使用了同义词 make promises/keep your word,刘殿爵使用了 stay clear of/lose,安乐哲与罗思文使用了 making good on/observing,森舸澜使用了重复词汇 comes close to,而且在注解中多次重复使用 trustworthiness(xin)与 rightness,并通过例子引导读者思考儒家"义"的本质内涵。

由上例分析可以看出,原文无形态变化,主要通过词汇手段表示时态、语态等语法意义,而英语译文则通过时态、语态、语气等方面的形态变化来展现。整体把握衔接形式有助于提高理解能力和表达能力。作为形式手段,衔接为译者快速获取原文信息提供了一个较为容易掌握的操作方法,同时也为译者提供了一种有效组织译文的谋篇布局方法。

(二) 连贯性

语篇的连贯性涉及文本深层世界各种概念及与之相关的方式(de Beaugrande and Dressler,1981)。连贯性关注的是文本深层结构所关涉的各种概念是否连贯,是文本使用者认知过程的结果,是语篇交际成功的重要保证之一。连贯的语篇"有一个内在的逻辑结构从头到尾贯通全篇,将所有的概念有机地串接在一起,达到时空顺序明晰,逻辑推进层次分明的效果"(李运兴,2001)。

张德禄指出了语篇连贯的主要因素与基本特点:首先,语篇内部各个部分在意义上是相互联系的,也就是说,是衔接的。其次,语篇的衔接形成的语义网络形成一个语义整体。最后,语篇必须适合情景语境,在语境中有适当的功能。前两者都受第三项的控制。据此,我们可以总结出语篇连贯概念的四个基本特点:分级性、连接性、整体性和功能性。因此,译者在处理原文形式与意义时,要对译文的连贯有构建意识:译者的思路要经历一个从原文连贯结构到译语连贯结构的转换。这种转换体现着两种语言、两种文化的思维定式的对应、对照甚至冲突,需要译者在思维方式上进行调整、变通,并把这种调整在译语语篇的连贯结构中表现出来(李运兴,2001)。

【例9】子曰:"能以礼让为国乎,何有!不能以礼让为国,如礼何?"(《论语·里仁》)(英语译文参考附录)

原文是指,孔子说:"能够以礼让治理国家吗?有何(人能够)?不能够以礼让治理国家,制礼又如何?""礼"代表了一种修身与治国相结合的文化精神。它是政治伦理与社会伦理的具体体现,也是治理国家的重要依据。孔子主张以礼治国,即用礼乐来约束君臣与官民的行为。

通过译文与原文比较可以看出,原文中的逻辑关系和线性顺序在译文中得到传递。具体而言,汉语句群的逻辑层次以意合形式呈现,而英语译文句群的逻辑层次明显具有形合关系。原文汉语的句群中没有看到逻辑标记,各词组、小句、句群间的逻辑关系都要依赖读者自己领会,但翻译成英语时,译者需根据英语表达习惯,将潜在的、隐性的逻辑关系表面化与突显化,并根据前后句关系增添相应连词。原文共两句,前后句关系是转折关系,但同时也是意义的推进关系,因此可以在译文中用层次指示词明确,如选用表示因果的 because/hence/therefore,表示转折的 but/whereas 等。

现在分析原文,原文第一句是感叹句,语言简练,使用对比结构,没有出现虚拟语气词语。而在译文中,除了辜鸿铭译文,其他译文都使用了 if 引导的虚拟语气从句,而且使用了对比结构,从而使译文逻辑清晰,如理雅各使用了 is able to/cannot 词语,刘殿爵使用了 is able to/is unable to 词语,安乐哲与罗思文使用了 are able to/but … are unable to 等词语,森舸澜使用了 is able to/on the other hand … not able to 等词语。辜鸿铭使用了 but 表示原文前后句群的转折,使语篇得以展开推进。但是整体来看,原文与译文结构表达仍然存在差异,如原文中的第一句是感叹句,而在译文中多是疑问句或陈述句。

由此可见,逻辑关系的重新确立以及线性顺序的重新思考是译者思维从原语语篇转换为译语语篇的重要思路,也是译者建构译文连贯结构的两大重要因素。因此,翻译过程不仅是语言表层的转换过程,也是语言内在逻辑关系与思维逻辑顺序的转换过程。这关系到译者思维的转换,也关系到译者对两种语言、两种文化思维的对照、对应甚至冲突的变通策略。

（三）意图性

意图性关注文本制作者的态度，是语篇制作者的意图在文本中的体现，即语篇制作者要将语言成分组织成具有衔接性、连贯性的文本，以有助于实现其制作文本的目的（de Beaugrande and Dressler，1981）。译者想要通过翻译行为达到所需目的，应考虑语篇意图，发挥译者主体性，否则将会影响译文接受。

语篇意图在语篇的各个层级上都有所体现。宏观上，从体裁来说，《论语》是语录体，语言对话占据了较大篇幅。中观上，从语域来说，可以根据言语行为理论来判断说话者的思维取向与意图是陈述、说教、评价、指令、鼓励还是批评（Austin，1975）。微观上，具体到语言的使用情况，如语篇的遣词造句与信息排列等都是语篇生成者的意向体现。

Halliday（1985）认为，语言功能主要有概念功能、人际功能和语篇功能。概念功能是指语言对人们在世界的经历进行表达的功能，即反映主客观世界所发生的事情，所涉及的人和物与时间、地点等因素。人际功能是指语言除了传递信息，还具有表达讲话者的身份、地位、态度、动机等功能。讲话者通过这一功能使自己参与某一情景语境，并表达态度，对他人施加影响。同时，此功能还表示说话者在情景语境中的角色关系，如提问者与回答者、陈述者与评判者之间的关系等。语篇功能是指在语意层中用各种语言手段将语言成分组织成连贯的语篇的功能。讲话者概念功能的意义潜势是否能够准确传递，依赖于人际功能与语篇功能是否能够实现。

根据 Austin（1975）的观点，人们的话语中包含了以下三种言语行为：（1）言内行为：指说出的话语具有可确定的命题意义，亦即说的内容。（2）言外（行事）行为：指说出的话语在交际语境中获得理解、引起反应的意义，亦即说的意图。（3）言后（成事行为）行为：指说出的话语能在听者的感情、思想或行动上产生（有益的或无意的）效果，亦即特定意图说特定的话后，有意无意产生的效果。这对我们了解信息的传递与接收、交际效果是否成功,以及其间所涉及的言语机制,具有重要的启示意义。

由此我们可以看到,广义层面的"意",既可能是讲话者言内行为传递的命题意义,也可能是讲话者言外行为意图要表示的延伸意义。而译者对"意"的阐释与翻译,实质上是讲话者的话语作为言后行为在译者认知语境中所实现的意义。如果译者所阐释的"意"与讲话者所表示的"意"吻合,则结果表现为译文的"达意"。而"意"是否能够准确传递,借助的不仅仅是词义层面的选词,还需要依靠通过句法层面的文本功能调度来呈现词语所携带的信息。《论语》是记录孔子及其弟子言行对话的语录体。因此,译者在《论语》翻译过程中要注意说话者的言语行为,注意交际语境、语篇意图与译者意图的影响。现在我们选取《论语》中的例子及其译文进行进一步分析。

【例10】子曰:"管仲之器小哉。"或曰:"管仲俭乎?"曰:"管氏有三归,官事不摄,焉得俭?""然则管仲知礼乎?"曰:"邦君树塞门,管氏亦树塞门。邦君为两君之好,有反坫,管氏亦有反坫。管氏而知礼,孰不知礼?"(《论语·八佾》)(英语译文参考附录)

原文意思是指,孔子说道:"管仲这个人的器量真是狭小!"有人问道:"管仲节俭吗?"孔子回答说:"他有三处豪华的藏金府库,他家里的管事也是一人一职而不兼任,怎么谈得上节俭呢?"那人又问:"那么管仲知礼吗?"孔子回答道:"国君大门口设立照壁,管仲在大门口也设立照壁。国君同别国国君举行会见时在堂上有放空酒杯的设备,管仲也有这样的设备。如果说管仲知礼,那么还有谁不知礼呢?"

通过原文句子分析可以看出,孔子学生用的小句数量少,孔子用的小句数量多,显然看出孔子在互动中的主导地位。此外,第一句是孔子感叹式的陈述,第二句与第三句则是师生间的对话:学生问,老师答。如果说话者之间的角色不能互换,则表示他们之间存在着不平等的权力关系(Eggins, 1994; Eggins and Slade, 1997)。原文中的感叹语气与师生间的亲密与不平等语气在译文中得到显化,一般来说,在不平等的关系中,只有权势高的说话者喜欢用责任性/可能性情态动词的高值,把握语气强烈,权势较低的说话者则会选用表示倾向/可能性的情态。理雅各使用了 indeed/how,辜鸿铭使用了 by no means/how,刘殿爵使用了 indeed/how,安乐哲与罗思文使用了 then,森舸澜使用了 how/then 等评价性的词汇,这些都反映了说话人对谈论对象的态度,而且森舸澜使用了 well 一词,把原文师生之间的亲密关系在译文中明晰化,使之更加贴近原文的语气。

现在分析原文中一些重要概念词的翻译,探讨各位译者的翻译意图在翻译过程中所起的重要作用以及译者的显化策略在翻译中的体现。

"器"原义是指器具,后引申比喻为"器量"。理雅各把"器"翻译为"器量"(the capacity),并作出注释:"器 see II. xii, but its significance here is different, and =our *measure* or *capacity*.";"礼"译为 rules of propriety。理雅各通过考证作出注疏,而且带有极强的基督教色彩,这是与他的翻译意图与工作使命分不开的。理雅各明确意识到,"一个从西方来到中国的传教士,如果未能完全理解掌握中国经典的内涵,未能亲自调查那些中国圣贤们所曾经涉猎的思想领域,并从中发现中国圣贤所建立的道德、社会和政治生活基础的话,就不适合他所担当的职责和正在从事的工作"(Legge,1991)。因此,理雅各在翻译过程中决定更注重原文内容而不是写作的文采。这并不是他对译文所使用语言的优美与地道的价值漠视,而是他期望能把诠释的准确性与译文风格的可接受性尽可能结合起来(Legge,1991)。正如他在序言中所述,"不以文害辞,不以辞害志。以意逆志,是为得之"。

辜鸿铭努力寻求两种语言文化之间的共通性,为了消除英语读者的陌生感,将辅佐齐桓公取得霸主地位的管仲比喻为统一了德意志帝国的政治家俾斯麦"a famous statesman (the Bismarck of the time)",借用了西方国家所熟悉的人物"the Bismarck of the time",以尽可能地消除英国读者的陌生感,增加他们对《论语》中人物的理解。辜鸿铭还在注释中引用了西方文学经典格言:Do, ut des。辜鸿铭通过唤醒英语读者所熟悉的思想经典,帮助他们深入理解原文含义。注释如下:

  令人惊奇的是,管仲这位古代中国的俾斯麦,在政治上竟然恪守着与那位著名的现代德意志帝国的奠基者同样的箴言"Do, ut des",汉语意为"欲取之,故与之"。

孔子称管仲"器小",辜鸿铭译为"Kuan Chung was by no means a great-minded man",意思是指管仲从思想与品德修养而言绝不是一个思想伟大的人。"三归"是指管仲修筑的"三归之台",辜鸿铭译为"magnificent Sansouci Pleasaunce"(壮丽的无忧宫乐园)。德国的无忧宫(Sanssouci Palace)是18世纪德意志王宫和园林,为普鲁士国王腓特烈二世模仿法国凡尔赛宫所建,位于德国波茨坦市。此外,辜鸿铭把"知礼"译为"a man of taste who observed the correct forms"(遵守正确礼义,举止得体)。此处,他用 taste 与 observe the correct forms 来解释"礼",即指人行为得体并遵守礼仪,而管仲却做不到。通过如此翻译,辜鸿铭拉近了英国读者与中华文化的距离,消除了英国读者对《论语》的陌生感。辜鸿铭如此翻译《论语》的直接动因是,他认为西方汉学家对中国历史文化没有深刻洞察,没有从哲学和文学高度深刻理解诠释中国儒家经典哲学。因此,辜鸿铭在序言中阐释了他的翻译策略:尽力按照一个受过教育的英国人表达同样思想的方式翻译孔子与其弟子的对话内容。

  刘殿爵把"器"翻译为 a vessel of small capacity,"礼"译为 rites,属于基本直译。刘殿爵强调在把这些儒家思想概念翻译成英语时,注意古汉语的简约、一词多义以及语境缺失的特点,不能仅仅局限于文字对应本身,而是要更关注作者的思想脉络、原文的思想内涵以及历史文化语境,结合文献、语义、语境、互文等多种考虑因素帮助读者准确把握原文思想内涵。

安乐哲与罗思文从中西哲学差异的视角把"器"译为 capacity。"礼"创译为 ritual propriety (li 礼)。安乐哲与罗思文认为,孔子所说的"礼"是关乎社会稳定的原则性秩序,可以指法律或行为标准,也可以指礼仪、礼貌与礼节等约束性行为,与西方的 propriety 的概念并不完全等同。安乐哲与罗思文在序言中指出,为了让读者充分理解《论语》的复杂深度,译者必须努力描述古代中国人所经历的世界。但这又是一项艰巨的任务,原因主要有以下几个方面:

(1) 现代英语语法与古汉语语法不同。

(2) 英语基本属于本质主义的语言,而古汉语更多属于事件性的语言。

(3) 汉语构词重视内在联系、普遍联系与新旧联系,而英文则更加重视单向线性原则,不太重视事物的内在联系,如汉语中的"树"会想到不同季节的树,而英语中的 the tree 则是特指某棵树。

(4) 中西存在不同的理念,中国强调"一多不分",而西方强调"一多二元"。例如,汉字是"一多不分"的体现之一:象形表义的造字方式,可以将中华文化的重要理念浓缩于一方汉字之中,人们利用汉字所包含的丰富信息,使中华文化传统得以流传。

(5) 中西基本观念不同,如中国人把修身求"道"当作己任,而西方人永远追求"超越性"的真理,如 god。译者通过语境阐释让中国儒家哲学呈现它自己的完整性。

森舸澜把"礼"译为 ritual,把"器"译为 vessel,并注释如下:"器"在字面上是指一种礼器,而孔子的迟钝的提问者显然只是从字面上看待他的说法:也许孔子的意思是管仲因节俭而使用小型、粗糙的礼器,或者是管仲使用小型礼器是因为仪式所需。提问者的这两个问题都给了孔子机会来评论管仲的道德缺陷,并清楚地表明,"器"在这里是比喻性含义,是指狭隘的专家或技术人员。

森舸澜曾在其译本前言中指出,自己之所以采用了大量注疏,主要原因是《论语》的深奥意义需要有领航人引导读者深入探索其中的奥妙(Slingerland,2003)。森舸澜选择程树德四卷本《论语集释》作为主要参考的中文底本,主要原因是该书注释丰富而且兼容并蓄。因此,森舸澜在译本正文中沿袭了《论语》的注疏传统,直接把注释放在各章译文之后,以供读者查阅。森舸澜在翻译时会增加注疏,提供相关评论与背景知识,注意给英语读者留有思考空间。这样,英语读者在读《论语》译本与理解儒家哲学时也在增强自己的思考辨别能力。由此可以看出,译者的翻译策略是与语篇意图和译者意图密不可分的。

【例11】子曰:"君子喻于义,小人喻于利。"(《论语·里仁》)(英语译文参考附录)

原文是指"君子通晓道义,小人通晓私利"。该句采用了对偶与对比的修辞手法,如"君子"与"小人"的对比。通过译文比较,我们看到译文也大都采取了相似的结构,使句式看起来整齐对称。

现在本书探讨原文中"君子""义"的理解与翻译。

(1) 关于"君子"的理解。先秦早期"君子"的解释主要是从政治角度立论的,多指"君王之子",着眼于社会地位而非道德品质。对"君子"一词的具体说明,始于孔子。孔子心目中的君子兼具高尚道德品质和完美人格,具有"仁者不忧,知者不惑,勇者不惧"的品德,是内在精神"仁"与外在规约"礼"的有机统一。孔子认为,君子具有以下特征:"君子不器"并重视自我修养,注意"知命""知礼""知言"能力培养。孔子认为,君子的精神追求就是行仁行义。"君子之于天下也,无适也,无莫也,义之与比。"(《论语·里仁》)君子应担道行义,以张扬仁义为己任,"见义不为,无勇也"(《论语·为政》)。子曰:"君子义以为上。"(《论语·阳货》)何谓义?《中庸》曰:"义者,宜也。"孔子认为,人有追求正当利益的权利,但孔子强调人对于利益的追求一定要符合正当性的要求。"不义而富且贵,于我如浮云。"(《论语·述而》)"富与贵,是人之所欲也,不以其道得之,不处也;贫与贱,是人之所恶也,不以其道得之,不去也。君子去仁,恶乎成名?君子无终食之间违仁,造次必于是,颠沛必于是。"(《论语·里仁》)孔子认为,人们可以追求富贵与正当权益,但不能因为追求富贵与权益而损害仁义。

通过比较"君子"的译文可以看出,理雅各将其译为 the superior man,辜鸿铭将其译为 a wise man。刘殿爵将其译为 the gentleman。安乐哲与罗思文认为,原文中"君子"的含义与英文词 the superior man 与 a wise man 的意义还存在一定差距,与 the gentleman 也有一定距离。因此,安乐哲与罗思文将其译为 exemplary persons (junzi 君子),并增添了拼音与汉字形式。安乐哲与罗思文指出,"做翻译和进行文化比较一样,都不能一厢情愿和简单化,而必须坚持主观与客观相结合,这是原汁原味地理解对方文化的一种必要意识。比如,对待儒家的'角色伦理学',我们首先需要做的是让儒家伦理学从西方伦理学的语境中脱离出来,使它返回到自己的语境中去,让它自己讲述自己"(安乐哲,2015)。因此,安乐哲与罗思文在翻译《论语》时,一方面充分利用西方的语言文化知识,另一方面努力还原原文语境,使儒家伦理学显示自己的主体性,尽量实现与西方哲学平等对话。

森舸澜把君子译为 the gentleman,并通过注解,解释了该儒家哲学概念的意义。森舸澜注解如下:

> 再次,"君子"不是外在利益的承诺,而是由儒家实践的内在的善行所驱动的。参见 4.2、4.5、4.9、4.11 和 4.12。一些评论认为,应该从社会阶层的角度理解"绅士"和"小人"的区别,因为"小人"在汉朝文本中常简单地用来表示"普通人"。很明显,孔子认为任何社会阶层的人都有可能成为绅士(6.6,7.7),而这种社会地位不一定符合实际的道德价值。而且很明显的是,至少在《论语》中,绅士/小人的区别是指道德品质而不是社会地位。

由此可见，森舸澜通过注解中的解释与互参，强调了儒家文化中的"君子"更加强调道德层面的区分，而不是地位高低的划分。森舸澜的注解一方面给读者提供思考的空间，另一方面又引导读者根据语境理解原文的内涵。

（2）关于原文中"义"的理解。古汉语中"义"的理解可归纳为以下三方面。

一是礼仪。《说文解字》曰："己之威仪也，从我羊。"注曰："义为古文威仪字，谊为古文仁义字。仪者，度也。谊者，人所宜也。"其中，"义"同"仪"，是指礼仪。

二是合宜。《释名·释言语》曰："义者，宜也，制裁事物使合宜也"。

三是合宜的道德、行为或道理，合乎道义。《礼·中庸》记云："义者，天下之制也"。由此可见，"义"最初强调"仪"与"宜"的意义，后来逐渐注重道德观念，这也是《论语》所沿用的意义。

《论语》中的"义"共出现了24次，大体分为以下几类：

第一，"义"体现了一个人的行为的正当性。孔子指出，"君子喻于义，小人喻于利"（《论语·里仁》）"君子义以为质，礼以行之，孙以出之，信以成之。君子哉"（《论语·卫灵公》）"有君子之道四焉：其行己也恭，其事上也敬，其养民也惠，其使民也义"（《论语·公冶长》）"上好礼，则民莫敢不敬；上好义，则民莫敢不服；上好信，则民莫敢不用情"（《论语·子路》）"今之成人者何必然？见利思义，见危授命，久要不忘平生之言，亦可以为成人矣"（《论语·宪问》）。子路评价一位隐士不愿做官时，说道："不仕无义。长幼之节，不可废也；君臣之义，如之何其废之？欲洁其身，而乱大伦。君子之仕也，行其义也。道之不行，已知之矣。"（《论语·微子》）

第二，人要朝着义不断努力、改变。例如，孔子说，"主忠信，徙义，崇德也。爱之欲其生，恶之欲其死。既欲其生，又欲其死，是惑也"（《论语·颜渊》）"夫达也者，质直而好义，察言而观色，虑以下人。在邦必达，在家必达"（《论语·颜渊》）"见善如不及，见不善如探汤。吾见其人矣,吾闻其语矣。隐居以求其志,行义以达其道。吾闻其语矣,未见其人也"(《论语·季氏》)。"勇"与"义"密不可分。孔子说,"见义不为,无勇也"(《论语·为政》)"君子义以为上。君子有勇而无义为乱,小人有勇而无义为盗"(《论语·阳货》)。

第三,不义会带来灾难。"德之不修,学之不讲,闻义不能徙,不善不能改,是吾忧也"(《论语·季氏》)"群居终日,言不及义,好行小慧,难矣哉"(《论语·卫灵公》)。

现在分析原文中"义"的翻译。理雅各将"义"翻译成righteousness,辜鸿铭翻译成right,刘殿爵翻译成moral,安乐哲与罗思文翻译成appropriate(yi 义),森舸澜翻译成rightness+注解。相较而言,理雅各的翻译受西方基督教思想的影响,因为righteousness(公义)是神的属性,与《论语》中的"义"的含义还有一定距离,并不完全对等。辜鸿铭翻译的right仍然是在西方思想的框架下互文对应。刘殿爵翻译的moral显然与"义"也不完全对等,因为moral更多从道义层面来理解,多与"自由""选择""应当""个人主义""困境"等意思相关。安乐哲与罗思文认为,《论语》中的"义"更多与"礼""仁""信"的意义相关,更加贴近"宜"(appropriateness)的意思(Ames and Rosemont, 1998)。因此,该词语作为一个文化空缺词,很难找到对应词,宜采用音译+汉字的翻译策略,从哲学层面翻译,以解释中西哲学内涵的不同。森舸澜通过意译+注解使英文读者对"义"的理解(应重视儒家思想实践意义的实质性好处,而不是只有口头许诺)更加深入、全面,指出语言行为在不同情境中所表达的不同意思。因此,从某种意义上来说,森舸澜的文化诠释策略能把丰富的中华传统文化内涵传递给西方,有利于英语读者了解中国的儒家思想。

综上所述,《论语》的体裁以及文本的神秘深奥性,使得《论语》读者需要借助历代学者的注疏和阐释才能理解原文本的内容。因此,译者在译文中增加丰富的注疏可以帮助英语读者理解原文语境的丰富性与文本的灵动性,还可以引导英语读者通过阅读大量的注疏熟悉原文作者与原文本内容。此外,由于缺乏当时的语境,《论语》非常晦涩难懂。孔子在传授知识时注重举一反三,常常引出弟子回答或发问,然后再纠正和评论,适当时候再给以启发引导。孔子强调,"不愤不启,不悱不发。举一隅不以三隅反,则不复也"。这种鲜活的语境却在《论语》文本中有所缺失,因此增加了读者理解原文意义的难度。从这个意义上说,《论语》的注疏和阐释是必要的。

由此可见,《论语》的语言文化特点以及时空距离与审美距离等因素,增加了《论语》语篇意图理解与翻译的难度。因此,译者需要根据语境使用相应的补偿翻译策略传递说话者的意图与文化内涵。译者的翻译行为会受社会语境的影响,并积极协调着作者与目标语读者的互动过程。翻译过程最直观地体现了译者主体性的发挥。从原文的理解到译者翻译策略的选择,再到译文的阐述,处处受译者翻译意图的影响。同时,译者的语篇意识、认知心理结构、翻译目的、社会文化背景等都会影响译者的翻译意图,并最终影响译作的产生、传播与接受。

(四)可接受性

可接受性是指语篇接受者的态度,这一系列连贯的语篇对语篇使用者来说应该有关或者有些关联(de Beaugrande and Dressler,1981)。译文在某种意义上体现着原语文化和目标语文化之间的时空差异,而正是这种时空错位为读者提供了多种解读的可能性。因此,译者在翻译过程中需要考虑读者的阅读期待。

【例12】孔子谓季氏:"八佾舞于庭,是可忍也,孰不可忍也。"(《论语·八佾》)(英语译文参考附录)

原文是指,孔子评论季氏在自己家庙的庭院里用了天子的八佾奏乐舞蹈,说他这样的事情都忍心做,那还有什么事情不敢做呢?孔子表达了他对这种破坏周礼等级的僭越行为极为不满。其中,"八佾"是古代奏乐时的舞蹈,每行各八人,成为一佾。天子礼乐可用八佾,也就是六十四人；诸侯六佾，四十八人；大夫四佾，三十二人。季氏身为大夫应用四佾，此处用八佾就是僭越了礼乐。

关于"八佾舞于庭"的翻译，理雅各、辜鸿铭、刘殿爵、安乐哲与罗思文、森舸澜分别译为：had eight rows of pantomimes in his area, employed eight sets of choristers (an Imperial prerogative) in their family chapel, use eight rows of eight dancers each to perform in their courtyard, use of the imperial eight rows of eight dancers in the courtyard of their estate, have eight rows of dancers performing in their courtyard。

其中理雅各在注释中增加了佾（a row of dancers, or pantomimes rather, who kept time in the temple services）、庭（the front space before the rasied portion in the principal hall, moving or brandishing feathers, flags, or other articles. In his ancestral temple, the king had eight rows, each row consisting of eight men, a duke or prince had six, and a great officer only four）以及相关背景知识与上下文语境的注释。辜鸿铭使用了文内注释皇帝特权（an imperial prerogative）。刘殿爵增加了文外注释皇帝特权（a prerogative of the emperor）。森舸澜则作了大量注解：根据后来的礼文，在典礼场合，社会上不同阶层的人允许在祠堂外由不同数量的舞者进行表演：天子允许八佾，诸侯允许六佾，大夫允许四佾，官员允许两佾。虽然季氏实际上是鲁国的统治者，但他只正式担任大夫的职务，这里使用八佾就代表了他对周王礼仪特权的无耻篡夺。

此外，关于原文中"忍"的理解与翻译，理雅各翻译为"bear"，辜鸿铭翻译为"allow"，刘殿爵翻译为"tolerate"，安乐哲与罗思文以及森舸澜翻译为"condone"。根据《牛津高阶英汉双解词典》（第7版）解释：（1）bear：to be able to accept and deal with something unpleasant. （2）allow：to let sb/sth do sth; to let sth happen or be done. （3）tolerate：to allow sb to do sth that you do not agree with or loke.

(4) condone: to accept behaviour that is morally wrong or to treat it as if it were not serious. 从原文的文化语境来看,孔子一向推行"君臣父子"的封建礼教,对于季氏擅用天子之礼仪这一严重违背礼教的行为,感到十分愤怒。因此,安乐哲与罗思文以及森舸澜翻译的 condone 最为贴切。

由此可以看出,为使原文成功译介给英语读者,使读者理解原文的文化内涵,译者的注释翻译策略可以缩短译文与读者之间的距离。根据 Jauss(1984)的观点,读者解读文本时往往受以往的审美经验(如体裁、风格、语言)与以往的生活经验(社会历史人生)的双重制约,翻译活动不仅涉及译者对原文本的理解表达,还涉及译入语读者的理解接受。因此,译者身兼原文读者和译文作者双重身份,在翻译过程中需充分考虑译入语读者的阅读期待、审美距离与文化历史背景,采用合适的显化翻译策略,增强译文的可接受性。

【例13】子曰:"三军可夺帅也,匹夫不可夺志也。"(《论语·子罕》)。(英语译文参考附录)

原文是指,一个军队的首领可以改变,但是一个有志气的人的志向是不能被改变的。这句话强调了人格的高贵,旨在教育学生,一个人应该坚定信念,矢志不渝。

从读者的角度来说,"三军"与"匹夫"的理解需要译者准确作出诠释。三军是"军队的通称,古制,12 500人为一军",匹夫"在古代是指平民中的男子,后来泛指平民百姓"。对于"匹夫"的翻译,安乐哲与罗思文将其翻译为 common peasants,不是很贴切,其他译文 common man, common people, commoner 则比较准确。因此,译者对原文的准确理解是至关重要的。关于"三军"的翻译,理雅各的译文 the forces,辜鸿铭的译文 an army 与刘殿爵的 the three armies 的译文表达欠准确,而安乐哲与罗思文的 the combined armies 与森舸澜的 the combined forces of an entire state 的译文更加准确。森舸澜在译文注解中通过比较"三军可以夺帅"与"个人意志的顽强",对人的意志的不可动摇性作出强调。

由此可见,由于文化的多元复杂性以及"文化他者"之间缺少普遍沟通的可能性,在翻译过程中,原文词句的意义在目标语中不可能得到完全表达。此外,具有不同文化背景的读者具有不同的生活经验和认知框架,这会促使读者对译文形成不同的预先期待,影响其对译文的理解与接受,并最终会影响译者在考虑读者需求时所选择的翻译策略。森舸澜的译文有助于译者和目标语读者在目标语的政治文化语境中增强对"异域他者"的理解,从而将原文的丰富涵义融入目标语的文化语境。

总之,译者在"他者"和"共通性"之间努力,在文化互动中使译文在异域和本土之间具有更强的张力,进而潜移默化地影响目标语读者的思维。译文中的异域因素以及"异化"策略,可以使翻译得以延伸与扩展,并可以丰富滋养目标语文化。因此,理想的译者应当保留原作字里行间所蕴含的各种意义的可能性,并将丰富的信息传递给身处特定文化背景的目标读者。因此,翻译的效果不仅仅取决于译者,在一定程度上也取决于目标语读者。

(五) 信息性

信息性关注文本传递的信息情况,是指对篇章的接受者而言它所承载的信息超越或低于期望值的程度,也就是篇章中的事件在多大程度上是预料之中的还是出于意外的,是已知的还是未知的或是不确定的(de Beaugrande and Dressler,1981)。在《论语》内容的翻译传播过程中,信息性主要体现在《论语》内容信息的选择及其内容信息的准确传递。

【例14】有子曰:"礼之用,和为贵。先王之道,斯为美;小大由之。有所不行,知和而和,不以礼节之,亦不可行也。"(《论语·学而》)(英语

译文参考附录)

原文是指,有子说:"施行礼制的作用,应当达到和谐的目的。古代圣明君主在治理国家的时候,在这一点上做得很好。无论大事小事,他们都会依循礼制而行。但在遇到行不通的问题时,如果只是单纯追求和谐,而抛却礼法的节制,也是行不通的。"

首先,通过分析原文与译文的信息布局结构可以看出,原文的信息布局是意合结构,是话题突出的语言结构,采用了话题+评论的句式。而在译文中则是由许多连词连接而成的形合结构,是主语突出的语言结构,主语+谓语的句式贯穿全文。从汉语结构到译语结构转换调整的过程就是译者信息思维转换的过程。另外,从语篇的信息推进程序来看,译文与原文语篇结构大体一致。这可能与译者尊重原文的权威性与学术性有关。李运兴(2001)也曾经指出:"翻译的学术目的越强,对语篇结构进行变动的趋势越小;源语语篇作者的权威越大,译者对语篇结构进行变动的余地就越小。"

其次,分析原文的信息内容"礼"。《论语》的核心思想可以概括为"仁"与"礼":仁为内容,礼为形式,以中庸为准则,以和为最终目的。"礼"可以理解为一种礼制,可以协调各种社会关系,约束人们的行为规范,进而保证社会秩序有条不紊地运行。"礼"的内容主要包含两方面:"一是国家机关、社会组织内部的各种规章制度,二是社会上人与人之间的尊卑等级,以及与这种等级相关的行为规约(范敏,2017)。"礼"的作用与最终目的则是追求社会的和谐与安定,包括国家、社会与民众的和谐,如君臣关系、官民关系的和谐、社会上人与人之间的和谐等。孔子曾说:"居上不宽,为礼不敬,临丧不哀,吾何以观之哉?"(《论语·八佾》)。这句话的意思是,"居于统治地位的人,倘若不能宽以待人,行礼的时候不够恭敬严肃,遭遇丧葬之事不是真的哀痛,对此我怎能看得下去呢?"

由此可以看出,在孔子看来,"礼"的含义与功能体现在方方面面,它不仅体现在礼仪思想与礼仪仪式的结合,而且可以用来作为治国理政、社会安定与处世之道的政治策略。孔子强调,领导者需要深谙礼制,具有为人处世的做事原则与管理策略,才能更有效地推进事业的进步。由此可见,儒家的"礼"的学说涉及个人与社会之间的关系,在某种程度上存在着一种与自由观念的紧张关系的儒家思维,其中所涉及的中国社会政治思想的讨论关注问题也都与此相关,包括"个人生活和社会生活的修养、基于传统的礼仪活动(礼)在再造社会政治和谐的过程中的作用、通过对名字次序的安排来规定和协调社会政治角色、文化模仿的功效、正当抗议的方式,等等"(安乐哲,2006)。这是与西方国家强调诸如"个人与社会的关系、私人活动与公共活动的范围,自然法与实体法的地位、权利与义务的性质、国家的强制权(合法权威)、正义的含义"等等有所区别(范敏,2017)。

再次,关于"礼"的翻译,理雅各、辜鸿铭、刘殿爵、安乐哲与罗思文、森舸澜分别将其译为 the rules of propriety, art, rites, ritual propriety (li 礼)/ritual propriety, ritual/rites。理雅各将"礼"翻译为 the rules of propriety,但在注释中指出"礼"字的概念其实很难在西方语言中翻译,因为"礼"字含有与上级相处时应该"事之宜"的含义。理雅各指出,在该例句中,"礼"与"道"是相通的。

辜鸿铭的译文选择 art 这个词,认为它有五个含义:艺术品(a work of art);艺术实践(the practice of art);与"天然"相对的"人工"(artificial as opposed to natural);与自然"质"相对的人文"文"(the principle of art as opposed to the principle of nature);严格的人文规范(the strict principle of art)。辜鸿铭指出,最后的第五个含义即表达了"礼"的"事之宜"之意。儒家思想重视诗书礼仪,强调"行有余力,则以学文"与"文质彬彬,然后君子"。在这个意义上,"'礼'与质相对的'art(as opposed to nature)'的意义是相通的,辜鸿铭翻也因此将"礼之用,和为贵"译成了'In the practice of art, what is valuable is natural spontaneity'"(刘雪芹,2010)。

刘殿爵、安乐哲与罗思文、森舸澜则强调中国的各种社会关系是由"礼"相联的,这与西方社会的基督教思想中上帝创造并影响人类等一多二元的关系不同,强调"由礼所建构的社会不仅是一个世俗的社会,而且是儒教经验的场所,是由礼的各种规约而构成的各种角色和关系"(范敏,2017)。不同的是,安乐哲与罗思文采用"意译+拼音+汉字"的策略,启动英语读者的联想,达到文化传播的目的。森舸澜则在注释中进行了解读,强调个人与社会的关系以及"礼"的终极目的"和"的作用。林语堂曾指出:"'礼'字一方面指'仪式''礼节',在广泛意义上指'礼貌',在至高无上的哲学意义上则指各安其所的理想社会秩序,尤其是合理的封建秩序。"(Lin,1938)因此,"礼"的本质是一种行为规约,对个人可以修身养性,所谓"克己复礼为仁";对国家可以用来建设精神文明,所谓"道之以德,齐之以礼,有耻且格"。

我们再看"有子"的翻译,理雅各、刘殿爵、安乐哲与罗思文以及森舸澜分别翻译为 the philosopher Yu、Yu Tzu、Master You、Master You。辜鸿铭省略人名的翻译,而代之以 a disciple of Confucius,虽然理解上比直接音译加注的处理更加简单明了,减轻了读者对于信息处理的负担,消除了读者的"陌生感"。然而需要注意的是,人不同于事物和地方,人是活的,是有个性和思想的,而这种个性和思想又必然体现在其言行之中。尤其《论语》中各位弟子的言行各有特点,而孔子与他们的对话也是因材施教。虽然辜鸿铭把颜回和子路别译作 the favorite Yen Hui 和 the intrepid Chung Yu,但其他诸多弟子的鲜明个性都如本例中的译文一样。因此,就这层意义而言,辜鸿铭译文的信息是不完整的。

由此可见,译者在《论语》翻译过程中经常受翻译目的与文化背景等的影响。我们需要注意以下几点:首先,译者对《论语》原文正确理解,进行严格的训诂、考据和义理求证。其次,对于《论语》中很多中国古代文化特有的事物,如人名和地名的翻译简化往往带来损失,归化又会常常导致误解,因此,译者需根据情况,灵活处理。最后,儒家学说自成体系,很难用西方文化体系中的概念去诠释,因此译者在翻译儒家思想体系中的关键词汇时,需要仔细斟酌中西文化差异。

【例 15】子曰:"人而不仁,如礼何?人而不仁,如乐何?"(《论语·八佾》)(英语译文参考附录)

原文是指,孔子说:"做人若没有仁德之心,应当如何对待礼仪制度呢?做人若没有仁德之心,又该如何对待文学和音乐呢?"孔子认为,礼乐属于文化的范畴,"仁"是人们内心追求的道德修养,用恭敬的态度表现出来就是"礼"。只有心怀仁德,行之于外的"礼"才是真正有礼。

"仁"字从词源上来说,是指对他人的尊重和友爱,强调人们彼此依存、友好相处、互助互爱。儒家把"仁"的学说与政治关联,形成"仁政"说,对中国的政治思想产生了重要影响。"仁"是儒家思想的核心,是儒家学说的最高道德准则。"仁"的最初含义是指人与人的一种亲善关系。孔子把"仁"定义为"爱人",并解释说"夫仁者,己欲立而立人,己欲达而达人","己所不欲,勿施于人"。"仁"逐渐演变为具有多义性、内涵丰富、意义深刻的概念,包括社会、群体与个体等生活思想、行为的理想人格修养体系。具体来说,它既包括内在的如何达到"仁"的境界,也包括外在的如何实现"仁"的方式方法;既包括个人理想人格的培养,也包括治理国家的理想社会行为。

关于"仁"的翻译,理雅各、辜鸿铭、刘殿爵、安乐哲与罗思文、森舸澜分别将其译为 humanity(侧重仁义),moral character(侧重道德),benevolent(侧重善心),authoritative(ren 仁)(侧重汉语本意),Good(大写,侧重广义的良善)。由此可以看出,各位译者为我们研究《论语》的哲学概念提供了不同的视角,尤其是安乐哲与罗思文以及森舸澜在译文中提供了大量的信息,使我们更深刻地理解儒学的内涵。

安乐哲与罗思文认为,authoritative 具有权威、创作、威信、礼貌等多种功能,能贴切地表达出"仁"的多层含义,因为"仁代表一个人的整体认知:表现在一个人仪式化的角色和关系中,具有修养的认知、审美、道德和宗教意识。它是一个人的自我领域,是重要关系的总和,构成了一个坚定的社会人。"仁"不仅是精神上的,而且是身体上的:包括姿势和行为,手势和肢体语言"(Ames and Rosemont,1998)。译者还指出,"如果把仁译为 benevolence,就会因缺少人类的心理体验,成人之路的复杂含义不能突显,使得意义不完整"(Ames and Rosemont,1998)。安乐哲与罗思文的翻译揭示了"仁"作为本质内化的过程。

森舸澜将"仁"译为 Good,并在注解中阐释了做一个善人的标准与实现"仁"的途径,指出如果一个人纵使有很多才能,如果没能实践"礼、乐"也不能称作"Good"(仁)。森舸澜在注解中指出,虽然这是一个关于内在性情与儒家实践关系的一般性陈述(参见译本 3.12 和 17.11),但这一评论可能更具体地针对译本 3.1 和 3.2 中批评的季氏家族和鲁国其他主要家族。森舸澜还引用汉史的解释,强调一个没有仁德之心的人没有办法运用自己。他不能练习仪式和音乐,即使他有许多其他的才能,也只会被用来做不好的事。在孔子生活的时代,鲁国大臣们攻击仪式和音乐,贪婪篡夺国王特权,相互遵循既定腐败习惯,践行错误,导致正不压邪,人们缺乏仁德之心。

【例 16】父在观其志,父没观其行,三年无改于父之道,可谓**孝**矣。(《论语·学而》)(英语译文参考附录)

这段话包含了孔子对"孝"的深刻认识:当父亲还在世的时候,要观察一个人的志向(因为他无权独立行动),而在他父亲死后,要考察一个人的行为——如果是他长期不改变他父亲的合理的处世之道,这样的人才可以说是尽孝了。

通过对比原文与译文发现,辜鸿铭的译文出现理解的信息错误。辜鸿铭将其翻译为 When a man's father is living the son should have regard to what his father would have him do; when the father is dead, to what his father has done. 辜鸿铭在翻译原文中的"父没观其行"时,强调"在父亲去世三年之后,仍能终生保持父亲的做事准则,这样的儿

子,可以成为孝子"(辜鸿铭,2013)。但是原文中隐含的意思是儿子要"承续父业,不轻易改动,这是氏族传统的要求;即使改动,也得要慢慢来,所以要'三年'及多年之后才动"(李泽厚,1998;唐翼明,2016)。因此,原文强调"过程"的含义未能在译文中表达。

通过对比分析不同译文,我们可以发现安乐哲与罗思文的译文内容更加准确:While a person's father is still alive, observe what he intends; when his father dies, observe what he does. A person who for three years refrains from reforming the ways (dao 道) of his late father can be called a filial son (xiao 孝). 其他四个译文隐含的意思是,如果儿子遵循父亲的"道"大约三年不变,就是孝子,这意味着儿子可能以后仍然保持遵循父亲的"道"不变。此外,英文 filial 带有基督教含义,表示"对上帝虔诚"。因此,安乐哲与罗思文的译文使用了"reform""filial (孝)"等词语,隐含着儿子必须首先严格尊崇传统的礼节,在完全吸收理解"父道"之后,在合适的时间、在合适的环境下再进行改革的意思。这一译文强调了儒家哲学顺序的过程性特点与临时性特点,阐明了儒家哲学中"人能弘道,非道弘人"与"当仁,不让于师"的深刻道理。

孔子认为,"孝悌"是儒家思想的重要内容,是中国古代处理家族内部两大关系的基本要求。"孝"是指尊敬顺从父母,"悌"是指尊重兄长。孔子还认为,"孝"是仁之本,不孝就是不仁。即要实行仁,必须从"孝"做起,这也奠定了"孝"在儒家学说中的重要地位。孔子所讲的"孝"主要有三层含义:一是"敬而能养"。孔子认为,敬、爱才是"孝"的本质,只是在生活上赡养父母并不是"孝",要有真正的孝心、爱心等真情实感。二是绝对地服从父母的意志,听父母的话,即使知道父母错了,也要好言相劝、和颜悦色地顺从父母。三是"三年无改于父之道"。孔子要求人们对待父母"生,事之以礼;死,葬之以礼;祭之以礼"。孔子对"孝"的理解体现着尊敬、赡养、真诚的仁爱之心,贯穿着社会的礼制与礼仪规则。当然,我们也应该认识到其孝道有一定的局限性。安乐哲(2017)

认为,汉语中的"孝"不等于英语文化中的"filial",汉语中的"孝"字由"老"和"子"构成,不仅蕴含了情感的传承,体现了晚辈对长辈的尊敬和供养,是人们至臻完善的源头与人类社会和谐的基础,还集中体现在语言、价值观念、哲学思想等文化与历史的传承性上,具有丰富的意义,因此把"孝"阐释为"filial(孝)"。

由此可见,在《论语》翻译过程中,原文信息的充分理解以及准确、通顺、地道地传递显得非常重要。因此,译者需要深刻理解《论语》的文化内容,熟悉英汉语篇的转换规律,根据英语读者需求、共有知识情况、语言习惯表达等调整想要表达的信息内容,提高译文的可接受性,有效实现译文的成功译介。

(六) 情境性

情境性是指产生文本的各种情境因素(de Beaugrande and Dressler,1981)。一般来说,各种社会文化语境、语言语境与各种情景语境都会影响语言的表达与功用、语篇体裁的使用与功能。同时,各种语言体裁以及语言表达又是各种语境环境下的产物。

Halliday(1964)指出,语域对于语言选择与使用具有重要作用,并探讨了语域分析的三个变量:语场、语旨与语式。语场是指所发生事情主题以及相关社会活动的性质与特点;语旨是指发生社会活动的交际者及其基本情况、地位、角色以及关系等;语式是指语言在交际过程中所起的作用,包括交际途径与修辞方式。语场、语旨、语式与语言的功能密切有关:语场体现了语言的概念功能,语旨体现了语言的人际功能,语式体现了语言的成篇功能。进一步说,与语场相关的概念功能又要由语言的及物性结构来实现,与基调相关的人际功能由语言的情态系统来实现,而与语式相关的成篇功能则由主位—述位结构以及衔接手段等来实现。

李运兴(2010)指出,翻译语境是指译者在翻译过程中瞬时生成的语境视野,并把翻译语境主要分为译者的语境视野和翻译研究者的语境视野,将重点放在研究者上,指出语境是一个心理架构,是听者关于世界假设的子集。翻译语境本质上是认知的,是指翻译事件发生时,为完成交际意图,译者所调动起来的心理世界因素与所摄入的语篇世界和外部世界的相关因素的总和。翻译并非在真空中产生,它会受到各种文本内外因素的影响。这些限制或者在文本转换过程中的各种操纵过程成为翻译研究工作的主要焦点。为了研究这些过程,翻译研究已经改变了研究路线而因此变得更加广阔(Bassnett and Lefevere, 2001)。

现在我们分析语言语境、心理语境与社会语境对译者翻译策略的影响:

【例17】子曰:"学而时习之,不亦说乎?有朋自远方来,不亦乐乎?人不知而不愠,不亦君子乎?"(《论语·学而》)(英语译文参考附录)

原文意思是,孔子认为,学习后经常温习所学知识是一件令人愉悦的事情;有志同道合的人能从远方来也是一件令人高兴的事情;而且如果别人不了解我,但我不生气,这也应该算是道德上有修养的人。

原文中有很多古今异义与一词多义现象,翻译时需要注意。古今异义词汇有很多,例如,"学"在《论语》中出现多次,更多与德行密切相关,与孔子所推崇的"忠""孝""信"等君子品质相联系,逐渐达到"敏于事而慎于言,就有道而正焉",具有孔子"修习君子"的特定方法论内涵,而不是现在一般意义上的"学习"或"学问"。在该例中,"学"主要是指学习西周的礼、乐、诗、书等传统文化典籍。"君子"古义是指有道德修养的人,与现代意义"泛指品德高尚的人"有所区别。"时"古义是指"按一定的时间",今义是指"时间"。"习"古义是指"温习、实践",今义是指"学习"。一词多义的现象也比较常见,例如,"知"在《论语》中出现很多次,是指"了解""获得""知道""智慧"等含义,在本例语境中的意思是指"了解"。因此,译者在翻译过程中根据语境选取正确的词汇至关重要。

现在重点分析"学"与"知"的翻译。

(1)"学"的翻译。作为儒家思想经典的《论语》,其内容博大精深,思想除了包括伦理道德范畴"仁"、社会政治范畴"礼",还包括认识方法论范畴"思学"等。在《论语》中,孔子认为,"学"是一个不断思考、改造自然生命,使其发展、完善的过程。孔子重视学习传统与人文素养,重视向贤人智者学习,以提高自身素质。在"学"的内容及目的上,孔子指出,"子以四教:文行忠信"(《论语·述而》),"贤贤易色;事父母,能竭其力;事君,能致其身;与朋友交,言而有信。虽曰未学,吾必谓之学矣"(《论语·学而》)。孔子曾说:"颂《诗》三百,受之以政,不达;使之四方,不能专对,虽多,亦奚以为?"(《论语·述而》)孔子依此认为可以培养"志于道,据于德,依于仁,游于艺"(《论语·子路》)的君子,此即"学"之目的。孔子认为,在学习过程中还要学以致用,知行合一,有所担当,"仕而优则学,学而优则仕"(《论语·子张》),这也是《论语》中"学"思想的意旨。这样通过学习传统人文,把个体生命与传统文化相融合,并通过见贤思齐、认知思考与修己养身使自己成为真正意义上的"君子"。

通过比较译文可以发现,关于"学"的翻译,理雅各、辜鸿铭、刘殿爵、安乐哲与罗思文、森舸澜分别将其译为 learn, acquire knowledge, learn something, study/learn 与 learn。理雅各认为,learn(学)重在强调一种教育体系的显著与辉煌。刘殿爵认为,learn 强调学习的实践性,强调学习者本身能力的提高;而 study 强调学习的内容,因此他将"学"翻译为 learn something。安乐哲与罗思文在尾注中指出,中华传统文化中对于"学"的认识,更多强调一种过程与任务(study),而非注重习得结果(learn),因此根据语境采用 learn 或者 study。森舸澜在脚注中指出"学"的古今之区别,强调"学"的古汉语意义在于"修身养性",与现代普通意义的"学习知识"有所不同,通过"学""习"最终成为有技能有涵养的人。通过译文比较可以发现,辜鸿铭的译文 acquire knowledge 显然只是翻译了原文的部分意思。

(2)"知"的翻译。"知"是儒家学说中一个非常重要的概念,《论语》中的"知"字共出现了118次。在《论语》中,"知"字多以"了解""知道""获得""知识"为义,例如,"子曰:'不患人之不己知,患不知人也'"(《论语·学而》),"不知命,无以为君子也"(《论语·尧曰》),"子曰:'温故而知新,可以为师矣'"(《论语·为政》)。在此基础上,"知"又引申出"赏识、任用"的意思,如"子曰:"以吾一日长乎尔,毋吾以也。居则曰:'不吾知也!'如或知尔,则何以哉?"(《论语·先进》)。

在本例中,"知"是指"欣赏、认可、了解"的意思。理雅各、辜鸿铭、刘殿爵、安乐哲与罗思文、森舸澜分别将其译为 take note of, notice, appreciate, acknowledge, understand。在上下文语境中,刘殿爵、安乐哲与罗思文、森舸澜的译文更加准确。

此外,"知"通"智",有"聪明""智慧"的含义,如"知者乐水,仁者乐山"(《论语·雍也》)。再看下例中"知"的翻译。

【例 18】原文:子曰:"由,诲女知之乎! 知之为知之,不知为不知,是知也。"(《论语·为政》)(英语译文参考附录)

原文是指,孔子说:"子路,教给你对待知和不知的态度(即对待学问的态度)吧,知道就是知道,不知道就是不知道,这样才是真正的智慧。"这句话被后世用来提醒人们用诚实的态度对待知识问题,要养成实事求是的学习态度。这句话也隐含着另一层意思:变不知为知需要努力获取知识,很少有天才生来就有知识,大多是后天通过学习典籍文化而得知识。

最后一句中"是知也"中的"知"通"智"(智慧的意思)。Austin(1961)指出:"一个词语从不(几乎从不)离开它的词源和形成时的状态。尽管它的涵(含)义会变化万端,增减不已。最初的涵(含)义将会保留下来,并渗透于和支配着这些变化不定的增减。"

我们知道,荀子对"知"与"智"曾作出明确区分,指出"所以知之在人者谓之知,知有所合谓之智"(《荀子·正名》)。这种观点认为,"知"是认识能力,"智"是认识结果。从"知"到"智"的过程就是由知识体验向智慧德性的转化过程。也就是说,含有"智"意味的"知"既是一个认知范畴,也是一个道德范畴。在儒家看来,"智"是在人格成就不同层次上所体现出来的对人性道德和世界的高度自觉认知,而且应是"知行合一"的高度体现。

《论语》中孔子直接言说"知"(智)约有14次,大概分为三类情况。

其一,指某人聪明、有智慧,如子路问成人,子曰:"若臧武仲之知,公绰之不欲,卞庄子之勇,冉求之艺,文之以礼乐,亦可以为成人矣。"(《论语·宪问》)(子路问怎样才算是完人。孔子说:"像臧武仲那样有智慧,像孟公绰那样不贪求,像卞庄子那样勇敢,像冉求那样有才艺,再用礼乐来增加他的文采,就可以算个完人了。")

其二,解释"知"(智)的含义。例如,樊迟两次问"知",孔子两次言"知者不惑"。从孔子回答中可以看出,"辨"是"知"(智)的一个重要内涵,也就是说,"智"本身包含着辨别是非的认知判断能力。与仁者"爱人"相比,智者"知人"有所选择,能够分辨对错并举直错枉。

(1)樊迟问知。子曰:"务民之义,敬鬼神而远之,可谓知矣。"(《论语·雍也》)(樊迟问怎样才算有智慧,孔子说:"致力于让民众趋向于义,对待鬼神既要尊敬,也要远离,这样才可以称得上是智慧。")智者应当重视力行,能够区分可知和不可知,所当知和所不当知,应当秉承先难而后获的修德理念。

(2)樊迟问知。子曰:"知人。"樊迟未达。子曰:"举直错诸枉,能使枉者直。"(《论语·颜渊》)(樊迟问什么是智,孔子说:"善于知人。"樊迟没有完全理解。孔子说:"选拔正直的人,罢黜邪恶的人,这样就能使邪者归正。")

(3)子曰:"知者不惑,仁者不忧,勇者不惧。"(《论语·子罕》)(孔子说:"智慧的人不疑惑,仁德的人不忧愁,勇敢的人不畏惧。")在儒家传统道德中,智、仁、勇是三个重要的范畴,是君子的基本品质。

(4)子曰:"仁者不忧,知者不惑,勇者不惧。"(《论语·宪问》)(孔子说:"有仁德而不忧愁,有智慧而不迷惑,有勇敢而不惧怕。")

其三,"知"与"仁"比较。例如,"知者乐水,仁者乐山。知者动,仁者静。知者乐,仁者寿"(《论语·雍也》)(智慧的人爱水,仁义的人爱山;智慧的人好动,仁义的人爱静;智慧的人容易快乐,仁义的人容易长寿。),这里采用了互文的手法,意指"知者和仁者都喜欢山水"。水性使人相通,高山使人感到厚重。这里的"智者"和"仁者"都是指有修养的"君子"。在"仁"与"智"的关系中,"智"主要是作为达"仁"的手段而存在的。这也就是说"知"或"智"具有更鲜明的道德情感,"知之为知之,不知为不知"是"智",因而在这个意义上的"知"是具有道德意义的自知与成己,是更高意义上的重塑与创新。

通过比较五译本可以发现,理雅各、辜鸿铭、刘殿爵分别将"知"翻译为 knowledge,understanding,to know,不符合原文的本意。安乐哲与罗思文、森舸澜的译文更准确,分别将"知"翻译为 wisdom(zhi 知)。森舸澜在注解中补充解释"知/智"的内涵意义:谨言慎行与诚实守信等。森舸澜在注解中指出,荀子版本中有关下面故事的更详细版本:子路的穿着在孔子看来有些自命不凡,子路因此受到责骂。当子路赶紧换上更朴素的衣服出现时,孔子教育他,如果一个人不谨言慎行就会变得浮夸与炫耀。其本质是,君子如果知道某事就说自己知道,如果不知道某事就说自己不知道。举止的完美是,君子如果能做某事就说自己能做,如果不能做某事就说自己不能做。《荀子》的这句话对我们也很有帮助,即"言而当,知也;默而当,亦知也",知道什么时候说话以及什么时候保持沉默。

综上所述,由于时代变迁以及中西语言文化差异,译者在理解与处理《论语》中的儒家文化概念时也有所不同。译者在翻译过程中会受其文化教育背景与所处社会文化语境的影响。文化背景知识虽然常由一定文化读者共享,并且成为理解翻译的共有基础。然而这种共有背景知识常常随着时空差异而变化,随着时间的推移,有些共有的背景知识不再共享。因此,上下文语境与社会语境的补充很重要。孙艺风(2016)指出,翻译是一种试验性探索,若同时还要保留原作的准确度和真实性,翻译任务的难度的确很大,循序渐进地增加文化信息才是可行之道,并强调译文在跨文化语境(而不仅仅是文化语境)中要重视可读性。因此,有效的跨文化交际需要译者跨越不同民族的文化障碍,调整好跨文化交际的心态,同时认清形式与功能等值之间的差异,力求做到再现原作的艺术质地与情感,吸引更多译入语读者,让我们的文化真正"走出去"并传播到世界各地。因此,理想的译者应当考虑翻译过程中的多种因素,如文本体裁、文化背景、读者情况、阅读期待等,尽量保留原作字里行间的各种意义的可能性,并将丰富的原文信息传递给身处特定文化背景的目标读者。

(七) 互文性

互文性是指既定语篇的产生与接受依赖于参与者对其他语篇知识的了解,强调语篇意义的产生是在与其他语篇相互参照、相互指涉的过程中产生的(de Beaugrande and Dressler,1981)。就《论语》的语篇特征而言,互文性主要涉及《论语》的文本互文以及译者所要处理的各种翻译互文关系。

王宏印(2006)把翻译中的互文关系分为三种:(1) 共时性互文关系:原文本和正在生成译文本之间的翻译互文关系。(2) 历时性互文关系:文化语言系统内部的渊源互文关系,这是建立在原文本自身社会历史文化与语言系统中的互文关系之上,是原文本赖以生成的文化文本的语言文化资源、运作机制与译文本在译语文化中潜在的、可以依赖的语言文化资源、运作机制之间的互文关系。(3) 转换性互文关系:文本转换过程中产生的互文,即体现在原文本中的互文因素是否有必要或者是否有可能全部转移到译文中去。

【例19】子曰:"《诗》三百,一言以蔽之,曰:'思无邪。'"(《论语·为政》)(英语译文参考附录)

【例20】子曰:"兴于《诗》,立于礼,成于乐。"(《论语·泰伯》)(英语译文参考附录)

【例21】子贡曰:"贫而无谄,富而无骄,何如?"子曰:"可也;未若贫而乐,富而好礼者也。"子贡曰:"《诗》云:'如切如磋,如琢如磨',其斯之谓与?"子曰:"赐也,始可与言《诗》已矣,告诸往而知来者。"(《论语·学而》)(英语译文参考附录)

【例19】、【例20】与【例21】都出现了《诗》这一语篇隐喻,也就是说,由《诗》构成一个源域,用于映射或者衔接一个后续的语篇或一个语境中的事件。《诗》即《诗经》,约成书于春秋中期,是我国历史上最早的诗歌总集,在我国文学史上占据着重要的地位。孔子重视《诗经》的教导作用,多次引用《诗经》,强调其在为人处世方面的重要作用,并教诲弟子要学《诗经》。孔子曾说,'不学《诗》,无以言'(《论语·季氏》)。这里的"言",是指"温柔敦厚"的雅言,且有着"乐而不淫,哀而不伤"的文化特质。孔子还强调《诗经》的教化作用,指出诗以言志,礼以立身,"诗,可以兴,可以观,可以群,可以怨。迩之事父,远之事君;多识于鸟兽草木之名。"(《论语·阳货》)。当人们熟诵《诗经》,理解其中的文化底蕴并将其内化为自己的言语时,便能呈现出"温柔敦厚""知书达礼"的人格品性。只有理解并使用雅言,才能在言语中构建出儒家经典所创造的至善至美的世界。

【例19】原文意思是,孔子说:"《诗经》三百多篇,可用一句话来概括它,就是思想纯正,没有邪念。"原文看似写《诗经》,其实强调"为政以德"的"德",是用《诗经》的"思无邪"来培养人的道德品质,也就是《大学》中的"正其心,心正而后修其身"。【例20】原文意思是,孔子说:"(人的修养)开始于学《诗经》,自立于学礼,完成于学乐。"孔子重视诗、礼、乐,而且指出了这三者的不同作用,要求学生不仅要修炼个人修养,而且要有全面的知识和技能。【例21】原文意思是,子贡说:"贫穷而能不谄媚,富有而能不骄傲自大,怎么样?"孔子说:"这也算可以了。但是还不如虽贫穷却乐于道,虽富裕而又好礼之人。"子贡说:"《诗经》上说,'要像对待骨、角、象牙、玉石一样,切磋它,琢磨它'，就是说的这个意思吧？"孔子说："赐呀，你已能从我讲的话中领会到我还没有说到的意思，举一反三，我可以同你谈论《诗经》了。"孔子希望他的弟子以及所有的人都能够达到贫而乐道、富而好礼这样的理想境界，因而在平时对弟子的教育中，就把这样的思想传授给学生。贫而乐道，富而好礼，社会上无论贫或富都能做到各安其位，便可以保持社会的安定了。

这三个例子中典故与引语的使用体现了历时性翻译互文关系，同时也体现了转换性互文关系：首先，译文本身就是对原文互文的体现；其次，对于原文中引用《诗经》的话本身就是互文，翻译是更进一步的互文体现；第三，对于其中所指如《诗经》的理解，译文也都进行了翻译。例如，【例19】中，五译本译文分别将《诗经》翻译为 The Book of Poetry, The book of Ballads, Songs and Psalms, The Odes, The Songs。【例20】中，五译本译文分别将《诗经》翻译为 the Odes, poetry, the Odes, the songs, the Odes。【例21】中，五译本译文分别将《诗经》翻译为 Book of Poetry/the Odes, Poetry, the Odes, The Book of Songs, the Odes。有的译者还在注解中解释了"诗经"的含义，如【例19】中，理雅各、刘殿爵与森舸澜作了互文注解，并在上下文中形成互文关系。理雅各在注释中指出，《诗经》的篇数大约为300，而且请参考《诗经》第四章第二部分，这样形成了各种互文关系。刘殿爵在注释中指出，原文中的这句话出处来源于《诗经》，本意是指一群马意志坚决，直奔向前，不会左右摇摆。森舸澜在刘殿爵注释释义的基础上进一步指出该典故的深层含义——无违"儒道"。这些互文体现明确了原文意思，加强了英文读者对原文的理解。

现在把三个例子中的注释列举如下进行对比：

【例19】注释：

Legge：The pure design of the book or poetry. The number of compositions in the Shih-ching is rather more than the round number here given. 思无邪, see Shih-ching, IV. ii. 1. st. 4. The sentence there is indicative, and, in praise of the duke Hal, who had no depraved thoughts. The sage would seem to have been intending the design in compiling the Shih. A few individual pieces are calculated to have a different effect.

Lau: This line is from *Ode* 297 where it describes a team of horses going straight ahead without swerving to left or right.

Slingerland: The quoted phrase is from *Ode* 297. The original reference is to powerful war horses bred to pull chariots and trained not to swerve from the desired path. The metaphorical meaning is that one committed through study to *the Odes*—"yoked" to them, as it were — will not be lead astray from the Confucian Way.

【例 20】注释：

Legge: The terms 诗, 礼, 乐 have all specific references to the Books so called.

Slingerland: Here we have a more succinct version of the course of Confucian self-cultivation described in 2.4. The translation of the first phrase follows Jiang Xi's interpretation of xing 兴 as "to inspire, stimulate": "Gazing upon the intentions of the ancients can give inspiration to one's own intention." Bao Xian takes xing to mean, more prosaically, "to begin": "The point is that the cultivation of the self should start with study of *the Odes*." "Taking one's place" through ritual involves, as discussed in 2.4, taking up one's role as an adult among other adults in society, something that requires a mastery of the rituals governing social interactions. Steps one and two thus represent, respectively, cognitive shaping through learning and behavioral shaping through ritual training. Finally, the joy inspired by the powerfully moving music of the ancients brings the cognitive and behavioral together into the unselfconscious, effortless perfection that is wu-wei. Mencius 4:A:27, which invokes the metaphor of dance, represents perhaps the best commentary on this passage:

 The substance of benevolence (ren) is the serving of one's parents; the substance of rightness is obeying one's elders; the substance of wisdom is to understand benevolence and rightness and to not let them go; the substance of ritual propriety is the regulation and adornment of benevolence and rightness; and the substance of music is the joy one takes in benevolence and rightness. Once such joy is born, it cannot be stopped. Once it cannot be stopped, then one begins unconsciously to dance it with one's feet and wave one's arms in time with it.

 Some commentators take all three nouns in the passage as titles of classical texts—"Take inspiration from *the Book of Odes*, take your place with *the Book of Ritual*, and perfect yourself with *the Book of Music*"—but it is unlikely that such books existed in Confucius' time.

【例21】注释：

Slingerland:

"Cutting and polishing" refer to the working of bone and ivory, while "carving and grinding" refer to jade work: cutting and carving being the initial rough stages, and polishing and grinding the finishing touches. Here the task of self-cultivation is understood metaphorically in terms of the arduous process of roughly shaping and then laboriously finishing recalcitrant materials. Zigong's quotation of this ode shows that he has instantly grasped Confucius' point, explained quite nicely by Zhu Xi:

> Ordinary people become mired in poverty or wealth, not knowing how to be self-possessed in such circumstances, necessarily leading to the two faults of obsequiousness or arrogance. A person who is able to be free of both knows how to be self-possessed, but has still not reached the point of completely transcending poverty and wealth ... When a person is joyful he is relaxed in his mind and physically at ease, and therefore forgets about poverty; when he loves ritual, he is at peace wherever he goes and follows principles in a cheerful, good-natured fashion, being equally unconscious of wealth. Zigong was a businessman, probably starting out poor and then becoming rich, and therefore had to exert effort to remain self-possessed. This is why he asked this particular question. The Master's answer was probably intended to acknowledge what Zigong had already achieved while at the same time encouraging him to continue striving after that which he had yet to attain.

Zhu Xi also notes that Zigong's quotation reveals not only that he has grasped Confucius' specific point-that he, Zigong, still has quite a bit of "finishing" work to do-but also serves as a general statement of the Confucian view of self-cultivation: that one "should not be so satisfied with small achievements that one fails to urge oneself on" (5.8). This instant grasping of the larger point to be taught is an excellent example of a student" being given three corners of a square and coming up with the fourth"(7.8).

由此，我们还可以看出，森舸澜的注释贯穿到每一章每一节，整体与部分互文都更加明显。例如，在【例20】、【例21】中，很多译者之前注释过了，就不再进一步注释。而森舸澜则对原文中提到的《诗经》中的内容根据语境再进一步注释，如【例21】中强调自我修养的提高需要一个艰苦的过程，普通人只有做到遵守各种礼制，做到仁义而知礼仪才能真正达到"无为"的境界。

【例22】尧曰："咨！尔舜。天之历数在尔躬，允执其中。四海困穷，天禄永终。"舜亦以命禹。曰："予小子履，敢用玄牡，敢昭告于皇皇后帝：有罪不敢赦。帝臣不蔽，简在帝心。朕躬有罪，无以万方；万方有罪，罪在朕躬。"周有大赉，善人是富。"虽有周亲，不如仁人。百姓有过，在予一人。"谨权量，审法度，修废官，四方之政行焉。兴灭国，继绝世，举逸民，天下之民归心焉。所重：民、食、丧、祭。宽则得众，信则民任焉，敏则有功，公则说。（《论语·尧曰》）（英语译文参考附录）

原文是指，尧让位给舜的时候说："上天的大命已经落到你的身上，你要真诚地持守那中庸之道。天下的百姓如果困苦贫穷的话，上天赐给的禄位就会永远终止了。"舜让位给禹的时候，也说过这番话。商汤说："我这个小子履，恭敬地用黑牛祭祀，向伟大的天帝祷告：有罪的人我不敢擅自赦免，您的臣仆的善恶我也不敢隐瞒，都由天帝的心来分辨定夺。我本人若有罪，不要连及天下万方；天下万方有罪，都由我自己承担。"周朝大封诸侯，让善人富有起来。周武王说："我虽然有至亲，却不如有仁德之人。百姓如有过错，应该由我来承担。"谨慎统一重量、容量单位，审定长度单位，治理废缺的官职，全国的政令就会通行了。复兴灭亡的国家，承续已断绝的世系，举用隐逸的贤人，天下的老百姓就会心悦诚服了。所重视的事情：百姓、粮食、丧礼与祭祀。宽厚就会得到民众的拥护，诚信就会得到百姓的爱戴，勤敏就会有功绩，公平就会使百姓心悦诚服。

以上这段文字选择性地记述了自尧帝以来历代先圣先王的遗训。

孔子在这段文字中大量引用古文《尚书》,是为了强调虽然时代在变,但政治传统没有变。这段文字可以分为四部分。第一部分是尧将地位禅让给舜时,对舜的告诫之辞,重点是"允执其中"。尧舜时,帝王是上天选来管理天下万民的人。王位意味着一种责任,而不是荣华富贵。衡量这个使命的完成,要看是否"四海困穷",如果百姓走投无路,君主也会"天禄永终"。第二部分是商汤祷告上天的一段话,重点是"朕躬有罪,无以万方;万方有罪,罪在朕躬"。这里是告诫后世帝王,作为天下苍生之主,应该有敢于担当的勇气。第三部分是武王伐纣后分封诸侯时的一段话,重点是"虽有周亲,不如仁人"。这里讲的是重视人才,要想赢得天下苍生的支持,就应该争取能力出众的人的支持,这样,事业才能长盛不衰。第四部分是孔子对三代以来的美德善政作了高度概括,"谨权量,审法度,修废官"。原文意思是指要建立一套行之有效的制度,不管是度量衡、法律法规还是官员任免的制度,都是为了有法可依。"兴灭国,继绝世,举逸民"说的是对已有传统的继承。"所重四者"是围绕百姓生活的四个方面来说的,"宽、信、敏、公"则是围绕着人的品德来说的。这一部分可以说是对《论语》中有关以人为本与治国安邦平天下的思想的深刻总结,对于君主治国安邦与民众为人处世等产生了很大的影响。

上述典故与引语的使用也体现了历时性翻译互文关系,同时也体现了转换性互文关系:首先,译者的译文本身即对原文互文的体现;其次,对于孔子引用《尚书》的话本身就是互文,翻译是更进一步的互文体现;最后,对于其中所指,如"咨!尔舜。天之历数在尔躬,允执其中。四海困穷,天禄永终";"予小子履,敢用玄牡,敢昭告于皇皇后帝:有罪不敢赦。帝臣不蔽,简在帝心。朕躬有罪,无以万方;万方有罪,罪在朕躬";"虽有周亲,不如仁人。百姓有过,在予一人"的引用与理解,译文也都进行了诠释与翻译,并在上下文中形成互文关系。

刘殿爵与森舸澜的译文对历史背景知识的注解与其译文正文以及原文的内涵形成了相互关联的互文关系。需要说明的是,森舸澜对每段话都进行注解，本书只选取其中第一个注释如下。

Lau：

1. It has been suggested that these are the words used by King Wu in enfeoffing feudal lords, and may have been used, in particular, in the enfeoffment of T'ai Kung of Ch'i. This whole passage consists of advice to kings or declarations by them. These kings all founded new dynasties. Shun founded the Yü 虞, Yü 禹 founded the Hsia 夏, T'ang 汤 founded the Yin 殷, and King Wu founded the Chou. It must have been taken from *the Book of History*, although only the saying of T'ang is found quoted in ancient works. (See *Ch'en Meng-chia, Shang shu t'ung lun*, p. 23, and n. 4 on p. 25.) This kind of material was probably used for teaching purposes in the Confucian school.

2. The paragraph up to this point is also found in XVII. 6 where instead of *min* (common people) the text reads *jen* (fellow men).

3. This passage is not attributed to any speaker. It seems to consist of a number of unconnected parts on various aspects of government. Although one of these parts, as we have just pointed out, is, indeed, attributed to Confucius in XVII. 6, it would be rash to infer from this that Confucius must have been responsible for everything else as well.

Slingerland：

The occasion of this remark is Yao's passing on of the throne to Shun. This address of Yao's does not appear in Chapter 1 ("The Canon of Yao") of the current *Book of Documents*, but pieces of it can be found in the probably spurious Chapter 3 ("The Counsels of the Great Yu"), where they are presented as Shun's words to Yu. The translation of the second half of the passage follows Zhu Xi, who understands it as a warning to Shun: if Shun should fail to care for and protect the people, Heaven's favor will be withdrawn from him. Bao Xian takes it somewhat differently: "If you can faithfully hold to the mean, you will be able to exhaustively extend [your rule] throughout the Four Seas, and Heaven's emoluments will last forever." Huang Kan follows Bao Xian, elaborating: "If Shun is able to internally hold fast to the Way of the correct mean, then his Virtuous instructive influence will externally cover the Four Seas, so that everyone will submit and be transformed, and there will be nowhere that this influence does not reach." Zhu Xi's reading seems preferable, however, better fitting the context in which these lines appear in the received version of the *Documents*, and allowing a less forced reading of the text.

通过比较两个译文的注释策略，我们可以发现，刘殿爵的注释策略运用了很多互参，森舸澜在该注释中给出不同评论，从而形成各种共时、历时与转换性互文关系。例如，刘殿爵指出，这段话与说话者没有任何关系，而是似乎由关于治国理政的各方面一些不相关的部分构成。尽管正如上文所指出的，其中有一部分确实是归属于《论语》的第十七章第六部分，但是如果从这一点推断孔子也对其他一切负责，那就太草率了。森舸澜指出，这是尧让位给舜时说的话，认为朱熹的观点更可取，也就是说，"尧对舜警告"应该理解为"如果舜不关心和保护人民，上天的恩惠就会从他身上撤回"，而不应该理解为"如果舜坚守中庸之道，那他将恩泽天下"。

互文性还体现在不同译者对原文的复译上,这是对以前译文的继承与创新(cf. Plett,1991)。《论语》的英译不仅仅是两种语言之间的转换,更是一种跨文化的交际活动与社会实践。《论语》译者受各自历史文化环境的影响,因此出现了《论语》译本的不同声音。例如,理雅各等传教士出于传教目的,将《论语》中的儒学基督教化;辜鸿铭等译者为探索儒家之道对儒家思想重新诠释;随着"汉学热"的升温,刘殿爵、安乐哲与罗思文、森舸澜等译者在多元文化背景下对《论语》进行重译,从文化学、哲学、历史学等角度启发读者理解儒家之道,促进《论语》英译朝跨学科方向发展,这在一定程度上证明了典籍重译的必要性,也在一定程度上解读了《论语》英译的互文性。

综上所述,通过分析《论语》的语篇特征及其翻译中的显化现象,我们可以看出,由于《论语》通过孔子与其弟子的对话,传达了为人、处世、伦理、政务等内容,语言上多用对偶、排比、比喻等修辞手段,蕴含了无穷的哲理。《论语》"不是完全由语录构成,但具有语录体的基本特征"(黄国文,2011)。根据 Snell-Hornby(1988)的观点,这类语篇的翻译更加强调语言的创造性,因此,译者应注重强调文学理论、文化史、历史语言学等的研究,注重语言的创造性理解与传达以及视角转换等。此外,基于《论语》的语篇特点,根据 Reiss(1971)对语篇类型特征与功能的划分,可以推断《论语》属于表达型语篇与感染型语篇,语篇功能以表情功能与感染功能为主,同时也具备信息型语篇特点,兼具信息功能。因此,在《论语》翻译过程中,译者在注重传达原文的信息功能的同时,也要注重传达原文的表达功能,准确传递原文内容,提高读者接受度。

【例23】太宰问于子贡曰:"夫子圣者与?何其多能也?"子贡曰:"固天纵之将圣,又多能也。"子闻之,曰:"太宰知我乎?吾少也贱,故多能鄙事。君子多乎哉?不多也。"(《论语·子罕》)(英语译文参考附录)

原文是指,太宰问子贡说:"孔夫子是位圣人吧?为什么他这样多才多艺?"子贡说:"这本是上天想让他成为圣人,而让他多才多艺。"孔子听后说道:"太宰怎么会了解我呢?我因为少年时地位低贱,才学会了许多卑贱的技艺。君子会有很多的技艺吗?不会有很多的。"子贡作为孔子的学生,认为自己的老师是天才。但孔子并不承认自己是圣人,并坦诚讲述了自己的苦难经历。同时,孔子认为,只要德行高尚,技艺懂得多少并不重要。

原文通过对话形式,使用了"与、何其、也、固、纵、又、乎、故"等词语,表达了子贡对孔子的尊敬与感叹,具有强烈的感染功能;同时又表达了子贡对孔子的认知及其观点,具有一定的信息功能。通过对比五个译本,笔者发现,森舸澜的译文通过添加注解与评论增加了背景知识等显化策略,使读者更多地了解孔子谦虚低调的为人特点,从而更容易了解原文。

(1) 信息功能:宏观上,五译本都基本准确地传递了原语篇的信息功能。微观上,以"太宰"的翻译为例,五译本在实现信息功能时所使用的翻译策略各有不同。太宰是古代官名,原名太师,掌管国君宫廷事务。理雅各、辜鸿铭、刘殿爵、安乐哲与罗思文、森舸澜的译文分别将其翻译为"a high officer""a minister of a certain state""the t'ai tsai (This is the title of a high office. It is not clear who the person referred to was or even from which state he came)""grand minister""the prime minister"。刘殿爵采用了文内注释的翻译策略,在遵循原文的语言形式的同时,也把语言的意义告诉读者。其他译者都采用了意译的翻译策略,使英语读者能容易理解这一文化术语的内涵。此外,森舸澜还增加了注释,进一步阐释了该词语的含义:这里提到的首相的身份有大量的评论性辩论,但没有一个论点是完全令人信服的。首相大概很熟悉孔子的许多技术能力,显然很难将其与孔子自己的"君子不器"的教导相协调。子贡试图巧妙地回答这个问题,但孔子却认为他的技能并不是自己努力做一个有抱负的绅士所迫切需要得到的结果,而是自己出身卑微而不断努力的结果。虽然技能对一个还没有被派上合适用场的人来说可能会有用。

(2)感染功能与表情功能:理雅各、辜鸿铭、刘殿爵、安乐哲与罗思文、森舸澜的译文分别使用了"may, how, certainly, and, moreover, must, such" "what, certainly, besides, therefore, but, merely, much" "surely, otherwise, why, so many, however, in addition, how well, should, not at all" "then, how, definitely, many, certainly" "how, then, so many, surely, how well, so"等感叹词、语助词与连接词,把原文的感情色彩、表达特点与衔接意义传递给英语读者,使读者感受孔子的为人及其弟子对老师的敬佩之情。

综上所述,时空差异、译出语与译入语的语篇特征、读者认知差异以及翻译目的与翻译策略等都会影响译作的最终产生,并影响语篇翻译的交际功能的实现。因此,在《论语》翻译过程中,译者往往采用显化翻译策略,以帮助英语读者理解原文内涵。因此,译文的语篇特征与交际功能能否最大程度实现,取决于译者作为沟通者与协调者的交际目的,及其为实现交际目的所采用的翻译手段与相关交际互动因素。

三、《论语》中的文化特征及翻译

文化是指"世世代代通过个人与集体习得的知识、经历、信仰、价值、行为、态度、意义、阶级、宗教、时间概念、角色、空间、宇宙概念以及人工制品等的积累与沉淀"(Samovar, Porter and Stefani, 1997)。本书将结合定性与定量分析,主要从《论语》的高语境文化特征、《论语》的哲学特征以及《论语》的儒家文化概念及翻译三个方面进行论述。

(一)《论语》的高语境文化特征

不同的社会学家与人类学家对文化都有不同的分类。例如,Nida(2001)从语言、宗教、物质、社会、精神与生态等领域对文化进行分类。

Hofstede(2010)用"文化维度"定量研究文化因素,主要包括五个层面:个人主义与集体主义(individualism/collectivism)、权力距离(power distance)、不确定性规避(uncertainty avoidance)、刚柔性(masculinity/femininity)和长/短期方向指数(long-term orientation index)。结合《论语》的文化特征,《论语》的文化维度可以划分为"仁爱心、长期导向、和谐性与道德规则"(范敏,2015),而且"这几个维度相互影响,互为补充,共同构成《论语》的文化维度价值观,并对传播和谐世界理念,解决世界政治、经济、文化与信仰差异所导致的冲突等问题能提供丰富的文化资源"(范敏,2015)。

美国人类学家 Hall(1976)把文化分为高语境文化(high context culture)和低语境文化(low context culture)。例如,美国文化属于低语境文化,而中华文化属于高语境文化。在低语境文化中,信息的意义通过语言可以表达得很清楚,大量的信息置于清晰的编码中,语境不再是重要的因素;而在高语境文化中,信息的意义寓于传播环境和传播参与者之间的关系中,在传播过程中,语境是推测信息的重要因素(陆雄文,2013;霍尔,1988)。换句话说,高低语境文化的差异主要表现为低语境文化的人清晰、明朗,信息明确编码;而高语境文化的人含蓄、内敛,信息倾向于内化。此外,低语境文化以个人主义为价值取向,而高语境文化以集体主义为价值取向。

《论语》作为中国儒家经典代表作,其文化思想内容丰富,语言含蓄隽永,微言大义、寓意深刻,是典型的高语境文化的产物。《论语》包含一套具有系统性、高浓缩儒家文化内涵的伦理学词汇。这些词汇概念构成一个意义完整、有所贯通的思想体系,而且具有高度的哲理性、普遍性、抽象性与互文性,对这些概念意义的准确认知离不开语言语境和社会历史文化语境。

表3-4是笔者利用字频统计工具对《论语》中的高频次出现的具有儒家文化核心概念进行统计的结果。

表 3-4 《论语》中具有儒家文化核心概念字频表

类别	统计	
	核心儒家文化词语	次数
1	知	118
2	仁	110
3	君子	108
4	道	89
5	礼	75
6	善	42
7	德	40
8	信	38
9	贤	25
10	命	24
11	义	24
12	直	22
13	孝	19
13	天	19
14	忠	18
15	勇	16

本书将从集体主义与含蓄内敛两个方面,结合表 3-4,进一步分析《论语》中儒家文化的高语境文化特征。

1. 集体主义

儒家文化所体现的集体主义主要体现在家庭与社会两个层面。基于 Hofstede(2010)的文化维度论的观点,我们发现,儒家文化的集体主义理念在《论语》文化的仁爱心维度、长期导向维度与道德规则三个维度中体现尤为明显。

由表 3-4 可知,"仁"在《论语》中出现的次数仅次于"知"。冯庆华(2012)指出,在一个文本里使用频率特别高的词语。用一个词语在整个文本中所占的百分比或者该词语在整个词频中所占的前后位置来决定该词语是否为高频词。每个文本大小不一样,因此选择或定义相关文本的高频词的百分比或排序位置也会有所区别。"知"体现了孔子重视知识、智慧与教育的思想。孔子主张"有教无类",认为"学而优则仕",把培养为统治阶级服务的知识分子作为目的,以"六经""文行忠信"作为施教的主要内容,强调"温故而知新以及"学"与"思"的关系,注重启发,强调循序渐进、因材施教。"仁"的相对高频则体现了《论语》重视修养与为政以德的主要哲学思想。

仁爱心维度中的"仁"是孔子思想的核心。"仁"最初是指人与人的一种亲善关系,"《论语》中的'仁'常常理解为一种从家庭出发的体现尊卑长幼、贵贱亲疏、带有阶级差别的爱。而这种'爱'体现在孝、悌、忠、信的道德礼教以及君臣与父子的奴隶制秩序上"(范敏,2015)。孔子重视个人修养以及仁德的价值和力量,认为仁德应是第一位。孔子把"仁"定义为"爱人",而要实现"爱人"需要具有仁、道、礼、善、德、信、义、孝、忠等基本品质。例如,孔子曰:"能行五者于天下,为仁矣。""请问之。"曰:"恭、宽、信、敏、惠。恭则不侮,宽则得众,信则人任焉,敏则有功,惠则足以使人。"孔子认为,一个人首先应该具备爱人的能力:爱父母,爱兄弟,爱朋友,爱大众,爱人类,只有这样才能亲近仁。统治阶级不仅要体恤民情,还要遵循"夫仁者,己欲立而立人,己欲达而达人""己所不欲,勿施于人"的"忠恕"之道。他认为,"仁"是每个人必须具备的道德修养,同时也是治国安邦的治理准则,因此强调"爱人、关心人",以仁政、德政的方式来达到治理天下的目的。

长期导向维度主要体现在人们的坚持、学习、积累、节俭与尊重传统等生活态度上,以及儒家的"先天下之忧而忧,后天下之乐而乐"等行事理念。孔子不仅自己修身养性,而且教育弟子勤勉、努力、隐忍、顾全大局。孔子强调"学而时习之,不亦说乎"(《论语·学而》),"知之为知之,不知为不知,是知也"(《论语·为政》)。孔子的弟子曾子也特别强调自省的重要性,每天"三省吾身"。孔子还为从政者指出治国理政之道,指出从政者必须勤勉忠诚,"居之无倦,行之以忠"(《论语·颜渊》),处理政务时应当慎重,"多闻阙疑,慎言其余,则寡尤;多见阙殆,慎行其余,则寡悔。言寡尤,行寡悔,禄在其中矣"(《论语·为政》)。孔子认为,道德规则维度在为政中至关重要,"富与贵,是人之所欲也,不以其道得之,不处也;贫与贱,是人之所恶也,不以其道得之,不去也"(《论语·里仁》)。可见,孔子强调获得富贵必须通过正当的手段和途径去获取,否则宁守清贫而不去享受富贵。再如,齐景公问政于孔子。孔子对曰:"君君,臣臣,父父,子子。"公曰:"善哉!信如君不君,臣不臣,父不父,子不子,虽有粟,吾得而食诸?(《论语·颜渊》)这段话的译文如下。齐景公问孔子如何处理国家政事。孔子回答说:"国君要像国君,臣子要像臣子,父亲要像父亲,儿子要像儿子。"齐景公说:"讲得好啊,如果真的国君不像国君,臣子不像臣子,父亲不像父亲,儿子不像儿子,即使有粮食,我能吃得到吗?"这段话阐述了孔子理想中的社会礼法制度,强调了人尽其责在社会中的重要作用,以及摆正人与人之间的名分关系对维护社会秩序的重要性。但是齐景公后来并没有付诸实践,最终他未能明确接班人,导致陈氏家族刺杀其主并篡夺国家控制权这一事件的发生。

2. 含蓄内敛

儒家文化所体现的含蓄内敛特点也是儒家文化高语境文化特征的体现,主要体现在自省修身、为人处世等方面。表3-4中,君子、道、礼、善、德、信、贤、义、直、孝、忠等文化高频词都体现了这一特征。

孔子强调,真正的绅士需要品德修身,"君子欲讷于言而敏于行"(《论语·里仁》),"战战兢兢,如临深渊,如履薄冰"(《论语·泰伯》),"先行其言而后从之"(《论语·为政》),"仁者,其言也讱"(《论语·颜渊》)。孔子还赞赏颜回安贫乐学的贤德,注重内在儒道而不是外在的物质,注重内心修炼而不是琐碎的小事,追求内心真正的平和而不是外在的浮夸,正所谓"君子食无求饱,居无求安,敏于事而慎于言,就有道而正焉"(《论语·学而》)。这里可以看到孔子对于人格的重视,他强调君子应该克制自己追求物质享受的欲望,注重培养自己的道德品质,以成就自己的高尚人格。

在处世方面,孔子强调"道",指出君子实行"仁、圣"的重要原则是

"己欲立而立人,己欲达而达人",需要"推己及人"。例如,子贡曰:"如有博施于民而能济众,何如?可谓仁乎?"子曰:"何事于仁!必也圣乎?尧舜其犹病诸!"这里孔子强调,仁者要推己及人,要自己站住脚、发展强大,也要帮助他人一同发展强大。孔子还认为,中庸之道是人们立身行事的最高标准,指出"文质彬彬,然后君子","质胜文则野,文胜质则史",强调不可则止,处理事情要注意分寸,不要使行动突破质的规定,注意避免"过"与"不及",认为"过犹不及"。孔子强调变通,因地、因时、因人制宜,但都要遵循认同最高标准——"中"。子曰:"野哉由也!君子于其所不知,盖阙如也。名不正,则言不顺;言不顺,则事不成;事不成,则礼乐不兴;礼乐不兴,则刑罚不中;刑罚不中,则民无所措手足。故君子名之必可言也,言之必可行也。君子于其言,无所苟而已矣。"(《论语·子路》)这里孔子强调君子要慎重对待自己的言行,如果名分不正,说起话来就不顺当合理,说话不顺当合理,事情就办不成。事情办不成,礼乐也就不能兴盛。礼乐不能兴盛,刑罚的执行就不会得当。刑罚不得当,百姓就不知怎么办。

另外,儒家文化的含蓄内敛的高语境文化特征还体现在对理想的价值追求等方面,这在《论语》的和谐性维度方面体现得尤为明显。理想的实现需要由"礼"约束,因此"礼"是维持良好社会秩序的重要哲学思想。"礼"的范围很广,"上自宗法社会的政治、经济、军事、文化等方面的典章制度,下至人们的生活日用、风俗习惯和行为规范"(夏传才,2017)。孔子崇奉周礼,认为礼的精神主要体现为"仁""恭""敬""善""德"等方面。孔子主张以礼义来约束道德,达到"仁"的道德境界。他主张"克己复礼",就是说要克制自己,使自己符合"礼"要求。"礼"的最高境界则是"和",就像有子所说:"礼之用,和为贵"(《论语·学而》)。例如,在《论语·先进》中,曾皙与孔子谈论志向时勾画了一幅"浴乎沂,风乎舞雩,咏而归"的春天郊游图,展示了世界的和谐平安,受到了孔子的称赞,这也是中华民族文化含蓄、内敛、平和与延续的体现。

(二)《论语》的哲学特征

《论语》的哲学特征主要表现为具有丰富深厚的儒家哲学思想及其所具有的最高概括性和普遍性。根据《中国儒学百科全书》的解释,儒家哲学思想主要是指,"儒家对宇宙(自然)和人生(社会、个人)等问题的原则看法,又称内圣外王之道,是儒家认识自然界和人类社会的指导思想和方法"(中国孔子基金会,1997)。儒家哲学关注"人与社会",并非"自然与科学",因而建立了具有永恒价值的思想体系。儒家哲学对世界的观察都是服务于其伦理学,以人为中心,更多强调德行修养与自我提升。

林语堂指出:"孔子的哲学要义是以人为本,儒家思想的整套礼乐哲学是以个人道德修养的完善为基础。人们只要按照伦理道德的方法去实行,就是初步奉行儒家的为人处世与治国之道。"(Lin,1938)在林语堂看来,孔子的思想代表了一个理性有序的以"齐家治国平天下"为目的的社会,强调了个人道德修养与伦理道德,并以德政与礼仪为施政基础。《论语》中所体现的哲学思想不只是"处世格言",更是一种深沉的道德理性思索,一种对人生意义的执着追求,一种对社会秩序建构的理想探求。相较而言,西方哲学是以世界为中心。在西方语境下,形而上学始终是第一哲学,其思路是由外而内,首先关注宇宙构成,其次关注宇宙中的人。《论语》儒家哲学思想主要包括天命观、天人观、人道观、道器观与思学论等。

1. 天命观

天命观来源于"远古人类自然崇拜和祖先崇拜。古人以天为上帝,而上帝是自然神和祖先神的统一。天命即上帝的命令或天道的意志,指不能为人力所支配的事情"(中国孔子基金会,1997)。

儒家"天命"思想,即尊天信命,赞成敬鬼神,对鬼神既不盲目肯定,也不盲目否定。例如,儒家的经典文献中含有很多为人处世的教导,如"君子理想"与"修身齐家治国平天下"等,都是强调个人在生活中的个人道德修养提升与修身实践行为,而不是形而上的对宇宙起源与生死等问题的论述。在孔子的思想中,天和天命都带有神圣庄严的性质。孔子认为,"孔子曰:'君子有三畏:畏天命,畏大人,畏圣人之言。小人不知天命而不畏也,狎大人,侮圣人之言。'"(《论语·季氏》)"畏天命"居于首位。重要的一点是,遵循自然规律,保持乐观,将天道运用于人道,承担起社会责任。孔子以是否敬畏天命来区分君子与小人。子曰:"大哉尧之为君也!巍巍乎!唯天为大,唯尧则之。荡荡乎!民无能名焉。巍巍乎其有成功也!焕乎其有文章!"(《论语·泰伯》)。孔子指出,尧之所以成为圣君,是因为其以天为法则而陶冶自己的伟大人格,并在道德文章和政治事功方面都受到人们的景仰。因此,孔子都把"知天命"都当作奋力追求的目标,并在"五十而知天命"(《论语·为政》)中强调,一个人的富贵贫贱与生死存亡与天命有关。孔子说,"不知命,无以为君子也"(《论语·尧曰》)。

同时,在孔子看来,天命也不是被动的、宿命的。一个能够积极追求生命意义、驾驭社会生活与世界外部力量,勇于承担自己的社会责任,同时又能够发挥自己内在潜能与能动性的人,才能正确对待个人的命运起伏,并对天命、天道与人道有所敬畏,把"天"做主宰化为人做主宰。孔子认为,"天生德于予,恒其如予何"(《论语·述而》)。

此外,孔子具有一种因"知天命"所获得的继承文化传统的神圣使命感以及社会历史文化融入个体生命后所形成的一种社会精神,例如,"文王既没,文不在兹乎?天之将丧斯文也,后死者不得与于斯文也;天之未丧斯文也,匡人其如予何?"(《论语·子罕》),"不然,获罪于天,无所祷也"(《论语·八佾》)。

由此可见,孔子对"天命"的思想有着深刻的哲学意义与人文关怀。孔子一方面认为"天"具有神秘性,要求人们对"天"与"天命"有所敬畏,另一方面要求人们由"畏天命"上升到"知天命",按照"天道"与"儒道"尽力而为。

2. 天人观

天人观是指"儒家围绕着天与人的关系问题所发挥的观点,是儒家哲学思想的重要组成部分"(中国孔子基金会,1997)。儒家哲学中的"天人合一"思想是中华民族精神的核心内容,同时也是中国哲学的基本精神和主要特点。它不仅影响人们的思维习惯、观念信仰、生活习俗等方面,还影响人文、社科、天文、艺术、地理等领域。

古代哲学理论中"天人合一"哲学的实质是为人设定一个价值本体即"人道/天道"的形而上的本源。孔子"天人观"的特点在于保留了天的有意志的属性而使之伦理化,并为自己的伦理思想作论证,表现了一种人文主义的倾向。只有从人的视角把握天以及天与人之间的关系,才能深入理解古代天人合一理论的哲学要义。

天人观需要从两个方面来理解:一方面,孔子把天(自然以及神格化、人格化的自然)看作化生万物的自然运行的过程,如,孔子说,"天何言哉?四时行焉,百物生焉。天何言哉"(《论语·阳货》);另一方面,孔子把天看作道德理想的最高依据,是人理解(超越)自身的对象性的参照物与中介物,同时强调人在天地间的能动性,实现道德理想需要依靠人的主观努力。例如,孔子主张,"仁远乎哉?我欲仁,斯仁至矣"(《论语·述而》)。孔子强调"不怨天,不尤人,下学而上达"(《论语·宪问》)。不怨天即信天命而又不提倡宿命论;下学上达是指通过学习知识而通达天理。听天命和尽人事要相辅相成,这也是孔子天人观的人文精神的关键所在。

3. 人道观

人道观是儒家关于人类行为规律和伦理道德规范的学说。儒教观的立足点"不是神学,也不是无神论,而是人学;以人为本,将天与人、生与死、人与鬼神、祖与子孙进行一体化;皆纳入人道的系统,把神道鬼事看成人道的继续和组成部分"(中国孔子基金会,1997)。

"人道"是儒家哲学的重要范畴,与"天道"相对应。一般认为,"人道"与"天道"一致,以"天道"为本。也有人主张强调"人道"与"天道"的区别,认为"天道"无为,"人道"有为。

人道观的核心内容是孔子、孟子创立的仁义论和以"亲亲""尊尊"为原则的人伦秩序和道德规范,以及人生理想和价值追求。也有人主张,强调人伦道德和物质欲求统一,把厚生利用纳入人道范畴(中国孔子基金会,1997)。孔子对人道有系统的论述。他说,"吾道以一贯之"(《论语·里仁》),"道不同不相为谋"(《论语·卫灵公》)。这里所说的"道"就是指他的"人学"——"人道"。孔子还说:"朝闻道,夕死可矣。"(《论语·里仁》)在这里,孔子强调"闻道"的重要性:人类之所以为人,是因为人类能认识世界,能掌握自然与社会规律,并能利用掌握的规律为人类服务。如果人们领悟了生活的真谛与宇宙中的真理,纵然朝闻夕死,也会觉得不虚此生。

孔子强调,"人能弘道,非道弘人"(《论语·卫灵公》)。在这里,孔子强调人必须先提高自身的修养,才可以把道发扬光大。孔子之所谓道,必须有正确的知识支持,并重视艺能在生活与行为中的意义,所以特别提出"游于艺",进而由这种意义来提升人生的价值,使人真能成为《论语》中所谓的"成人"与"君子"。孔子告知子路,君子治理国家需要先正名分,"野哉,由也!君子于其所不知,盖阙如也。名不正,则言不顺;言不顺,则事不成;事不成,则礼乐不兴;礼乐不兴,则刑罚不中;刑罚不中,则民无所措手足。故君子名之必可言也,言之必可行也。君子于其言,无所苟而已矣"(《论语·子路》)。由此可以看出,儒家的人道治理观及其构成性关系模式,即人与自然、人与社会、人与团体的相互依赖关系,也就是人借助与社会的有效关联与实施行为来改良社会。

孔子人道观的核心是"仁":以仁为最高道德准则,以仁为人道之本。"仁"主要包括以下几层意思:

(1) 爱人。樊迟问仁,孔子答曰"爱人"(《论语·颜渊》)。具体而言,"仁"便是"己欲立而立人,己欲达而达人"(《论语·雍也》),"仁者先难而后获,可谓仁矣"(《论语·雍也》),"唯仁者能好人,能恶人"(《论语·里仁》)。

（2）克己复礼。颜渊问仁。子曰："克己复礼为仁。一日克己复礼，天下归仁焉。为仁由己，而由人乎哉？"(《论语·颜渊》)具体而言，"仁"则是"非礼勿视，非礼勿听，非礼勿言，非礼勿动"(《论语·颜渊》)，"弟子，入则孝，出则悌，谨而信，泛爱众，而亲仁。行有余力，则以学文"(《论语·学而》)，"出门如见大宾，使民如承大祭。己所不欲，勿施于人"(《论语·颜渊》)，"居处恭，执事敬，与人忠。虽之夷狄，不可弃也"(《论语·子路》)，"仁者，其言也讱"(《论语·颜渊》)，"唯仁者能好人，能恶人"(《论语·里仁》)，"仁者先难而后获，可谓仁矣"(《论语·雍也》)。

（3）"仁"涵盖"恭""宽""信""敏""惠""敬""义""刚""友""孝"等含义。例如，"子谓子产：'有君子之道四焉：其行己也恭，其事上也敬，其养民也惠，其使民也义。'"(《论语·公冶长》)这里的"君子四道"都属于"仁"。又如，"子张问仁于孔子。孔子曰：'能行五者于天下，为仁矣。''请问之。'曰：'恭宽信敏惠。恭则不侮，宽则得众，信则人任焉，敏则有功，惠则足以使人。'"(《论语·阳货》)这里的"五者"是实践"仁"的具体方案。再如，"子曰：'刚、毅、木、讷近仁。'"(《论语·子路》)"子曰：'工欲善其事，必先利其器。居是邦也，事其大夫之贤者，友其士之仁者。'"(《论语·卫灵公》)"有子曰：'其为人也孝弟，而好犯上者，鲜矣；不好犯上，而好作乱者，未之有也。君子务本，本立而道生。孝弟也者，其为仁之本与！'"(《论语·学而》)这些都是贯彻仁道的具体措施。

4. 道器观

道器观是"儒家哲学关于事物及其规律的学说。道指无形的法则或规律；器指有形的事物或名物制度"(中国孔子基金会，1997)。也就是说，事物和现象内在的、无形的规律是"道"，可见的事物和现象是"器"。

事物的规律是形而上的，它存在于形而下的事物之中，不能独立存在；具体的事物又受其内在的法则支配（中国孔子基金会，1997）。例如，"六艺"（礼、乐、射、御、书、数）是中国周朝的贵族教育体系，它是古人借助不同符号系统所表达的"自然之数"，同时也承载着"自然之道"。我们只有由"器"见"道"，在实践中通过力行"礼仪"，才能真正理解传统文化中的"义理"，并达成对家儒思想的体认。

《论语》中有很多相关论述，如孔子说，"君子不器"（《论语·为政》），"君子谋道不谋食。耕也，馁在其中矣；学也，禄在其中矣。君子忧道不忧贫"（《论语·卫灵公》）。这里孔子强调，君子应该从社会全局出发，有更高的追求，应该致力于立身行事、安邦治国。只有社会安定，士农工商各行各业才能正常运营，人们才会安康。如果社会秩序混乱，民不聊生，老百姓自顾不暇，将无心耕种。君子治理好社会，君主自然有所回报。

由此可见，君子是通过"谋道"来"谋食"，即孔子所说的"学，禄在其中也"。在孔子看来，人应该追求的是"道"。只有追求"仁道"，才能体现生命的意义与价值。而"食"指的是能够满足人们的基本生理需求的食物，以及人们赖以生存的其他物质资料。子夏说，"百工居肆以成其事，君子学以致其道"（《论语·子张》）。因为百工成事与君子致道都是通过自己的努力来实现的，所以子夏借助人们熟悉的百工成事比喻抽象的君子致道。各行业工匠每天在作坊里完成自己的分内工作可以看作"器"，君子终身学习从而实现道的目的可以看作"道"。通过努力学习实现理想，由"器"而达"道"，才能真正成事。

孔子说，"君子易事而难说也。说之不以道，不说也；及其使人也，器之。小人难事而易说也。说之虽不以道，说也；及其使人也，求备焉"（《论语·子路》）。这里的"器"作动词用，指按各人的才德适当使用。孔子在此强调做人的两种作风：君子严于律己，心中自有正道和操守，喜欢正道行事，能按各人的才德分配任务，故人乐为之用；小人则喜欢别人顺从取悦自己，但在用人时却对人求全责备。

5. 思学论

思学论是儒学认识论思想的重要内容之一,"认为思与学的结合,是求知的基本途径和方法的理论"(中国孔子基金会,1997)。孔子提出的思学结合以求知的理论,奠定了儒家思学论的格局。

在中国哲学史上,孔子最早提出思学范畴,"学而不思则罔,思而不学则殆"(《论语·为政》)。孔子所说的学包括多个层面。

(1) 多闻多见。例如,"子曰:'盖有不知而作之者,我无是也。多闻,择其善者而从之,多见而识之,知之次也。'"(《论语·述而》)"子曰:'多闻阙疑,慎言其余,则寡尤。多见阙殆,慎行其余,则寡悔。言寡尤,行寡悔,禄在其中矣。'"(《论语·为政》)

(2) 寻师访友。例如,"子曰:'三人行,必有我师焉;择其善者而从之,其不善者而改之。'"(《论语·学而》)

(3) 书本知识。例如,"子曰:'我非生而知之者,好古,敏以求之者也。'"(《论语·述而》)这里是指从古代文献与传统文化中学习知识。

(4) 学习目的。孔子强调学习不能盲目,要根据自己的特长有针对性地学习。例如,"樊迟请学稼。子曰:'吾不如老农。'请学为圃。曰:'吾不如老圃。'樊迟出,子曰:'小人哉,樊须也!上好礼,则民莫敢不敬;上好义,则民莫敢不服;上好信,则民莫敢不用情。夫如是,则四方之民襁负其子而至矣,焉用稼?'"(《论语·子路》)

由此可以看出,孔子强调社会有分工。在孔子看来,为政者应把精力放在如何修身立德,重视礼、义、信等;而耕作劳动之事是百姓分内之事。为政者做好分内的事,百姓就会主动来归附。孔子所说的思,"是指对所学到的知识加以思考,是一种理性活动"(中国孔子基金会,1997)。

孔子认为,"学"是"思"的基础和前提,同时"思"又是"学"的补充与升华。例如,"子曰:'吾尝终日不食,终夜不寝,以思,无益,不如学也。'"(《论语·卫灵公》)"子曰:'学而不思则罔,思而不学则殆。'"

(《论语·为政》)一方面,孔子重视学习,而且认为学习是人生的乐趣所在,如"学而时习之,不亦说乎"(《论语·学而》),要"学而不厌","发愤忘食,乐以忘忧"(《论语·述而》)。另一方面,孔子认为,仅靠所见所闻是不够的,还需要行之有效的方法。例如,"子曰:'赐也,女以予为多学而识之者与?'对曰:'然。非与?'曰:'非也。予一以贯之。'"(《论语·卫灵公》)这里的"一以贯之"即强调思考能力与掌握原则方法的重要性。

孔子提出,君子有九思,即视思明,听思聪,色思温,貌思恭,言思忠,事思敬,疑思问,忿思难,见得思义(《论语·季氏》)。在这里,我们看到孔子把"思"与眼、耳、面貌等表层认识的"思"与上升到理性认识的"思"结合起来以求知。这运用到教学活动中,便是启发式,例如,孔子说,"不愤不启,不悱不发。举一隅不以三隅反,则不复也"(《论语·述而》),"生而知之者上也,学而知之者次也;困而学之,又其次也;困而不学,民斯为下矣"(《论语·季氏》)。

综上所述,以"人"为中心的中国的儒家哲学更多强调"天人合一"与"自我的转化",而以"形而上学"为核心的西方哲学主要强调"探索世界的终极"。正是由于中西文化差异与读者认知差异,人们对异域社会价值理念的理解有所不同。不同国家之间的跨文化交流常常容易引发政治、意识形态与道德观念等问题的碰撞、冲突与融合,这些最终都可以归咎于文化诠释的问题。

(三)《论语》儒家文化概念及翻译

Koselleck 指出,"概念作为一种语境化指示,将历史、社会和文化知识结合起来"(汪亚利,2016)。中西文化的概念和术语是各自文化的思想、价值与情感的浓缩,彼此之间无法完全对等。安乐哲提出,《论语》中的概念术语翻译可以采用语境化方法,词和文本的理解和翻译"需要考证相关字词的词源,认真研读术语出现的文本,分析比较其意义,必要时根据具体语境一词多译"(郝大维和安乐哲,1999)。

安乐哲与罗思文认为,从事古代中国典籍的西方学者和汉学家们"在其翻译中使用了大量西方哲学史中的关键术语,结果中国的文本似乎不过是西方思想家在过去二千五百年中所作的稚嫩版本。在这种情况下,大部分哲学家都不认为中国的传统文化就是'哲学',因此可以说翻译家们对中国思想在西方引入的贡献微乎其微"(Ames and Rosemont,1998)。很多西方人类学家在试图使用"翻译"的汉语资料时,最大的障碍是系列的词汇,这些词汇渗透着西方文化的内涵而导致读者对中西哲学差异的漠视,进而降低对中华文化的理解质量。安乐哲与罗思文进一步指出,"对于作为一种范畴的普遍'人性'的缺少批判的假设,以及一些人对于巨大差异会导致无法比较的忧虑,都掩饰、模糊了这些巨大的差异度,然而如果考虑到中国同西方存在的距离,我们就应该承认中国人与我们的迥异特征。在中国文明的发展及其阐释中一直存在着另一种预设,而我们在翻译中未能挖掘、承认这一差别则使得中国的世界观看上去很熟悉,而这是有欺骗性的。当我们使得一种另类的哲学传统变成熟悉之物,且用于对它而言陌生的西方标准对其进行裁定,那么其他的哲学传统就只能成为西方文明的低等变体"(Ames and Rosemont,1998)。的确,在《论语》的英译历史中,很多译者都是西方传教士或汉学家,真正称得上哲学家的人为数不多,这必然导致一些译者对《论语》博大精深的哲学义理的理解存在问题。

1. 五译本儒家文化核心概念翻译

我们在翻译《论语》的儒家文化概念时,需要基于数据统计分析,结合《论语》中的文化特征与儒家哲学特征,根据这些儒家文化概念所处的语言语境与文化语境特点进行分析。

表3-5是对《论语》前16位的儒家文化概念(知、仁、君子、道、礼、善、德、信、贤、命、义、直、孝、天、忠、勇)的译文进行对比分析得出的结果。

表 3-5 五译本儒家文化核心术语翻译比较

术语	译者				
	理雅各	辜鸿铭	刘殿爵	安乐哲与罗思文	森舸澜
知	take no note of; know; acquire; wise; the wise; in the possession of	be noticed; know; understand; an intelligent man; men of intelligence	appreciate; Follow; see; understand; Keep; wise; The wise man; Knowledge	acknowledge; know; realize; wise persons (zhi 知); knowledge (zhi 知)	understand; realize; know; understood; recognize; see; wisdom; those who are clever
仁	excellence; virtue	excellence; moral character	benevolence; benevolent	authoritative persons (ren 仁); authoritative (ren 仁)	goodness; those who are good; good
君子	the superior man; a man of complete virtue	a wise man; wise and good man	gentlemanly	an exemplary person (junzi 君子)	The gentleman
道	practical courses; the way; men of principle; truth and right; the proper way; the right way; were well governed;	wisdom; the rules; principles; men of virtue; in government; the rule; the order and justice; the path of duty; order and justice; theology (天道);	the Way; guiding; the Way of Heaven (天道)	the ways; the way (dao 道) the way of tian (tiandao 天道)	the Way; To guide; the ways; the ancient Way (古之道)
礼	rules of propriety; perfect virtue	art; fine arts; education and good manners; a moral life; the ideal of decency and good sense	the rites; virtue; the spirit of the rites; benevolence	ritual propriety (li 礼)	ritual; virtue; returning to the rites (keji fuli 克己复礼)

(续表)

术语	译者				
	理雅各	辜鸿铭	刘殿爵	安乐哲与罗思文	森舸澜
善	the good; knew well how; excellence; politely good qualities; well; good	excel in anything; the excellence of moral grandeur; politely knew how; ability; good points	the good; excels in; goodness; tactfully inability (不善); strengths	adept (shan 善); felicitous (shan 善); good (shan 善) in; best (shan 善); be unable (不善); efficacious person (shan ren 善人)	the accomplished; perfectly good (shan 善); is good at; failings (不善); good, bad (不善); excellent
德	virtue; what is good; virtuous action	moral sentiment; moral worth; godliness; moral and intellectual power; moral greatness	virtue; benign rule; moral worth; moral virtue	virtue (de 德); excellence (de 德)	virtue; virtue
信	sincere; truthfulness; truthful	sincerity and trustworthiness; good faith; truthfulness; honest; confidence	trustworthy; being trusted; firm faith	word (xin 信); trust and confident	trustworthy
贤	the virtuous; worth; admirable; superior; men of virtue and talents; excellence	worthiness; heroism; men of ability and worth; superior; real moral worth	admirable; excellent; superior; men of talent; benevolent	exceptional character (xian 贤); superior character (xian 贤)	worthiness; worthy; a worthy man

(续表)

术语	译者				
	理雅各	辜鸿铭	刘殿爵	安乐哲与罗思文	森舸澜
命	the decrees of Heaven; appointed time; the appointment of Heaven; authority; decrees; report to the prince (复命); order; determined appointment; commission; the governmental notifications; orders of the state (国命); the ordinances of Heaven	the truth in religion; Died in the prime of his life (短命); God's will; religion; Summons; pre-ordained; Mission; the will of God; order and justice in the government of a country (国命); the Laws of God	the Decree of Heaven; allotted pan; Destiny; the fate of a state; lot; destiny; commission; command in a state (国命); the Decree of Heaven	the propensities of tian (tianming 天命); die young (短命); propensities; the command of a sovereign state; report to his lord (复命); lot; commission; a diplomatic treaty; circumstances (ming 命); command of the state (国命)	Heaven's Mandate (天命); allotted lifespan; fate; command; Heavenly Mandate; fate; ruler's mandate (君命) diplomatic orders; a matter of fate; message; the Mandate of Heaven (天命)
义	be right; what is right; duties; righteousness	be right; what is right; essential duties	rightness; right; what ought to be done;	appreciate (yi 义)	rightness; what is right; ensure social harmony
直	upright; straightforward; justice	just; honest, upright; integrity; justice; honestly straightforward	straight; forthright	true; candor; discipline; frank and direct	the straight; upright
孝	filial piety; be final	honor your parents	treat them with kindness	be filial to your elders (xiao 孝)	be filial; filial piety;
天	Heaven; heavens	God; Heaven	Heaven; sky	tian 天; sky	Heaven; heavens

(续表)

术语	译者				
	理雅各	辜鸿铭	刘殿爵	安乐哲与罗思文	森舸澜
忠	faithful; faithfulness; loyal; devotion of soul; undeviating consistency;	loyalty conscientious sincere	do one's utmost; do one's best; conscientious	do one's utmost; do one's best; do their utmost	be dutiful; dutifulness; good
勇	courage; boldness; daring; bold; bravery; valor	courage; daring; brave; valour; gallantry	foolhardy; courage; courageous; forthrightness	boldness; the courageous; bold	courage; courageous

通过对比与分析，结合《论语》语篇研究，我们可以看出，由于《论语》文本意义的开放性、不同文化语境影响以及翻译中的空缺和不对等现象，五译本的儒家文化核心概念都出现了多种翻译形式。因为《论语》大量陈述式言说省略了孔子说话时的具体语境，文言文言简意赅的特点以及古汉语语法的不稳定性又增加了翻译的复杂性。这些儒家文化核心概念在原文的不同语句里具有相通却并不相同的意义，即使在语内翻译中也很难用一个现代词汇来通译，因此在语际翻译过程中具有一定难度。这些最常见也是最重要的儒家文化概念构成了《论语》翻译最大的难点。

2. 概念词"天"及其搭配词的翻译分析

基于以上研究，以《论语》中的儒家文化概念"天"为例，本书对《论语》与五译本中的"天"及其搭配词的英译进行对比分析，探讨中西文化差异对译者翻译策略的影响。

第一，概念词"天"及其搭配词的内涵。"天"作为中华文化信仰体系的核心词，狭义仅指与地相对的"天"，广义是指"道、太一、大自然、天然宇宙"等。从造字本义看,天是指人的头顶上方的无边苍穹。它最初是指空间,与地相对,后引申为天空、太空。《道德经》云:"天长,地久。天地之所以能长且久者,以其不自生也,故能长生。"《说文解字》将其注释为:"(天)颠也。此以同部叠韵为训也。凡门闻也、户护也、尾微也、发拔也皆此例。凡言元始也、天颠也、丕大也、吏治人者也皆于六书为转注而微有差别。元始可互言之,天颠不可倒言之,盖求义则转移皆是。举物则定名难假,然其为训诂则一也。颠者,人之顶也。以为凡高之称。始者,女之初也,以为凡起之称。然则天亦可为凡颠之称。臣于君,子于父,妻于夫,民于食皆曰天是也。(天)至高无上,从一大。至高无上,是其大无有二也,故从一大。于六书为会意。凡会意合二字以成语。如一大、人言、止戈皆是。他前切。十二部。"由此可见,自古以来,天都是从原型位置高的现象出发进行诠释。

根据《中国儒学百科全书》(1997)的解释,在西周天命神学中,"天"指兼有自然和社会双重主宰身份的天神。这个天神不仅统帅日、月、星辰,为自然界的百神之长,而且无限关怀人世的秩序。春秋时期,原始形态的天人关系观点逐渐朝哲学的方向演变。儒家的"天人观"是直接继承西周以致春秋时期的天人观发展而来的。总体而论,儒家哲学世界观主要是以"究天人之际"作为哲学探讨的主题,以对"天"的理解以及天人关系的各种型态的可能性之优劣比较与选择等问题为基础,并且根据对二者关系的理解,建立一种天人哲学。这是一种高层次的思考,是对自然、社会、人生的整体性的把握,是一种囊括宇宙、统贯天人的完整的体系。傅佩荣(2018)指出:"'天'是儒家的信仰,也就是前面所讲的'二加一'的'一',是人类与自然界的来源归宿"。

孔子认为,人的意志、信念和信仰等都与"天"息息相关。在《论语》中,"天"出现了19次,"天"与其他词语搭配形成词组,如"天下"23次,"天命"3次,"天子"2次,"天道"与"天禄"各1次,如表3-6所示。

表 3-6 《论语》"天"及其搭配词频数

天与搭配词	频次	天与搭配词	频次
天	19	天子	2
天下	23	天道	1
天命	3	天禄	1

关于"天"的意义,孔子在"肯定'天'的超越性、道德性的同时,又把'天'看作自然的创化力量"(郭齐勇,2006)。孔子认为,"'天'有超越之天"(宗教意义的终极归宿)、道德之天(道德意义的秩序与法则)、自然之天(自然变化的过程与规律)、偶然命运之天等不同内涵"(郭齐勇,2009)。因此,从这个意义上说,天可以包括自然的"天",偶然命运的"天",道德义理的"天",自然之天与道德义理之天的交叉整合,以及有宗教神性或主宰意义的"天"。

一是自然的"天"。例如,子曰:"予欲无言。"子贡曰:"子如不言,则小子何述焉?"子曰:"天何言哉?四时行焉,百物生焉,天何言哉?"(《论语·阳货》)

在这里,"天"是指自然之天。通过以上对话,我们了解到孔子的无为的教育理念。子贡认为,老师如果不说话,那么做学生的就不能传述老师的思想。孔子认为,天也没有说话,然而四季却照样在运行,万物照样在生长。

二是命运的"天"。例如,司马牛忧曰:"人皆有兄弟,我独亡。"子夏曰:"商闻之矣:死生有命,富贵在天。君子敬而无失,与人恭而有礼,四海之内,皆兄弟也。君子何患乎无兄弟也?"(《论语·颜渊》)

当司马牛因唯独自己没有兄弟而感到忧愁时,子夏安慰他说:"人的生死由命中注定,富贵由天安排。君子严肃敬业、对人恭敬而有礼貌,天下的人到处都是兄弟。君子何必忧愁没有兄弟呢?"。从全章来看,子夏并不相信命运之说。但他引用的"死生有命,富贵在天"一句里的"天"与"命"都具有偶然命运的含义。

三是道德义理的"天"。例如,子曰:"天生德于予,恒其如予何?"(《论语·述而》)

公元前492年,当听说孔子从卫国去陈国会经过宋国时,桓魋就准备谋害孔子。孔子在学生保护下逃离宋国。在途中,孔子说出此话,是暗指桓魋不能伤害他,因为上天把仁德赋予了他。这里的"德"有先天赋予的味道,而且这个"天"似乎是有意志的。孔子自信有德,德来自天。此处的天已不是主宰之天的天帝,而是义理之天的天道。

四是自然之天与道德义理之天的交叉整合,不是纯自然也不是纯道德的天。天是万物之源,具有创造精神,却采取默运的方式运作。天的这一品格也赋予了人类,特别是圣人。尧舜都是以天为法则,无为而治的。孔子赞颂尧舜的功德以及发挥天的非人格性的观念。

子曰:"大哉尧之为君也!巍巍乎,唯天为大,唯尧则之。荡荡乎,民无能名焉。巍巍乎其有成功也,焕乎其有文章!"(《论语·泰伯》)孔子连用赞美之辞称赞尧帝。在孔子看来,尧帝顺应天道,建立了礼仪制度以及文化体制等,开启了中华的文明史,其恩德广大、功绩伟业足以值得世人称颂,这也是孔子及其弟子想要实现的终极理想。

子曰:"无为而治者,其舜也与?夫何为哉?恭己正南面而已矣。"(《论语·卫灵公》)孔子说,能够无为而治理天下的只有舜。其实他什么也没有做,只是庄严端正地坐在朝廷的王位上。这里看不到天的意志对自然人事的干预,无言、无为的自然之天与天道按自己的秩序运转,生成长养万物。同时,这种天是圣人的榜样,是道德的根源与根据。

五是保留有宗教神性或主宰意义的天。

王孙贾问曰:"与其媚于奥,宁媚于灶,何谓也?"子曰:"不然。获罪于天,无所祷也。"(《论语·八佾》)这是卫国大夫王孙贾引用古语,以灶神自喻,以奥神喻南子一派。古时尊长居西南,所以奥神的地位比灶神尊贵。孔子则认为,上天是万物的主宰,为人处世必须符合天意;他告诚大家对神的祭拜在于对"神"的敬畏,要忠孝仁义,多做善事,而不要仅寄希望于求神灵保佑。它表达了孔子的"顺天行道"以及"敬天意而远之"的态度。

子曰:"莫我知也夫!"子贡曰:"何为其莫知子也?"子曰:"不怨天,不尤人。下学而上达,知我者其天乎!"(《论语·宪问》)孔子认为,自己承担着替天传续斯文的使命,下学礼乐而上达天命。这种使命感在旁人眼中是知其不可为而为之,故孔子慨叹"知我者其天乎"。孔子呼天叹地,有把天作为有意志的神灵的含义,但不一定就以为天或天意在主宰其人,只是借天聊以自慰或宣泄情感。由此可见,在孔子看来,天具有丰富的认知意义与哲学意义。不同于传统的天命论,孔子在强调人格化、神格化与天命说的同时又强调人性的力量。

现在,我们主要探讨"天命"与"天道"的内涵。"天下""天子"与"天禄"等概念不再一一赘述。

《中庸》开篇提到"天命之谓性也"。这意味着"天命"是在上天赋予人生命的同时,也赋予某种需要个人来完成的使命。孔子认为,人是肩负着某种使命降临人世的;在上天赋予人"性命"之后,人也获得了一种独特的自觉完成使命的能动性。孔子认为,人不仅能够感知生命,而且能发挥自己的才能与智慧,主动地认知、回应并完成上天的使命,成就自己圆满的人生。基于这种认识,孔子认为,复兴礼制是上天赋予自己的人生使命,自己要为完成这个使命而竭尽全力。

"天道"是指天的运动变化规律,即万物的规则与道理,一切事物皆有一定的规则。孔子之道包括"人道""天道"以及"天人之道"。孔子认为,人道不同于天道,天人各有其道。孔子说:"天何言哉?四时行焉,百物生焉,天何言哉?"(《论语·阳货》)。天道之行,自有规律,与人道无关。此外,孔子还认为,人道无法超越天道。孔子说:"道之将行也与,命也;道之将废也与,命也。"(《论语·宪问》)。孔子指出,大道的兴衰成败都是天命的运作,无人能运作。人道的发展最终取决于天道的

运行,但是天道无法替代人道,人道自有其道。"人类受制于天道、人道之间,'天人之道'是其生存之道"(钱宁,2019)

第二,基于数据统计的概念词"天"及其搭配词的英译。首先,我们来看译本中"天"及其搭配词的翻译,见表3-7至表3-12。需要说明的是,因研究需要,译本的原文只保留正文,译文的前言、序言、附录、每章大标题及各译本中的注释与段落注解都没有统计在内。

表3-7 《论语》五译本中对"天"的翻译

译文	译者				
	理雅各	辜鸿铭	刘殿爵	安乐哲与罗思文	森舸澜
heavens	1	0	0	0	1
heaven	18	2	18	0	18
god	0	16	0	0	0
sky	0	1	1	1	0
tian 天	0	0	0	18	0
统计	19	19	19	19	19

表3-8 《论语》五译本中对"天下"的翻译

译文	译者				
	理雅各	辜鸿铭	刘殿爵	安乐哲与罗思文	森舸澜
world	2	8	1	14	22
empire	8	11	22	5	1
country	0	2	0	0	0
kingdom	12	0	0	0	0
land	0	0	0	3	0
wherever	0	1	0	0	0
everywhere	1	0	0	0	0
imperialism	0	1	0	0	0
tian 天	0	0	0	1	0
统计	23	23	23	23	23

表3-9 《论语》五译本中对"天命"的翻译

译文	译者				
	理雅各	辜鸿铭	刘殿爵	安乐哲与罗思文	森舸澜
the truth in religion	0	1	0	0	0
Laws of God	0	2	0	0	0
decrees of Heaven	1	0	3	0	0
ordinance of Heaven	2	0	0	0	0
Heaven's Mandate	0	0	0	0	1
Mandate of Heaven	0	0	0	0	2
propensities of tian（tianming 天命）	0	0	0	3	0
统计	3	3	3	3	3

表3-10 《论语》五译本中对"天子"的翻译

译文	译者				
	理雅各	辜鸿铭	刘殿爵	安乐哲与罗思文	森舸澜
Son of Heaven	2	1	0	0	2
emperor	0	1	2	2	0
统计	2	2	2	2	2

表3-11 《论语》五译本中对"天道"的翻译

译文	译者				
	理雅各	辜鸿铭	刘殿爵	安乐哲与罗思文	森舸澜
theology	0	1	0	0	0
way of Heaven	1	0	1	0	1
way of tian（tiandao 天道）	0	0	0	1	0
统计	1	1	1	1	1

表 3-12 《论语》五译本中对"天禄"的翻译

译文	译者				
	理雅各	辜鸿铭	刘殿爵	安乐哲与罗思文	森舸澜
Heavenly revenue	1	0	0	0	0
title and honour which God has given to thee	0	1	0	0	0
honours bestowed on thee by Heaven	0	0	1	0	0
Tian's charge	0	0	0	1	0
Heaven's emoluments	0	0	0	0	1
统计	1	1	1	1	1

表 3-7 至表 3-12 展示了五译本中对"天"及其搭配词语如"天下""天命""天子""天道""天禄"的翻译情况。通过译文比较可以看出,一般而言,理雅各倾向于宗教式的解读,辜鸿铭倾向于地道易懂的功能对等策略,刘殿爵注重原文经典的策略,安乐哲与罗思文采用"意译＋拼音＋汉字"的创造性策略,森舸澜则从字源考察认知的角度对原文进行诠释。

以"天"为例,理雅各、刘殿爵、森舸澜多将其翻译为 heaven、辜鸿铭多将其翻译为 god,安乐哲与罗思文多将其翻译为 tian 天。关于"天下"的翻译,理雅各多将其翻译为 kingdom,辜鸿铭多将其翻译为 empire 与 world,刘殿爵多将其翻译为 empire,安乐哲与罗思文以及森舸澜多将其翻译为 world。关于"天命"的翻译,理雅各、辜鸿铭、刘殿爵、安乐哲与罗思文、森舸澜分别将其翻译为 ordinance of Heaven, Laws of God, decrees of Heaven, propensities of tian（tianming 天命）、Mandate of Heaven。关于"天子"的翻译,理雅各与森舸澜都将其翻译为 Son of Heaven,刘殿爵都将其翻译为 emperor,安乐哲与罗思文都将其翻译为 emperor,辜鸿铭两次分别翻译为 Son of Heaven 与

emperor。关于"天道"的翻译,理雅各、刘殿爵与森舸澜都将其翻译为way of Heaven,辜鸿铭将其翻译为theology,安乐哲与罗思文将其翻译为way of tian(tiandao 天道)。关于"天禄"的翻译,理雅各、辜鸿铭、刘殿爵、安乐哲与罗思文以及森舸澜分别将其翻译为 Heavenly revenue, title and honour which God has given to thee, honours bestowed on thee by Heaven, Tian's charge, Heaven's emoluments。

第三,概念词"天""天命"的五种英译分析。本书将结合上述内容,从《论语》中选取相关典型译例,对《论语》五译本中儒家哲学概念"天"与"天命"的翻译策略进行对比分析。

【例24】子曰:"予欲无言。"子贡曰:"子如不言,则小子何述焉?"子曰:"**天**何言哉? 四时行焉,百物生焉,**天**何言哉?"(《论语·阳货》)(英语译文参考附录)

这段看似比喻的话,其实反映了古代的信念,就是以天为"造生者"与"载行者":天是万物的根源,也是维系一切的力量。天不讲话,四季照样运行。天有创造精神,是万物之源,却采取默运的方式运作。天的这一品格也赋予了人类,特别是圣人。此处的"天"具有自然之天与道德义理之天的交叉整合,以及有宗教神性或主宰意义的"天"的意义。同时,这种天是圣人的榜样,是道德的根源与根据。这里看不到天的意志对自然人事的干预;无言、无为的自然之天与天道(自然规律及人类社会规律)按自己的秩序运转,生成长养万物。通过比较五个译文可以看出,除了安乐哲与罗思文翻译为"tian 天",其他四位译者都翻译为Heaven,尤其森舸澜对该词的阐释(如无为而治)作了很多注解。

【例25】孔子曰:"君子有三畏:畏天命,畏大人,畏圣人之言。小人不知天命而不畏也,狎大人,侮圣人之言。"(《论语·季氏》)(英语译文参考附录)

孔子强调,君子要敬畏天命,敬畏地位高贵的人,敬畏圣人的话。

小人因不懂天命而不敬畏、不尊重地位高贵的人，并轻侮圣人之言。

"天命"是"天"字与其他字，如"命/道"等组合在一起构成双音节词时，变成具有新生命的词语。中国古代哲学中常把"天"当作神，天能决定人的命数。儒教中的"天命"思想，即尊天信命，主张畏天命，强调"天人合一"。君子有三畏，"畏天命"居于首位。重要的一点是，遵循自然规律，保持乐观，将"天道"运用于"人道"，承担起社会责任。"天命"意思是"天道的意志"，指不能为人力所支配的事情。

关于"天命"的翻译，理雅各、刘殿爵、森舸澜分别将其译为 ordinances of Heaven, Decree of Heaven, Mandate of Heaven。辜鸿铭将其译为 the Laws of God, 安乐哲与罗思文将其译为 propensities of tian (tianming 天命)。此外，理雅各、辜鸿铭与森舸澜对"天命"作了文外注释。

理雅各在注释中指出，"天命"是"上天"赋予人的道德本性。它超越了其他生物的本性，赋予人用以珍视和培养自己的巨大责任。老一辈的翻译家用"天命"来表示"上天"的奖惩道德管理。地位崇高、智慧高尚、德行高尚的"伟人"就是"上天"为教育和统治人类而培养起来的。

辜鸿铭在注释中指出，"天命"从字面上看是指"上帝的诫命"，因此他根据语境把"天命"翻译成宗教。"天命"不像摩西、吕库古、基督或孔子法则等仅仅是对上帝法则的解释，它在欧洲就是所谓的宗教。上帝的法则包含了一切，从简单的二加二等于四的法则，生姜在嘴里是辣的法则，日月星辰运行的法则到人类心中最高的是非法则。"但愿我的命运能引导我走上思想和行为神圣纯洁的道路，这条道路是庄严的法律所规定的，是在最光明的天空中诞生的法律……上帝的力量是强大的，不会老去。"

森舸澜在注释中进一步指出，认识或者理解"天命"是理解"道"与实现"无为"的基本步骤。"天命"隐含着服从命运与对政治上级表现出应有尊重之间具有异曲同工之处。个人无法直接控制的事情（财富、名望、健康、寿命）是由天国统治者"命令"或"授权"的，因此真正的绅士被比喻为忠诚的大臣,可以毫无焦虑或抱怨地服从这些"决定"。另一方面,小人则不尊重地位,不知道自己的位置,总是争先恐后地想获得成功。

其次,我们分析各位译者翻译策略背后的翻译目的与翻译原因。理雅各通过寻找基督教与儒教的相似性,采用经文辨读策略,从中国的知识体系与西方的基督教思想解读《论语》。理雅各认为,中华传统文化中的"天"等同于西方宗教思想中的"Heaven(上帝所在的天堂)",这密切了中西宗教的关系,但也存在一些争议。西方的宗教文化以基督教为主。基督教文化坚持精神世界服从上帝、信仰基督教的价值体系以及相关的精神和道德伦理观念。理雅各的翻译体现了西方的"一多二元"的思想。"自古希腊至今,'一多二元'的'一'是上帝式的唯一本源概念;'一'是主宰性的,'多'是由上帝创造的一切独立个体万物;'二元'表示'一'与'多'之间以及'多'个体之间对立的关系;'一'决定宇宙的秩序"(卜俊峰,2019)。

辜鸿铭努力按照受过教育的英国人表达同样思想的方式翻译《论语》。在【例25】中,他把"天命"翻译为 the Laws of God。辜鸿铭在翻译"五十而知天命"时将"天命"译为"the truth in religion",旨在帮助读者理解原文内容,以此消除英语读者的陌生感。其实,对辜鸿铭而言,"无论是他将'天'译为'宗教'还是'上帝',都有着同样的含义,那就是代指宇宙的根本规律"(王京涛,2019)。"在他眼中,中国哲学中的'天'在意义上相当于西方宗教哲学中的'上帝',都是宇宙中最高秩序或规律的代名词"(王京涛,2019)。

刘殿爵认为,"天"(Heaven)与"命"(ming)是近义词,蕴含着"道德的命令与道德的目的。天还有可能是判决的来源(Lau,1992)。"刘殿爵在处理'天'(Heaven)、'命'(Destiny)与'天命'(Decree of Heaven)这几个文化负载词时,虽然很难避免让英语读者联想到超自然的西方造物主及宿命论的观点,但译者对它们分别作了进一步解释,如'天命'是道德戒律(moral imperative),而'天'主要传达的是帮助万物生生不息的功用。'命'则是完全神秘莫测（mystery），着眼于命定的意义上"（许雷和屠国元，2014）。

安乐哲与罗思文对《论语》中的儒家哲学术语有着自己新的见解与诠释（Ames and Rosemont，1998）。他们认为，"天"有如下属性："天"不说话，却通过历史演变、神谕先灵与灾难等与人进行交流。如果把"天"译为"Heaven"，等于把中华民族塞入圣经中"亚布拉罕"的"上帝"体系。强加造成的事实是中华文化不是自己叙述自己，而是在西方话语的叙事结构中遭到肢解。因此，译者在翻译时不能望文生义，而要回到中国传统的阐释语境中去，才能准确理解其含义。安乐哲与罗思文在译本中解释不翻译"天"的主要原因在于英语基督教中"Heaven"的意象与中国"天"的含义不对等，"Nature"这个词语同样与"天"也不对等。原因如下：(1)"天"常用来表达"天地"，意味着"天"并不独立于世界。圣经中的上帝（God）——比喻意义等同于"Heaven"——创造了世界，但是古汉语中的"天"就是世界。"天"是造物主也是万物的场地。(2)"天"可以指"道"。(3)"天"具有神话历史化的含义，如"敬天祭祖"。(4)"天"不说话，却有效与人世间交流。因此，他们用哲学的思维把"天命"创造性地翻译为 propensities of tian（tianming 天命），以尽量传达原作所蕴含意义的可能性，最大限度帮助英语读者了解中国的语言文化特点与文化内涵。我们"总是预设了自己文化经验中的所熟悉的东西，而忽略了其他一些重要材料，恰恰正是它们，展示了作为文化之源的具有可比性的行为"（安乐哲，2002）。

森舸澜认为，"天"是可以与之交流、求助祈祷、具有无限潜力的神，并通过命令（mandate）来掌管人类事务（Slingerland，2003）。森舸澜从认知视角对"天"的"无为而治"作了阐释：在古时，天人合一的理想状态是统治者无需说话、无需行动，他只需按照"天道"谋其政，世界就会按照秩序正常运转。对此，森舸澜指出，该译本通过提供大量的连续评论，尝试为英语读者提供文本语境的丰富性，让读者了解到文本语录体的鲜活性。或许描述我所创造的这种经历的最好的途径是想像与一位了解古典汉语的朋友一起阅读《论语》,而且此人已对如何阅读该文本有些确定的观点。他能够引导读者快速浏览大量的注解、次要注解、文本注释、其他语篇注释以及与该文本相关的其他奥秘,也会偶尔对认为有用或是产生思想火花的地方欢呼,还能够为英语学术的进一步探索提供建议。虽然以上策略不理想,但是由于《论语》文本本身的奥秘特点,这种策略要比仅有一位译者序言+译文文本的策略更具有长远的意义(Slingerland,2003)。此外,森舸澜认为,由于东西哲学思想不同及读者认知差异,译者在翻译《论语》时,不应随意在译文中加入个人诠释和解读,而应充分尊重并保留原文的语义模糊性和多义性,以注释形式提供文本解释并注明出处,由读者辨析经典的原本面貌并做出最终判断与理解(Slingerland,2003)。

由此可见,译者策略会受到译者价值观与不同社会文化环境等诸多因素影响。成功的跨文化翻译需要译者调整跨文化传播心态,跨越各种形式的文化障碍,同时努力克服语言形式、文化差异与语用功能之间的差异,力求做到再现原作的原汁原味与艺术情感,吸引更多译入语读者。

第四,概念词"天道"的五种英译分析。孔子赋予"道"的含义似乎涵盖了有关宇宙和人类真理的全部,是一种非超越性的"天道"观。如前文所述,孔子之道包括"人道""天道"以及"天人之道"。"道"字由两部分组成:道=首+辶。"道"字似乎透露了古人对"人首蛇身(如伏羲女娲形象)"的图腾崇拜思想。从这个字的字形来看,"道"就是一个人在十字路口知道前进的方向,不迷惑,这就是道。从古今意义的深刻内涵来看,"道"都是指向生命的。因此,"道"应该是对生命的探讨。例如,老子说,道法自然,自然就是指生命。安乐哲(2006)认为,在理解孔子"道"的概念时,需要知道"道"来自人类活动,人不仅是"道"的继承者和传播者,而且是"道"的创造者。而"道"在英语中的诠释是超然的,由此可看出汉英语言之间的文化差异。

【例 26】子贡曰:"夫子之文章,可得而闻也;夫子之言性与天道,不可得而闻也。"(《论语·公冶长》)(英语译文参考附录)

原文是指,子贡说:"老师讲授的礼、乐、诗、书的知识,我们经常可以听到并学习,但是老师讲授的关于人的本性和天道的理论,我们真是很难听到。"这里强调孔子所讲的礼、乐、诗、书等具体知识可以学到,但孔子关于人性与天道等深奥的理论需要自己内心体验。在这里,"天道"是指有关自然、天地与宇宙的大道理。

通过五译文比较可以发现,理雅各、刘殿爵把"天道"译为 the way of Heaven。理雅各倾向于基督教式的解读,认为儒学与基督教义没有很大差异。刘殿爵强调准确性甚于文风的优美。由此可以看到,"在面对翻译过程中的语言及读者接受问题时,译者更倾向于原文本义与文化身份的直观呈现,而不是一种'为我所用'的文化殖民心态"(许雷和屠国元,2014)。

辜鸿铭把"天道"译成 theology。辜鸿铭通过分析儒家思想,尤其是《中庸》中的"天命之谓性,率性之谓道,修道之谓教"后指出,"与宗教相似,孔子的君子之道也是一套更纯粹、更规整的道德规范,比哲学家或伦理学家所提倡的道德准则(即哲学家的理性,伦理学家的良知)有更深刻的形态、更高的标杆。与宗教一样,孔子的君子之道要求我们恪守的是人类的真正法则"(辜鸿铭,2016)。因此,辜鸿铭认为,"儒教是中国的国教,相当于其他国家的教堂宗教。儒教也利用一种相当于教堂的组织来使人服从道德规则"(王京涛,2013)。

安乐哲与罗思文把"天道"译成 the way of tian(tiandao 天道),是以一种域境诠释的文化思维来翻译诠释儒家经典。安乐哲与罗思文强调中国哲学的特殊性,认为儒家哲学应从西方的文化语境中抽离,借助自身的叙事获得"主体性"和平等对话权。中国的哲学英译需要构建属于自身的框架和概念,并从词汇层的阐释入手。"天"作为儒学的核心概念,不具有超越性,是由持续发展的文化所产生的、聚集的精神性(郝大维和安乐哲,1999)。在安乐哲看来,"中国人具有宗教感,儒家思想是一种宗教,不过是一种以人为中心,而不是以超越的上帝为中心的另一种宗教。他认为,西方学者按照西方宗教观念来理解中国哲学,把中国思想基督化,并将中国的天理解为基督教中的上帝的观点是不对的"(范敏,2015)。因此,安乐哲与罗思文采用了创造性翻译策略译介"天道",体现了中国的语言文化特色。

森舸澜(2018)指出,虽然Heaven在英语里是天的标准译法,但是需要注意,"我们讨论的不是一个地点——如基督教概念中的天堂——而是神一般的人,它能发号施令,控制天气,决定战斗的胜负,褒奖并保护其信众。自周朝以来,天也被视为价值和善良的来源:显然,天想要的是善良。'道'也拥有这种内在的善,道的字面意思是指道路或通道——一种实实在在的路。推而广之,道也可以指做事的方法,在这种语境下,道指的是正确的道路。对古代中国人来说,道还有广大无边的意义:道是成为完人的途径,或者是忠实执行天意的途径。道是天道,是世上所有善或价值的依凭"。森舸澜在注释中指出,孔子更加关注"这个世界",即人类学习和自我修养的世界。孔子不太关心诸如"人性"或"天道"之类的理论与深奥的话题,并试图把弟子们的注意力集中在当前任务上,即获得成为绅士所必需的文化修养。有人认为,"人性"是指一个人出生时所获得的可变禀赋;在古典文本中,"天道"是指我们可称之为"运气"或"命运"的东西。按照这样的理解,"人性"和"天道"统称为人类无法控制的事物。而关键是,孔子强调人类所能控制的事物:注重学习并遵循儒道,注重自我修养的提高与完善。因此,森舸澜把"天道"译为the way of Heaven,并通过增加注释评论补充文化内容,从而以更广阔的文化视野让英语读者深刻领会原文的文化内涵。

我们再来看关于"天下有道"的翻译。

【例27】孔子曰:"天下有道,则礼乐征伐自天子出;天下无道,则礼乐征伐自诸侯出。自诸侯出,盖十世希不失矣;自大夫出,五世希不失

矣;陪臣执国命,三世希不失矣。天下有道,则政不在大夫。天下有道,则庶人不议。"(《论语·季氏》)(英语译文参考附录)

这段话的意思是,天下有道与天下无道的时候,制作礼乐和出兵打仗会有不同的阶层(天子/诸侯/家臣)做主。这段话反映了春秋战国时期诸侯国已不受中央控制,各自为政,中央政权名存实亡的状态。孔子通过对比天下有道与天下无道的情形,指出当时的政治状况。我们通过分析原文的意义、修辞对比以及语气词汇的使用,可以看出孔子对当时社会政权的担忧与焦虑。关于"道"的翻译,各位译者在该例句中的翻译如表3-13所示。

表3-13 五译本对"天下有道、天下无道"的翻译

译者	原文	
	天下有道	天下无道
理雅各	When good government prevails in the empire; When right principles prevail in the kingdom	When bad government prevails in the empire
辜鸿铭	In the normal state of the government of an empire; When there are order and justice in the government of a country; When there are justice and order in the government of a country	During abnormal conditions in the government of the empire
刘殿爵	When the Way prevails in the Empire; When the Way prevails in the Empire	When the Way does not prevail in the Empire
安乐哲与罗思文	When the way(dao 道)prevails in the world; When the way prevails in the world;	If the way does not prevail in the world
森舸澜	When the Way prevails in the world	When the Way does not prevail in the world

在翻译过程中,译者会发挥自己的主体性与能动性。由译文比较可以看出,理雅各认为,无论是人还是政府,都由"上天"或者"上帝"赋予了道德的品质,按照法则行事,用 principled 表示有道,用

unprincipled 表示无道,并运用了 good,right,bad,prevail 等词汇修饰加强他的基督教思想。辜鸿铭运用了 the normal state 与 order and justice 词汇,并增加注释:孔子所说的两种政府状态:第一种是欧洲所谓的"寡头政治",第二种是"民主"。根据这段话的意思,这两种政治都不可能是一个国家政府真正正常且永久的状态。中国古代的统治阶级或贵族可对应于英国的乡绅。辜鸿铭通过在注释中把当时的社会政治制度与西方国家政治制度对比,帮助英语读者理解原文含义。

安乐哲认为,如果"道"译为 the Tao,则变为西化"形而上学",引入了"一个不属于中国古代世界观的单一真理观念。'道'不应被'形而上学化'成个体品格应成就的某种单一、客观的普遍真理。世界从每一不同视角而得的观念语汇就是'道'——一条可从各种不同程度探寻到个别体存在与其域境和谐统一脉络的路"(杨朝明,2015)。安乐哲与罗思文考虑到儒家哲学思想的特征及其在中西文化交流中的困难,因而采用意译(the way)与汉语拼音(dao)加汉字(道)的创新性的翻译策略。他们的英译"成为对汉字的直述,成为原文的镜像,而不是以'翻译'的面目出现"(刘禾,2009)。这样,译者就给读者一种"身临其境"的感觉,在让读者感觉自己仿佛在读原文的同时,又让读者感受原文语言的异质特征与异国情调。

刘殿爵与森舸澜都用了大写的具有特殊含义的 Way 一词,区别于英语中的 way。森舸澜在注解中增加了文化语境,以帮助读者理解"无道/有道"的意义。森舸澜根据语境作出解释:前一种说法可能也是对鲁国现状的批评,后一种说法则反映了中国政府的传统理想。老百姓的政治辩论往往是政治混乱的表现。因为在一个国家正常运作的状态下,老百姓会很忙,很满足,也没有理由对国家的运行方式形成意见或者发表意见。老百姓可以更消极地批评或者辩论,在此情况下,老百姓可能会有积极表达观点的空间。

由于中西文化的多元复杂性以及"文化他者"之间缺少普遍沟通的可能性,译者需要准确理解原文的概念意义与内涵意义,注重"原作文化背景、原文作者的权威性、翻译的社会背景、翻译发起者和译者的文化观念以及译文读者群的文化接受心态等因素"(李运兴,2001),而这些因素又是相互关联、密不可分的。而在寻求最佳翻译策略"艺无止境"的动态过程中,译者也在翻译风格特征等方面不断"充分发挥各自的表现功力和主体的主导性潜能"(刘宓庆,2001)。

总之,不同语言文化之间存在的各种文化差异,导致人们对同一事物在各自独特的文化系统作用下产生不同的文化联想意义。在《论语》翻译过程中,译者需要把握文本背后的深层文化因素,准确在译文中体现《论语》的文化内涵与哲学思想。在《论语》翻译过程中,译者在"他者"和"共通性"之间努力,在文化互动中使译文在异域和本土之间具有更强的张力,进而潜移默化地影响目标语读者的思维。由于文化的多元复杂性以及"文化他者"之间缺少普遍沟通的可能性,在《论语》翻译过程中,原文词句的意义在目标语中不可能得到完全表达。此外,由于不同文化背景的读者具有不同的生活经验和认知结构,这必然促使读者对译文形成不同预先期待,影响其对译文的理解与接受,并最终会影响译者在考虑读者需求时选择相应的翻译策略。因此,译者需要考虑读者、文化、语境与时空等因素,提高翻译表达力与读者接受力。

四、《论语》中的修辞特征及翻译

《论语》以语录体为主,叙事体为辅,主要记录了孔子及其弟子的言行,其语录体具有丰富的语言表达形式与修辞手段,如比喻、对偶、排比等,使其表达形象生动。下文主要从《论语》的语体修辞、《论语》中的比喻及英译分析、《论语》中的类比及英译分析、《论语》修辞翻译策略等方面分析《论语》中的修辞与翻译,探讨《论语》的修辞特征及翻译中的显化现象。

(一)《论语》的语体修辞

语体是指"人们在不同社会活动领域适应语境和题旨的需要为实

现交际功能而形成的语言运用体式,常在词汇、句法、语法、语篇结构中体现"(Matthews,2000)。语体也可定义为:"用以确立和表达交际双方距离和关系的语言机制"(施春宏,2019)。修辞"原是达意传情的手段。主要为着意和情,修辞不过是调整语辞使达意传情能够适切的一种努力"(陈望道,2017)。

《论语》最为明显的语体特征是语录体。《论语》的语体"源自史官文献中以'王若曰''君子曰'为标志的'语'体"(过常宝,2007)。此外,"《论语》还继承了史官'述而不作,信而好古'的经典阐释方式,即通过'辞达'缩小自己与神圣文本之间的界限,让意义自我显示出来。《论语》总是通过鼓励学生接近真理,并指示路径,却从不直接表白最终真理"(过常宝,2007)。

《论语》的语录体"具有其自身的特点,是孔子及其弟子不同话语的记录或收集以及所处时代的描述"(Slingerland,2003)。《论语》的语言表达典范简约,具有"微言大义"的话语构建模式。《论语》运用了各种表现方式,使语言表达得准确、鲜明而生动有力。子曰:"辞,达而已矣一"(《论语·卫灵公》),是孔子对文章的基本要求。《论语》的语言"朴实无华、不事雕琢,有许多近乎于口语,却都是经过匠心独运的文学语言;话不多,道理越蕴含丰富,达到了言简意赅的艺术效果。在修辞手法上,《论语》最大的特点是善用比喻"(傅德岷,2017)。比喻"常常用于尊重以往个人的和文化的成就,以及现在的创新。它既揭示过去和现在之间的'同'和连续性,也揭示出它们的'异'和间断性"(郝大维和安乐哲,2018)。

在《论语》中,孔子大部分的话是讲给其他人听的。孔子在与他人的人际交流过程中,会恰当地表达意思,取得最好的表达效果,这就涉及修辞。孔子的交流有两个根本目的:"第一,说出某事物是什么或不是什么。第二,建议、比喻、暗示或者提及。第一种是表达的活动,第二种则是暗指"(郝大维和安乐哲,2018)。"暗指的语言由于不使用传统意义上的参指,因而就没有文字的基础。这种语言的功能主要是激发。

比喻和意象是交流的主要工具,但并不是从代替文字概念的意义上说的"(郝大维和安乐哲,2018)。孔子在与弟子的话语交流中,会经常使用特殊的类比方法来启发学生。这种方法主要是暗指比喻。暗指比喻的目的是在"模范关系中的两极间建立共鸣模范唤起活动,而这种活动又受模范的环境所制约"(郝大维和安乐哲,2018)。"君子曰"具备"官方所赋予的正当性,可以径直地褒贬人物言行"(刘承慧,2018)。

【例 28】 孔子曰:"见善如不及,见不善如探汤。吾见其人矣,吾闻其语矣。隐居以求其志,行义以达其道。吾闻其语矣,未见其人也。"(《论语·季氏》)(英语译文参考附录)

刘承慧引用 Lyons(1995)的话指出,"在言语活动中使用言说主观成分,显示发言者的立场与态度,即是基于某种社会和人际角色所作出的自我表达"(刘承慧,2018)。在该例中,孔子在言说活动中通过使用比喻表达了他对道德修养的立场与态度:"见到善的行为,就像怕赶不上似的去努力追求;看见不善的行为,就像手伸进了沸水中那样赶快离开。我看见过这样的人,也听到过这样的话语。隐居起来以求保全自己的志向,按照义的原则行事以贯彻自己的主张。我听到过这样的话语,却没见过这样的人。"孔子意在通过两种情况的对比告诉人们,行善修德重在自觉。人们不仅要自觉,还要去掉一切功利性目的,为修德而修德。孔子认为,学生应不断反省自己,要坚持不懈努力学习、勤勉工作,沿着儒道通往至善之路的用意。

【例 29】 定公问:"一言而可以兴邦,有诸?"孔子对曰:"言不可以若是其几也。人之言曰:'为君难,为臣不易。'如知为君之难也,不几乎一言而兴邦乎?"曰:"一言而丧邦,有诸?"孔子对曰:"言不可以若是其几也。人之言曰:'予无乐乎为君,唯其言而莫予违也。'如其善而莫之违也,不亦善乎?如不善而莫之违也,不几乎一言而丧邦乎?"(《论语·子路》)(英语译文参考附录)

该例通过会话分析的语轮转换、会话序列与话语修正,以及通过"一言以兴邦、一言以丧邦"的典故隐喻表达手段,使我们了解执政者应该怎样注意自己的言行。语言具有社会功能并能体现语言使用者的社会特征(Dubois,2012;de Fina,2006)。在这里,孔子以答疑解惑的话语形式表述自己的立场与观点。《论语》中很多类似孔子对礼法规则等行为的描述,都可以作为圣人如何灵活地将礼法原则与具体情境相适应的典范。

【例30】季康子问政于孔子曰:"如杀无道,以就有道,何如?"孔子对曰:"子为政,焉用杀?子欲善而民善矣。君子之德风,小人之德草。草上之风,必偃。"(《论语·颜渊》)(英语译文参考附录)

当季康子问孔子如何治理政事时,孔子回答,治理政事要行善,反对杀人,主张"德政"。原文中的风草比喻品德的不同,"在位者的品德好比风,在下的人的品德好比草",草随风向飘动。德风德草比喻统治者如能善理政事、用道德感化人民,人民就会像风一样顺从;而统治者如果无道,则必然遭到百姓反对。通过风与草的关系,强调执政者要修身养性,以德以礼服人,并对自己的行为谨慎负责,指出了儒家要以德治国的主张。对道德修养完美的人来说,合适的礼仪行为需要长期的努力达到"无为"后,不再需要有意识地思考或努力,而是由内心产生自动执行"道"的行为。

【例31】子路从而后,遇丈人,以杖荷蓧。子路问曰:"子见夫子乎?"丈人曰:"四体不勤,五谷不分,孰为夫子?"植其杖而芸。子路拱而立。止子路宿,杀鸡为黍而食之,见其二子焉。明日,子路行以告。子曰:"隐者也。"使子路反见之。至,则行矣。子路曰:"不仕无义。长幼之节,不可废也;君臣之义,如之何其废之?欲洁其身,而乱大伦。君子之仕也,行其义也。道之不行,已知之矣。"(《论语·微子》)(英语译文参考附录)

这段话语先叙述子路遇到荷蓧丈人的情况,接着是子路对"不仕无义,长幼之节不可废也;君臣之义,如之何其废之"的一番议论,然后是子路对"不仕无义"与"积极行道"的感慨。这样通过子路与隐士的对话、孔子与其弟子子路的对话、子路的评论话语,以及运用"四体不勤、五谷不分""不仕无义"等典故隐喻修辞手段,我们了解了隐士的观点、孔子的育人思想以及孔子"知其不可而为之"的人生处世态度。在儒家看来,君臣之间是恩义关系:君对臣有恩(赐其俸禄),臣对君就应有义(守其大义)。因此,像荷蓧丈人这样有才能、有学识的隐士理应义不容辞出来做官,帮助君主平定天下。我们在理解原文时,需要准确理解说话者的立场与态度,并注意语言文化内涵的传递。

由此可以看出,从语言表达和内容来看,《论语》中的儒家思想不是简单的教理问答。孔子与其弟子的师生关系,使得孔子处于某种上位关系,弟子处于某种下位关系。弟子在表达思想时常常表现出对老师的尊重,而孔子在评议他人时也常常表现出谦逊与明事理的姿态。这种用修辞等语言手段来调节和表达的交际距离,本质上是指"心理距离和文化距离而非物理距离,而交际关系正是这种心理、文化距离的体现,语体正是这种语距功能的语法表现"(施春宏,2019)。此外,孔子的传承教育的思想也提醒我们要"有责任去继承前人传给我的文化,有责任去理解传统、丰富传统,并使用传统来解决我们当前的问题,并使之传承到下一代去,告诉他们也这样做下去。当我们说'儒'时我们要知道我们在说什么。我们说的不是一套封闭的理念,而是一个特殊人群的社会责任"(卞俊峰,2019)。

(二)《论语》中的比喻及英译分析

《论语》中使用了大量修辞手段,尤以比喻为主。"比喻用于说理,能使抽象的理论,变成具体的概念,使人接受"(区永超,2018)。相对而言,就比喻的理解和翻译而言,译者在比喻等修辞理解的心理过程中所付出的心理努力要比非比喻等普通表达手段要高得多。因此,译者在翻译《论语》时,要注意修辞的翻译策略。在形式上,比喻一般由本体、喻体和比喻词三种成分组成。因这三种成分的异同和隐现,比喻可分为明喻、隐喻(暗喻)和借喻三类。

1. 明喻

明喻是指"思想的对象同另外的事物有了类似点,说话和写文章时就用那另外的事物来比拟这思想的对象的,名叫譬喻"(陈望道,2017)。明喻是用喻词连接本体和喻体,以表明相同或相似的关系。明喻的本体、喻词和喻体同时出现。《论语》中常用的喻词有譬(如)、犹、如、似等。

【例32】子曰:"为政以德,譬如北辰,居其所而众星共之。"(《论语·为政》)(英语译文参考附录)

原文是指,孔子说:"用道德的力量去治理国家,自己就会像北极星那样安然处在自己的位置上,别的星辰都环绕着它。"

"譬如北辰,居其所而众星共之"是孔子所作的比喻,用道德治理国家的统治者比作"北极星",意思是指施行"德"政的人,就像天上的北极星一般,受到满天星辰的拱卫。在古人眼中,北极星就是宇宙的中心,除了能够用它辨认方向,所有的星辰都以它为中心。"居其所"则是指代领导者不能逾越职权,要明白自己的职责范围。

关于这句明喻的翻译,五位译者分别使用了明喻,如 compare to、like 词语。理雅各、刘殿爵、安乐哲与罗思文使用了情态动词分别将其翻译为 may be compared to the north polar star, which keeps its place and all the stars turn towards it, can be compared to the Pole Star which commands the homage of the multitude of stars simply by remaining in its place, can be compared to being the North Star: the North Star dwells in its place and the multitude of stars pay it tribute,辜鸿铭、森舸澜使用了系动词,分别将其翻译为 is like the Pole-star, which keeps its place while all the other stars revolve round it, is analogous to the Pole Star: it simply remains in its place and receives the homage of the myriad lesser stars。此外,森舸澜在译文中还采用了注释,强调了无为与德政的重要作用,指出在自然界由天所带来的自然和谐,将成为人类统治者的典范。人类统治者将通过其完美道德美德的力量,以一种无为的方式,使世界安静地、必然地、无私地秩序化。

译者在翻译比喻"譬如北辰,居其所而众星共之"时,在理解、传递比喻时需要额外的认知努力。一般来说,注意力和行动需要努力;在正常情况下,行动的要求越高,维持某种效力所需的努力就越大。在正常情况下,努力的付出会随着需求的增加而增加,直到努力达到不再需要努力的最高点。翻译是一个复杂的认知过程,涉及两种语言与文化的转换。在这个翻译认知过程中,由于东西方语言文化差异,译者对比喻修辞以及两种文化的转换形成意义假设并为此作出努力。为了实现译文的最佳可读性和可接受性程度,译者的翻译策略可以反映译者在完成翻译任务过程中为解决具体翻译问题所做的有意识的计划和认知努力。

【例33】子曰:"譬如为山,未成一篑,止,吾止也。譬如平地,虽覆一篑,进,吾往也。"(《论语·子罕》)(英语译文参考附录)

原文是指,孔子说:"(锤炼自我修养)就像堆土成山,只差一筐土就可以完成,这时停下来,就会功亏一篑。又像平整土地,虽然只倒下一筐土,如果决心继续去做,最终会成功,那是坚持不懈、一往无前的结果。"孔子运用"堆土成山"与"填土平地"这两个比喻,说明了学习积累与持之以恒的深刻道理。他一再鼓励自己与弟子们,无论是做学问还是为人处世,都应自觉自愿地持之以恒。如果半途而废,只会前功尽弃,留下终身遗憾。

对于"譬如为山,譬如平地"的翻译,理雅各将其翻译为"The prosecution of learning may be compared to what may happen in raising a mound. It may be compared to throwing down the earth on the level ground"。辜鸿铭将其翻译为"Suppose a man wants to raise a mound; Suppose again a man wants to level a road"。刘殿爵将其翻译为"As in the case of making a mound; As in the case of levelling the ground"。安乐哲与罗思文将其翻译为"As in piling up earth to erect a mountain; As in filling a ditch to level the ground"。森舸澜将其翻译为"(The task of self-cultivation) might be compared to the task of building up a mountain; It might also be compared to the task of leveling ground"。

由此可见,关于原文中明喻的翻译,五译本都使用了排比结构与原文呼应。除了辜鸿铭使用 suppose 引导条件状语从句,引出所表示的情况不是事实,而是主观想象或夸大性的比喻,其他译者都使用了明喻修辞手段,如 compare to,as 等。他们在译文中增加了主语,根据语境调整了标点,体现了英汉语言的差异,进一步明确了原文中明喻词"为山"与"平地"的对比含义。斯坦纳作为一个外国人也曾指出中国语言的特点,"汉语注重意合,不注重形合,标点符号虽然也用来表示句子的逻辑关系和语法关系,但更主要的是用来表示停顿以调整呼吸"(刘禾,2014)。

此外,在原文内涵的理解上,相对于理雅各、辜鸿铭的译文,刘殿爵、安乐哲与罗思文以及森舸澜的译文不仅强调了个人能动性的重要性,而且强调了坚持不懈的重要性。森舸澜在注释中还借用孔子弟子颜回等具体实例,引用朱熹的理解对实践儒道所需的个人修养如决心、毅力、鼓励等精神作了解释补充,强调个人决心的力量在取得成就中的重要性,指出如果要彻底走上漫长而艰辛的儒家道路,就需要有不断努力与坚持不懈的决心,增强了译文读者对原文内涵的理解。

2. 隐喻

隐喻又叫暗喻。本体、喻体同时出现,它们在形式上是相合关系,所强调的类似点也更加鲜明突出。它一般用"为""即"等词代替"像"一类的喻词。译者在翻译过程中需要注意概念隐喻的翻译。George Lakoff 和 Mark Johnson(1980)认为,概念隐喻是指隐喻是从源始域向目标域的本体映射过程,即概念隐喻可视为以一个具体、熟悉的概念去理解和构建另一个抽象、模糊的概念。

【例34】仪封人请见,曰:"君子之至于斯也,吾未尝不得见也。"从者见之。出曰:"二三子何患于丧乎？天将以夫子为木铎。"(《论语·八佾》)(英语译文参考附录)

原文是指,仪封人请求把自己引见给孔子,说:"凡品德高尚的人到了这里,我还从来没有没去拜见过的。"随行孔子的学生把他引见给孔子。仪封人出来之后说:"诸位何必为孔子丧失官位担忧呢？天下无道已经很久了,上天将以孔夫子为圣人来号令天下、弘扬圣人之道。"

原文中的"木铎"是本体隐喻。朱熹的注释是"金口木舌,施政教时所振,以警众者也"。古代天子发布政令时用木铎召集听众,人们常用"木铎"来表示号令天下。天子需要按照天道行事,否则就会被剥夺权利。仪封人认为,孔子能够承担教化天下、维护天下秩序的重任,所以用木铎来作比喻,实现概念隐喻的转化过程。

关于"天将以夫子为木铎"的翻译,各位译者都采用了显化策略。由此可以看出各位译者在翻译《论语》时的严谨治学态度,他们对中国古籍的字词训诂,乃至每一词语在句子中的意思均细心揣摩,根据文化语境以及读者需求尽量选择合适的翻译表达方式。

理雅各将这句话翻译为"Heaven is going to use your master as a bell with its wooden tongue",其中"木铎"直译为"bell with its wooden tongue",非常形象生动。这与理雅各对中华文化的关注以及对中国先贤圣哲的认识分不开的。理雅各博士花费很长的时间,把中国人的生活作为活着的书籍去研究。理雅各努力打破语言上的障碍,冲破愚昧和偏见,努力接近中国人的内心。他以中国人在文化和教育上的标准来衡量自己,因为这些标准本身具有中国人独特而完整的智慧。他知道,那些让中国引以为荣的人们,都是些儒家学者,所以,他深入他们的领域,与中国人古老的传统和国学打交道(吉瑞德,2011)。

辜鸿铭把"天将以夫子为木铎"翻译为"now God is going to make use of your Teacher as a tocsin to awaken the world"。辜鸿铭认为,孔子生活的时代,社会秩序发生根本性混乱。这种秩序带来了世界的无序,而且造成了人们思想的混乱。有着中国精神的中国人试图建立新的社会秩序和文明,而孔子则为未来的世界文明奠定了一个真实合理的基础。辜鸿铭曾阐述:"所有伟人,所有富于智慧的人们,通常都信仰上帝。孔子也信奉上帝,虽然他很少提及它……然而,富于智慧的人们,其心中的上帝有别于常人。他们对上帝的信仰,就是斯宾诺莎所说的对神圣的宇宙秩序的信仰"(王京涛,2019)。因此,辜鸿铭把木铎译为 tocsin(警铃、警钟或者警报之意),并选用了 awaken(唤醒)一词。

刘殿爵将这句话翻译为"Heaven is about to use your Master as the wooden tongue for a bell"。同样,刘殿爵采用了直译,并把木铎译为"the wooden tongue for a bell",以保留原文的语言特点。其言简意赅的译作风格显然与英国哲学家吉尔伯特·赖尔(Gilbert Ryle)的影响分不开的。

安乐哲与罗思文将这句话翻译为"tian is going to use your Master as a wooden bell — clapper",并采用了文内注释的方式,如 a wooden bell —clapper。安乐哲认为,在翻译儒家哲学比喻时,注重"让关键哲学术语恢复其在本视域内的原初寓意。这一过程是'保守'的,如果用考古学意义比喻的话,就是尽最大努力将它恢复到原始视域中的那种情况;同时它也是'激进的',因为我们要做的是找出植根于中华文化土壤中的喻义,这些喻义本身是活的,是与其语义的树木生长在一起的。尽管我们还有实际的阐释性局限,我们必须能够做到何种程度就做到何种程度,符合'逻辑允许原则'(the principle of logical charity),充分发挥想象力,以使属于其他文化叙事的原典文献,显现自己的诗意——那深不可测属于自己的、未经染指的情节与独具的特色"(安乐哲,2017)。

森舸澜将这段话翻译为"Heaven intends to use your Master like the wooden clapper for a bell"。森舸澜采用了注释,解释将孔子比作木铎的原因:大多数评论认为,这是指孔子在鲁国失去职位——这大概是孔子和他的弟子离开鲁国的原因。有评论认为,边防官员能看到孔子作为隐身圣人的真正使命:在混乱和不道德的年代为了保护自己而采取卑微立场的贤人。"钟"可能是指流动的民歌收藏者和传播者所使用的钟,也可能是指官员用来在乡村发布官方公告所使用的钟。无论是哪种情况,边防官员的观点都是这样的:"天"故意让孔子失去官职,让他在整个王国游荡,传播"道"的教义,以唤醒堕落的世界。

【例35】子贡问曰:"赐也何如?"子曰:"女,器也。"曰:"何器也?"曰:"瑚琏也。"(《论语·公冶长》)(英语译文参考附录)

原文是指,子贡请教说:"我的表现如何呢?"孔子说:"你好比是一个器具。""什么器具呢?"孔子说:"是宗庙里面贵重的瑚琏。"

瑚琏是古代祭祀时盛黍稷的尊贵玉器,分别是夏、商两代祠堂中最重要的礼器。这里用作本体隐喻,比喻人特别有才能,可以担当大任。孔子以瑚琏比喻子贡,是说子贡对于国家社稷,乃是大器,具有超才、足堪重用、贮可裕养,容重厚德。但是孔子认为,"君子不器"。孔子的评论一方面说子贡不是普通的器皿;但另一方面则暗示子贡虽具有一定才能,但是如果要成为君子,还要进一步修身养性。因为瑚琏器皿既是古玩(不再用于周礼),又极为特殊(甚至在夏商时期也很少使用)。

关于"瑚琏"的翻译,各位译者采用了不同的翻译策略。本例中辜鸿铭没有使用注释,因此没有列出来对比。

通过译文比较,我们发现,理雅各的译文增加了对瑚琏作用的注释:瑚琏是装饰华丽的器皿,用于盛放王室宗祠/宗庙的谷物祭品。夏朝叫"琏",殷朝叫"瑚"。孔子没有给子贡"君子"的称号,而是用在重要的场合"有价值的瑚琏"代指。在这个译文中,理雅各出现了对瑚琏历史知识的误译,正确的说法应该是,夏朝叫"瑚",商朝叫"琏"。

刘殿爵强调瑚琏的材质:由玉制作的祭祀器皿[a sacrificial vessel (made of jade)]。

安乐哲与罗思文的译文强调瑚琏的功用:一件非常珍贵与神圣的器皿(a most precious and sacred kind of vessel),并在附录的注释中解释了什么是瑚琏:瑚琏分别是夏、商两代祠堂使用的祭器(The *hu* and the *lan* were sacrificial vessels used in the ancestral halls of the Xia and Shang dynasties respectively)。

森舸澜的译文增加了文化阐释,指出"君子不应是器皿"。也就是说,真正的君子不仅仅是专家:the gentleman is not a vessel (2.12)—i. e., the true gentleman is more than a mere specialist。在注释中,森舸澜还进一步阐释了孔子把子贡作为"理解"的听众的原因。自贡是一位成就卓著的政治家、能言善辩的演说家和成功的商人,但孔子觉得他似乎缺乏对他人的灵活变通与同情心。这也是孔子为什么选择子贡作为教学对象来讲授"理解"的含义:"理解"可以作为终身指导的教学。子贡的个性特点决定了他的功用,例如,他对礼节的严谨遵守,不知变通导致孔子称他为"具备有限能力、用来祭祀的瑚琏"。森舸澜还使用互参帮助大家进一步了解瑚琏的含义。

综上所述,理雅各的注释(文后注释)注重文本考证,刘殿爵的注释(文后注释)注重释义,安乐哲与罗思文的注释(文内注释与附录注释)注重传达中国语言的文化特色与哲学思想,森舸澜的注释(文后注释)注重历史文化背景与典故的阐释等。辜鸿铭在译文中很少用注释,偶尔用到也注重对西方文化的引用与诠释。

3. 借喻

借喻是比喻的一种,是比喻中的高级形式,是以喻体来代替本体,本体和喻词都不出现,直接把甲(本体)说成乙(喻体)。在特定语境中,由喻体可直接领会到本体,意义简洁、含蓄而深厚。

【例36】子曰:"君子不器。"(《论语·为政》)(英语译文参考附录)

原文是指,孔子说:"君子不能像器具一样,只有某一方面的用途,而应该博学多识。"

所谓"器",应该是道德状态的借喻。君子"不器",需要根据"道"来理解。孔子认为,一生学而不厌,求的就是"道"。《易经》里说:"形而上者谓之道,形而下者谓之器。"其意思是,道是无形的,器是有形的。但是,道器不离,无形的规律的道恰好就存在于有形的器物之中。这种由"人"实现"仁"和"君子"的过程是与过程性世界观分不开的,而"过程性世界观在根本上是域境性的,嵌入其中的特殊事物同它所处的环境既是相延续的,也是相区别的"(卞俊峰,2019)。

孔子强调,君子不能只是囿于一技之长,而应当"志"于"道",从变化多端的世界去感悟深奥的"道"。只有悟道,了解熟悉并按照儒道行事,实现"天道"与"本心"合一,才有驾驭各种复杂事件的能力,才能以不变应万变,才能担当修身、齐家、治国、平天下的重任。先秦早期"君子"主要是从政治角度立论的,多指"君王之子",着眼于社会地位而非道德品质。孔子心目中的"君子"兼具高尚道德品质和完美人格,具有"仁者不忧,知者不惑,勇者不惧"的品德,是内在精神"仁"与外在规约"礼"的有机统一。

由此可见,儒家哲学思想中的"道器观"强调有形事物与无形事物之间的相互依存,其核心内容是追求更高层面的"仁"与"道",以实现人生的价值;强调正确知识与德艺能在生活与行为中的意义,进而由这种意义来提升人生的价值,使人真正成为《论语》中所谓的"成人"与"君子";鼓励人们勇于承担自己的社会责任,发挥自己内在潜能与能动性,深入理解古代天人合一理论的哲学要义。

对于"器"的翻译,理雅各将其直译为utensil;辜鸿铭将其意译为make himself into a mere machine fit only to do one kind of work;安乐哲与罗思文将其直译为vessels;刘殿爵与森舸澜虽然都翻译为

vessel 并增加注释,以帮助读者进一步理解原文借喻的意义。但是相比较而言,森舸澜的翻译更加准确、通顺、易懂。刘殿爵增加的注释为:也就是说,他不应只是专家,因为每个器皿都是为某个特殊目的而设计的(i. e. he is no specialist, as every vessel is designed for a specific purpose)。森舸澜增加的注释为:"器"是指用来完成某个特殊功能的仪式器具或者工具,也常用来比喻为专门从事某项特殊任务的专家。君子应在技能的掌握上不该受限。相对于艺术的习得与任务的完成,君子治学更应该强调美德与善行的完善。如果拘泥于君子能做什么、不能做什么,就会落于"器"思维的困境。

此外,"器"的翻译是否成功也需要看上下文语境的衔接与连贯,如"君子"的翻译。"这些互系关系是否有成效,取决于它们在多大程度上成为喻义增加或是减少的来源"(安乐哲,2017)。理雅各的译文 accomplished scholar 更加突出"建树"与"技能"层面,没有把"君子"的道德层面含义凸显出来,因此读者在理解"器"时也会有所偏差。与此相类似,辜鸿铭将"君子"翻译为 A wise man,刘殿爵与森舸澜都将其翻译为 The gentleman,也都没有把"君子"的道德层面含义凸显出来。安乐哲与罗思文把"君子"创译为 Exemplary persons (junzi 君子),强调原文汉语中的"君子"更加注重道德层面的区分,而不是地位高低划分这一含义。

(三)《论语》中的类比及英译分析

类比是将两个本质上不同的事物就其共同点进行比较(如通过围墙高度了解人的能力深浅)。通过使用类比,译者可以通过许多平行的相似来扩展阐释,说服读者相信由于两种事物在许多方面很相似,一种事物得出的结论暗示另一种事物也可以得出同样的结论。通常类比的事物是人们所熟悉的。

类比有别于明喻和暗喻。在句子结构方面,明喻与暗喻是在相似的一点上进行比较,而类比则是在几个共同特性或相似点的两种不同事物之间进行平行比较。在作用方面,明喻与暗喻是通过描述、阐明和说明来提高效果和增强主题。而类比则是用劝说或解释说明一种观点或思想。

【例37】叔孙武叔语大夫于朝,曰:"子贡贤于仲尼。"子服景伯以告子贡。子贡曰:"譬之宫墙,赐之墙也及肩,窥见室家之好。夫子之墙数仞,不得其门而入,不见宗庙之美,百官之富。得其门者或寡矣。夫子之云,不亦宜乎!"(《论语·子张》)(英语译文参考附录)

这段话的意思是,叔孙武叔在朝廷上对大夫们说:"子贡比仲尼更强些。"子服景伯把这话告诉了子贡。子贡说:"就用围墙作比喻吧,我家围墙只有齐肩高,从墙外可以看到里面房屋的美好。我老师的围墙有几仞(1仞=1.8米)高,找不到大门走进去,就看不见里面宗庙的雄美、房屋的富丽。能够找到大门的人或许太少了。所以叔孙武叔先生那样说,不也是很自然的吗?"这段话通过叔孙武叔的话语,子贡与子服景伯的话语内容的补充解释让我们了解到孔子的弟子对老师的内心赞美与崇敬之情。原文通过比喻帮助说明道理或描述某种复杂情况。

现在分析原文中的类比"譬之宫墙"的翻译。通过比较译文可以发现,五译本都使用了直译策略。五译本分别将其翻译为 the comparison of a house and its encompassing wall, the comparison of two buildings, take outer walls as an analogy, take a perimeter wall as an analogy, use the analogy of a residence surrounded by a wall。其中,理雅各与辜鸿铭使用了 the comparison of 词组,刘殿爵、安乐哲与罗思文以及森舸澜译文都使用了 analogy(类比)一词。

值得一提的是,相对而言,辜鸿铭与安乐哲和罗思文的《论语》译本中在更大语境上使用了许多类比策略。辜鸿铭为了让西方人容易理解,在书中对诸多中西人物与事件进行了大量类比。例如,他以《旧约》中的先知摩西或古希腊立法家梭伦比作周公,以一生传奇的英国海军上将西德尼·史密斯(1764—1840)比作祝鲍。以英国的政治家、外交家及文学家查斯特菲尔德(1694—1773)比作当时的宋国公子朝,以"古代中国的法兰西"称呼齐国。安乐哲与罗思文则是系统性、创造性地翻译中国伦理学词汇。在此情况下的类比翻译策略在很大程度上有了另一种意义,即扩大了《论语》中某些概念的外延,使文本进一步扩展并让新艺术升华到世界地位,有助于我们从多角度了解《论语》的精神价值。

【例38】子曰:"夏礼,吾能言之,杞不足征也;殷礼,吾能言之,宋不足征也。文献不足故也,足则吾能征之矣。"(《论语·八佾》)(英语译文参考附录)

原文是指,孔子说:"夏朝的礼,我能说出来,它的后代杞国不足以作证;殷朝的礼,我能说出来,它的后代宋国不足以作证。这是它们的历史文件和贤者不够的缘故。若有足够的文件和贤者,我就可以引来作证了。

"礼"是一个时代人文文化的最突出表现,知道"礼"就等于知道一个时代的文化。孔子说知道夏礼、殷礼,又说描述夏礼、殷礼的文化典籍贫乏,这有两层含义:一是意在让人们领悟礼的本质是不变的,从传统文化中可以整理出一脉相承的文化精神,再把这种文化精神与时代生活相结合,才能创造出适合时代的文化;二是提醒质疑者学习周礼要参考当时文献与礼仪活动,借此用心领悟礼的本质以及学习遵循周礼的道理。

通过比较五个译本,我们发现,辜鸿铭不仅增加了文内注释,如 say the Greek civilization, say modern Greece, say Roman civilization, say Italy 与文外注释,如互参(参考2.23),而且增加了 during, modern 等词,以突出时代的发展变化。文中杞、宋分别是夏殷的后代诸侯国。这样,辜鸿铭通过比拟的手法,帮助西方人理解,把夏朝时的艺术与文明比作希腊文明,把现在的杞国比作现在的希腊,把殷朝时艺术与文明比作罗马文明,把现在的宋国比作意大利。也就是说,把"杞"与"夏"的关系比喻为"现代希腊"与"古希腊"的关系；把"宋"与"殷"的关系比喻为"意大利"与"古罗马"的关系，进一步拉近了英语读者与原语言文化的距离。此外，辜鸿铭还把"礼"翻译为"the state of the arts and civilization"（文明与艺术的状态）。辜鸿铭认为，这里所说的"礼"，是指整个朝代或社会的文明与艺术状态，并与《论语》的第 2 章第 23 节"殷因于夏礼"翻译相近，形成互参。

安乐哲与罗思文创造性地把"礼"翻译为 ritual propriety（li 礼），增加了 during, descendant 等词，以突出时代的发展变化。安乐哲与罗思文认为，"跨文化理解必须以类比开始，每一传统必须在它自己的文化资源中找到一套词汇，这套词汇能重申这一传统，用总有些不完美的方式来理解什么是该传统的哲学和文化资源，这也使它更好理解自己"（安乐哲，2017）。因此，安乐哲与罗思文运用类比法，使中西哲学在持续的对话之中，彼此创造性地解读对方，在给对方文化以及儒家文化的意义增值的同时也丰富了世界文化。

总之，《论语》的修辞翻译体现了译者的翻译目的与翻译思想。译者需要考虑语体修辞特点与读者认知思维差异，思考社会文化因素在《论语》修辞翻译过程中所体现的语言变异、文化变异以及区域变异中的作用，通过适当的翻译修辞表征，提高译文的可读性与可接受性。

（四）《论语》修辞翻译策略

《论语》中修辞的翻译策略与译者措辞选择，句长使用以及修辞时的用语特点都密切相关，需要考虑文本分析、译者意图与读者接受等因素。译者在翻译过程中需要思考各类修辞在翻译过程中的理解与认知，以及读者在理解译文修辞时所作的努力，从而采取相应策略。此外，译者具有不同的翻译思想，表现出较强的译者主体性，而且受译入语语言与文化语境的影响，因此翻译策略各具特点。

1. 语义翻译

语义翻译是指，"在译文语言与结构所允许的范围内，尽可能传递原文的语境意义"(Newmark,1981)。语义翻译策略可以保留原文的意象,使译文形象生动,因此,它是修辞翻译过程中首先考虑的翻译策略。

【例39】 子曰:"苗而不秀者有矣夫!秀而不实者有矣夫!"(《论语·子罕》)(英语译文参考附录)

原文意思是,孔子说:"庄稼有只长苗而不开花的吧!有开了花却不结果实的吧!"孔子在此处用"苗""秀""实"来比喻生命和修养。谷始生曰苗,成穗为秀,成谷曰实。孔子认为,学无止境,不能半途而废,因此借庄稼的生长、开花到结实的过程来比喻一个人学习的过程。地里的庄稼从播种、拔苗再到开花结实来完成生命历程。但是,有的庄稼只长苗而没有开花——"苗而不秀",有的开了花、长了穗却没有结果——"秀而不实"。人的成长也是如此,有的人树立了志向,却没有行动,就像只长苗不开花;有的人,立志并进行了修行,却半途而废,就像庄稼开花而没有结果。只有那些既树立远大志向,又积极行动,并能够坚持到底的人才会有所成就。

对于原文中"苗而不秀、秀而不实"的翻译,五译本都采用了保留原文形式的语义翻译策略。例如,理雅各将其翻译为"the blade springs, but the plant does not go on to flower; it flowers but fruit is not subsequently produced"。辜鸿铭将其翻译为"some only sprout up, but do not flower; some only flower, but do not ripen into fruit"。刘殿爵将其翻译为"(there are) young plants that fail to produce blossoms, and blossoms that fail to produce fruit"。安乐哲与罗思文将其翻译为"(there are indeed) seedlings that do not flower, and there are flowers that do not fruit"。森舸澜采用了语义翻译+注释的翻译策略。森舸澜将其翻译为"(there are) some sprouts that fail to flower, some flowers that fail to bear fruit"。森舸澜在注释中指出,从汉朝到唐朝的评论常把这段话与《论语·子罕》篇中的9.20和9.21一

起指颜回的英年早逝。而朱熹则把这段话与《论语·子罕》篇中的9.17和9.19一起指对自我修养的评论,强调君子治学要注重自我激励。这两种解释似乎都有道理。森舸澜在注释中给出不同评论供读者思考,帮助读者理解原文隐含的意义。

2. 交际翻译

当语义翻译会引起读者误解或者译文晦涩难懂等情况时,译者可以采用交际翻译策略。交际翻译是指:"使译文读者产生与原文读者读原文尽可能相似的效果"(Newmark,1981)。交际翻译策略可以拉近译文读者与原文的距离,提高译文的可接受性。

【例40】子曰:"鲁卫之政,兄弟也。"(《论语·子路》)(英语译文参考附录)

原文是指,孔子说:"鲁国和卫国的政治,就像兄弟一样。"

通过比较五个译文可以发现,在对原文中"兄弟"的意象进行表征处理上,大部分译者采用了语义翻译策略。例如,理雅各将其译为:"The governments of Lu and Wei are brothers."刘殿爵将其译为:"In their government the states of Lu and Wei are as alike as brothers."安乐哲与罗思文将其译为:"The governments of Lu and Wei are elder and younger brother respectively."森舸澜将其译为:"In their forms of government, the states of Lu and Wei are like elder and younger brother."并在注释中补充了孔子时代鲁国和卫国因衰落而变得相似的背景知识。

与其他译者都采用语义翻译策略所不同的是,辜鸿铭采用了交际翻译策略。辜鸿铭没有把原文中"兄弟"的意象进行表征,而是把原文中的"鲁、卫两国政治状态大致形同"的深层意思翻译出来,译为:"(the state of government of his own State and that of another State in his time) The one is about the same as the other."[(孔子在谈到他的国家与同时代另一个国家的政治状态时说)"一个与另一个大致相同"]

由此可见,语义翻译强调保留原文内容,尽力帮助目标语读者理解原文意思。交际翻译则关注目标语读者,根据目标语的语言、文化和语用方式传递信息,而不是尽量复制原文文字。在语义翻译中,译者尽力追踪原作者的思想过程,而不是努力阐释;交际翻译则更加强调译文"效果",尽力使译文通顺易懂,规范自然。

3. 创造性翻译

创造性翻译策略不同于传统意义上的翻译策略,是根据语言文化的本质差异特点采用一种富于想象的创造性的翻译策略,如运用汉语的音、形、义的语言特点,在翻译原文意义内涵的同时,通过增加拼音与汉字以表征原文的语言文化特点。

【例41】哀公问社于宰我。宰我对曰:"夏后氏以松,殷人以**柏**,周人以**栗**,曰,使民战**栗**。"子闻之,曰:"成事不说,遂事不谏,既往不咎。"(《论语·八佾》)(英语译文参考附录)

这段话的意思是,鲁哀公问宰我,土地神的神主应该用什么树木。宰我回答道:"夏朝用松树,商朝用柏树,周朝用栗子树,用栗子树的意思是使老百姓战栗。"孔子听到后说:"已经做过的事不用提了,已经完成的事不用再去劝阻了,已经过去的事也不用再追究了。"

原文选自《论语·八佾》。这部分内容主要涉及"礼"的问题,孔子主张维护礼在制度上、礼节上的种种规定。"礼在中国古代特别重要,它有三层含义:第一,宗教的含义;第二,政治的含义;第三,伦理的含义"(傅佩荣,2019)。"礼(禮)"字是由"示"(代表日、月、星)字与"丰"("豐",是二玉在器之形,桌上两块玉,下面的"豆"字是祭桌)字组成,表示与祭祀有关。"礼者,理也"(《礼记》),"它的本质是区分尊卑上下,把社会里的人分成一个一个的层次,也就是等级,或说伦理"(唐翼明,2016)。

例如,上文中涉及的祭礼、葬礼都与祭祀有关,反映了对祖先的态度,类似于宗教的功用。其中隐含的政治含义是,鲁哀公问社的目的是想除去三家权臣,宰我也以隐语回应。牌位用什么木材去做本来是一种自然的选择,但宰我引申到政治含义解释,周人树栗是取其谐音,为让老百姓望而生畏、臣民战栗,隐喻周代老百姓因苛政而生活不安定。此外,该例句中隐含的伦理含义就是人类社会的行为应有约束。这也是为什么孔子认为宰我借题发挥对前辈圣人周王不敬,或者认为三家专权的局势形成已久,再说无用,因此作出既往不咎的评论。

通过对比原文与译文可以看出,各位译者尽可能采用创造性翻译策略力求突出原文隐喻中的双关语含义。例如,在翻译"栗树"与"战栗"这一隐喻中的双关语时,理雅各在注解中指出,"栗, the chestnut tree,'the tree of the existing dynasty, is used in the sense of li 慄 to be afraid'. he suggested a reason for its planting which might lead the duke to severe measures against his people to be carried into effect at the altars"。辜鸿铭将其翻译为 the li (chestnut) 与 awe (li),刘殿爵将其翻译为 the chestnut (li) 与 tremble (li),安乐哲、罗思文在译文中增加了汉字,翻译为 the chestnut (li 栗) 与 fearful (zhanli 战栗),凸显了原文的语言特色与文化底蕴。因此,安乐哲与罗思文在翻译《论语》时,坚持主观与客观相结合的策略,一方面利用西方的语言文化知识,另一方面努力还原原文语境,从而使儒家伦理学显示自己的"主体性"。森舸澜将其翻译为 the chestnut tree (li) 与 instill fear (li 栗),并在注解中对该隐喻的双关语的含义作出解释:Zai Wo is playing upon a graphic pun between li(栗)chestnut and li(栗)fear, awe(later distinguished with the heart radical,慄)。这种"意译+拼音+汉字"的策略把中国的特色文化词汇传递给英语读者,使译文在异域和本土之间具有更强张力,进而潜移默化影响英语读者的思维。

4. 注疏策略

在《论语》翻译过程中,对于一些修辞的翻译,如果采用直译策略不能使读者理解,或者想让读者了解更多的文化背景知识,译者可以采用注疏(包括注解、注释等)的方式加强翻译显化策略,减轻英语读者对原文理解困难的负担。注疏策略常常与其他策略融合在一起使用。

【例41】中,关于其历史背景、典故与双关的注释,理雅各与森舸澜采用了"文内翻译＋文外注释"的策略。理雅各不仅在译文中对栗树作了文化解释,还在注解中对社、哀公、宰我等历史考证作了简单解释。森舸澜不仅采用创译策略翻译栗树,还进一步在注释中对其他如松、柏等相关树木的双关语进行诠释,如 pine（song 松）being graphically similar to rong（容）(accommodating) and having the phonetic gong 公（just, public; lord）and cypress（bo 柏）being similar to po 迫（to press）or pa 怕（quiet, still; to fear）。

现在我们比较理雅各与森舸澜的注疏策略：

Legge：

哀公, see Ⅱ. xix. Tsai Wo, by name 子, and styled 子我, was an eloquent disciple of the sage, a native of Lu. His place is the second west among the wise ons. 社, from 示（ch'i）, 'spirit or spirits of the earth,' and 土 means 土地神主, "the resting-place or altars of the spirits of the land or ground Wo simply tells the duke that the founders of the several dynasties planted much and such trees about those altars. The reason was that the soil suited such trees; but as 栗, "the chestnut tree, 'the tree of the existing dynasty, is used in the sense of li 慄 to be afraid,'. he suggested a reason for its planting which might lead the duke to severe measures against his people to be carried into effect at the altars. 其他如夏后氏、殷人、周人的注解略。

Slingerland：

The *Annals* tells us that the altar to the soil in the state of Lu was destroyed by fire during the fourth year of the reign of

Duke Ai (Legge 1994d: 804). This is probably the reason for his questioning of Zai Wo, who at the time was apparently being employed by the Duke as a ritual specialist. In his answer, Zai Wo is playing upon a graphic pun between *li* 栗 "chestnut" and *li* 栗 "fear, awe" (later distinguished with the heart radical, *li* 慄).⑭ There are many ways to understand this passage. Perhaps the simplest interpretation is that of Kong Anguo and others, who see it as a rebuke of Zai Wo's reckless speculation: different states used different trees to mark their altars because of variations in local growing conditions; to derive significance from a pun as Zai Wo does is both foolish and insulting to the ancients. Alternately, Confucius saw Zai Wo's comment as being critical of the Zhou, and thus a violation of ritual pro priety — especially when speaking to one of the Zhou's direct descendants, Duke Ai. Perhaps more interesting are interpretations that see this exchange as a coded reference to current affairs. In addition to their sacrificial function, altars to the soil doubled as sites of public executions. Some commentators see the Duke's question as an oblique way of suggesting that he use force against those in the state who oppose him, and Zai Wo's answer ("it is said they wanted to instill fear in the people") as an implicit approval of this strategy. There is some variation in which commentators identify as the specific players in this drama, but the explanation of Liu Baonan is representative:

It seems to me that "that which is already past" refers to the actions of Ji Pingzi.⑮ Pingzi did not act as a minister should, even going so far as to force Duke Zhao from power. No doubt Duke Ai saw this "past action" of Pingzi's as the root of his current troubles, and wished to announce his crime in order to bring punishment down upon his descendents. This is an example of "trying to censure what is already past." However, the loss of favor experienced by the Ducal House and the devolvement of real power into the hands of the ministers was not brought about in a single day. Duke Ai does not yet realize that "one should employ one's ministers in accordance with ritual" (3.19), and furthermore he was not yet capable of employing Confucius. Instead, he impatiently wants to make a show of power in order to vent his anger, and thinks he can rely upon this to recapture his lost power and influence. This, of course, will not work at all, and this is why the Master tries to restrain him with his comment.

⑬ The altar of the soil, one of the most important religious sites in a state, was marked with a sacred tree.

⑭ It is possible that the other tree names had similar double meanings as the result of puns: "pine" (*song* 松 being graphically similar to *rong* 容 ("accommodating") and having the phonetic *gong* 公 ("just, public"; "lord") and "cypress" (*bo* 柏) being similar to *po* 迫 ("to press") or *pa* 怕 ("quiet, still"; "to fear").

⑮ The Ji Family head who is the probable target of 3.1 and who, with the help of the other infamous Three Families, attacked his lord, Duke Zhao, and forced him from office.

通过比较可以发现,两译文都采用了互参,且对原文的双关意义进行阐释。不同的是,森舸澜在翻译《论语》中的比喻时,采用音译加汉字加注释的创造性策略翻译《论语》文化内容,并在注释部分体现自己对原文的解读,通过增加历史文化背景,以最大限度地帮助英语读者了解中华文化。

森舸澜采用注解、次要注解与文本注释,帮助英语读者深刻了解原文中隐喻的文化内涵。注解与注释字数远远超过原文字数。森舸澜通过翻译原文隐喻中典故的字面意义、引申意义与语用意义,把原文的文化内涵传递给国外读者。森舸澜通过提供历史背景知识并从修辞、释义等多角度解释原文的文化内容,使当代英语读者了解当时文化背景,同时体会孔子处事周全而不失原则以及作为教育家的宽厚仁爱之心,赋予读者内心新的启迪与思考,对于当前时代也有着重要的教育意义。

森舸澜在注解部分(包括引用理雅各的观点)对一些关键人物和事件作了解释,如孔子学生"宰我"借助双关语与树木的象征意义回答鲁哀公问题,孔子对该事件的几种不同认识与观点等;在次要注解中对孔子的回答"既往不咎"的典故及其隐含的意义进行诠释。森舸澜在注释中对"社"作了解释,它是指祭祀后土的地方(庙或场地),常用来种植象征该国精神的树。同时,森舸澜在次要注释中对松柏树作为隐喻的双关意义以及季平子这个人物作了解释,以帮助英语读者理解原文内涵。例如,森舸澜在注释中指出,"松"与"容(宽容)"形相似,又与"公(公正)"音似;"柏"与"迫(迫害)"或者"怕"(害怕)相似。

森舸澜采用这样的注解和注释是与译者的翻译目的分不开的。森舸澜在译本序言中曾指出,由于《论语》文本本身的哲理奥秘,该译本的评论能够引导读者快速浏览大量的各种注解以及与该文本相关的其他奥秘,并为英语学术的进一步探索提供建议(Slingerland,2003)。因此,森舸澜在翻译时,尽量注意在《论语》翻译过程中不把个人观点"隐藏"在译文中。

接下来我们探讨比喻中代词等语言点的翻译注释。例如,颜渊喟然叹曰:"仰之弥高,钻之弥坚。瞻之在前,忽焉在后。夫子循循然善诱之,博我以文,约我以礼,欲罢不能。既竭吾才,如有所立卓尔。虽欲从之。末由也矣"(《论语·子罕》)。可以看出,颜回对孔子的评价既客观又有真情。颜回认为,孔子无论是在人格上还是学问上,都是别人难以企及的,"仰之弥高,钻之弥坚"。孔子作为老师不仅有着伟岸的人格、渊博的学识与深厚的道德修养,同时还有着坚定而灵动的教育智慧和循循善诱的教育方法,"博我以文,约我以礼"。对于原文中明喻"如有所立卓尔"的翻译,辜鸿铭将其直译为 would still stand clear and distinct away from me,理雅各、刘殿爵、安乐哲与罗思文、森舸澜把原文的明喻修辞手段在译文中也明确体现出来,分别将其翻译为 seems something to stand right up before me, seems to rise sheer above me, as though something rises up right in front of me, seems as if there is still something left, looming up ahead of me。而对于隐喻"仰之弥高,钻之弥坚"中指代词"之"语言点的翻译,刘殿爵与森舸澜两位译者则在注释中注明如下。

Lau:

　　Throughout this chapter the "it" refers to the way of Confucius.

Slingerland:

　　The "it" referred to by Yan Hui is most likely the Confucian Way. This passage represents the most dramatic expression in the text of the difficulty of self-cultivation and the incredible strength of will needed to remain on the path—especially because it comes from the mouth of Yan Hui, the most naturally gifted of Confucius' disciples. Many esoteric and mystical interpretations of Yan Hui's words have been offered by traditional commentators, but Huang Gan is correct in rejecting them: The Way of the sage is certainly high and brilliant, expansive and great, so that it is indeed difficult to reach, but it still does not transcend our basic human nature. The details of one's movements and expressions; the tasks of eating and drinking, rising and resting, interacting with others and meeting one's social responsibilities; the standards that govern relations between ruler and minister, father and son, elder and junior, and husband and wife; going out in public or remaining at home, resigning or accepting office, declining or accepting reward, taking this and discarding that, along with everything else up to the implementation of government regulations— none of this lies outside the scope of the Way. The difficulty does not lie in the Way's transcendental nature, for it is right in front of us (7.30), in the details of everyday life. The true challenge is the almost superhuman stamina and determination required to walk it to its end. Cf. 8.7 and 9.19.

通过森舸澜对语言点"it"的注释,我们了解到孔子所奉行的儒道体现在方方面面,如日常生活、行事礼仪以及为政施教等。还有重要的一点是,儒道的坚持也是至关重要的。这让我们认识到孔子作为圣人所拥有的优良品质。

由此可见,语言作为文化的载体,反映了该民族的文化价值观。由于中西文化差异,汉语与英语的词汇体系中存在许多词义空缺的现象,反映中国特色的典故、双关语、比喻等很难在英语中找到相应的表达方式。从这个意义上来说,典故、双关语与比喻等在一定程度存在某种不可译性。由于有些文化障碍是无法逾越的,如果在翻译过程中依然坚持注重形式,势必导致译文的晦涩难懂,令读者不能理解原文。因此,我们也要认识到,"翻译是指在译语中用最贴近的自然的对等语再现源语的信息,首先是在意义上,其次是在文体上"(Nida and Taber, 1969)。在这种情况下,译者只能退而求其次,而采用注重传达内涵的翻译策略。这样通过采用适当的翻译策略,使原文中的典故、双关语与比喻等力求在译文中得到恰当表达,从而实现中西文化的交流与互动。

因此,在典故以及各类修辞翻译过程中,译者需考虑读者群体以及文化语境等因素而采用显化策略。译者在典故以及双关、比喻等修辞翻译中经常采用的显化翻译策略,即通过采用注释策略与创造性翻译策略以及修辞手段的明朗化等,把原文修辞中所包含的历史背景、语言难点、文化空缺等进行分析讲解,从而增强读者对文本的可理解性。我们的翻译目的是准确地传达原文的文化内涵,克服中西文化差异,帮助英语读者能更好地理解这些具有特殊文化色彩的词语,从而实现中西文化共沟通交流的功能。因此,我们在翻译过程中,要注重使用灵活的变通翻译策略,注意内涵意义的传递优先于语言形式表达的重要性。

五、小结

本章以《论语》汉英双语平行语料库为基础,结合定量与定性分析,通过多层面考察,将《论语》及其五译本在文化特色词、句子、语篇、文化、修辞等层面的基本特征进行比较与探讨,分析了《论语》及其五译本在文化特色词、省略句、倒装句、被动句、判断句等特殊句型以及在语篇、文化、修辞等方面体现的特点及其翻译异同,探讨了翻译规律与译者风格,揭示了五译本的翻译显化策略的表现及其原因,指出具有不同文化背景的读者因具有不同生活经验和认知框架而对译文有不同期待,影响读者对原文文化的理解与接受,所以译者在翻译过程中要注重对译出语与译入语的语篇特征、文化内涵与修辞特点等因素进行深入分析,增强译入语读者的理解与接受效果。

第四章 《论语》英译传播与海外接受

《论语》蕴含丰富的儒家哲学思想,也是国外了解中华文化的重要圣典。在当前国际寻求融通发展与文化交流的背景下,《论语》中儒家哲学的翻译传播需要重视不同历史、社会与文化差异对儒家哲学概念的理解及其诠释的影响。因此,翻译传播者需要考虑时代背景、文化差异以及读者接受等多种因素,以助力中西融通的翻译话语体系建设,并推动中华文化的对外传播。

一、《论语》英译传播历程

《论语》英译历史源远流长。现在主要从历时角度,按照历史文化语境、译者文化背景以及译者翻译策略划分,通过聚焦《论语》典型译本的翻译传播,讨论《论语》英译传播历程的演变特点。

《论语》翻译传播历程大体可以分为以下四大主流发展阶段:基督教诠释阶段、以西释中阶段、注重原典阶段和哲学诠释阶段。需要补充的是,以一个理论点来命名某个阶段,主要是为了说明这个理论点的研究在该阶段最突出。当然,《论语》译介过程中还存在一些非主流情况,在此不再阐述。从这四个主流发展阶段讨论《论语》英译历程,主要研究目标不是简单叙述《论语》英译历程,而是通过探讨《论语》英译本的传播历程与外在影响因素来进一步探索《论语》翻译传播的大体发展路径、演变趋势、传播启示与机制创新策略。

（一）基督教诠释阶段（1809—1897年）

《论语》在西方的译介即始于西方传教士在中国的传教（包括由欧洲其他语言如拉丁文等翻译成英语时期）。其间有节译本和全译本共十多部，较有名的译者有马士曼（Joshua Marshman，1809）与理雅各（James Legge，1861）等。

这个阶段所有的译本都是由西方传教士完成的，其中理雅各译本堪称经典。这些传教士为开启和推动《论语》的英译传播研究作出了重要贡献。我们在肯定这些汉学家对儒学研究作出贡献的同时，也要结合他们的时代特征与身份特征以及经典文本的多元诠释特点对这些译著的翻译传播作出客观评价。

自1809年英国人马士曼出版的第一部直接译自中文的《论语》英译本（实际只有半部，只含《论语》前十篇的翻译）到1861年英国传教士、汉学家理雅各于1861年出版译著《中国经典》第一卷（包含《论语》《大学》与《中庸》）的问世，儒家经典的英译工作主要是由西方传教士完成的。

理雅各作为一名传教士，在传教过程中发现了"中国古老文明的深厚底蕴与普世价值。他不顾教会的反对，坚决声称：'在中国的传教事业必须与尊重中国的古老传统习惯，与传统的民族理念结合起来'"（吉瑞德，2011）。理雅各"发现'没有任何一个国家像中国那样崇拜学术上的卓越，世界上没有一个王国会把学问推崇到如此崇高的地位'。理雅各还发现，大众的礼仪和习俗以前所未闻的程度受古老的典籍中的格言来规范。要想了解中国这个国家，就必须了解它的古代典籍"（吉瑞德，2011）。正是由于理雅各对中国古老文明的热爱，他才能让自己专心致志从事中国经典的翻译传播。

理雅各认为，《论语》等中国经典的翻译会大大促进未来的传教工作，"藉此，世界可以了解中国，在华传教工作也可以知己知彼，收到永久成效。系统、全面译注出版儒经必将大大惠及以后的传教工作"（王辉,2003)。因此,理雅各翻译《论语》,旨在让欧洲人尤其是在华传教士全面地介绍中国的文化体系、政治道德、伦理思想与价值观念,也极力使人们相信中国的儒教与道德理念等同于西方的基督教理念。由此可见,"在他苦心造诣为人类的服务中,他试图进入包含在中国经典内的亚洲人的内心世界。他打开了通向中国人内心世界的大门"(吉瑞德,2011)。

理雅各在翻译《论语》时会常常受基督教的影响,因而其译本带有明显的宗教价值取向。理雅各认为,儒学与旧约和新约的基督教义没有很大差异。他把孔子诠释为"上帝的信使",把儒学看成中国古代的宗教,将"帝"等同于西方基督教的 God。所以,在将《论语》翻译成英文版时,理雅各将"天"译为 Heaven,将"帝"和"神"译为 God,把基督教中一神论的概念传递到译文中;同时,他将"孝"译为 filial piety(对上帝虔诚),将"忠"译为 faithful(ness)、loyal、devotion of soul,增加了译文的宗教意味。此外,理雅各在翻译和评注《论语》时经常与《圣经》和基督信仰作比较,且经常在译著中表现出对儒家思想的偏见。

综上所述,传教士积极将儒学经典传入西方,推动了《论语》在世界范围内的传播,在近代中西文化交流中发挥了重要作用。但是我们也要认识到,他们用基督教思想解读《论语》译本,在某种程度上消解了《论语》中的哲学思想。

(二) 以西释中阶段(1898—1950 年)

在这一时期,中国和西方的政治、经济、文化都发生了较大改变,中西文化在冲突中碰撞与融合,导致译者对《论语》进行重新阐释。其间共有 20 多个译本,主要译者有辜鸿铭(Ku,1898)与威利(Arthur Waley,1938)等。

辜鸿铭是第一个独立完成《大学》《中庸》《论语》三部儒家经典英译的中国人。与理雅各等传教士所不同的是,辜鸿铭翻译儒家经典的目的是向西方国家传播中国的儒家思想。辜鸿铭在序言中曾解释说,"理雅各的译著在内容与形式上所体现的中国的思想与智慧会使绝大多数英国读者感到古怪"(Ku,1898)。辜鸿铭认为,西方文化并不优于中华文化,他期望自己的译介工作能改变西方国家对中华文化的偏见态度。辜鸿铭在序言中指出:"期望那些不辞辛苦阅读我们译作的、受过教育、拥有思想的英国人,能够重新思考他们迄今为止对中国人持有的固有观念。这样做,不仅能让他们重新修正对中国人的成见,也能从个人和国家层面改变对中国人以及中国的态度"(Ku,1898)。辜鸿铭为了便于英语读者理解儒家思想,没有采用逐字逐句的对照翻译,而是采用归化的翻译策略诠释《论语》。

因此,辜鸿铭采用英国读者表达同样思想的方式翻译《论语》,经常用《圣经》中的人物和故事比作《论语》中涉及的人和事。例如,辜鸿铭把孔子的学生"颜回"注释为 The St. John of the Confucian gospel, a pure, heroic, ideal character, the dispel whom the Master Loved, 将"易"译为 Chinese Bible, 将"太庙"译为 the State Cathedral, 将中国的"舜"和"禹"翻译为西方的 Issac, Jacob 和 Abraham。为了加强英语读者对《论语》的理解,辜鸿铭在英译人名等专有名称时经常使用省译策略。例如,他将"王孙贾"译为 an officer in a certain state, 将"子游"译为 a disciple of Confucius, 将"子夏"译为 another disciple, 将"孟武伯"译为 a son of the noble, 将"孟懿子"译为 a noble of the Court, 只把人物的身份或地位翻译过来。辜鸿铭在翻译中还经常引用西方著名学者的话对原文进行诠释,其中包括歌德、卡莱尔、爱默生、莎士比亚、华兹华斯等人,从而吸引那些了解这些作家或者作品的英语读者,并帮助他们回想已经熟悉的西方文化思想。

威利于1938年首次出版了《论语》英译版本。该译本一直是英语世界较为通行的译本,并多次再版。威利译本较为大众化,译文通俗易懂。威利多用平实简洁而诗性的语言、丰富而多样化的词汇、通俗易懂的注释方式翻译《论语》。威利英译本使用大量的小词、短词、短句,对话体特征明显,翻译风格更加口语化和简洁;而且译语语篇的构建方式不受制于原文,非常灵活。《不列颠百科全书》这样介绍威利:"他是20世纪前半个世纪中的最杰出的东方学家,也是将东方文种译为英文的最杰出的翻译家。……他的译作使中国文学易于为英语读者接受了。"

(三) 注重原典阶段(1951—1997 年)

在该阶段,译者为了让英语读者更好地理解儒家文化的神圣性与权威性,在翻译过程中尽可能还原《论语》的语言文化特色。主要译者有英国诗人、翻译家埃兹拉·庞德(Ezra Pond, 1951)和中国学者刘殿爵(D. C. Lau, 1979)等。

20世纪初的西方社会各种矛盾激化。庞德作为一名批判西方文化的现代主义文人、学者,逐渐在中国的儒学中找到精神家园。庞德认为,中国的儒教优于基督教,并期望儒学译介到西方后,能有助于重建西方人与社会的理想秩序和社会价值体系。1951年,庞德翻译出版了《孔子:大学、中庸与论语》(*Confucius: The Great Digest, The Unwobbling Pivot, The Analects*)。后来,该书多次再版。庞德用简洁的意象式的语言,创造性地翻译《论语》,向英语读者诠释《论语》中内涵丰富的抽象概念。"庞德这种极富创造性的翻译主要有两大特点,一是从中华文化出发,富有创意的'拆字法',也称为'表意文字法',在他心里,中国的汉字具有表意及形声等多种功能,一个个文字仿佛是一幅幅活生生的图画,构成各种具体意象。另一个特点则是异化的翻译方法"(李钢和李金姝,2013)。庞德的翻译能让英语读者发现中国儒家文化的特点,也体现了他作为译者对孔子的恭敬以及对中华传统文化的尊重。

刘殿爵的译本于1979年出版,主要面向现代普通读者。刘殿爵的翻译思想一直受中华文化、东方观念以及英国哲学家吉尔伯特·赖尔(Gilbert ltyle)的影响。相对于优美的风格,刘殿爵更加强调对原文理解的准确表达,在翻译过程中力求儒家思想的翻译充分性,对于一些文化关键词采用音译加注解或直译加注的方法,最大限度地保留中华文化特色。

刘殿爵阅读大量原始文献,充分向英语读者传播孔子和儒家文化。例如,刘殿爵在引论中对一些儒家哲学概念作出解释,认为"天命"的理解应追溯到公元前2世纪末周朝的建立。"天"非常关心老百姓的福利,因此特意设置皇帝来提高他们的福利水平。皇帝凭借"天命"来行使权力,如果他不能履行这个职责,"天"就会撤销命令,把皇帝这个位置让给其他更有能力的人。因此,从这个意义上来说,"天命"是一个道德命令。后来,到了孔子时代,"天命"不再仅仅限于皇帝,每个人都受天命的约束。"天命"要求他有道德,符合"天命"的要求是他的责任。孔子说,"五十而知天命"。"天命"作为道德的命令,关注人们应该做什么;而从命运的意义上来说,"命"关注会发生什么。"天命"虽然难以解释,但还是可以理解的,而"命"则是个谜。"天命"命令我们的,我们理应遵守,而属于"命"的,我们就不要管了。例如,"义"与"天命"相关,应该遵守;而"利"与"命"相关则不要刻意追求(Lau,1992)。

(四) 哲学诠释阶段(1998年至今)

这个时期的《论语》英译主要特征如下:译者主要从社会哲学与社会认知语言学等视角对《论语》儒家哲学思想进行阐释,并在翻译过程中使用了很多中西结合的创新表达手段。这个阶段的代表译者主要有安乐哲与罗思文(Roger Ames and Henry Rosemount,1998)、森舸澜(Edward Slingerland,2003)。

安乐哲与罗思文认为:"西方人文主义者在试着解读中国经典哲学文献的过程中,不经意间植入了他们的臆断,使表述中国哲学的词汇带有特定的色彩,这已经是司空见惯的现象。西方读者所熟知的中国哲学,首先经过'基督教化'的洗礼,然后又被渲染了'东方化'玄妙神秘的色彩,这与我们所追求的理性启蒙是相悖的"(杨朝明,2015)。此外,安乐哲认为,儒家重视集体而不是个体的观念,以及重视家庭和社群在社会中的作用,因此发挥了西方人权观念所起到的某些作用。安乐哲和罗思文从比较哲学角度对儒学进行阐释,试图让西方学界认识到中国的哲学特色:是人与人之间的"一多不分"的哲学思维,而不是理雅各的神与人的"一多二元"框架的西方基督教思维(温海明,2018)。安乐哲把他对中国哲学独特的理解和翻译思想体现在《论语》翻译过程中,不仅传递了中国的哲学思想,而且逐渐改变了西方人对中国哲学的认识。

森舸澜的《论语》译本是一个聚焦中国古代哲学思想的学术型译本,其最大的特色在于充分尊重并保留原文的语义模糊性和多义性。森舸澜考虑到普通读者的需求,从不同地域读者认知差异的角度翻译《论语》的儒家哲学思想,因而,读者在其译文中会看到大量历史文化背景知识阐释。森舸澜强调,经典的翻译应尽量尊重和保留原文的字面意义。因此,该译本多以注疏的形式提供多种文本解释并注明出处,由读者进行辨析和取舍。森舸澜在为原文提供多种文本解释供读者选择的基础上,也在注释中提出了自己对原文的解读及其相应的考证理据,帮助英语读者进行思考和理解。

由此可见,在《论语》英译的初始期,传教士英译《论语》主要是以基督教意识形态为取向,以西方文化为中心;在《论语》英译的过渡时期,早期西方汉学家和海内外华人在社会政治文化因素的影响下,以自己的理解和思维方式诠释儒家思想,《论语》的英译历程开始转向以中华文化为中心的趋势;在《论语》英译的成熟时期,不同身份和文化背景的译者从多个视角对《论语》文化进行阐释,促进《论语》英译朝着多元化方向发展。由此可以看出,在中西文化交流的不同历史阶段,《论语》英译呈现不同特点,大体趋势是由原来"西方化"的儒学向具有"中国特色"的儒学转变,并朝着多元化方向发展。

因此,《论语》翻译传播的历史演变特点可以归结为:儒家哲学意义的不断重新阐释,主要表现为由原来西方化的基督化精神诠释逐渐转向具有现代性中国特色的哲学诠释精神的转变,并朝着多元化方向发展。我们应正确认识翻译传播规律,在新的历史环境下积极有效地传播优秀儒家文化。我们也应认识到,这些动向特点对《论语》翻译传播的创新发展具有重要的指导意义。

综上所述,《论语》翻译传播历程一方面体现了译者根据时代需求、文化差异、读者需求对传统文化的不断重新诠释,力求实现传统文化与现代读者的沟通与对话,另一方面反映了时代需求对译本文化内涵诠释策略的呼唤。此外,译者本身的翻译动机、翻译目的、主观能动性与翻译能力也是促进《论语》对外传播与海外接受的重要因素。

二、《论语》英译传播模式

翻译传播模式是指对翻译传播过程所作的概括性描述,以及对翻译传播活动规定的一套标准的操作程序。该翻译传播模式旨在揭示翻译传播过程中各系统要素之间的结构关系、作用原理以及与外部环境的联系,从而有助于我们把握翻译传播规律以及预测进展过程和结果。

美国学者哈罗德·拉斯韦尔于1948年提出了传播过程的"5W"传播模式:谁、对谁、通过哪些渠道、说什么、取得的效果(哈罗德·拉斯韦尔,2013)。其中,"谁"就是传播者,负责信息的收集、加工与传递;"对谁"是指传播的对象,即受众;"渠道"是信息传递所需要的手段与路径,如广播、电视、新闻、书刊等媒介;"说什么"即传播的内容;"效果"是指受众在接受信息后的认知情感、行为等的反应,是传播是否成功的重要检验石。但是,作为一个典型的线性模式,它似乎把传播过程看成是一个单向传递信息并呈直线形态的过程,而且对传播的社会条件等外部环境缺乏关注,对跨语言文化传播及其反馈也考虑不足,似乎割裂了传播过程与社会之间的联系。拉斯韦尔的线性传播模式如图4-1所示。

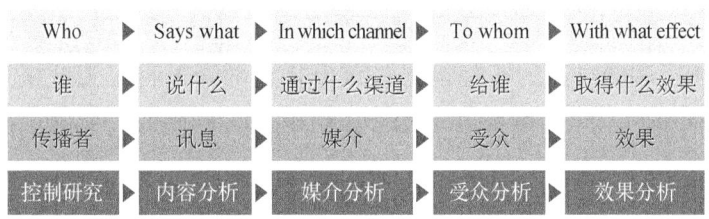

图 4-1　拉斯韦尔的线性传播模式

德国学者马莱茨克（Maletzke）于 1963 年提出的大众传播模式从社会心理学角度切入，将社会系统与传播系统中各因素及其之间的关系进一步细化，并对可能影响传播各环节的各因素进行了分析。这些因素既包括个性、心理、社会环境等制约传播者与受传者的因素，也包括内容加工、受众选择等制约媒介与信息的因素；既包括各种显在的社会影响力因素，也包括各种潜在的社会心理因素。这些因素相互作用，构成了复杂的社会传播系统。这一模式的优点"不仅在于深化了对'社会过程'（在传播中的作用）的认识，同时还在于深化了对'心理过程'（同一作用）的认识"（张国良，2018）。马莱茨克的大众传播过程模式如图 4-2 所示。

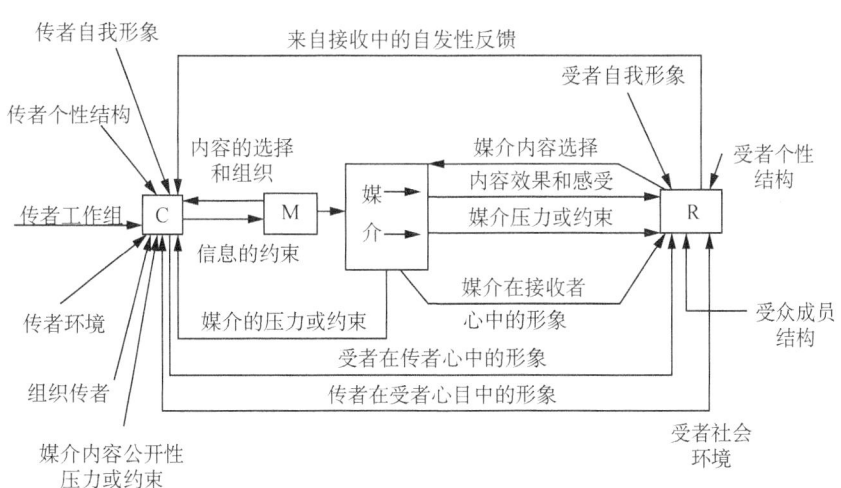

图 4-2　马莱茨克的大众传播过程模式

英国学者 Bell 于 1991 年以心理语言学、认知学和人工智能为基础,构建了翻译过程的心理模式。该模式将翻译过程分为分析过程和合成过程两个阶段,包含以下步骤:译者接收发送人包含信息的信号 1、识别代码 1、解码 1、获取信息、理解信息、译者选择代码 2、译者通过代码 2 编码信息、译者选择信道传输、译者传递给接收人包含信息的信号 2。Bell 强调"该模式中需要两种解释:一是心理学解释,尤其用在译者解码、编码时;二是篇章语言学或社会语言学的解释,尤其用在译者在理解表达意义时"(Bell,1991)。Bell 的翻译过程模式如图 4-3 所示。

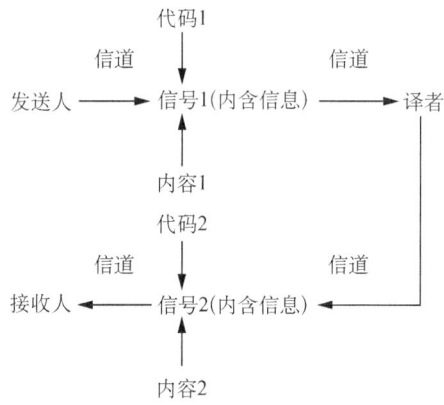

图 4-3　Bell 的翻译过程模式

由此可见,传播过程主要包括信息的传送、接收及反馈三大环节,翻译过程实质上也由原文和译文的传送、接收和反馈三大环节构成。翻译的本质是跨文化传播行为,或称为翻译传播行为,它以跨文化的双语转换为手段,以信息传播为目的。翻译作为跨文化交流的重要桥梁,对于信息的传播具有重要的作用(Wilss,2001;Nida,1964/2001;Newmark,1981/1988;Snell-Hornby,1988;Nord,1997)。

因此,传播过程与翻译过程有相似之处:它们都属于一种社会信息的传递,表现为传播者、传播渠道、接收人之间的一系列关系,是一个由各传播关系组成的动态、系统的信息传递过程。但是,由于翻译涉及两种语言的转换,参与传播行为的主体除了赞助人(如政府、出版社)、媒介,还包括原作者、译者和译作受众三方,因此它是一种独特的传播形式,包含了译文与原文、译者与原作者、译文受众与原文等其他传播形式所不具有的特殊关系。翻译传播过程模式如图4-4所示。

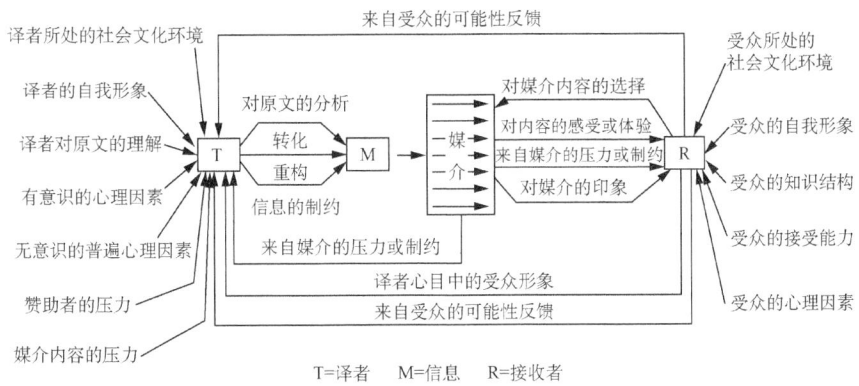

图4-4 翻译传播过程模式

该翻译传播过程模式是在拉斯韦尔的线性模式、马莱茨克的大众传播模式和贝尔的翻译过程模式的启发下,结合社会学与心理学的成果思考设计而成的,它全面系统地展示了翻译传播作为一种特殊的大众传播过程的复杂性。

由图4-4所示,翻译传播是一种复杂的社会行为,是一个变量众多的社会互动过程,涉及翻译传播主体,如译者、受众(包括读者、听众、观众、网友等)以及翻译传播路径(如翻译、广播、电影等)与媒介(如印刷媒介、视听媒介、电子媒介、网络媒介等)等多种因素,并受这些因素的影响与制约。

若将该翻译传播模式与马莱茨克传播模式结构相比较,我们发现,后者的传播者与信息之间除了来自"信息的约束"和"媒介的压力和约束",没有任何阻碍。而翻译传播模式则不同,译者与译文之间有一个屏障——原文,而且是硬性存在的。如果没有原文,翻译行为就成了无源之水。此外,因为增加了目标语的受众,受众可接受性的考察需要从多维考量。该翻译传播模式有助于进一步研究翻译传播者与接受反馈效果、翻译传播者与社会心理因素、译者与媒介、媒介与受众以及译者与受众之间的互动关系,尤其是译者与受众之间的关系。

(一)翻译传播影响因素

翻译传播是一种动态的开放交际行为,先对译者施加影响可以更好地获得翻译传播的接受效果。影响译者的具体因素主要来自社会文化环境、个性结构和自我形象约束、心理因素、赞助者要求、受众特征以及媒介传播制度等。

第一,译者在社会文化环境中生活,社会道德规范、社会文化规范和翻译规范都有着控制和制约作用,而且大众媒介组织的宗旨意图也是重要环境因素。

第二,译者要考虑自己的行为准则在公众中的形象,如译者的人格意识、个性结构、感情色彩、翻译风格、翻译目的都会影响其对原作的理解与诠释。

第三,各种有意识与无意识的心理因素都会潜移默化地影响译者的态度与策略。社会心理因素考量深化了译者对心理因素在翻译传播过程中的影响的认识。

第四,译者会受赞助者的制约。赞助者可以是宗教团体、政党、某个社会阶层、皇室、出版社、媒体等,他们可以决定文学作品的发行,其主要目的是维系整个社会体制的稳定(Lefevere,2004)。在这种情况下,一方面,译者可以根据赞助者的合理要求选择适当的翻译策略,将中国典籍作品成功译介到西方国家。另一方面,译者有权利和义务维护自己的翻译责任与翻译规范,应有道德、有原则地从事翻译工作。由此可见,译者的自由程度会受工作群体的约束和社会价值观的限制。

第五,受众的舆论可以反映他们对译者的态度,而且受众心目中的译者形象也会部分决定受众对译文的重视程度和评价倾向。因此,译者在翻译之前需要了解受众的自我形象、个性特征、教育程度、接受能力、心理因素及其所处社会环境等。

第六,在市场调研与媒介发布中要考虑受众的媒介接受习惯,以及媒介与受众之间的关系,尤其要考虑媒介的影响力与传播力,注重媒介品牌形象。

(二)翻译传播过程模式

现在我们来探讨翻译传播过程模式,重点探讨《论语》翻译传播过程中,译者在分析原文、传达翻译内容、选择翻译策略时所发挥的主体性与能动性作用,以及译文受众接受和媒介传播影响等内容。我们将从译介主体、译介内容、译介过程、译介受众四个方面进行论述。

在译介主体方面,译者应以文化沟通与交流为出发点,努力建构跨文化认同,尽量使译文符合目标语读者的习惯和要求。译者需要分析作品内容、历史背景、读者接受以及社会环境的互动关系,揭示翻译活动与权力话语的相互作用问题,使《论语》中的文化内涵在异域文化语境中成功接受。

《论语》较为晦涩难懂,即使汉语读者读原文也要依赖历代注疏。随着时代发展与中西文化交往的不断深化,越来越多的英语读者对中华传统文化充满了期待。因此,《论语》译者需考虑英语读者对中华文化的求知心理,在翻译过程中注重体现中国哲学本质与特色的新内容,以满足他们对异质文化的心理需求。译者需采用文化补偿策略补充翻译语境,对《论语》中的文化内涵准确阐释,并确保《论语》通达流畅,同时再现中国特有语言文化特色。

此外,受不同文化背景与认知差异的影响,读者会对《论语》中的文化概念有着自己的理解与认识。《论语》译者应针对不同时代、不同层次、不同地域的读者的需求,使传播方式多样化、层次化,使传播不断深化、不断普及、不断趋近原文本,使不同地域的受众顺其自然地接受中国的儒家哲学思想。

但是,我们还要注意,译者会受赞助者与媒介等的影响。为了有效实现跨文化翻译传播,增强英语读者对译文的理解,译者在翻译过程中,要注意具体问题具体分析,采用适当翻译传播手段,让不同地域的读者理解《论语》中的儒学精神。

在译介内容方面,译者需要考虑《论语》文化典籍的文本特点、文化内涵、修辞特征、历史背景与读者需求,有针对性地对译本内容作出适应性调整。

作为集中华古文化之大成的典籍文本,《论语》富含历史、人文、典故等文化积淀,而且言简意赅、含义深刻。《论语》丰富的儒家哲学术语包含了大量的哲学思想、人文精神与社会价值观念。《论语》中哲学术语的有效诠释、翻译与认同,是向世界传播中华文明的关键所在。

译文与原文存在时空"错位",从而使译文具有无限的诠释性与可读性。很多核心哲学术语在不同时期有不同的理解与诠释,因此有着复杂难以传达的含义,译者需要进行创造性的诠释,而不仅仅是借用西方的哲学术语以实现中西思想文化简单地等同。另外,《论语》中的很多成语典故常蕴含着丰富的历史文化内涵,是经过社会长期发展而形成的生活哲理。译者要考虑中西文化差异与文化语境,不能简单字面直译,而是通过增加注释与阐释文化背景等方式,使英语读者能顺畅理解原文中的儒家哲学概念或者历史典故信息内容。译文因增加了注释(文内注释或者是文后注释)而使其信息量和篇幅都变得较为丰厚。

在译介过程方面,《论语》的翻译过程受很多外部环境因素的制约。《论语》的翻译过程可分为语内翻译与语外翻译两个阶段。首先是语内翻译,译者可以通过研究史学,借鉴吸收历代注疏的成果,准确、完整地把《论语》原文的意思用现代汉语表达出来。其次是语际翻译,译者在语内翻译的基础上,根据《论语》的语录体特点与修辞等文体特征,考虑社会文化语境,采用适当的翻译策略把原文意思表达出来。译者需要充分发挥自身的主体性与能动性作用,在对原文分析、转换与重构的翻译过程中,还要考虑"特定手段、特定范围、特定语层、特定文体、特定时空、特定问题"(Holmes,1988)等参数的影响与制约。

(1) 特定手段:《论语》是具有文学特征的典籍翻译,言简意赅,注重语言形式与意义的传递,需要译者具有高度的翻译素养与文化创造力。

(2) 特定范围:《论语》翻译属于典籍汉译英翻译,具有特殊性,原文文本意义不确定,阐释空间大。因此,译者在《论语》翻译过程中需要借助训诂学、翻译学、篇章语言学、社会语言学与跨文化传播等理论进行诠释。

(3) 特定语层:译者在《论语》翻译过程中,需要注重以语篇作为视角,以语言为导向,处理特定语言层次(如词、词组或句子等),结合翻译语义学、翻译句法学、翻译语用学、翻译修辞学、翻译文体学与翻译功能语言学等理论进行研究。

(4) 特定文体:《论语》是具有语录体特征的文学文本,译者在选择翻译策略时应区别于其他类型的文本如科学与新闻文本。

(5) 特定时域:如同其他典籍英译一样,译者在《论语》翻译过程中需要经历从古典文言文到现代白话文再到英语翻译的过程,需要注意经典重释问题。

(6) 特定问题:《论语》中大量的哲学术语、成语、谚语、典故的使用等会加剧翻译的困难程度,因此译者应使用相应的翻译策略以解决翻译问题,在翻译过程中应该具体问题具体分析。

《论语》译介过程还会受译者及其所生存的社会意识形态的影响,即"一种包含着在被一定时期一定社会所认可的观点与态度的概念性框架,读者与译者借助该框架能够着手处理语篇"(Bassnett and Lefevere,2001),并使原作中带有民族文化特性的东西在翻译过程中受到影响。

意识形态是一套系统的观点,能够强烈地影响人们的思维方式与社会行为。意识形态也是社会历史文化的重要组成部分,是一定社会和文化的产物。在不同的历史时期和不同的文化语境下,人们的意识形态往往不同。Shelby(2003)曾对意识形态的两种最根本的使用惯例作了区分:非评价性使用与评价性使用。非评价性使用是指意识形态是实用的,在道义上是中立的。这主要用来描述与解释。例如,一些社会科学家与历史学家常用该含义指某一特定社会群体、社会或历史时代信仰体系的世界观。它有时还指某种特定的政治教义或者政治行动计划。评价性使用常常暗含着某种形式的批评意义。

Thompson认为,意识形态有不同程度的理解:(1)描述性的使用:社会群体的职位、态度、观点、视角。这常常与权力、统治等相关。(2)批评性的使用:世界各方面的表达有助于建立、保持或者改变权力、统治与探索等社会关系。社会文化还可以通过文本中识别的意识形态表达。这些表达可能会有框架性的结构,能够代表每一群组的自我形象,展现各成员之间的组织结构、目的、活动、规则与资源等。意识形态还常受制于社会官方政策与体制结构。同时,意识形态又对社会活动产生深远影响。

译者的教育背景、文化倾向和社会环境也会受意识形态的影响。Bassnett和Lefevere(1990)指出,意识形态随时都在影响译者的思维和行为。Lefevere(2004)认为,有两个重要因素操纵着翻译过程,按照重要性顺序,依次为译者的意识形态与译文产出时代接受文学中占统治地位的诗学。对于"意识形态",Lefevere(2004)将其简单地表述为有关社会应该是怎样(或者说可以是怎样)的主导观念,并强调"意识形态是指由形式、习俗与观念等组成的支配我们行为的观念体系"。也就是说,意识形态是社会的、政治的思想观念或世界观,它存在于社会阶层的各个层面。Lefevere(2004)认为,文学作品通过翻译树立形象,在很大程度上取决于译者的意识形态,这种意识形态可以是译者本身认同的,也可以是赞助人或者出版社强加给他的。不同的意识形态作用于翻译过程中,会造成原作的文化在译作中的改写现象。

此外,在《论语》翻译完成之后还要尽量寻求目标语国家知名度和信誉度高的出版社出版译作及其相关书评,例如,刘殿爵《论语》译本选用的企鹅出版社(1979)或者香港中文大学出版社(1992),道森(Dawson)《论语》译本选用的牛津大学出版社(1993),从而增加了英语读者对译作的认同度。

在译介受众方面,译者要考虑读者个人形象、教育程度、接受能力与心理特点等因素。在《论语》的翻译传播过程中,译文读者是传播的对象,也是传播的目标。翻译传播是一种交际过程,即翻译的最终目的是使译文得到接受。译文信息只有被译文读者接受,翻译传播过程才得以完成。因此,了解英语读者对《论语》翻译传播内容信息的态度,将有助于译者进行相应的调整,从而提升翻译传播效果。影响译文读者对信息的理解活动的因素,主要包括文化立场、自我形象、知识结构、接受能力与心理因素等。例如,英语读者在接收《论语》译文信息时,必然站在一定的文化立场上对之进行阐释,其理解的信息不可避免带有自身社会文化背景的烙印。

读者的自我形象主要是指性别、年龄、个性、智力、经历、兴趣、爱好等个体特征。具有不同个体特征的人对信息感知的广度和深度都是不同的。例如,某人一旦对儒家文化经典产生兴趣,其在进行选择性注意、理解和记忆时,自然就倾向于该类文化经典。但是,即使是同一信息内容,其对经历不同的受众也会产生不同的认知效果。一般来说,符合经验认知范围的信息比较容易接受,完全陌生的信息很难接受,因此需要在两者之间寻找最佳结合点。

译文读者的教育水平、知识结构与接受能力也影响其对译文的接受。如果英语读者是专业研究者、高校学生,要求内容严谨周密严肃,信息量大,译者可采用学术翻译策略。例如,森舸澜译本通常附有序言、导读、注释与索引等,一般提供与原作相关的文化背景信息,评论和解释原作中重要的文化概念。又如,安乐哲与罗思文从哲学视角进行文化诠释,在翻译典故、成语、比喻时注意在译文中补充添加语境。如果是普通读者,希望内容简单明了,信息内容轻松,信息量不大,则可采用归化翻译策略,尽量使译文准确、通畅、易懂,降低阅读难度。再如,辜鸿铭引用了很多西方学者的话语进行诠释,注重信息传递的易懂性。

译文读者的心理因素在读者接受信息时起着至关重要的作用。译文读者在接受信息时,往往有所选择、有所侧重。译文是否能够实现传播,在很大程度上取决于是否符合译作读者的选择性心理。每个人所处社会环境和经历不同,造成个人心理、认知与思维等方面存在很大不同,这就决定了不同读者在信息接受与理解时有不同的选择。

从某种意义说,译文阅读就是一种文化建构,是人类社会中特有的一种精神活动。译文读者群体往往有一定的阅读目的,根据社会文化环境与自身特点有意识地选择接受翻译内容。这种阅读目的就是心理活动的反映。另一方面,文本意义常受读者诠释共同体因素制约。费什(2004)认为,诠释共同体是由具有共有诠释策略的人们所组成的阅读群体。诠释策略不是指通常意义的阅读文本方式,而是关于写作文本、构造文本特性、指定文本意图的策略。诠释策略先于阅读行为而存在,并且决定了所读之物的意义和形态。

因此,为了使英语读者容易理解接受中华文化,达到有效的接受效果,译者在英译时需要考虑读者认知差异与读者层次需求,结合《论语》特点与社会环境等因素,有意识地在翻译过程中有所选择,认真考虑译文读者反馈,翻译出符合译文读者选择性心理特点的译文。如果是为了满足读者的研究心理,译者需要根据《论语》的古汉语特点与文化哲理的深奥性,以及缺失语境的语录体文本特征,在翻译过程中可采用增加序言、前言、注释、评论、附录等内容,并采用相应的全译策略。如果是为了满足读者的欣赏心理,译者可采用相应的变译策略。奈达与泰伯(1969)指出,如果译文读者不能完全理解,可以改变或补充信息内容,以在某种程度符合译入语的接受文化。黄忠廉也指出变译策略可实现译文信息的功能对等,强调"变译的灵魂是变通,这也正是它与全译的差别之所在"(黄忠廉,2002a),是"译者据特定条件下特定读者的特殊需求所采用的翻译手段"(黄忠廉,2002b)。

综上所述,在《论语》的翻译传播模式中,译者、受众、媒介等翻译过程和传播过程的各要素起着重要作用。译者、受众与媒介彼此互动,共同构建语言文化体系,助力儒家文化的翻译传播。同时,传播者的自我形象、受众的接受能力以及媒介形象等因素在《论语》翻译传播中的作用也不容忽视。

三、《论语》英译传播途径

随着中西文化交流的不断深入,《论语》英译传播途径也在逐渐拓展。《论语》翻译传播途径不仅包括语际翻译,而且包括符际翻译,并通过纸质印刷出版、会议交流与数字技术等多种形式进行对外传播。语际翻译本身是通过另一种语言对文学符号作出的解释(cf. Jakobson, 1971),如《论语》英译。符际翻译是通过非词语符号系统对文字符号作出的变异解释(cf. Jakobson, 1971),如电影《孔子》中英文版、蔡志忠漫画中英文版、Kindle电子图书、国际媒体对《论语》经典译文的引用等。本书主要从以下五个方面探讨《论语》英译传播途径:翻译传播主体译介《论语》,开展国际合作与国际联合出版,构建国际学术交流平台,建设国际儒学文化在线平台,积极举办与参加国际书展。

(一) 翻译传播主体译介《论语》

翻译传播主体(主要包括译者、书评者与相关书籍作者)对《论语》的译介在其翻译传播过程中发挥了重要的作用。《论语》的译介内容只有到达目标语读者并为之接受,译文的成功传播才能真正得以实现。因此,译者在翻译《论语》时应选择恰当的翻译策略,努力促进中西方文化之间的融合与互补。相关评论者与作者应实事求是地推介《论语》译者与译作,帮助英语读者客观、全面地了解中国典籍。翻译传播主体应借助合力,增强《论语》的海外传播力度。

《论语》翻译的副文本是帮助我们了解翻译传播主体译介《论语》的重要资料。我们不仅可以通过译本的正文本,而且可以通过译本的副文本理解译者表征出来的儒家思想。副文本"是为文本有意识精心设计的门槛,它可能影响文本的接收方式"(Batchelor,2018),在帮助人们理解原文内容时起着至关重要的作用。Genette(1988)进一步指出,所谓"副文本"是指"围绕文本的所有边缘的或补充性的数据。它包括各种形式:与作者和编辑相关的(如标题、插图、题词、前言和注释);和媒体相关的(如作者的访谈,官方的概要);私人的(如通信、蓄意或非蓄意的秘闻)以及和文本生产与接受的物质手段有关的内容,如分段等"(耿强,2016)。副文本主要包括以作者名、标题、前言、序言、图片、注释、附录等随书一同出现的内副文本(peritext)和以访谈、对话、书信、日记、书评、书刊广告、相关书籍等为代表的外副文本(epitext)。由此可见,副文本既包括言语也包括非言语,在正文本和读者之间起着重要的沟通、协调与补充作用。

《论语》翻译的副文本可为翻译研究提供重要参考依据,有助于我们了解原文本核心思想、译者翻译思想以及译本所产生的外部社会历史环境,因此对于《论语》的翻译传播起着重要作用。译者通常会在译文的内副文本中介绍译本背景、文化语境、翻译目的、历史知识以及《论语》相关学术思想,并将相关历史文化材料与之关联,表达自己的翻译意图与翻译思想,这在之前的译例分析中都有体现。外副文本主要是指介于文本与读者之间有助于加深读者对原作和译本理解的其他文本,如书评与相关作品。现在主要介绍有代表性的《论语》五译本的外副文本,思考译介主体在《论语》翻译传播过程中所做出的努力。

理雅各的外副文本如《朝觐东方:理雅各评传》(吉瑞德,2011)与理雅各女儿海伦·蔼蒂丝·理所著的《理雅各:传教士与学者》(又名《汉学家理雅各传》)(理,2011)对于我们理解理雅各的译作具有重要的作用。其中,吉瑞德将精炼娴熟的传记叙事与扎实严谨的学术考证结合,将理雅各的文化生涯分为传教士、朝圣者、异端者、阐释者、比较学者、翻译者、教师等方面,对理雅各的传教士生涯和作为汉学家的学术经历、精神历程进行了细致探究。海伦·蔼蒂丝·理的书中提供了大量书信、日记等珍贵史料,对于后人理解理雅各的翻译思想起到了重要作用。理雅各在《中国经典》中找寻圣经,突破基督教与儒教的壁垒,采用尊重原文又融合基督教思想的翻译策略传播中国儒家经典,使得欧美人士由此可以了解思考中国传统儒家文化,并对西方的哲学思想、伦理思想与文学思想产生了一定影响。

辜鸿铭外副文本如《中庸》英译本(辜鸿铭,1906)、《辜鸿铭讲论语》(辜鸿铭,2013)与《中国人的精神》(辜鸿铭,2016)有助于我们进一步理解辜鸿铭的《论语》翻译思想。辜鸿铭在《中庸》译本序言中阐释了中国文明及其对世界文明的影响,在正文中引用了大量西方宗教、哲学、文学经典对《中庸》诠释与解读,以增进英语读者对中华传统文化的认识。《辜鸿铭讲论语》不但语言精练,词意精达,而且在讲解过程中援引歌德、卡莱尔、阿诺德、莎士比亚等西方著名作家和思想家的话注释某些经文。辜鸿铭在注释中将该书提及的中国人物、中国朝代与西方历史上具有相似特点的人物和时间段作横向比较,帮助那些对中国文化知之甚少的英语读者更好地把握儒家经典。《中国人的精神》一书主要探讨了中西方文化思想的比较,通过介绍中国的儒家文化思想及其在中国社会中的地位和作用,向英语读者阐释了中国统文化的社会价值观。辜鸿铭发现,儒家文化在促进世界进步与解决西方社会主要问题方面具有重要的作用。因此,辜鸿铭引用西方文化经典翻译中国儒家思想,旨在提高中华传统文化在海外的理解与接受程度。

刘殿爵外副文本如《语言与思想之间》一书(刘殿爵,1993)可帮助我们理解刘殿爵的《论语》翻译思想。刘殿爵(1993)认为:"我们可以看见日常语言每每用一种隐喻的方法作为形容的手段,这隐喻一用上便有许多涵义可以慢慢引申出来。同时超感性的领域,比如说内心的现象的形容是常常要用上隐喻的,因为超感性的领域不可捉摸,只能用比拟去说。我的看法是语言采取这种或是那种比拟方法，只是语言在长期发展中偶然的结果，并无处心积虑于其间"。这在刘殿爵的《论语》译文注释中的互文中可以得到验证。

安乐哲与罗思文的外副文本有很多，例如，《道不远人：比较哲学视域中的〈老子〉》（安乐哲和郝大维，2004）与《孔子哲学思微》（安乐哲和郝大维，2018）从比较哲学的视角翻译诠释中国传统文化。安乐哲和郝大维长期从事中西哲学文化的比较研究，论及了跨文化交流和理解的难题。在安乐哲和郝大维看来，由于西方人尤其几百年来的汉学家把西方传统的"超越性思维"附加于中国思想，西方对中国文化的理解存在严重"误读"。安乐哲和郝大维从中国文化自身出发，去思考、理解中国传统文化，并努力把中国思想"原汁原味"介绍给西方世界，以便消除这种"误读"。《安乐哲比较哲学著作选》（温海明，2018）主要通过安乐哲关于中国哲学核心问题、中西哲学比较的思考，帮助读者思考如何以西方视角关照中国哲学，并以中国哲学反思西方文化，以求二者相互借鉴、共同发展。《儒家角色伦理学》（安乐哲，2017）主要是以家庭角色和关系作为切入点，强调儒家伦理的关系性、协作性与社会性，认为儒家思想对于社会生活中关系和角色的表述可引导人们思考中西文化差异。《豁然：一多不分》（卞俊峰，2019）主要结合历史的儒学及其现代命运，探讨了安乐哲的学术探索之路、"一多不分"的翻译理念，以及安乐哲与罗思文的使命担当。其中，"一多不分"强调宇宙万物天地人之间的密切关联与互相依赖的关系，强调人需要从与他人、万物、世界的恰当关系出发，对社会、政治、经济与历史问题进行宏观整体思考"（卞俊峰，2019）。

森舸澜的外副文本如《为与无为》（森舸澜，2018）体现了中国先哲的内在修养与文明和谐相处的古老智慧。森舸澜指出，儒家的"无为"思想之所以有用，是因为人在克己修身进入"无为"状态后，是在执行天意、遵循天道，之后会获得一种天赐予的力量，也就是"德"。拥有"德"的圣人具有感召力与吸引力。"为与无为"的思辨可以修正以自我价值为中心的现代生活方式和思维方法。森舸澜指出,"重新找回古代中国思想,拥抱无为理念,提倡轻松自如,必定会矫正现代世界观推崇的那种亟待矫正的、极端的个人主义。无为这一理念更适合我们目前所知的人类心智。无为与德(魅力)内在的性质,也能彰显与自我息息相关的社会性和角色感"(森舸澜,2018)。

综上所述,翻译传播主体在译介中华传统文化以及相关著作中所反映的翻译思想不仅蕴含着丰富的理论研究价值,而且对于促进《论语》中儒家思想的传播、提升中西跨文化认同以及建构中外融通话语体系具有重要的现实指导意义。同时,我们在重视中国典籍翻译副文本的同时,也要认识到副文本可能对读者造成的误读与误解。有些儒家哲学在西方世界的接受困境与接受的问题,有时是受某些副文本所造成的影响。

(二) 开展国际合作与国际联合出版

《论语》的翻译和传播,很多情况下得益于国外汉学家与国内汉学家的合作,也离不开国内出版社与国外出版社的联合翻译出版。很多国外汉学家受到走向世界的中国学者对中国哲学思想的启发而受益无穷。

例如,国外汉学家理雅各与中国学者王韬的合作。王韬是晚清时期沟通中西文化的重要人物,曾为理雅各担任中国经典《中国经典》的助译。王韬协助理雅各搜集相关书籍与参考文献,担任理雅各的译经顾问和研经同伴角色。王韬不仅为理雅各答疑解惑,而且经常在辩论中给理雅各以思想的启迪。因此,理雅各在《中国经典》译注中常征引王韬的意见,从而为读者提供另一种解读的可能。

安乐哲与罗思文合作翻译《论语》,其译文所展现的儒家哲学思想与他们对中国哲学家唐君毅等思想家的哲学传承分不开。安乐哲与罗思文有相似的价值观,他们在长期合作中尽力在学术研究中同时融入汉学与哲学研究的经验。为了实现"让中国来言说自身",他们提出了"角色伦理"观点,并对一系列中国儒学核心词汇作出新的阐释与解读。他们合作翻译《论语》的主要目的是展现儒家思想的社会价值,从而使中国哲学可以与西方世界对话并力争在世界有一定地位。安乐哲与罗思文认为,中国传统思想的核心是哲学,儒学宗教性的核心是"礼",不是西方意义的"上帝",重礼的传统在中国特别普遍。因此,他们从中国思想文化本身的框架出发,在翻译过程中采用了很多有别于传统的翻译方法,主要目的包括:(1) 辨别西方传统对儒家思想的解读;(2) 让中国哲学呈现出其完整性(3) 向西方哲学界宣传儒家哲学的内涵,从而在加强中西哲学深层次对话方面作出重要贡献。

安乐哲与罗思文的哲学翻译理念传达了唐君毅等人的"一多不分"的世界观。中国儒家哲学所强调的天命观、天人观、人道观等哲学理念都是"一多不分"的世界观。"一多不分"观指的是"一个生生不息"的"道"的世界观。安乐哲与罗思文的儒家哲学思想在田辰山等中国学者的合力推动下,得到了进一步推广与传播。例如,田辰山参与安乐哲译作的校对,学术思想的传播,通过著书立说多次强调中国人的世界观,如注重天人合一,世界的流动变化与生生不息,人与人之间、事物与事物之间以及事物和人之间关系的相互依赖(cf. 田辰山,2003/2008)。正因为中西哲学思想存在显著差异,所以安乐哲与罗思文力图采用自觉性阐释策略让英语读者"再现"中国儒家思想。

此外,《论语》作品的成功译介,也离不开国内外众多主流出版社的支持,如 Clarendon Press, Kelly and Walsh, Ballantine, Hackett Publishing Company, Oxford University Press, Chinese University Press 等。作为跨文化传播的一种重要手段,编辑、校对、出版等深度加工策略在《论语》典籍的译介出版中得到了一定应用。深度化的编辑出版策略是译者深度化翻译策略的延续,两者的结合对《论语》的翻译出版及其跨文化传播效度的提高具有重要的作用。通过《论语》五译本研究,例如首页排版、形式符号、文内插图以及附录与文末注释的编排等,可以看出,编辑者和出版者在面对如何在译本中最大限度地实现中国典籍的文化保真和有效传播等方面作出了很大努力。

(三) 构建国际学术交流平台

政府、高校、学术组织、外宣部门等单位定期举办线上与线下国际学术研讨会或国际文化交流活动,以弘扬中华优秀文化、促进中外文化交流、推动世界不同文明之间交流互鉴为目的,构建学术性、国际性与开放性相结合的国际学术和文化交流平台。

近年来,在国家重视中华传统文化的传承创新以及注重中华文化"走出去"的政策推动下,国际儒学联合会与北京外国语大学国际中国文化研究院举办了一系列"国际儒学与中华思想文化跨文化传播国际学术研讨会",以推进中外文化交流机制、国际传播能力与对外话语体系建设研究。会议议题包括国际儒学文化传播与话语体系建设,中华文化走向世界战略探究,中华传统文化的海外传播研究,新时代儒家文化的发展,跨文化传播的理论与实践,中华文化"走出去"与对话话语体系建设等。该系列学术活动还多次邀请北京大学人文讲习教授、世界著名中西比较哲学家安乐哲,澳门大学哲学系教授、德国著名汉学家 Hans-Georg Moeller,美国洛杉矶罗耀拉大学哲学终身教授 Robin Wang 等专家学者,在中西比较两大传统阐释视野下探讨文明交流互鉴,用"人与人"的哲学思维,将被误读的中国传统从利玛窦的"神与人"的西方特设哲学框架中解放出来,带领人们重归"原汁原味"的中国经典。

此外,在国家汉办指导成立的孔子学院组织的孔子学院大会,一直被誉为教育"达沃斯"。孔子学院大会是全球孔子学院的盛会。截至2020年,孔子学院已经举办了十三届孔子大会。其中,2018年第十三届孔子大会邀请校长与众多学者专家以"改革创新促发展,携手同心创未来"为主题,主要围绕"孔子学院办学模式和管理机制创新""汉语+与孔子学院特色化发展""孔子学院数字化建设""培育多元化合作伙伴关系"等议题展开讨论。孔子学院大会为增进人们对儒家文化了解,增进世界文化交流,促进不同文明之间相互学习借鉴起到了重要作用。

另外,在山东曲阜定期举办的国际孔子文化节是国际思想文化交流的重要平台。该文化节以开展不同文明对话、弘扬中华优秀文化以及促进中外文化交流为使命。会议主题一般围绕利用儒家文化讲好中国故事、文明相融与人类命运共同体等内容,强调以儒家思想为代表的中华文化是参与世界文明对话的重要力量。这对于推动中华优秀传统文化的创造性转化与创新性发展,增强中华文化在国际的传播力与影响力以及促进世界文化交流等方面起到了重要作用。

(四) 建设国际儒学文化在线平台

目前,国际儒学文化在线平台的建设主要是通过建设儒学特色网站实现对外传播儒家文化。这些在线平台充分利用融媒时代的互联网技术,以承续儒家文明、促进中国学术繁荣、推动中华复兴为己任,致力于儒学的对外传播和研究应用,对于弘扬中华优秀传统文化、推动世界文明交流互鉴起到了重要作用。

为了推动儒家文化的翻译传播,有很多网站有英文版,如"一多不分"在线网站(http://www.yiduobufen.com)用中英文版介绍中国的"一多不分"的世界观、中国话语的阐释、安乐哲的翻译思想以及最新的儒家文化翻译传播学术交流活动等内容。孔子学院在线网站(http://www.hanban.org/confuciousinstitutes/)则有英语、法语、西班牙语三种语言,设有孔院论坛、魅力孔院、图说孔院等专题,对于儒家文化的传播起到了重要推动作用。

此外,很多在线网站对于推动儒家文化对外传播也起到了重要作用,如中国儒学网(http://www.confuchina.com)、传统文化网(https://www.zhwh365.com/article_cate_94.html)、中国孔子网(http://www.chinakongzi.org)与国际儒学网(http://www.ica.org.

cn/)等。

有些在线数据库网站,如儒家经典数据库、儒家文化数字馆以及儒家图书馆等仍在建设完善中。这些数字化工程的落地落实,对于《论语》文化翻译的国际传播及研究应用都会起到重要的推动作用。

(五) 积极举办与参加国际书展

国际书展是发布新书、展示国家文化、探讨全球出版业发展动态的平台,可以为中国作家和海外作家、图书经销商、出版商、译文读者之间的沟通搭建平台,增加面对面交流的机会,有助于中国文学作品走出国门参与交流(潘震,2015),因此,它也有助于中国典籍翻译作品的对外传播与海外接受。

例如,在上海每年举办的上海书展作为一个全国性的重要文化盛会吸引国内众多读者参加。在2018年由孔学堂书局承办的"安乐哲新书分享与签售会"上,国际知名比较哲学家、汉学家安乐哲现场与读者分享哲学的深奥与智慧,成为上海书展的热门话题。

在国外,伦敦国际书展是全球英语国家中最大的专业书展。作为全球图书业最重要的盛会,每年都会吸引众多国家的参展商参会。中国国际出版集团等对外文化传播机构可利用这个机会与伦敦书展主办方合作策划与中国市场相关的中国典籍推介会,推广中国典籍图书翻译传播活动,包括新书发布、书刊广告、访谈对话、签约赠书、座谈交流以及翻译专业论坛在内的各项主题活动。

总之,《论语》的英译传播途径对于中华传统文化的传播起到了重要作用。其中,译者的主体作用尤为重要。译者优先选择具有民族特征、普世意义和经典价值的儒家经典进行译介,有利于促进世界各民族文化的交流与合作。同时,译者根据文本特征、文化语境与读者接受选择翻译策略,确保译作能在异域国家的读者受众中得到认同与接受。此外,政府、高校、文化部门、媒体等单位积极构建国际学术及文化交流平台,加强中外作家与翻译家的合作与交流,充分利用电子图书、在线网络等现代多媒体的传播媒介平台,丰富了《论语》的翻译传播途径,也推进了中国典籍对外传播的译介进程。

四、《论语》英译海外接受调查

我们研究《论语》英译海外接受调查,可使我们更好地从他者的视域来反观自身,了解《论语》在当前世界多元文化背景下的异域接受情况。读者接受情况是"判断中国文化是否成功"走出去"的重要衡量标准。因此要深入研究《论语》的海外传播与信息反馈情况,提高《论语》在世界文化多元化语境背景下的异域接受,推动全球文化趋同化与本土化的互动与认同"(范敏,2019)。

(一)实地调研与问卷调查

2018年,笔者在英国实地调研时,尝试借助《论语》英译典籍研究路径的可行性来进一步推动中华文化的对外传播。内容包括实地考察,书籍出版与阅读等。笔者在英国调研时发现,中国的典籍文化在一定程度上受到重视。例如,英国及欧洲最大规模的中国研究中心"牛津大学中国中心"有大量专家学者从语言文化、思想艺术、历史地理等视角全方位研究中国问题,当然也包括中华传统文化。在牛津大学图书馆,关于《论语》的电子文献有很多,内容多与《论语》文化译介有关。而在英国大型书店,更多见到的是国外汉学家的《论语》译本,如牛津大学出版社出版的 R. Dawson(1993)翻译的 *Confucius: the Analects* 等。

笔者曾于2018年通过问卷调查对不同国别(主要是中国与欧美国家)、年龄、性别、受教育程度、工作性质等对《论语》感兴趣的受众进行抽样。此次调查遵循定量的研究方法,注重对读者深层洞察和理解,通过设计《论语》文化内容接受、翻译策略、海外传播与接受等问题,获得有效样本600份,样本有效率100%,得到了他们对《论语》海外接受的不同维度的反馈。在该样本中,年龄在30岁以上的具有硕士学位的人数占总人数的96.8%。男女比例相差不大,男士占51%,女士占49%。海外华人、留学生等以英语为主要交际语言的人占总人数的34%,相关中国研究学者、学生等占总人数的66%。关于《论语》译本接受的问卷调查结果显示,读者对译文可接受度与《论语》的对话体裁、读者层次、译文语言地道程度以及译者文化背景有关。其中,高层次、受教育程度较高人群、海外华人更加喜爱带有中华文化符号、能体现中国特色的文本,如安乐哲与罗思文、森舸澜的《论语》译本。这说明,随着中国在世界地位的提升以及中华传统文化的日益崛起,海外民众对中国话语的喜爱度、认知度、理解度大幅上升,一些中华传统文化词语如"孔子""道"等进入英语话语体系。这一方面说明中国的传统文化思想逐渐受到英语读者的关注,另一方面也说明中国的儒家文化思想正在影响、改变着世界。

值得一提的是,在所测试的受众中,读者大致分为专业型读者与非专业型读者。前者具有较高的文化教育程度,较强的跨文化交际能力与审美能力。后者是一般普通读者。通过调查发现,前者常常尊重经典原文的权威性,后者在接受异国文化信息时,往往喜欢地道的语言、通俗易懂的阅读,具有消遣文化的特点。由此可见,如果《论语》英语读者的期待视野与译文阅读实际一致,就可以很快完成理解过程,读者的直接期待就会得到满足;如与译文的阅读实际发生偏离或冲突,读者的理解就会产生审美距离的问题。当然,不可否认,读者在阅读过程中既受《论语》译文质量的制约,又受自身主客观条件的制约,而这两种制约都会在《论语》译文审美的过程中有所体现。

(二)被引频次、图书出版与读者评价

通过调研《论语》英译典籍的版次信息、读者网络购买《论语》英译

书籍的购书情况、英语国家对《论语》研究文献的引用、评论与介绍,我们发现,在成功的《论语》翻译传播与海外接受中,译者往往采用西方国家易懂的语言和方式,围绕中西方传统文化的思维观、价值观和语言文化,实施中西思想文化融合的语言和方式。

笔者通过统计《论语》五译本在 Google Scholar 数据库中的被引情况以及在美国亚马逊(Amazon)图书网上的销售情况与读者评价,了解各译本的被引频次以及销售量与评价排名,以进一步考量各译本的流传程度和传播效果。

Google Scholar 的数据来源主要包括学术出版商、数据库提供商、专业团体、各大学及其他学术组织的经同行评议的文章、图书、摘要等,它为科研用户提供了一个强有力的学术搜索工具。尽管该搜索引擎具有一定的局限性,但由于目前国内外仍缺乏针对图书被引频次统计的权威和完善的数据库,Google Scholar 经常被用作替代的引文分析工具(Harzing,2008)。亚马逊图书网是全球性的专业网络图书销售平台,具有高质量的数据库和便捷的图书检索系统,可通过纸质书、Kindle 电子书、购买者评论、星级数等多种途径向读者推荐图书,是国外读者购买图书的主要渠道之一。此外,亚马逊根据机器学习模型而不是原始数据平均值来计算商品的星级评分。该模型考虑了各种因素,包括评分的年龄,评分是否来自经过验证的购买者,以及确定评审者可信度的因素。因此,通过调查亚马逊图书网站《论语》五译本的销售情况与读者评论,有助于我们了解《论语》五译本的海外出版与接受情况(cf. Fan Min,2021)。

通过表 4-1,我们可以发现,《论语》五译本中在 Google Scholar 被引频次最高的是理雅各译本,然后依次是安乐哲与罗思文译本、刘殿爵译本、森舸澜译本、辜鸿铭译本。通过表 4-2,我们发现,《论语》五译本在亚马逊网销售量最高的是刘殿爵译本,然后依次是森舸澜译本、理雅各译本、安乐哲与罗思文译本、辜鸿铭译本。Kindle 版本除了理雅各与森舸澜译本顺序稍有调整,其他顺序保持不变。通过表 4-3,我们发现,《论语》五译本在亚马逊网的用户排名最高的是森舸澜译本,然后依次是安乐哲与罗思文译本、刘殿爵译本、理雅各、辜鸿铭译本。

表 4-1 《论语》五译本在 Google Scholar 的被引频次排名(截至 2020 年 12 月 25 日)

排名	被引频次	题名	作者	首印年份
1	1 665	The Confucian Analects, the Great Learning and the Doctrine of the Mean	理雅各	1861
2	1 136	The Analects of Confucius: A Philosophical Translation	安乐哲与罗思文	1988
3	1 037	The Analects	刘殿爵	1979
4	402	Analects: with Selections from Traditional Commentaries	森舸澜	2003
5	77	The Discourses and Sayings of Confucius: A New Special Translation, Illustrated with Quotations from Goethe and other Writers	辜鸿铭	1898

表 4-2 《论语》五译本在亚马逊网站的销售量比较(截至 2020 年 12 月 25 日)

排名	亚马逊销售量名次	译者	出版/再版情况(出版社/出版时间)	Kindle 图书在 Kindle 商店排名
1	1(孔子学说)	刘殿爵	Penguin Classics; 1st edition (1998.9)	181 065
2	5(孔子学说)	森舸澜	Hackett Publishing Company, Inc.; Hackett Classics Series edition (2003.9)	419 202
3	12(孔子学说)	理雅各	Create Space Independent Publishing Platform (2016.9)	414 001
4	43(孔子学说)	安乐哲与罗思文	Ballantine Books; Illustrated edition (1999.9)	453 559
5	1301(经典历史著作)	辜鸿铭	Kessinger Publishing, LLC; Facsimile Edition (2008.11)	1 546 315

表4-3 《论语》五译本用户在亚马逊网站的评价比较(截至2020年12月25日)

亚马逊用户排名	译者	星级数(满分5分)	买家评论数	5星	4星	3星	2星	1星
1	森舸澜	4.7	73	82%	7%	11%	0	0
2	安乐哲与罗思文	4.5	76	77%	9%	10%	1%	4%
3	刘殿爵	4.4	523	70%	15%	8%	3%	4%
4	理雅各	4.1	42	59%	12%	19%	3%	7%
5	辜鸿铭	3.6	2	52%	0	0	48%	0

结合读者评论,我们发现,在五译本排名中,辜鸿铭的译本被引频次、销售量与用户排名都最低。这可能与出版社的出版质量(如句中有评论、存在打印错误)有关。译本出版质量差很可能导致读者阅读感受差、评分低甚至读者购书数量下降。其他四个译本中,刘殿爵的被引频次居中,而译本销售量最高,可能与刘殿爵译本便于快速阅读、思想犀利有关,也可能与企鹅出版社有关。企鹅出版社是世界最著名的英语图书出版商,在世界媒体业排行第10位,国外读者更加信赖该出版社的图书出版质量,更容易接受该出版社出版的《论语》译本。刘殿爵的译本被誉为具有里程碑的意义,已经成为长销不衰的"企鹅经典"。刘殿爵译本结合了中国的儒家思想和英语的语言表达,使其具有很高的可读性,促进了《论语》在国外的传播。理雅各译本在Google Scholar被引频次最高,而在用户排名中落后于其他三个译本,在亚马逊网销售中居于中间位置。这可能与理雅各的译本比较久远,但又具有经典学术价值有关。同时,理雅各译本从西方基督教的思想进行诠释,因此其与安乐哲和罗思文译本以及森舸澜译本相比较,在儒家核心概念的重新诠释与理解方面存在一定距离。当前的用户读者更倾向于学习如何跟中国这样历史悠久的古老文明进行现代对话。安乐哲与罗思文的译本被引频次与用户排名都位列第二,而在销售方面居于中间稍后位置,这可能与学术性读者对该译本的学术价值认可有关,也与其翻译传播团队坚持不懈

的学术推广有一定关系;但是相对森舸澜的译本而言,安乐哲与罗思文译本的哲学诠释使普通读者阅读起来有一定难度,因此,这些普通读者更倾向于购买能提供大量文化背景知识的森舸澜译本。这也是森舸澜译本被引频次落后于安乐哲与罗思文等译本,但是用户评价排名第一,销售量排名第二的原因。这也可以解释很多普通读者阅读森舸澜译本是为了获得《论语》儒家文化知识,而不一定是为了从学术的目的去学习或者研究。森舸澜译本从读者认知科学的视角出发,考虑了普通读者的认知需求,因此更加容易被英语读者理解与接受。

综上所述,《论语》译本依托国外知名度与信誉度较高的出版社出版译作,并利用 Kindle 电子书等对于其译介的多元化传播都起到了一定推动作用。同时,我们也要注意《论语》译本是否具有学术性、读者是否具有针对性、出版质量是否具有权威性、译本评论是否具有积极性等因素都会影响《论语》英译的传播情况以及读者对译作的认同与接受。

因此,中华传统文化的翻译传播应注重加强对国际文化市场的调查研究,以提升国际视野和跨文化传播的适应性,并根据不同国家的社会风俗习惯调整翻译传播策略,组织有效书评资源提高读者接受度,从而让不同文化背景的人能准确理解所传播的文化内容,增强中华传统文化的吸引力,提高跨文化传播质量与国际影响力。

五、小结

从历时与跨文化视角探究《论语》英译传播历程、英译传播模式、英译传播途径与海外接受调查,思考《论语》的英译传播与海外接受对策,注重历时语境、文化背景、传播策略与读者接受等多种因素在国际文化交流中的重要作用,不仅可使英语读者更好地理解中华传统文化,有力提升中华优秀传统文化的接受程度,推动各国之间互相尊重,而且可以提升异质文化之间的借鉴、吸收与转化,使不同文化个性的人类文化相互促进、共同发展,有效加强国际交流。

第五章　中国典籍翻译传播机制创新探索

中国典籍的翻译传播一直是中西文化交流的重要内容、重要途径与重要方式。本章基于《论语》个案的翻译传播与海外接受的研究，进一步探索中国典籍翻译传播的机制创新问题。本章主要从中国典籍翻译传播的现状、中国典籍翻译传播主体的多元化、中国典籍翻译传播的路径创新、中国典籍翻译传播人才培养模式的创新等方面进行分析，探讨重构中国对外传播话语体系、提高文化国际表达力、提升中国典籍翻译海外接受程度以及提升中国典籍翻译传播人才培养质量等问题，以进一步推动具有国际影响力的中国典籍文化翻译传播，并促进中西文化的沟通与交流。

一、中国典籍翻译传播现状

中国历代圣贤撰著的中国典籍是中华优秀传统文化的核心和载体，也是我们传承发展中华优秀传统文化的基础。中国典籍主要是指经过时空考验，在推动中华民族文明与世界文明发展中发挥过重要作用的文献书籍。这些文献典籍经过历代学者的研究、增补、阐释及传播，表现出极强的生命力和永恒的社会价值。中国典籍的翻译传播需要注重其中的社会价值与意义，进一步加强中西文化的对话与交流。目前中国典籍的翻译传播情况如下。

（一）主要成绩

1. 学术地位逐渐提高

21世纪以来,随着中华文化软实力的建设以及中华传统文化的对外输出,中国典籍翻译传播已逐渐上升为国家工程,并受到国家高度重视。国家层面推出的《大中华文库》工程(1995)、中国图书对外推广计划(2004)、中国文化著作翻译出版工程(2009)、经典中国国际出版工程(2009)等项目对于推动中国典籍翻译事业的发展起到了重要推动作用。其中,《大中华文库》工程是我国历史上首次向世界推出外文版中国典籍的国家重大出版工程。其内容选自先秦至近代的文化、历史、哲学、经济、军事、科技等领域最具代表性的经典著作100多部,力求系统、全面展示中华传统文化的基本情况与文化成就。

2. 研究领域逐渐拓展

随着语言学、传播学、文化研究等跨学科研究的发展,中国典籍翻译研究的领域已从仅仅强调字词翻译技巧的内部研究逐渐转向中西文化对比研究以及翻译与传播的外部研究,更加注重从比较文学和跨文化研究的角度探讨中国典籍的翻译传播问题,研究中国典籍在异域文化的变异性,以"'中国文化'作为研究的'客体',以研究者各自的'本土文化语境'作为观察'客体'的基点,在'跨文化'的层面上各自表述其研究的结果"(严绍璗,2006)。

3. 研究队伍逐渐壮大

随着"大中华文库"等文化翻译工程以及相关重要相关研究课题项目的启动,从事中国典籍翻译事业的中外学者逐渐增多,而且有越来越多的硕士生与博士生有志于从事中国典籍翻译传播的研究。中国典籍翻译传播研究队伍的壮大有力推动了中国典籍翻译传播事业的发展。

（二）主要问题

本章主要从中华传统文化吸引力需进一步提升、中西文化交流不平衡、中国典籍翻译传播研究与翻译选材范围有待提高、中国典籍翻译传播传媒有待加强、中国典籍翻译传播人才严重缺乏等方面分析中国典籍翻译传播过程中存在的主要问题。

1. 中华传统文化吸引力需进一步提升

中华传统文化作为东方文化的代表在西方国家有很高的知名度。西方民众对中华传统文化充满了好奇心与各种想象。但西方人对中华传统文化的想象不成体系,并带有西方文化中心主义的"他者"形象。

在国外,中国的武术、杂技、舞动的狮子、元宵的灯笼、春节的剪纸等,以象征符号的功能展示了中华传统文化的特色,迎合了西方的审美期待,在西方国家得到了广泛传播与接受。但是中华传统文化的很多智慧未能被充分挖掘。

相对于中国古典小说如《红楼梦》与当代小说如《蛙》《狼图腾》等在海外的传播,儒家哲学经典《论语》在海外的接受程度还是相对较低。这说明,我们还缺乏用具体生动的故事彰显中华传统文化力量的能力,导致中华传统文化在国外的接受情况不佳。

如何坚定文化自信,建构自我文化身份,实现中华传统文化现代转型,促进文化产业发展,以及向世界展示中国形象等成为当前中华传统文化传播面临的重要任务。

2. 中西文化交流不平衡

在当前世界,中美两国由于缺乏深度沟通和相互理解,还存在某种认识的误区。随着中西文化交流的深入,中国引入了西方文化中的一些新方法、新理论、新思想,但是中华文化对外输出较少。这种中西文化交流的不平衡让我们不得不重新思考跨文化传播中的文化失语与文化误读等现象。

早期中国典籍在国外的翻译传播主要得益于海外汉学家与海外华人的翻译传播。与国内译者相比,他们在目标语语言的运用和对读者阅读期待把握等方面更胜一筹。但是由于缺乏对中国具体文化现象的了解,在翻译过程中有时也会产生误读和误译。很多中国人不能用英语表达中华传统文化,尤其对中华传统文化的表达不够自信,这种失语症现象导致了中华文化的对外传播不足。中华文化的失语,除了语言的相对弱势、学术话语与社科体系话语的失语以外,更重要的是文化价值观的失语。

另外,西方国家一直对中国存在偏见以及对中华文化存在误读现象。一方面,在西方国家强势文化影响与西方媒体的垄断下,很多国外受众对中国的了解是片面的。另一方面,目前中华文化在对外传播过程中仍存在忽略西方国家对中华文化的不同兴趣和真正需求的现象,缺少"对国际化传播与国际文化市场的调查研究,忽视了对不同国度的文化兴趣和与中华文化的可容度之类的精神要素、价值观研究"(曲慧敏,2017),从而导致跨文化传播不够顺畅。

由于中西语言文化固有差异,中国典籍中具有中国儒家哲学思想的概念很难在西方文化中找到对等词语。中国典籍中很多作为中华传统文化的身份标识的术语体现了一多不分的哲学观。这些术语与西方文化中的一多二元的术语表征有着明显差异。但是很多中外译者一直习惯于用英语中现有的词语替代中国典籍中的哲学术语。例如,中国经典中经常出现的词语分别被翻译为仁—仁慈—benevolence,义—正义—justice,礼—礼节—propriety,但结合上下文理解时,就会发现这些对应的英语词汇表意并不充分,没有涵盖对应的汉字的全部含义。以"仁"的翻译为例,辜鸿铭认为,"另一个词,'人道(humanity)',反倒可能是汉语中'仁'字最确切的对应词,但必须对humanity"做与其英语的一般用法所不同的解释(辜鸿铭,2016)。安乐哲认为:"'humanness'比译为'benevolence'似乎好一些,因为'仁'指的是整体性的个人行为:一个人的修养而得的认知感、审美感、道德感和宗教感;这些是通过'角色'和关系喻意的行为结合在一起,即一个人的品格。正是这样的'域境自我'——充满意义的关系发源地——构成了一个人,一个不可简约的社会人。'仁'不仅是智能与精神的,也是形体的;它包括一个人的仪态与举止,一个人的举手投足与身体语言交流。我认为,将'仁'译为'benevolence',是狭隘地对待一个来自传统的广义得多的思想,是将它心理学化;而产生'仁'观念的传统在其认识与提升人本身经验的努力中是不需要'psyche'(灵魂)这个理念的"(安乐哲,2017)。因此,安乐哲进一步指出,"虽然'benevolence'的某些意思,也是'仁'的重要方面,但是把它当成标准翻译则会削弱'仁'观念,相当于从众多道德性格层面,只孤立地截取其中一个单一面,其代价是牺牲了由做人、成人这一错综复杂事物而结合在一起的太多的其他意义"(安乐哲,2017)。

由于英汉语言文化与思维差异,当中国典籍翻译传播时,我们需要思考中国人向国外讲述中华传统文化的最佳途径,在文化比较中通过阐释语境体现儒家文化形态的表现方式,以及中西语言文化差异在不同译本中的不同体现及其价值意义,从而实现中西文化平等对话。

3. 中国典籍翻译传播研究与翻译选材范围有待提高

"由于对域外汉学研究的跨文化属性,从比较文学的角度来看,无论在基础建设还是在理论建设上都亟待深入和提高"(张希平,2013)。目前,中国典籍翻译传播理论与实践脱节的现象仍然存在,借鉴跨学科、跨文化最新成果的研究有待进一步加强,整体性与系统性研究以及定量与定性相结合的研究有待进一步开展,尤其是中国典籍海外传播的机制创新研究有待进一步探索,以帮助翻译传播主体根据出版商、赞助商、英译读者与海外市场需求选择最佳翻译策略(如节译、编译还是全译)以及合适的翻译传播路径和方法。此外,目前中国典籍翻译的选材以文学、哲学、军事类典籍为主,如有些中国典籍作品如《红楼梦》《论语》《孙子兵法》等有许多英译版本,相关书评、媒介及相关文化产业对这些典籍作品的翻译传播起到了重要作用。而其他文体的选材如科技、法律、医学等中国典籍的翻译传播需要结合国外市场需求与英语读者接受等因素进行拓展。

4. 中国典籍翻译传媒有待加强

在全球化时代,传媒超越时空,承担着文化传播与文化交流的重要功能。因此,我们应加强中国典籍翻译传媒建设,努力构建国内外翻译传播平台合作共赢的新机制,促进中华传统文化的对外传播。

但是,中国传媒相对于英、美等西方国家来说较弱,这主要是因为:第一,中国媒体传播渠道单一,限制了传播广度,无法与国际媒体竞争。第二,传播内容过于专业化导致西方受众文化接受难度增加。第三,有关部门对自媒体引导不够,传播能力和话语掌控能力有待提高。第四,新技术在文化领域未得到充分运用,新技术的开发与运用落后导致中华文化与科技融合不够。第五,中华文化产业中高附加值的中华文化品牌缺少吸引力,有待进一步开发。

因此,中国媒体需要更新传播手段,不要强力灌输中华文化,而要用多元化且西方人喜闻乐见的手段传播中华文化。例如,针对普通读者,我们可通过电视、网络、微博、动漫、报纸、杂志等多渠道发表关于中国典籍译本的评论,吸引他们关注、阅读、传播这些译本。针对专业读者,我们可通过线上与线下学术研讨会、学术出版发行会等形式,通过沟通对话与正面积极引导,促使更多学者关注中国典籍的翻译传播。此外,还可以采用其他一些手段,如将中华传统文化的文字、图像、符号等通过数字化技术展现出来,以吸引更多英语国家读者。由此可见,中国在运用传播媒介来树立中国形象以及增加吸引力和影响力等方面任重而道远。

5. 中国典籍翻译传播人才严重缺乏

中国典籍在海外的传播力和影响力逐渐增加。但是在国外看到的中国典籍翻译作品多是由国外汉学家与海外华人承担,较少见到国内大陆译者的翻译作品,这可能与国际表达力、国际出版以及海外传播途径等方面有关。

国外汉学家与海外华人既精通英语等语言,又了解中华文化,并且有着深厚的文学修养。但是很多中国典籍中的微言大义即使是精通汉学的外国学者也难以理解。而在国内,很多较低水平的翻译不能满足国际需求,能够成为国际跨文化交流的经典翻译作品也较少。此外，一些反映中华传统文化的影视若在海外传播，需要高质量的英文字幕翻译以吸引更多的海外受众，这就需要大量典籍高端翻译人才提高翻译质量。中国翻译团队的水平和数量在很多情况下滞后于跨文化交流的需要，这种供需矛盾导致翻译工作滞后于翻译事业的发展。另外，中国典籍的对外译介也需要高质量的对外传播人才采用适当的传播手段进行对外传播。

因此，中国典籍翻译传播人才的培养特别重要。高质量的中国典籍翻译传播人才是中华传统文化翻译传播的重要主体与坚实后盾。在我国，培养具有较强的国际文化交流意识又具备较强的人文素养、专业素养与技术素养的中国典籍翻译传播人才是当前译学界与教育界面临的重要任务。

由此可见，中国典籍的传承、发展及其翻译传播与社会文化环境、翻译传播主体、受众接受等因素密切相关。因此，在翻译传播过程中，我们应注重发掘影响中国典籍翻译传播的社会深层因素，探讨主体与受众、文本和社会历史环境间的互动关系，注重揭示译者、权力话语与翻译活动间以及媒介传播环境与受众间的互动。此外，翻译传播主体需要在全球化语境中肩负起对儒家文化精神和价值进行正确阐释的责任与担当，以积极的心态努力改变海内外受众对中华传统文化的误读，在世界文化中重构中华传统文化的魅力与价值。

二、中国典籍翻译传播主体多元化

中国典籍的翻译传播过程是翻译传播主体通过大众传播媒体，跨越两个或两个以上国家，或不同文化体系之间进行跨文化交流和沟通对话的过程。中国典籍翻译传播的主体呈现多元化特点，包括译者、受众、政府、企业和各种社会组织等。其中，译者又包括国外汉学家、中外合作译者、加入中国籍的原籍译者、旅居海外的华裔译者以及中国译者等。中国典籍翻译传播主体的多元化研究应结合政策、外交与传播策略,以中西文化交流的互利共赢与和而不同为最高原则,以提高中国典籍翻译的传播与海外接受为最终目标,思考译者、受众、政府、企业与社会组织等翻译传播主体的翻译传播经验,进一步增强中国典籍翻译传播主体的创新活力。

(一) 译者

译者作为翻译活动的主体,在翻译传播过程中发挥着重要作用。译者的翻译行为是一种有目的、有意识的跨文化传播行为。译者是社会环境的一部分,并处于动态交际过程的中心地位,协调着原文作者与目标语读者的互动过程。

译者的主体性贯穿翻译的全过程。查明建和田雨(2003)指出:"译者主体性是指作为翻译主体的译者在尊重翻译对象的前提下,为实现翻译目的而在翻译活动中表现出的主观能动性,其基本特征是翻译主体自觉的文化意识、人文品格和文化、审美创造性。"屠国元和朱献珑(2003)指出:"译者的主体性就是指译者在受到边缘主体或外部环境及自身视域的影响制约下,为满足译入语文化需要在翻译活动中表现出的一种主观能动性,它具有自主性、能动性、目的性、创造性等特点。"王宏印(2003)以彦琮"八备"说为例,对译者在中国传统译论中的主体性作了论述,强调译者的主体地位。由此可见,译者主体性可以发挥创造性与能动性,提出可行、有效的翻译策略。

译者主体性的发挥会受到很多因素影响,这不仅体现在译者对原文本的理解、诠释和语言层面的艺术再创造,也体现在翻译目的与翻译策略的选择等方面。Hatim 与 Mason(1990/1997)指出,译者作为翻译过程的协调沟通者,会受文本特征,译者的各种干扰活动,译文翻译实践过程中的翻译原则以及统治诗学和意识形态等因素的影响。因此,译者的翻译生态环境、文化立场、翻译目的、读者考量、审美创造性等不可避免地会影响其文本理解与翻译决策。

译者的翻译生态环境对译者主体性提出了挑战。译者主体性必然受其历史局限性及所处翻译生态环境的制约。译者并非在真空中生活,译者作为翻译主体要适应并选择翻译生态环境。翻译生态环境是"由原文本、原语言与目的语言构成的世界,包括翻译的语言、交际、文化与社会等层面,以及作者、赞助商与读者等层面"(胡庚申,2004)。翻译传递的"不仅仅是基本意义,其本身也需要跨越历史、语言、社会和文化的距离"(孙艺风,2016)。中国典籍的译者需要跨越时空距离与原作者的思想进行对话,再根据读者需求进行选择性翻译活动,从而在某种程度上限制了主体性的发挥。例如,中国主要受儒家思想影响,强调家庭与集体等思想;而西方国家则主要受基督教思想以及人权平等思想的影响,强调个人力量与自由权力的获取。这些文化差异必然会给不同历史阶段的译者以不同的翻译思考。

因此,中国典籍的译者要注重两种文化的互动与交流,尊重、沟通并适应两种文化语境之间的转化,根据翻译语境与历史环境进行相应调整,做到译文、读者与环境的相互协调与适应。谢天振(2014)强调,在翻译过程中需要考虑很多因素,包括目标语国家读者的阅读习惯、审美趣味、目标语国家的意识形态、诗学观念,以及译介者自己的译介方式、方法、策略等因素,否则预期结果很难预料。

在中国典籍翻译对外译介的前期阶段,译者可在重视原文权威性的基础上,采取适当的"归化"翻译策略。这会在一定程度上减少目标语读者的"排斥"心理,并尽量减少文化差异导致的理解偏差与障碍。例如,辜鸿铭的翻译[天命(the truth of religions)]更多采用符合英文习惯的表达手段传递给英语读者,使译文符合英语读者的阅读习惯,从而最大限度获得他们的认同和接受。而随着中西文化交流的增加,在中国典籍对外译介的较成熟阶段,译者可以逐渐采取适当的"异化"翻译策略,通过富有民族特色的文采表达,采用文外注释的翻译手段更深层次地传递中华民族特有的文化内涵,如安乐哲的翻译[propensities of tian(tianming 天命)],以更加有效地加强东西异质文化间的交流与对话,并丰富世界文化。

译者的文化立场和译文读者的文化立场都会影响译者主体性的发挥。译者在面对中西方文化的矛盾和冲突时，表现出不同的态度：(1) 偏向原语中国典籍文化的立场，保留原文化的语言特色和风貌，带领读者向原文化靠拢；(2) 偏向译入语文化，考虑译文读者的文化接受立场，以译入语文化为归宿，降低译文读者的阅读障碍。当然，在具体翻译过程中，译者可视具体情况而作出分析。为了既能够彰显原文特色，又能够使译文自然流畅，译者可在尊重文化差异的情况下，有选择地采用翻译策略，以使译文得到最高限度地传播与接受。同时也要注意，文化直入或者文化归化策略在弱势民族文化向强势民族文化的译介初期似乎是一种必要的译介手段，但随着弱势文化地位的逐渐强大以及双方文化交流的深入推进，译者可以选择各种翻译补偿策略传达这种文化差异。

译者翻译目的对其主体性的重要影响也不容忽视。如果译者的翻译目的是力图使目标语文本的语言特征与目标语的文化规范契合，就会采用归化策略，目标语文本就会表现出传统化趋势，如辜鸿铭译文。如果译者的翻译目的是忠实再现源语文本所体现的源语文化，就会采用异化策略，目标语文本就会呈现明显的陌生化趋势，如安乐哲与罗思文译文；此外，如果译者将普通读者视为目标语文本读者，通常会更多采用解释性翻译方法，使目标语文本通俗易懂，如森舸澜译本。译者在翻译过程中，常在考虑译入语读者的阅读期待与审美距离的基础上，根据文化翻译语境选择不同的翻译策略。

如何使中国典籍中具有国际特征的文化内涵获得英语读者的认同与接受，需要译者在翻译的过程中发挥译者的主体性、创造性、主观能动性与自我认同身份重构。译者可从以下三个方面进行努力：

一是在表达方式上强调国际化，注重运用国际社会容易理解和接受的方式传播中华文化。"国际表达"包括三层含义：(1) 根据英语读者的思维习惯、接受方式、信息需求选择翻译传播策略；(2) 通过中西融通的方法表达和解读中国典籍的文化内容；(3) 借用国际惯例和规则对中华文化特色内容进行解释和说明,从而增强彼此的理解与信任。

二是在表达手段上注重创新,需要考虑翻译目的、社会环境、英语读者阅读期待、时空距离和审美距离等因素,如安乐哲与罗思文在翻译时所采用的"意译+汉语拼音+汉字"的手段有助于提高当前国外受众对中华文化的感知,增强国外受众加强对中西文化的沟通、交流。

三是译者可以借助国家、政府与社会的大力支持,包括中国政府对汉译外典籍事业的支持,国家所提倡的语言政策的支持,以及社会现代化的互联网等传播媒体的支持等,创新翻译传播手段,通过纸质、网络、影视等多种媒介形式,传播中国典籍文化。

由此可见,由于中西语言文化传统的差异,以及不同受众认知的差异,中国典籍中蕴含的哲学思想如果要与西方国家实现最大程度的平等对话,译者需要准确理解原文含义,把握翻译规律,立足新文化传统,借助传播媒介体系,尽力构建中外融通的话语体系,帮助英语读者深入了解中华文化内涵。此外,国际环境、国家战略、市场需求与翻译话语实践的复杂性对译者能力提出了更高的要求和挑战。译者需要根据时代形势、翻译目的与读者期待,创造出既有民族特征,又有全人类共性的新文化,使中华传统文化内容与世界文化相适应、相协调,并通过翻译得以延伸、扩展、丰富、滋养目标语文化。

(二) 受众

受众也称为"受传者""接受者"和"传播对象",在翻译传播过程中处于主体地位。受众是完整的传播过程的有机组成部分,在传播活动中处于与传播者同样重要的地位。受众不是被动的、消极的,而是具有很强的主动性,决定着翻译传播活动的基本方向。中国典籍的翻译传播受众是中国典籍翻译信息的接收者的总称,也是翻译传播活动的积极参与者和传播效果的有效反馈者,具体包括读者、听众、观众、网民等。

中国典籍的翻译传播的受众在很大程度上决定着传播活动的主

要因素:内容、形式、媒介、方法、效果等。我们根据受众的阅读目的,把译文受众的心理类型主要分为认知心理、好奇心理、从众心理、欣赏心理、研究心理等方面。这几个方面彼此联系,又有自己的特征。

(1) 认知心理:它是指受众普遍存在的、寻求信息的心理现象。阅读中国典籍译本的每一个读者都有一定的求知欲,他们希望不断从经典的译本及相关材料中获得文化信息。如果媒介的信息不能为译文读者提供真实、必要的知识和经验,就无助于他们获取相应信息,因而不能提高其认知行为的有效性,这必然导致翻译传播行为不能达到预期的传播目的。此外,我们还要认识到由于中西文化差异,中西方读者的认知心理存在很大差距,这也会影响他们对文本中文化知识的理解有所不同。

(2) 好奇心理:好奇心理与认知心理密切相关。一般情况是,人们总是乐于接受新颖、罕见、异常的信息。除了信息内容的新鲜,信息形式如遣词造句、修辞手段、图文搭配、篇章结构的创新也可以满足读者对信息量的期待。例如,《论语》五译本中的副文本编排、安乐哲与罗思文的创新翻译策略都能满足译文读者对儒家文化的求知需求。

(3) 从众心理:生活在群体中的个体往往受外界人群行为的影响,而在言行态度上表现出符合于公众舆论或多数人的行为方式。群体中的意见或价值标准往往通过群体中的权威集中体现出来。一方面,正确的从众心理有利于维护社会稳定与文化传播;另一方面,我们也要认识到盲目的崇拜与迷信也会导致诸多社会问题。当今世界文明程度的差异已愈发明显地体现为科技进步与创新能力,而从众特征则是创造与创新的阻碍。对于中国典籍中的儒家文化的对外传播,译者需要思考如何用适宜的方式路径去传播,正确地引导人们的从众心理。

(4) 欣赏心理:读者往往在工作之余,为了调剂精神生活而进行欣赏阅读,而且人们都愿意欣赏健康积极向上的作品。因此,我们可以思考如何打造儒家文化品牌及其多元化文化途径的传播。例如,中国学者蔡志忠与Brian Bruyan合作的中英版《论语》漫画选择了《论语》中有代表性的由70章改写成的70个主题鲜明的漫画小故事来阐释儒家文化,用简洁生动的线条塑造《论语》中不同的人物形象,同时使用图像隐喻的手段突显人物的身份和地位,增强儒家文化的对外传播。另外,人们也可通过视听、电子、网络等多种媒介进行赏析。

(5) 研究心理:研究心理类型读者以从事科研活动的读者为主体。他们的共同特点是:具有较深的专业理论知识,较高的学术研究能力,担负一定的科研任务并具有较强的责任感。对于研究心理类型的读者而言,他们更喜欢学术性强的文化典籍翻译。他们可以在求知、研究的过程中发现某一值得研究的问题,再通过跨学科的思考找到解决问题的办法。

当外界信息进入传播过程时,受众会根据自己的心理需求进行有选择性的注意、有选择性的理解和有选择性的记忆。因此,翻译传播者需要了解受众的信息需求和参与翻译传播活动的基本动机,掌握他们的信息接受习惯和熟悉的媒介和传播形式。

要使中国典籍信息对受众有较大的吸引力,引起他们的注意,译者在信息的内容和形式上需要把握以下原则:一是信息的易得性。为使受众容易获得信息,译者需要考虑翻译传播内容(国际性、引导性、准确性)、翻译传播方式(纸质、电子、网络等)等因素。二是信息的对比性。人们的好奇心常引导人们对那些新鲜有趣的信息产生兴趣。对自己需要而翻译传播过程中没有的信息,受众还会主动向媒介或者传播者寻求信息。因此,中国典籍翻译及其传播策略对于吸引受众的注意力发挥着重要作用。三是信息的引导性,即在传递信息的过程中让受众无意识地把信息与自己的实际情况(如名誉、地位、前途)等结合起来。如果是有利于自己的正面信息则愿意接受,否则就会遭到排斥。在此情况下,中国典籍翻译的传播者需要思考如何让典籍品牌文化内涵和典籍品牌影响力得到进一步提升。

在中国典籍翻译传播过程中,受众在接受信息后将面临再一次选择:选择性理解。也就是说,受众只对其中的一部分信息进行深层次的认识、思考与应用,对其他信息则停留在曾经注意的阶段,不再做进一步探究。而这些能引起人们进一步关注的信息往往与受众本人的生活、兴趣、价值观等直接有关的信息,或是对人们产生了强刺激的信息,导致不同认知结构的人产生了不同认识。面对选择性理解,中国典籍翻译传播者要有意识地引导与控制所传播的信息。一是通过增加注释等翻译补偿策略尽量减少或消除可能造成受众对翻译信息产生误解和歧义的因素,降低信息理解的难度。二是翻译的信息力求准确。译者在翻译过程中增强哲学术语等信息符号在语境一致情况下的专用性、系统性和统一性,必要时利用相关内容或其他传播方式对所传播的主导内容进行说明,消除可能被人们曲解的因素。三是在序言等副文本中通过说明预防有人有意识地对翻译信息进行曲解并将这种曲解的结果再次传播。

每个人都有自己的特殊信息记忆库,即在特殊生活工作环境中通过学习和实践积累的知识经验等,一方面用于指导自己的行为,另一方面用于解读新的信息。记忆信息库的内容常常表现出个人独特的风格,同时也是在不断调整更新变化的。一般来说,在选择性记忆中,人们倾向于记忆那些感兴趣的、与自己价值观一致的信息,有意或无意忘记那些尽管重要但是与自己观点相悖的信息。选择性信息是在人们的潜意识中进行的。面对选择性记忆,中国典籍翻译传播者要有意识地引导与控制所传播的信息。一是帮助受众提高文化素养,树立正确的价值观。二是增强翻译符号的易记性与易懂性,加强受众对翻译符号体系的掌握。三是创新翻译传播接受方式,让受众在寓教于乐中掌握所学知识。

每个翻译受众所处的文化传统、社会环境不同,造成个人的种种差异。即使是在完全相同的翻译传播环境中,面对相同的媒介和传播内容,不同的受众也会有不同的反应。翻译受众的性别、年龄、国籍、政治态度、文化信仰、受教育程度等都是影响他们对信息接收的不同选择、理解、记忆以及行动的重要因素。例如,相对普通受众而言,专业性受众对翻译信息有较高的专业化要求。他们参与翻译传播就是要得到自己在工作、生活、科研中所需要的信息,参与传播活动的目的性和功利性很强。在这种情况下,学术性阐释的典籍翻译策略更适合这些专业受众。翻译传播者可以通过更新翻译传播理念与策略作用于受众所处的社会文化环境,对他们产生影响。一是需要提高认识,不仅社会是不断发展变化的,而且受众作为有强烈的主动意识的群体在对传播过程施加控制力的同时,也处在不断变化之中。二是通过文化教育与文化规范等措施,使受众的观念发生变化,让他们认识到中国典籍翻译传播的重要价值与意义。三是对受众开展调查研究,了解他们的兴趣、爱好以及媒介接触习惯等,采用文字、电子、网络等翻译传播方式,保证翻译传播活动的顺利进行。

由此可见,受众作为翻译传播活动的主体,是传播环境的重要组成部分,在翻译传播过程中发挥着重要作用。他们通过积极参与干预翻译传播活动的内容与形式,影响翻译传播活动的过程,并决定翻译传播的效果。因此,在中国典籍的翻译传播中,我们要注重考虑英语读者的价值观念与心理特征,探索受众参与翻译传播活动的基本规律与动机,分析受众在不同翻译传播语境中的接受情况,保证中国典籍翻译传播的顺利进行。

(三) 其他主体

中国典籍的翻译传播不仅需要译者、受众作为传播主体,还需要政府、企业与社会组织等传播主体。在这些传播主体中,只有国家或政府的信息可以通过大众传媒直接向外传播,而企业与其他社会组织向外传递信息,均要在国家的主体框架下进行。

政府是国家进行统治和社会管理的机关,是国家权力的执行机构,具有一定权威性。由于政府具有特殊的地位,在国际传播中,它始终是主导性的传播者,即所谓"强势主体"(程曼丽,2006)。中国典籍的翻译传播离不开政府的主导把控,并与国家利益与中国话语权密切相关,因而也带有一定的政治色彩。

企业是从事生产、流通与服务等经济活动的营利性组织。企业会通过广告、公共宣传对外宣传自己的企业产品,参与国际竞争。企业通常会加强与国际国内媒体的交流合作,加强企业自媒体建设,结合业务扩大宣传,吸引大量外国受众,在全球市场中发挥越来越重要的作用。因此,我们可以把中华传统文化精神融入企业产品,用心打造带有中华传统文化符号的企业品牌,展现中华传统文化的魅力,推动中国企业与国际社会相互交流。

社会组织主要是指政府与企业之外的,不以营利为目的的组织机构和团体,也称为"非政府组织"或"非营利组织"。社会组织旨在推进社会的公共利益,主要包括各种形式的协会、学会、研究会、学校、文化艺术团体等。例如,孔子学院、国际儒学联合会(International Confucian Association, ICA)与中国孔子基金会等。孔子学院致力于适应世界各国(地区)人民对汉语学习的需要,增进世界各国(地区)人民对中国语言文化的了解,加强中国与世界各国教育文化交流合作,发展中外友好关系,发展儒家文化,促进世界多元文化发展。国际儒学联合会是国际性学术文化联合组织(国际非政府组织),由中国、韩国、日本、美国、德国、新加坡等国家和地区与儒学有关的学术团体共同发起。中国孔子基金会旨在通过募集基金,组织或支持国内及海外儒学研究,为弘扬中华优秀传统文化、促进海内外华人团结、加强各国文化交流而服务。随着全球化的推进,社会组织在各国社会生活中以及国际交流中发挥着越来越重要的作用。

总之,中国典籍翻译传播的主体应充分激发主体活力,发挥主体性与创造性,合力开展中国典籍对外传播研究,在使用中西融通的哲学思维开展工作的同时,也要尽力创新翻译传播表达手段,使用对方能听懂的语言阐释中华文化语言特色,以增进国外对中华传统文化的了解,并有力推动中西文化沟通与交流。

三、中国典籍翻译传播路径创新

中国典籍翻译传播的路径创新主要是指,为增强《论语》等中国典籍翻译传播而在国家政策指导下,在运营机制与激励措施等方面进行的创新活动。结合新时代我国文化建设的主要使命与任务,围绕现代性儒家哲学重新阐释这一主题进行,表现为多路径、多模态、联动式,本书主要从提升中国典籍文化软实力、增强跨文化认同、深化翻译传播理念,提高翻译传播水平,注重翻译传播内容、创新翻译传播途径、提高翻译传播效果七个方面展开论述。

(一)提升中国典籍文化软实力

提升中国典籍文化软实力是增强国家文化软实力的直接体现,也是中华优秀传统文化翻译传播的创新目的与动力。中国在经济、政治上处于上升趋势,亦迫切要求文化地位崛起;如果文化地位微弱,经济与政治的崛起将难以持久。因此,中华传统文化的软实力文化建设具有重要意义。

"软实力"来源于"对一个国家文化、政治理想或者各种政策的吸引力。当我们的政策在其他人眼里看起来合法时,我们的软实力就得到了提高"(Ney,2004)。Ney认为,一个国家的软实力主要来源于三种资源:文化(在某些地方更吸引他人时)、政治价值观(能够在国内/外践行这些政治价值价值时)及其外交政策(看起来合法而且具有更多权力时)(Ney,2004)。Ney进一步指出,"如果一个国家的文化与意识形态是吸引人的,其他人就更加愿意追随。如果一个国家能够形成与其各种利益与价值一致的国际规则,在其他人看来,它的各种行动看起来会更加合法"(Ney,2004)。因此,软实力是通过吸引力而非强制力影响其他国家的行为。

文化软实力是对"软实力"的改造与拓展。文化软实力是依靠文化自身的巨大魅力与吸引力而发挥作用。杨淳伟(2011)认为,"文化软实力"的重点在"文化"和"力"上,"文化"是资源,"力"是资源能量由内而外的表现,文化软实力是一种因文化的巨大魅力而产生影响力、吸纳力的政策手段和工具,它以内藏的吸引力发挥作用,以足够的内在能量吸引他人的趋近。文化是作为文化力的资源和依托而存在的,文化力则是文化影响力的外现。

因此,文化软实力作为一种具有隐形性的能推动社会发展的精神力量,能够直接影响一个国家的社会、政治、教育、文化等各个领域,并成为综合国力的重要组成部分。文化软实力是一种因文化魅力对他人产生的影响力、吸引力与感召力。因此,从某种意义上说,文化软实力就是一种隐形的和间接的动力。如果一个国家的社会价值观能够得到人们的普遍价值认同,它就可以对内增强凝聚力、提升硬实力,并对外产生感召力,提升国际话语权。

儒家文化经典是中华传统文化中有助于提高中国典籍的文化影响力的重要组成部分。儒学"所提供的哲学财富,不仅是中华文化焕发活力、走向复兴的资源,而且是更广大性的文化利益资源"(安乐哲,2017)。儒学中的优秀思想不仅具有深远的凝聚力与感召力,而且作为影响了中华文化数千年的儒家文化具有顽强的生命力。典籍文献的流传是"读者对典籍文本不断进行阐释的合集,是传统与现代的对话,聚合而成民族文化软实力"(辛红娟,2009)。通过提升中国典籍的文化软实力与加大对外译介力度,"到绵延不绝的儒家传统中发掘可促成与其他文化实行建设性对话的元素,并加深认识,进行阐释,将其付诸实践,那么儒家哲学在今天可能成为充实我们思想与生活方式的重要资源。而且,同其他文化会通将是'儒学'获得更进一步内外提升的体现,提供有利其本身创造性成长与创新的机遇"(安乐哲,2017)。

由此可见,提升中国典籍的文化软实力是加强中国典籍翻译传播的重要路径之一。这不仅能够以优秀中华传统文化思想为中介,丰富世界文化,也有利于在西方学界为中国典籍探寻一条可促进社会文化发展、以儒学为底蕴的现代化之路,并在中西文化交流中达成更深层次的共识。

(二) 增强跨文化认同

跨文化认同是指一个群体中的成员在民族共同体中长期共同生活所形成的归属于本民族的文化身份或感觉,是成员自我概念和自我认知的一部分,既具有个体的特征,又具有同一文化身份的相同文化成员群体的特征,与国籍、种族、宗教、社会阶层、世代、地域或任何有自己独特文化的社会群体有关(Ennaji,2005)。

跨文化认同是民族认同和国家认同的重要基础,是维系整个民族、国家文化群体的精神支柱,同时也是维系整个民族、国家向心力的动力与源泉。跨文化认同的建构常借助创造的异国形象来促使读者对异域社会的文化认同,即借助他者发现自我和认识自我以及对自我文化身份进行重构的一个过程。这通常可以借助于读者的心理调适、文化意象转换与认知思维调整来提升文化认同。Wan 与 Tajfel 指出,"在跨文化交流的语境中,文化身份能够赋予主体一种深层次的归属感,帮助其获取、处理和分享相关的文化信息,也可以帮助主体认识自身与他者,确立一定的文化价值取向,并在寻找自身优于其他群体文化特征的过程中,提升自信心,建立更好的自我形象"(周晓梅,2017)。

在跨文化传播过程中,始终存在着彼此文化是否互相认同的问题。陈国明(2010)指出,"文化间差异越明显,传播的跨文化程度就越高"。王东风(2002)认为,文化认同是指"触发文化的文化因子在被引入目标文化之后,安全度过排异期,最终被目标文化所吸收"。范正宇指出,两种文化在长期的全面接触之后会在价值体系与行为模式上出现相互接近的现象。若双方文化力相当,文化融合的进一步趋势往往是产生第三种文化,若双方力量不等,则可能导致一种文化被融进另一种文化的现象。当然,也存在这种现象,即不相邻的区文化未经实际接触而在一段时间内会逐渐向相同的方向发展,直至变为相似或相同的无中介共项变化现象。文化群体或文化成员承认群内新文化或群异域文化因素的价值效用符合传统文化价值标准的认可态度与方式后,这种新文化或异文化因素将更容易被接受与传播。全球化背景下,不同民族间的跨文化交流容易引发政治、意识形态与道德观念等问题的碰撞、冲突与融合,这些最终都可以归咎于文化认同的问题。

根据历史唯物主义的观点,人们的认同感和归属感是根据历史环境与时间的演变而变化。中国提出的"一带一路"和"人类命运共同体"的理念基于"天下""和、仁、礼、大同、世界主义"等理论框架,注重中西文明交流互鉴,民心相通与文化认同、共同发展与共享共治等内容,对于当前全球化时代的跨文化翻译传播有着重要的指导意义。2015年《推动共建丝绸之路经济带和21世纪海上丝绸之路的愿景与行动》指出,在21世纪以和平、发展、合作、共赢为主题的新时代,面对复杂多变的国际形势,合作重点要以政策沟通、设施联通、贸易畅通、资金融通、民心相通为主要内容。其中,作为"一带一路"建设社会根基的民心相通理念坚持以人为中心,以增进好感为基础,以文化价值交融为导向;而文化认同则是实现民心相通、促进国际交往的基础与保障。此外,2011年《中国的和平发展》白皮书曾提出要以"人类命运共同体"为新视角,寻求人类共同利益和共同价值的新内涵,即在追求本国利益时兼顾他国合理利益,在谋求本国发展中促进其他各国共同发展。2017年习近平在党的十九大报告中进一步提出,要推动构建"人类命运共同体",并提出要相互尊重、平等对话、普惠共赢,要尊重世界文明多样性,要文明交流、互鉴并共存(习近平,2017)。

由此可见,在当前全球化时代,跨文化认同不仅没有失去意义,而且逐渐成为国际交往与跨文化传播的创新理念。在当前中华文化"走出去"的文化战略影响下,中国的优秀传统文化思想也越来越受到社会的关注。从跨文化认同视角思考话语体系重构既是一个对既有文学价值观、文学经验观与文学审美观的挑战,也是一个有助于中国典籍在海外地位从边缘到中心的过程。

跨文化认同理论有六个基本观点(陈国明,2010)。(1)文化认同构成跨文化认同的基底,任何形式的跨文化认同都需要地方文化的支撑。(2)文化认同根植于人类的历史传统,被特定的地理与社会环境所塑造,既有其理性的层面,又受情感因素的影响。它是集体的造物和多元的统一,既不能被完全化约为个人特性,也不能彻底升华为普适性的原则或观念。(3)在建构跨文化认同过程中,文化的差异性与同一性都不可或缺。每个群体内部的同一性以及它与外部群体的差异性是文化认同的两个基本要素。文化认同的两个方面为文化主体性的确立提供了必要条件,它们相互依赖、相互促进、相辅相成。(4)跨文化经验的积累可以帮助交际者摆脱中心主义的束缚,培养他们的跨文化意识。(5)地方性意义框架构成历史与社会事实,不能彻底地颠覆和清除,但能加以扩展和更新。(6)跨文化认同建构不能够彻底消除差异与冲突,但能够缓解矛盾,使文化纷争变得更易调和与掌控,使交际者获得创造性转化的潜力。

文化发源于特定时空,并且在特定的历史文化背景下发育、生长和传播。因此在跨文化传播时,跨文化认同只有获得异域文化的认同与接受才能获得稳固的基础与发展的潜力。但是,跨文化认同需要依靠文化自身的吸引力、合作力与感召力,即文化软实力,而不是依赖于文化的强迫力与威逼利诱。习近平总书记曾多次强调,中华优秀传统文化的丰富哲学思想、人文精神、教化思想与道德理念等,可以为认识和改造世界提供有益启迪,可以为治国理政提供有益启示,也可以为道德建设提供有益启发。中国典籍跨文化传播的内容选择、传播路径与质量高低等都会影响国际社会对中国形象、中国观点与中国声音的理解与认识。

因此,增强跨文化认同需要做到以下几个方面:第一,中国典籍的跨文化传播需要深入挖掘理解中华传统文化的精髓,要坚持古为今用,因势利导,深化研究,结合当前语境推动传统文化创造性转化、创新性发展,提升中华传统文化的吸引力与凝聚力。第二,我们需要认真借鉴其他国家文化的优势,注重中华传统文化主体的整体认同,采用多元恰当的途径,向世界展示当代的中国精神及其价值理念,提升中华传统文化的吸引力与感召力。第三,为了促进中华传统文化的翻译传播与接受,我们需要努力实现包容创新,"通过继承传统、包容现代、创新未来三部曲,打造符合时代要求与普遍公益的国际话语体系"(王义桅,2014),在融通中外的过程中寻找新概念与新表述,增强中华文化的国际影响力。

为此,我们既要放眼世界,具备国际视野,又要立足中国与当下,根据目标语读者与社会语境来调整中国典籍文化翻译传播策略,增强中国在国际学术界的话语权。翻译传播主体不仅要重视翻译在中国典籍翻译传播过程中的重要作用,而且要重视社会语境、出版制度、国际形势等外部因素的重要影响。"翻译作为交流文化、沟通思想的桥梁,对中国文化'走出去'战略的实现无疑发挥了至关重要的直接作用(即内部路径)。除此之外,与翻译工作相关的间接因素(即外部路径)对文化战略的实现起着不容忽视的影响,也是值得探讨的议题"(李伟荣,2015)。

综上所述,增强中西跨文化认同可促进中国典籍的海外传播,展现中华传统文化的魅力,使其在新时代条件下发挥积极作用。因此,我们可以通过增强中华优秀传统文化在国外的跨文化认同,促进中华文化的对外传播与海外接受,增强中国优秀典籍文化在世界文化中的吸引力与感召力。

(三) 深化翻译传播理念

从世界范围看,"中国文学'走出去'的语境比以往任何时候都有了巨大变化。从某种程度上来说,这种变化,得益于文学全球化(literary globalization)格局的发展、变化"(张西平,2016)。同样,中国典籍翻译传播的日益增强也是与文化全球化的变化趋势分不开的。一方面,文化全球化格局为中国典籍的翻译传播带来了机遇与挑战,可以促使中华传统文化与西方文化一起在"融合"和"互异"的同时作用下,在全球范围内以各种方式流动;另一方面,中国典籍的翻译传播必将为促进中西文化交流、探究跨文化交流与重构对外传播话语体系提供新的思考路径。

当前,我国翻译传播逐渐由"西学东渐"转向"东学西传",而且逐渐重视对中华传统文化的重新认识与发扬。因此,译学界需要考虑许多新的问题,例如,"翻译在此转变中应承担怎样的责任?翻译在此转变中如何定位?翻译研究者应持有怎样的翻译观念?以研究'外译中'翻译历史与活动为基础的中国译学研究是否要与时俱进,把目光投向'中译外'的活动?中国文化'走出去',中国要向世界展示的是什么样的'中国文化'"(许钧和李国平,2018)等。

我们知道,一个国家的文化价值观对该国家的社会发展以及国际交流都具有重要的影响作用。儒家文化作为中华优秀传统文化的代表,可以为当前的社会、政治、经济、文化的发展、社会价值建构以及国际交流体系的完善提供参照,能够形成无形的国家力量,对内增强民众的凝聚力,对外增强对他国的感召力与影响力。优秀的中华传统文化始终是我们对外发声音、传形象、讲故事的重要内容,是国际社会从文化的层面认识中国、了解中国、理解中国、欣赏中国的主要内容。中国要重视中华传统文化的传承创新及其对外传播,提升自己的国际形象与地位。中华传统文化要"走出去",中国典籍的翻译与传播是重要路径。

因此,我们要做好翻译传播工作,向世界阐释好中国的历史文化,做好中国经典文化的价值重构,促进中外文化的互动、交流与互鉴。在中国典籍翻译传播中注重保持中华文化主体地位可以增强中华文化自信,是"增强国家文化软实力的直接体现,也是现代性儒家哲学重新诠释的动力"(范敏,2019)。我们一定要树立文化自信,坚持文化自觉,从中西文明交流互鉴与促进世界文化繁荣的高度定位中华传统文化外译,促使中国典籍外译有力推动中外文化平等与文化交流。

当然，我们也要认识到，儒家文化在人性、个体与价值观等方面与西方文化中的自由、人权等思想存在很多差异。但是，这并不意味着儒家思想与现代人权思想的矛盾与不可调和。例如，《论语》文化维度中的仁爱思想、天人合一思想都非常具有普适性现代意义，尤其是对于当前的人文思想以及环境问题都具有重要的指导意义。安乐哲指出，"儒学其实更具包容性，它指的是一个社会阶级和世代对文化的传承，并非专指孔子这个人的生活和精神遗产。虽说文化典籍把儒学实践的'目标'确定为求'道'，事实上，'道'似乎更意味着一种有明确'方向'的世代传承转化的旅程，而不是某个'终点'"（杨朝明，2015）。因此，我们在翻译传播儒家文化时，需要对《论语》中的思想辩证地理解和诠释，对《论语》中的儒家文化还要创造性地转化与发展。

此外，在中国典籍的翻译传播过程中，我们还需要考虑社会历史环境与时代特征进行文化阐释，"因为人类文化都会随着自己所处的环境而发生改变，这就是《易经》所谓'穷则变，变则通，通则久'的'变易'之道，所以我们不仅要尊重变化和差异，也要对文化传统的延续性身份做出一个厚重的概括"（李文娟，2017）。此外，"每一代人都会选择一些思想先驱，按照自己的想象对其进行重新塑造。每一代人也会根据自己的需要重新建构世界哲学经典。我们也不可避免地处于特定的时空。就算是对中国哲学原典的谱系式、历史主义理解，我们也得承认受到了时空的限制"（杨朝明，2015）。

综上所述，中国儒家文化中的优秀价值观不仅影响着中国人的世界观与价值取向，也影响着世界对中国形象的认识。中国传统的儒家哲学具备一套与西方超验主义截然不同的思想体系，我们在翻译传播中国典籍中的儒家哲学理念时，需要正确理解中华传统文化的思想内涵，辨明西方传统对儒家哲学思想的误读。只有这样，才能真正走进儒家哲学。因此，在中国典籍对外传播中，我们要根据社会文化环境与时代特征，注重在中西比较哲学视野下增进中西文化对话。中国典籍翻译传播如何"既体现中国文化的民族特色和精神，又符合世界的审美观"(范敏,2019),成为中华传统文化走向世界所面临的问题。

(四)提高翻译传播水平

在当代国际交往中,一个国家的话语权与国际形象不仅依赖于政治、经济等实力,更取决于文化软实力与思想认同感。在当前中国崛起环境下,国际社会需要了解中国的价值观与文化理念。因此,提高翻译传播水平变得越发重要。

第一,一个国家政策所遵循的意识形态和文化理念,直接决定它的向心力和凝聚力。中华优秀传统文化一直是国际社会从文化层面认知中国、理解中国与欣赏中国的主要内容之一。当前,国家支持中华优秀传统文化走向国际化,以促进西方受众对中华文化的接受。中国典籍中所包含的中华优秀传统文化既具有民族性,又具有世界性,对世界文化产生了重要的影响。

在中国典籍翻译传播过程中,我们认识到中西文化差异不是障碍,而是创新的推动力。但是,当前中国典籍翻译传播存在的诸多问题,很多都可以归结于文化的问题。因此,我们需要提高翻译传播水平,不仅要把文化发展放在重要地位,把《论语》《道德经》等中国经典文化作为国家文化软实力建设的一部分,而且要注重儒家文化翻译传播的海外接受及其国际影响力。

第二,我们要不断加强对中国典籍中的儒家哲学的辨证吸收与现代阐释,进一步发掘儒家思想中潜在的创造力。中国典籍的翻译传播需要以传播中华优秀传统文化价值观为基础,只有这样,"才能有助于避免中国文化在西方国家遭受误读甚至曲解,有助于树立真实的中国形象"(刘云虹,2015)。也只有形成了明确、有力的中华传统文化价值观,中国典籍的翻译传播才能真正从文化交流与对话的意义上发挥作用。

习近平新时代中国特色社会主义思想和文化要求中国必须有自己的话语,必须建设属于自己的思想文化话语体系,其中必须贯穿具有马克思主义哲学高度的、具有颠扑不破的内在联系性和真理性的描述。这个要求将必然呼唤比较中西两大传统阐释的大视野,对比"一多不分"与"一多二元"两大文化语义环境,对人类的基本认识进行划分(卞俊峰,2019),从而进一步克服西方世界对今天"儒学"的误解与误读。

第三,需要关注中国典籍的翻译传播策略研究,即为提高中国典籍的影响力与受众接受度,译者作为主体应怎样选择、翻译与传播文化内容,从而有助于中华文化的传播与接受。提高翻译传播水平的重要内容还包括其他翻译传播主体如何借助翻译传播技术等途径向世界传播中华优秀文化、塑造良好国际形象以及提高受众接受等。例如,怎样加强国际话语体系建设,建构融通中外的新概念、新思想与新表述,传播好中华传统文化;怎样提升翻译水平,传播正能量,正确引导国外受众客观全面认识中华传统文化,促进中西跨文化沟通与交流;怎样进一步完善相关教育政策,推动翻译人才培养以提供人才支撑以及推动翻译理论创新以提供学术支撑等。

因此,我们要提高翻译传播水平,首先掌握儒家文化的精髓和核心概念,做到首先立足本国、本民族的文化,保持本国民族特色;然后再借助译者、媒介、政府、高校等各界力量使世界认识我们独特而具有一定普适性的中华文化,从而推动中华传统文化走向世界并与世界进行平等对话。

总之,中国典籍文化的翻译传播应以中国的国家利益和人类的共同利益为最高原则,强调与异域文化互利共赢、和谐共处、求同存异以及与政策、外交、技术与人才等相结合。随着跨文化交流的日益加深,越来越多的学者认识到中华优秀传统文化在促进世界文化交流中所发挥的独特作用。

(五)注重翻译传播内容

中国典籍翻译传播必须注重翻译传播内容,突出思想文化内涵。

中国典籍中蕴含着大量的优秀传统文化价值观。在跨文化传播过程中，应摒除传统文化的消极因素，创造性地吸收消化传统文化的内涵，把中国典籍中的优秀文化与人文精神传递到国外。

中国典籍文化博大精深，对国人的价值观、世界观、思维方式与为人处世都产生了重要影响。儒家文化中的天人合一的精神思想、自强不息的进取精神、以人为本的民本思想和止于至善的崇高追求，在当下中国治国理政、对外交往、参与全球治理等方面仍发挥着重要的价值引领作用。中华传统文化是人类文明的共同财富，对世界也会产生深远影响。因此，若要中华传统文化走向世界，译者需要发挥主体性作用，根据海外受众的情况与需求，采用世界性书写的途径，把其中的优秀文化内容准确、通达地介绍给海外受众，并能使海外受众乐于认可、接受中华文化。

在重释中国典籍文化内容时，译者要根据时代发展与文本特征采用中西融通的话语体系。我们需要根据中国典籍文本的最初产生历史语境，努力还原和厘清其历史文化价值内涵，选取那些具有世界价值的概念内容作出现代解读，使其为今所用，并在当今的文化语境中得到新的阐释和发展。正如每代人都会有选择地继承先哲的学术思想，并以自身的形象来重塑先哲，以自身的需要来重构古代经典。因此，中国典籍翻译传播的主体需要跨越时空，以文化自觉的途径去理解、传播中华优秀传统文化。

例如，安乐哲与罗思文运用文献学和哲学的研究方法，对《论语》中的哲学思想进行阐释，然后再把这一阐释背景应用到原典的哲学翻译中去，注重把一些关键词通过增加一些具有提示性的符号，帮助英语读者理解汉语。森舸澜运用文献学与认知语言学的研究方法，对关键词的翻译通过增加文化历史知识注释，帮助英语读者理解中国的哲学传统。译者借助大量历史考证与文献注疏，通过增加副文本，补充文化背景，尽量采用既能表达原文又能让英语读者容易接受的方式帮助读者理解原文。我们在译文中也能发现很多互参现象，这有助于读者理解文本内容与语篇内各部分之间的关联。对此,刘宓庆指出,除了把握语言交流中的语境、扩大交流中动态化的语义,"翻译理解还包括析出文本的'潜意识',即所谓次文本——co-text)。文本的词语、句子、语段的意义不仅是语境化的"、动态化的,而且是多层次的。这是因为意义处于这样一种联立的动态关系中可隐、可显、可半隐、可半显,从而使一个文本可能析出多层涵义、衍生出多重文本(刘宓庆,2012)。刘宓庆进一步指出译者对文本求证的重要性。

> 究竟哪一种解读比较贴近 SLT 的原意,一切取决于译者的悉心求证,包括:(i) 文本内证。文本内证是重要的文本解构分析法之一。在很多情况下文本是自释的,即文本内部的前后关联或交错关联。如作者在文本的前面解释了后面提出的问题(或相反)。交错关联也很常见,即文中存在或明或暗的互指(或预指 anaphora,即前面的部分可以解释后面的部分;或后指 cataphora 即后面的部分可以解释前面的部分)。(ii) 文本外证。文本外证是极重要的文本解读手段,其中包括:(a) 人文互证,即从研究"作者其人"来印证"其文"的真义:(b) 互文性(intertextuality),即将作者的若干著作进行对比来印证其文的真义;也指将此一文本与别的作者的作品进行比较研究以显示、论证其真义。(刘宓庆,2012)

由此可见,译者根据当代文化语境,做好中国典籍的考证、理解与现代阐释工作特别重要。我们还需要借助语言学、文体学、历史学、传播学、哲学等知识,从语义、句法、语篇、文体、修辞、文化及社会背景等多维度展开对中国典籍进行全方位解读和研究,以此发挥中国经典文化在世界文化建构中的重要作用,为中国典籍进一步走向世界奠定坚实基础。

此外,在内容信息量的选择上,译者可以根据读者水平与读者兴趣选择采用全译、节译法或者编译策略来实现。例如,译者可选取《论语》中耳熟能详的经典名句,通过故事漫画的形式、结合现代技术并突出时代特征,将中国传统的主要儒家思想介绍给初级读者,吸引更多的国内外普通读者,促进中华优秀传统文化的对外传播。

总之,文本的选择、诠释与翻译是一个开放与建构的过程。在中国典籍翻译传播过程中,原文不断被研究、诠释、解构与重构,促使原文与译文不断地碰撞、理解与融合。因此,我们需要把内容传达放在重要位置,充分考虑目标语国家的文化传统、文化语境及受众接受等因素,注重中华传统文化思想内涵的对外传播,依托高质量的经典翻译作品,实现中国典籍在西方世界的对话交流与融合。

(六)创新翻译传播途径

一个国家的文化影响力,不仅取决于该国文化的独特魅力,也取决于其强大的传播能力和先进的传播手段。尤其在当前信息化时代,创新翻译传播途径是中国典籍翻译传播的重要路径之一。

第一,译者需要有使命感与担当意识。译者要有全球视野,在当代和全球化的环境下作出重释,注重儒学思想"内圣外王"传播,在创新中发展儒家文化。"内圣"与"外王"是互为关联、内在统一与不可分割的关系。"内圣"需以天下为己任、必须敢于承当;"外王"要有全球视野与高境界的"内省、内圣"。注重儒学"内圣外王"思想,可以影响中华文化的创造性转化与创新性发展。

第二,拓宽中国典籍翻译传播学术交流渠道。学术交流是文化的重要载体,也是文化传播最有效的渠道。我国的高校、学术组织与文化单位等部门应集思广益,定期举办各种具有创新意识、主题鲜明与立意深远的国际学术研讨会或国际文化交流活动,通过学术交流推动中华文化"走出去"。

在国际学术交流中,学者需要用自己的独特思想与世界交流和对话,注重儒学传播的文化自信。如果儒学对外传播失去自信,就会失去其存在价值与意义。儒家哲学思想有其独特的文化魅力,是中华民族对社会人文进行长期探索和理性思考的结果,不仅是中华文明的宝贵精神财富,而且是世界文明的重要组成部分,对于促进中西文化交流起着重要作用。

我国的高校、学术组织与文化单位等部门还应积极组织、举办、参加媒体峰会、国际书展、国际文化节等跨文化交流活动,通过策划各种创新主题活动,加强与国内外出版机构和研究机构的交流与合作,努力构建国际学术与文化交流平台,进一步推动中国典籍翻译传播与海外接受,促进人类文明共同进步。

第三,提升信息技术环境下的国际输出创新能力。一个国家的文化影响力不仅取决于文化内容和表现形式是否具有独特魅力,而且取决于文化传播输出能力的强弱。以数字化、网络化为代表的现代信息技术推动了传播方式的巨大变革。国家要采取措施进一步创新翻译传播途径,充分利用互联网等现代传媒,推动跨文化传播与信息科技创新驱动发展,进一步增强中华文化的国际影响力。

只有推动中国典籍翻译传播途径的不断创新,才能使中华优秀传统文化理念和价值观念得到有效传播。这是因为,提升中华传统文化影响力,"并不只是一种对文化的宣传、包装与推广策略,而是一种文化的自我建构战略"(辛红娟,2009)。如果中国典籍传播的形式单一、内容不够有吸引力,受众较少,就达不到应有的翻译传播效果。

中华传统文化传播不仅可以通过中外译者合作与中外出版机构联合出版优质的中国典籍翻译版本,而且可以通过注重提升中华优秀传统文化的有效输出,充分利用各种传播媒介构建多元互补的翻译传播模式,充分利用新媒介和新技术助推国学典籍的翻译传播,以最大限度地提升翻译传播效果,从而提升中华传统文化的吸引力、国际竞争力和国际影响力。

中国典籍的出版需要有相关专业人士分工合作,在文字编辑、排版设计、插图制作等方面实现一体化与系统化。很多中国典籍纸质图书都可以采用电子文本形式进行保存以及在线或者线下销售。出版社或者书店等单位可以开发打造典籍文化创意产品开发销售一体化平台,力图实现从中国典籍元素提取到产品设计直至成品落地的全流程追踪,并通过线上与线下营销体系,既拓展文创产品的宣传和售卖覆盖面,又保证联盟文创品牌价值输出的连续性、统一性,让中国典籍变得时尚而且接地气,推动优秀文化产品的市场转化。

此外,以互联网为代表的现代高新技术在中华传统文化传播方面蕴藏着巨大潜能。例如,中华传统文化的翻译传播可以通过展览中国典籍,运用静态图文+投影互动等科技手段,向人们展示中国古籍的考证、整理、译介、出版等工作取得的重要成果。中华传统文化的海外接受需要借助有效的媒介传播途径和手段才能实现,如借助海内外网络媒体、社交媒体、传统平媒(电视、电台、报纸)以及在线教学国际平台(Coursera、Udacity、edX)等。在新媒体融合大背景下,我们可以在传统阅读的基础上,通过学习强国、超星学习通、网络学习、微信公众号、听书等途径来加强中华传统文化的传播,也可以把典籍改编成电影、歌剧、音乐剧、戏剧、卡通漫画等方式传播中国典籍,让不同层次的外国受众以直接、有效的方式来了解中华传统文化。我们还可以不断建筑与完善中国儒学特色网络文化网站,增加英文版网站,充分运用先进科学技术拓展中华传统文化的传播渠道,增强中华传统文化的影响力。

我们可以借鉴现有信息化技术进一步建构完善数字化工程,如借鉴"中华思想文化术语术语库"(http://www.chinesethought.cn/TermBase.aspx),建构中国典籍术语库,聘请权威专家制定中华思想文化术语、遴选、释义、翻译规则,邀请知名汉学家参与英译文审稿工作。中国典籍术语库可汇聚中国典籍中具有中华传统文化特征和民族思维方式,以及体现中国核心价值的思想文化术语,用易于口头表达交流的简练语言客观准确诠释,便于受众理解接受。同样借鉴"儒家经典数据库"(http://db.chinakongzi.org/index.php?m=books&c=source)与儒家文化数字馆(http://dp.chinakongzi.org)的思路,利用科技创新进一步建设完善中国典籍数据库和中国典籍文化数字馆等。此外，还可以借助科技创新提升《论语》《道德经》等中国典籍文化产业的品牌效应，开发相应的图书软件、新媒体图画书与各类虚拟现实技术互动体验功能，全方位、多模态地呈现中国典籍内容，吸引更多国外受众，以提升中国文化软实力。

第四，推进中华传统文化体制改革创新。政府要努力推进中华传统文化体制改革，需要转变体制机制，同时也要解放思想、转变观念。政府要加快中华传统文化体制改革，这成为促进中华传统文化发展与繁荣、增强国家文化软实力、激发中华传统文化对外传播生机活力以及形成中华传统文化"走出去"可持续动力的迫切要求。

深化中华传统文化体制改革创新的基本思路是把公益性的中华传统文化事业与经营性的中华传统文化产业区分开来，通过国家政策使文化事业与文化产业相互促进。政府不仅要发展公益性文化事业，还要促进传统文化产业发展。政府不仅要构建公共文化服务体系，引导社会资金投入公共文化事业，同时也要努力完善市场体系，在实践中开拓创新，积极推动文化产品的内容创新与形式创新。强大而有竞争力的文化产业和公共文化事业应成为增强国家文化软实力的重要载体。例如，我们可以发展中国典籍文化产业，如图书出版业、动漫产业、电影业、文化旅游业以及完善孔子学院建设等措施。我们可以在科学评估与市场调研的基础上确定这些文化产业的营销策略和销售渠道，推进市场化的对外传播机制建设。我们要努力构建传输快捷、覆盖面广的中国典籍文化传播体系，促进中国典籍的文化产业与公共文化事业的创新发展，打造具有核心竞争力的创新文化产品和文化市场格局。

第五，充分发挥社会团体的力量。我们不仅要发挥国家、政府、高校的作用，而且要发挥文化单位、民间团体和企业单位的作用，进一步构建完善的中国典籍翻译传播体系，借助中国典籍中优秀文化的传播使中国成为文化强国。要大力提升中华传统文化教育，开展提升中华传统文化的软实力教育工作；把主流文化价值与民族精神融为一体并将其内化为自身需要,推动中华优秀文化内化为民族素质,提高人们的人文素质内涵,促进全民族素质的提高,以此增强人们对民族文化和国家文化的认同,凝聚人们对中华优秀传统文化的统一认识,并进一步以国外受众能接受的方式使其理解中国典籍所体现的社会文化价值观。

(七) 提高翻译传播效果

翻译传播效果是指译文通过一定的媒介渠道到达译入语受众后,所引起受众思想和行为的变化。受众是中国典籍翻译传播的接受主体和反馈主体。受众的接受情况是检验中华传统文化对外传播效果的重要衡量标准。中国典籍的翻译传播受众反馈在很大程度上反映了其翻译传播效果。

英国传播学家麦奎尔把传播效果模式分为六类:(1) 按照传者与受者的意图和动机不同,传播效果可分为预期效果和非预期效果。(2) 按照时间层次不同,传播效果可分为长期效果和短期效果。(3) 按照外在形态不同,传播效果可分为传媒效果(media effects)、传媒效能(media effectiveness)与传媒效力(media power)。(4) 按照效果的内在性质不同,传播效果可分为心理效果、文化效果、政治效果与经济效果等。(5) 按照传媒影响力的作用范围,传播效果可分为对受众个体的影响、对小团体和组织的影响、对社会机构的影响和对整个社会及整个文化的影响。(6) 按照传播效果的种类,传播效果可分为受众个体主动有意或被动无意的反应、传媒群的社会动员、新闻传播、创新和文明传播、知识传播等。另外,传播效果各层次和取向之间是彼此相联与共存互动的关系(Mcquail,1996)。

由此可见,传播效果模式不同,受众接受效果也存在一定差异。提高中国典籍的翻译传播效果需重视受众的接受反馈,通过提高受众接受度来加强中华传统文化形象在国际社会的理解与认知,从而保证中国典籍翻译传播取得良好效果。

翻译传播效果反馈可以通过设计标准在线问卷调查以及实地调

研等获得对中国典籍翻译传播海外接受情况的反馈。在线问卷的调查内容涵盖调查受众的身份、年龄、性别、学历、从事笔译工作年限、主要翻译领域以及调查受众对中国典籍译本的案例评析、译者策略选择以及对翻译传播影响力等参数的选择与建议等。问卷调查设计需要注意尽量设计中、英两个语言版本,也就是说,不仅考虑海外的中国受众,也要考虑海外的外国受众。此外,还要明确受众是普通受众还是专业性受众。受众不同,所采用的翻译策略必然有所不同。要尽可能保证在线网络调查的信效度,保证受试者提供信息的真实性以及受试者的信息如年龄、职业、教育背景、语言能力、经验积累与出国经历等参数的同质性。

根据 2018 年中国外文局的在线问卷调查《中国话语海外认知度调研报告》,当前海外民众对中国话语的认知度、理解度大幅上升,一些中华传统文化词语以汉语拼音的形式进入英语话语体系,如"孔子""老子""阴阳"等。这说明随着中国的先贤思想越来越深刻地影响世界,中国人的思维与话语方式也正在悄然影响、改变着世界。中国道路和中国方案也得到越来越多理解和认同,如"中国梦""一带一路""命运共同体""中国道路"。此外,2018 年当代中国与世界研究院开展的在线问卷调查《中国国家形象全球调查》发现,中国的国家形象仍然以历史悠久、充满魅力著称,而且"人类命运共同体"等中国方案与治国理念对全球发展都大有益处,从而进一步展示了新时代的中国形象。因此,为了提高中国典籍在外国的受众接受度,需要注重中华传统文化在国际交流中的传播效果。

由此可见,翻译传播活动是在特定时空与特定的社会语境中进行的。传播过程中的各种要素,如社会环境、受众接受、心理特点、传播内容、译者策略、国际输出能力等,都会对翻译传播效果以及受众反馈产生影响。社会环境在某种意义上也可以说是一种生态环境,是由原文本、原语言与目的语言构成的世界,包括翻译的语言、交际、文化与社会等层面,以及作者、赞助商与读者等互联互动的整体,强调生态平衡与适应选择等理念

(胡庚申,2013)。不同的生态环境会对翻译传播产生不同的影响。

在当前,随着中国经济的发展,中国在国际的影响也逐渐增强。中国的国际化过程与中国的改革开放过程使翻译传播成为国际社会不同文化交流最有吸引力的部分。在此情况下,西方受众对中国信息的需求也逐渐凸显出来。一方面,西方受众需要了解中国的文化、思路与价值观,这些都对翻译传播提出了要求;另一方面,中国典籍中的传统特色文化与价值观的成功传播与有效接受,都需要翻译传播主体的努力。而翻译传播质量的高低会直接影响国际社会对中国形象、中国观点与中国声音的认识。

在此情况下,中国典籍的翻译传播工作也应与时俱进,尽可能考虑翻译传播反馈及其效果,采用中外融通的翻译话语表达,提高英语受众对中华传统文化的接受能力,加强中华优秀传统文化与世界的对话。翻译传播主体应该形成合力,根据中西受众差异,针对海外受众群体,对中国典籍中具有中国特色的儒家哲学思想采用相应翻译传播策略,善用外国受众容易接受的方式,帮助他们了解与体验中华文化,并助力中华文化走向世界。

提高中国典籍受众接受能力是提高翻译传播效果与获得反馈的重要措施。受众接受能力是指译文通过一定的媒介渠道到达受众后,受文化程度、欣赏水平、审美习惯、民族心理等因素的影响,受众在接收译文过程中产生的能否接受和接受多少的限度。翻译作为交际行为是一种双向的动态过程,如果交际双方的个人因素(如受教育程度、文化背景、时代因素)、交际双方的因素(如共有知识、彼此认可程度)和交际的社会背景与场合等不一致,那么交际目的就可能出现障碍。Widdowson(1990)指出,语篇的意义不在于语篇本身,而在于受话者对语篇的理解,是以受话者为中心的。因此,语篇交际功能的实现在很大程度上依赖于发出者与接收者双方的共同努力。

因此,在国际寻求融通发展与对话交流的背景下,翻译传播主体应以文化传播与交流沟通为己任,尊重中国典籍翻译传播规律,考虑中西文化差异与受众认知差异,在新时代语境背景下探讨中国典籍的翻译传播与海外接受。这不仅包括中国典籍为什么能够生存、发展与创新,而且包括为了能够让西方受众能够读到具有原文语言文化特色而且地道的译文,翻译传播主体应该怎样建构中国典籍译语话语权,怎样根据社会文化语境提高中国典籍的翻译传播效果反馈,从而让西方受众能够更加容易接受中国的传统文化。

此外,为了提高中国典籍翻译传播效果反馈,加强国际输出传播能力也是十分重要的。在当代国际交往中,国家之间成功的跨文化交流不仅取决于中西文化思想的相互融合,还取决于文化思想在异域国家的理解和接受。中华文化"走出去"以及能走多远,在很大程度上取决于翻译传播主体的素养和对对方文化的了解程度。翻译传播主体的翻译传播能力常常影响着中国的文化、形象与声音是否能被国际社会成功接受。为了在国际交往中促进中外融通与文化交流,中国典籍翻译传播主体应借助现代传媒手段,努力构建中西融通的翻译传播话语体系,采用受众容易接受的翻译传播策略,把中华优秀传统文化思想翻译传播到国外。在信息化时代,应用翻译传播技术在很大程度上有助于提高中国典籍的翻译传播效果。

总之,在信息化时代,中国典籍的翻译传播主体、翻译传播途径和翻译传播能力等已经成为中华传统文化对外传播与国家文化软实力提升的重要影响参数。因此,我们要借助译者、高校、国家、政府、企业与社会等众多力量,创新翻译传播路径,提高中国典籍翻译传播质量。此外,我们要重视中国典籍信息媒体传播能力建设,扩大中国典籍的文化学术交流,促进产业发展与出版销售,借助中国典籍翻译传播的文化软实力的作用,让中华优秀传统文化走向国际。

四、中国典籍翻译传播人才培养模式创新

中国典籍翻译传播质量高低影响国际社会对中华文化的理解,因

此加强中国典籍翻译人才和国际传播人才队伍培养可为提高中国典籍翻译质量提供有力支撑。当前高质量的中国典籍翻译传播人才缺乏。虽然很多院校开设了翻译专业或者相关课程,着力培养复合型翻译人才,但相对翻译传播人才需求而言,课程设置、培养理念以及教学方法等仍然需要不断探索与创新。当前中国典籍翻译传播的人才培养需要遵循能力导向OBE(outcome based education)的翻译教育培养理念,不断探索创新的人才培养模式,以适应"面向现代化、面向全球化、面向未来"的要求。笔者基于中国典籍翻译传播人才的培养模式,探讨此类人才的培养理念、培养路径和培养效果评价等内容。

(一) 培养理念

优秀的中国典籍翻译传播人才培养是当前教育界面临的重要任务。教师在设计与实施教学时,应注重培养具有良好的专业素养、人文素养、技术素养(cf. 范敏,2016/2018)以及具有较强的翻译能力、跨文化传播能力与信息技术传播能力的复合型翻译人才,能站在世界文化、民族文化和跨文化全局以及思想文化创新的高度审视中国典籍译介工作,并能以良好的理性态度、宏阔的学术视野和较高翻译传播能力适应当前的多元文化环境。

1. 专业素养

专业素养的培养主要是指,我们在培养中国典籍翻译传播人才时,要注重他们对专业知识技能的掌握以及获取专业知识的素质与能力。在全球化时代,中国典籍翻译传播人才的专业素养不仅包括对翻译学知识的掌握应用程度,而且包括对传播学等知识的掌握应用程度。

翻译学知识的熟练掌握是中国典籍翻译传播人才专业素养的重要组成部分,是经过长期翻译教育与实践过程发展而成的具有专门性、指向性与指导性的翻译知识体系。优秀的译者应该具有多方面的专业素养(Chan, 1995; Baker, 1998; Shuttleworth, 2004; 孙迎春,

1999；王宏印，2006)，如对所译作品有深入的理解，对目标语语言和文化的良好把握，对审美、道德、文学批评等方面的良好修养等。优秀的中国典籍翻译传播人才不仅需要精通译出语与译入语语言及其相互转化能力，而且需要掌握翻译理论、跨文化传播理论、古典文献文化理论、古代汉语、现代汉语等精深的专业知识；不仅对原文能够进行正确理解、批评与鉴赏，而且能够准确地表达原文的语言与文化内涵，如此才能将中华优秀传统文化有效地传递给国外受众。

翻译理论的职能在翻译传播者的专业素养中的作用也是不容忽视的。翻译理论的职能可以分为认知职能、执行职能与校正职能(刘宓庆，2005)。认知职能也就是翻译理论的启蒙作用，能对翻译规律进行深入、系统的探讨，其目的在于使翻译只能"神而明之"的技能和技巧成为可知的客体、可掌握的规范和条理化的体系。执行职能也就是翻译的能动性和实践性，能指导译者凭借翻译理论的科学论证及方法论的引导，在实践中有选择地"实施"翻译理论所提供的"参照性指令"。校正职能也就是翻译理论的规范性、指导性，这与前两个职能都是相关的，而且翻译理论的对策性既体现了其实施职能，又体现了其校正职能。由此可见，系统的翻译理论知识有助于译者认识、掌握和运用翻译规律，并与实践相结合，有效提升翻译实践能力。

此外，优秀的翻译传播者还应具备较强的跨文化传播能力，能借助适当的机会、通过适当的传播途径有效地对外传播中国典籍。具有中国特色的中国典籍如果要进入国际文化市场，则需要依靠文化产品的价值。因此，译者需要认识到中国典籍作为文化品牌对外传播的重要作用，而且需要掌握一定的传播学知识，如跨文化传播的意义、功能、类型、内容、受众与效果等知识。译者需要通过不断主动学习传媒类学科知识、现代国际新闻传播教育等专业知识，熟悉国际传播形势以及文化传播力途径，不断完善知识结构，进而提升自身翻译传播能力，包括语言转换能力、跨文化传播能力与公众演讲能力，以满足中华优秀传统文化对外传播的需要。

2. 人文素养

人文素养的培养主要是指在培养中国典籍翻译传播人才时注重培养他们的道德素养、人生价值观以及文化修养等。

首先,中国典籍翻译传播人才应有底线思维,具备较高的道德素养。《国家中长期教育改革和发展规划纲要(2010—2020年)》指出,坚持以人为本、推进素质教育是教育改革发展的战略主题,是贯彻党的教育方针的时代要求;坚持德育为先。道德素养需要教师在教学过程中进行有意识的培养。这需要教师研究教育理论思想,通过思政教学让学生认识到中国典籍及其翻译传播的重要性。当然,道德人文素养可在翻译教育过程中不断进行改造、重组与提升,译者可通过大量翻译实践如《论语》《道德经》《尚书》等中国典籍的知识学习与翻译实践来提高个人的社会道德觉悟与翻译能力。当面临道德和价值观之间的抉择时,译者能够作出正确判断,自觉抵制与修正各种不良信息。

其次,中国典籍翻译传播人才应具有正确的价值观。学生可以通过翻译工作坊、专题讨论等各种活动来培育志趣情怀;通过分工合作,弥补性格差异,了解自己与他人,并通过翻译作品与译文比较鉴赏等活动影响和改变自己和他人在实际生活中的人生观与价值观。学生还可以通过准时上课签到、按时在超星学习通系统提交作业,积极参与互评等学习活动培养担当精神与人文素养。这样,中国典籍翻译传播人才的培养不仅着重提高学生的翻译传播能力,更注重将爱国主义和担当精神教育融入教学全过程,在教学育人过程中加强学生的家国情怀教育、人类命运共同体等的教育,增强学生的自信和担当意识。

第三,优秀的中国典籍翻译传播人才需要具备较强的跨文化传播能力与人际交往能力。在教育信息化时代,信息技术的进步加速了跨文化交际的发展。由于中西文化差异,人们对异域社会价值的认同会有所不同。忽视东西语言文化差异的交际可能导致跨文化交际的失败,引发政治、意识形态、道德观念的碰撞、冲突与融合等问题。因此,全球化时代中国典籍翻译传播人才的跨文化交际能力的培养需要经历三个阶段。初级阶段:能够熟悉不同文化背景人士的文化特征与交往方式,学会比较、分析与评价文化差异。中级阶段:能够具有海纳百川的积极态度,摒弃文化偏见,尊重并接受多元文化群体的宗教信仰、习俗行为与价值观,用客观的态度进行跨文化交流;高级阶段:能够具有正确的价值观与优秀的跨文化思辨能力,能够从中西文化互鉴的角度翻译传播《论语》《道德经》《尚书》等中国经典,能与国际翻译家沟通与交流,了解他们翻译策略背后所蕴含的哲学思想,解决中西跨文化传播过程中的具体问题。

简言之,中国典籍翻译传播人才的人文素养的培养任重而道远,需要注重道德素养、人生价值观、跨文化思辨能力与跨文化沟通能力的培养,注重"典籍文化素养+道德素养+跨文化能力"的结合,并能够以理性的态度和灵活的思辨能力适应多元的文化环境。

3. 信息技能素养

在教育信息化时代,随着信息技术的应用,知识更新速度越来越快,信息技能素养已成为信息化时代人们需要具备的基本能力。信息技能素养的培养是指在培养中国典籍翻译传播人才时注重培养学生的信息技术能力,如信息搜索、语料库建设与新媒体传播技能等,以培养他们的职业翻译能力。

教师通过课程设计,注重在教学过程中利用网络与超星学习通平台等在线资源传授课程知识。学生在学习专业知识的同时,可以不断增强信息检索能力与超文本阅读能力,掌握使用网络通信工具获取资料的途径、方法和重要性,提升网络认知能力、信息判断能力和逻辑推理能力。学生还可以借助超星学习通等在线资源与信息技术工具掌握翻译市场所要求的翻译技术持续发展的学习能力,能主动地从社会生活中不断地查找、探究新信息,能够将新信息与原有的翻译知识体系进行融合,扩充自己的知识库,最大限度地发挥自己所掌握信息的效益,能够在各种情境下理智自信地运用信息解决各种翻译问题。学生还要掌握计算机辅助翻译软件的使用,如应用计算机辅助翻译工具与语料库工具等进行翻译实践与数据分析等。柴明颎(2010)指出:"对专业翻译工作者来说,除掌握翻译所使用的两种或两种以上工作语言之外,还必须熟悉与翻译业务相关的知识。除此之外,译者还必须了解翻译流程、项目管理、职业操守,以及与翻译相关的其他知识和技能。"此外,中国典籍翻译传播人才还需具有较强的创新意识和进取精神,能够通过信息技术进行引领性的翻译研究,通过互联网与海外中国典籍汉学专家积极进行联系,提高持续开展科研探索的能力。

因此,学校可以借助现代化翻译技术教育平台,创建良好的教育环境,改革传统的中国典籍翻译传播人才培养思路,培养具有较强的专业素养、人文素养、信息技能素养,能借助利用现代教育技术手段从事中国典籍翻译传播工作的高端复合型人才。

总之,为了提高国家文化软实力,我们应该重视中国典籍翻译传播人才的国际化培养,思考中国典籍翻译传播人才适应对外传播需要所应具备的人才素质。结合当前信息化时代特征、文化战略以及对外传播市场的需求,中国典籍翻译传播人才的培养需要从专业素养、人文素养与信息技能素养等方面考量,注重翻译能力、跨文化传播能力以及职业能力的培养。

(二) 培养路径

在信息化时代,现代信息技术融入教学。中国典籍翻译传播教学需围绕中国文化"走出去"的战略大局,科学设计课程、创新教学手段,努力培养优秀的中国典籍翻译传播人才。为此,高校的中国典籍翻译传播教学需要做到与时俱进,通过拓展人才培养路径,实施素质教育和实用技能教育,培养适应社会竞争以及具有应用型、创新型、复合型的高素质翻译传播人才。下文主要从课程建设、课堂教学与政校企协同育人三个层面进行分析。

1. 课程建设

为了提升学生的翻译传播能力与综合素养,让学生掌握信息化时代所应具备的"跨文化＋人文素养＋专业素养＋信息化素养＋传播能力",中国典籍翻译传播课程的建设主要包括课程设计理念、课程规划方案与课程设置内容等方面。

首先,教师在课程体系设计时需要按照"一致性建构"等教学理念,在构建翻译课程体系,确定教学方法,开展教学评价时都需认真思考和科学设计,以建设高质量的中国典籍翻译传播课程。教师通过线上与线下构建中国典籍翻译课程目标与学习活动、学习测评等各要素之间的一致性,让学生明确自己应该学什么,怎样学以及达到怎样的标准;并通过在教学过程中精心设计课程教学愿景,通过思政教育提高学生的人文素养与人格培养,引领学生成长,让学生认识到学习该课程的重要性,全面提高学生的翻译能力与传播能力。

其次,中国典籍翻译传播课程的规划需要根据学校人才培养特点与教学目标,依据教育心理学,规划课程实施方案。教师可根据社会需求,借助智慧教育技术,认真分析教学情境,包括课程性质、学生特点、课程体系、本校的教学要求以及国家社会的人才培养要求,根据当前教育信息化时代特点与市场需求,在专业课程设置时遵循多元化、专业化、系统化等原则,注重通过经典文化课程提高学生的人文素养。中国典籍翻译传播专业的各课程之间应有一定的相关性、连续性和层级性,使教学培养理念、课程内容、教学资源在教学系统中更好地得到优化,从而达到整体提升教学质量的功效。

最后,根据课程建设原则,结合当前市场对高素质典籍翻译传播人才的需求,中国典籍翻译传播课程设置内容如下:

(1) 文体翻译课程:文体翻译课程在于培养学生对各类文体特征的认识,掌握各类文体翻译的原则与方法、语篇翻译的交际功能与翻译策略,提高学生的翻译能力。授课内容可包括(但不限于):翻译专题、典籍翻译、文学翻译、公关文献翻译、新闻翻译、政府及公共事务翻译、大众传媒翻译、广告翻译、高级双语翻译与写作。

(2) 典籍文化素养课程:《国家中长期教育改革和发展规划纲要

(2010—2020年)》强调要坚持以人为本、推进素质教育,坚持德育为先,把德育渗透于教育教学的各个环节,把优秀的社会道德价值体系融入国民教育全过程,如中华传统社会文化课程("中华优秀传统文化""中西经典文化""经典文化赏析")、中华传统文化翻译传播课程、文化百科知识课程、英美社会与文化课程、跨文化交际课程等。

(3)典籍翻译技术课程:该课程旨在帮助学生掌握有利于中国典籍翻译传播的翻译技术,如通过搜索技术查询有关语料库网站如"语料库在线",借鉴现有的一些汉英平行语料库在线,英国国家语料库(British National Corpus,简称BNC)等网站,探索《论语》等中国典籍翻译语料库的在线建设路径等。授课内容可包括(但不限于):语料库知识、语料库构建、术语管理、搜索技术、团队协作等。

(4)传播学课程:传播学课程旨在帮助学生学习中国及全球媒体的理论与实践,批判分析媒介在不同社会及语境下的角色。通过理论课程的思维训练,学生应努力成为具有良好的文化素养、理论修养与跨学科知识结构,掌握系统的新闻学、传播学知识与较强的表达能力,能够分析社交媒体与现代社会的复杂互动,同时具备国际视野和交流能力,推动中国典籍翻译传媒事业走向世界的优秀人才。授课内容可包括(但不限于)传播学研究理论与方法、媒体导论、国际传播、跨文化传播研究以及新媒体、文化与社会等课程。

总之,我们必须从中国典籍翻译传播人才培养目标、中国典籍翻译课程设计以及中国典籍翻译课程评价等各个环节和要素着手,进行系统的、整体的建设与改革,通过系统的教学大纲设计与教学计划培训,真正促进中国典籍翻译传播课程建设的逐步完善。

2. 课堂教学

中国典籍翻译传播课堂教学需要有卓有成效的教学方法,才能将自己的知识有效地转化为学生的知识,取得理想的教学效果。教师在教学过程中可以结合现代教育理念采用以下教学方法:

首先,教师依据美国教育心理学家布鲁纳提出的四个原则——动机原则、结构原则、程序原则与强化原则(Bruner,1961)以及澳大利亚教育心理学家比格斯(Biggs and Tang,2011)提出的一致性建构原则,思考教学目标、教学愿景与教学课程之间的关系,以中国典籍翻译传播为主线建设相关在线课程资源,优化课程目标,设计与教学目标一致的学习活动与学习测评建构的一致性。

动机原则主要是指教师的引导作用,关注学生的强烈的学习动机,注意为学生设计最适当的学习环境与最合适的学习策略。教师要充分认识自己在教育中的地位和作用,要富有责任感。教师需要重视教育的目的与社会作用,因为它对教育的性质、内容和途径都具有决定性的意义。例如,教师可以通过课堂思政教育,让学生通过中华传统文化的学习,了解儒家的德育过程大致分为知、情、意、行四个阶段,儒家的教育目的在于"大学之道,在明明德,在亲民,在止于至善"。儒家的教育思想是以道德教育为中心的,在孔子看来,"据于德"方能"游于艺","行有余力"而后"则以学文"。学生通过学习儒家文化可以陶冶道德情感,可以知仁、知礼、知道。

结构原则主要是指教师需要具备有效的资源整合及应用能力。儒家教育重在学以致用,强调将已学的知识应用于实践,以达真知。学生在学习过程中,注重"博学而笃志,切问而近思,仁在其中矣"(《论语·子张》)。在教学过程中,教师可有效利用各种线上与线下信息资源,将教育教学过程与信息技术应用相结合,为学生构建高效灵活的课堂学习环境。例如,教师可创建教学科研"云"环境与中国典籍网络学习平台,利用共享教育资源库,实现网络协作互动交流。

程序原则是指教师在教学过程中应分析教学情境,注意设计、选择最佳教学程序使学生能够顺利掌握中国典籍的相关翻译传播知识与技能。我们在教学中要循序渐进,"循循然善诱之"(《论语·子罕》)。孔子教导学生凡事要循序渐进。孔子曾自述自己学习与修养不断提高的过程是随着年龄增长思想境界不断提高的过程。教师在教学中可以依据程序原则,设置教学愿景与学生学习目标,让学生有自主学习的动力,循序渐进帮助学生掌握英语基本功、中西文化常识、英汉互译转换技巧、文体翻译分类与中国典籍的翻译传播策略。

强化原则是指教师在教学过程中利用超星学习通等教学软件,通过练习、测试等形式使学生强化自己的学习结果,如"学而时习之,不亦说乎?"(《论语·学而》),"温故而知新,可以为师矣"(《论语·为政》),"敏而好学,不耻下问"(《论语·公冶长》)。学生通过反复实践不仅可以提高自身翻译能力,还可以通过不断反思与有效及时总结调整自身翻译理念和方法,提高自身翻译水平与中国典籍对外译介策略。

一致性建构原则强调深层次的、高质量的学习应该是学生自己建构知识的过程(Biggs and Tang,2011)。教师应充分发挥引导作用,在课程设计时,在分析教学情境的基础上明确该课程的预期学习目标,再紧扣这一目标设计相应的学习活动和学习测评。"学习目标—学习活动—学习测评"的一致性建构是课程设计的质量保障。通过学习目标、学习活动与学习测评的系统化使学生树立远大目标,增强学习使命感,做好职业规划,进一步提高学习动力。具体而言,就中国典籍翻译课程设计来说,学习目标描述学生在该课程结束后可以获得相应的人文素养、中华传统文化知识与较强的职业翻译能力。在学习过程中,如翻译工作坊与小组讨论等各种学习活动应服务于这些学习目标,以调动学生的互动和参与,提高学生的学习效率。学生的学习评价应以形成性评价为主,结合诊断性评价与终结性评价,帮助教师与学生本人跟踪学生的学习情况,了解学生在实现既定学习目标方面所取得的进展情况,能够达到与该课程目标相符的学习评价,从而促进学生的身心成长与能力提升。

其次,课程思政教育可以潜移默化提升学生的思想高度,让他们认识到这门课的实用价值与现实意义,帮助他们更加系统进行职业规划,更加具有远大志向、拼搏精神与团队精神。教师在课程中通过思政教育,让学生更加喜爱这门课程以及与这门课程相关的内容。例如,学生通过学习分析中国典籍译文背后的中西文化差异,开阔学术视野,学会接触不一样的价值观点与思想认识;通过中国典籍翻译鉴赏逐渐树立正确的人生观与价值观,锤炼学生的毅力品格,还可通过各种翻译活动改变影响他人的态度,学会坚忍、稳重、乐观向上,从而提高自身的学习能力与沟通能力。

教师还可通过分析教学情景因素与教学目标,注重启发式教学,让学生通过思考社会需求、学校教育培养要求与所学课程之间的关系,鼓励学生理论联系实际,提高学生的思辨能力以及自我成长能力等。在信息化时代,教师可借助形式多样的信息化教学手段帮助学生认识提高翻译能力、应用能力以及学以致用能力的重要性。例如,教师可利用网络教学平台进行师生间的答疑互动交流。教师可在超星学习通资料库上传《论语》《道德经》《尚书》等译文评析、译者资料及相关作品资料,要求学生在学习通讨论区回答问题;学生在学习通作业平台上传相关作业,与老师、同学进行互动反馈等。这样,学生借助学习通、多媒体等电子资源,进一步掌握系统的翻译学知识、接受美学知识以及传播学知识,进一步提升人文素养、专业素养与技术素养,为他们将来从事翻译传播实践打下良好基础。

教师在教学思政教育的过程中,还要注意对待学生的态度,如人格尊重,因材施教,注重启发引导等,把学生的学习努力看作成才的关键条件。孔子曾说,"不愤不启,不悱不发。举一隅不以三隅反,则不复也"(《论语·述而》),教师要让学生懂得"学而不思则罔,思而不学则殆"(《论语·为政》),学会"博学于文,约之以礼"(《论语·雍也》)。

最后,课程设计需要注重突出以"学"为中心的教学理念,通过促进学生全面主动学习的策略,如头脑风暴、探究式学习、翻译真实项目、随堂学习报告等,提高学生的学习主动性,提升学生的主动学习效果。

学生拥有自主学习权,对于他们在自己的成功中发挥着重要作用。因此,如何调动学生的学习积极性,提升学生的学习动力至关重要。教师应给学生创造更多互相学习、共同学习的机会,设计、丰富学生的学习实践活动。在当前教育信息化时代,教师需要结合现代教育技术与在线教学平台,充分利用在线智慧教学系统辅助翻译教学,设计学生的翻译工作坊、小组协作主题讨论、拓展练习等翻译教学活动。当教师"注意以下这两方面时,好的小组活动经历才更有可能产生:小组动力和小组任务以及结构的设计"(玛丽埃伦·韦默,2006)。因此,教师设置奖惩标准与考核评价标准,对于促进学生学习以及提升学生的综合能力至关重要。教师要注重从学生的学习目标维度选择翻译测评方法,系统结合多种测评方法和测评任务,兼顾形成性测评与终结性测评,注重测评方案的科学性与有效性,并通过结合学生测评与教师点评促进学生的主动学习,提高学生的学习成效。此外,教师还要精心设计小组话题与小组实施途径,通过创造学习氛围鼓励学生积极参与课堂互动、小组任务等活动,提升学生在中国典籍翻译传播学习过程中的体验,提高学生的思辨能力。

下文主要以两项教学活动翻译工作坊与翻译作业为例,结合学生以"学"为主的教学方法探讨。

第一,翻译工作坊。翻译工作坊是学生在教师指导下,按照研究兴趣分组,完成某一专题的课堂展示。每组课堂展示时间一般为10～25分钟。"教师鼓励学生的课堂展示内容与其毕业论文的研究课题相关,这样有助于激发他们学习、研究的积极性,达到事半功倍的学习效果。翻译工作坊可以把传统的以老师'教'为主的课堂教学转变为以学生'学'为主的课堂教学"(范敏,2020)。

学生参加翻译工作坊,通过与小组同学一起研讨,聆听其他参加研讨的人的意见,学会用不同的眼光看待世界,这样有助于学生发现新的观点。学生通过课下研讨、课堂积极展示与教师点评等活动会认识到各种问题、课题或主题的偶然性、复杂性和模糊性,坚定他们的持续思考与研究。学生在老师的指导下学习 Peter Newmark(1981/1988、1991)、Neubert(1992)、Katharina Reiss(1989/2000)等人的理论,鼓励学生按照不同文体类型进行分组讨论。再基于 Anna Trosborg(1997)、Hatim 与 Mason(1990)、Hatim 与 Munday(2004)、Kelly(2008)等人的观点,教师可以鼓励学生们在翻译过程中思考以下问题:(1)语篇类型在理解翻译过程的优势是什么?译者是如何在翻译实践中处理语篇类型的?(2)在跨语言文化中,语篇类型在何种程度及何种范围上等同?原语篇与译语篇比较时有何相似性与差异性?这样从语篇翻译类型与语篇功能视角切入,有助于学生们根据语篇类型宏观把握翻译策略,提高语篇类型分析能力。老师通过启发式引导,帮助学生通过主动构建知识、自主个性化学习与接受反馈提升翻译能力。同时,学生在学习翻译理论以及翻译实践的过程中还要认识到理论与实践的关系"并不限于指导与被指导的关系,理论对实践还有描述、解释、规范、启发和预测的作用;世上并不存在放之四海而皆准的翻译理论,每一种具体的翻译理论都来自于与之相关的特定的翻译活动及其结果,因此每一种翻译理论都有其时空上的局限性"(曹明伦,2019)。

学生基于语篇类型翻译理论,根据自己的研究兴趣,可分成以下一些主题小组:(1)信息型语篇:如有关《论语》翻译的新闻报道、官方文件、教材、论文、报告等。其主要功能强调"真实性",通常用不带个人特色的现代语言写成,所以比较客观。在翻译此类文体时,译者应准确全面地译出原语篇的内容,并且译文风格的选择也应遵循目标语言文化的主流规范。(2)表情型语篇:如有关《论语》翻译的权威性言论以及相关自传、散文及个人信函等。其主要功能是说话者或作者运用这些话语表达其思想感情,可对读者产生一定的美学效果。在翻译时应忠实地传达原作的思想内容,同时还应保留原作中带有作者个人风格的文体语言特征,以传达原作风格。(3)呼唤型语篇:如《论语》翻译的宣传画册以及相关辩论性文本等。这种类型语篇的主要功能是以信息功能与呼唤功能为主,号召读者们按照作者的意图去行动、思考、感受。在翻译此类文体时,译者应注重把读者的同等反应作为核心,注重可读性与实用性,多采用编译策略,做到译文通俗易懂。

小组同学在课堂展示后可以采用学生互评与教师评价。学生互评有助于培养学生互帮互助的合作精神,有助于学生在相互学习交流中分享心得、获得灵感和知识。但是为了帮助学生在互评时尽量做到客观公正,教师在课程开始时应明确告知学生评价标准,设置小组贡献分、PPT 制作分、观点正确分等分值比例,如《论语》学术性翻译策略与《论语》宣传画册的交际翻译策略是不同的。教师在给学生评价时,要注意情感态度,要与学生心理个性特点相符,应根据学生的不同思维情况,循序渐进、运用启发式语言对学生进行有针对性的引导。

由此可见,翻译工作坊注重翻译学习过程。学生们通过主题选择、案例分析以及合作完成课题,不仅有利于提升学生主动学习的积极性,培养小组认同感,鼓励民主习惯,而且有利于加强师生互动。

第二,翻译作业。翻译作业是众多教学活动的一种,与其他教学活动相辅相成,共同营造良好的学习氛围,帮助学生提高自己的专业能力与职业能力,培养学生成为自主、有责任的学习者。

教师通过学习通平台给学生布置适量中国典籍的课外作业。学生是否按时提交、是否独立完成、作业质量如何反映他们的学习态度与学习情况。例如,教师选取《论语》《道德经》《尚书》的部分篇章让学生翻译,或者让学生思考语录体散文《论语》与古典小说《红楼梦》的翻译,或者让学生赏析不同翻译名家《论语》《红楼梦》译文,并分析不同文体、不同译文的翻译策略背后的原因。教师可以通过课下分析学生作业,总结出学生出现错误的各种原因;并在下节课开始时,结合学生作业错误向学生讲清楚这些错误的深层次原因。教师也可以适时让学生互评,以增强学生之间的学习互动,激发其学习兴趣,并在老师的指导下提升作业质量,增强对翻译学习的乐趣。

老师通过让学生高质量完成作业可以培养学生的责任感,给学生创造独立解决问题的机会。老师要教育学生承担起作业细节的责任,如是否按时完成、是否独立完成、是否作业清晰、差错少等。如果学生的作业质量与学生的态度相关,如拼写错误,格式不规范等,教师可以设置一些规章制度约束学生的作业行为,但这不是全部。更重要的是,教师需要创造一种学习氛围或者提供一些激励机制如形成性评价,让学生对作业情况及时反馈,以激发学生通过认真完成作业提升学习效果的动力。如果学生的作业质量与学生的能力有关,如语言表达能力(如语法错误、词汇误用)、文化能力(如《论语》中"义"译成"righteousness"引起误解)、与语篇表达能力(如语篇衔接与连贯不畅,内容重组不到位),教师需要教会学生在仰望星空的同时也要脚踏实地,从职业愿景的视角鼓励学生充分认识到自己应肩负的责任,认真分析自己作业错误的原因并通过主动学习探索提升语言驾驭能力、文化洞察思考能力与语篇翻译能力,从根本上提升自己的中国典籍译介能力。此外,教师在课堂布置完作业后,可要求学生做一个备忘录以准备下节课检查。备忘录中要说明他们完成翻译作业的主要步骤、应该完成的任务、解决问题的策略以及对翻译批评的反馈思考等。

总之,教师让学生通过翻译工作坊与完成作业等学习活动,在主动探索、发现解决问题以及启发引导的学习过程中提升学生的翻译专业能力与人际沟通能力。同时,老师注意在教学过程中创造以学为主的学习氛围,让学生学会承担自己的责任,并赋予学生自己解决问题的权力。

3. 政校企协同育人

政校企协同育人主要是指政府、高校、企业以合作共赢为目的建立的可持续发展的人才培养机制。政校企协同育人一般由高校作为主体,政府作为支持,企业积极参与,即在政府的文化战略政策支持下,充分利用学校的教学资源和企业的实践环境,以互利互惠为最终目的,通过政府、高校与企业三位一体深度融合的协同育人路径,培养出适应市场需要的优秀翻译传播人才。下文主要从联合培养、翻译传播大赛与翻译传播实践基地三方面探讨中国典籍翻译传播的人才培养。

(1) 联合培养。政校企可共同合作,通过慕课制作,计算机辅助翻译语料库共建、信息传播技术指导等形式多样的联合培养形式,让现代技术赋能中国典籍翻译传播知识创新,为中国典籍翻译传播智能教育拓展空间,培养市场所需的中国典籍翻译传播人才,实现中国典籍翻译传播人才培养目标。

在教育信息化时代,学习革命与高等教育变革给全球带来挑战。现在的教育生态环境已被重新定义,教与学也应采用多元化的形式。这就要求政校企三方共同探索中国典籍在线优质翻译教育资源的教学创新模式。学校不仅可以邀请政府与企业的专家到校讲学指导,而且可以利用在线教学技术应用创新提升中国典籍翻译教学质量,促进中国典籍翻译教育优质资源的共享力度。在政府部门政策的指导下,高校教师可以借助超星等企业单位的专业慕课制作平台及其团队,以智能技术的翻译慕课教育学习方式,更加高质量地完成优质在线中国典籍翻译传播教学课程,并推动中国典籍翻译传播教育变革引擎。在信息化时代,在线教育具有极大优势,可以满足人们对跨学科知识的信息需求。教育信息技术给传统的中国典籍翻译传播教学模式提出了新的挑战。教师可借助政校企的通力合作,进行中国典籍的翻译传播教学模式改革,以学习者为中心,让学生通过教育技术体验新的学习路径,如通过现代信息技术体验中国典籍所呈现的时尚性,以激发学生的学习兴趣。

因此,政校企要携手合作、实现共赢,充分考虑学生的认知学习特点,共同制订培养方案,借助互联网等前沿科技共同提高学生的专业素养、人文素养与信息技术素养,提升学生的个性化学习效果,让学生学到更专业、更实用的翻译传播技能,为中国典籍翻译传播人才的培养提供优质服务。

(2)翻译传播大赛。中国典籍翻译传播大赛旨在以赛促学、以训促学,促使人们重视中华传统文化传播,传递中国声音。通过翻译大赛,政校企之间可以进一步加强沟通,促进共同发展。同时,学生们也能够进一步地了解中华传统文化传播,学会用自己的方式传播中华传统文化,向世界发出自己的声音。

在政府部门与企业等相关单位的支持赞助下,学校可以举办中国典籍翻译传播大赛。大赛秉承"学术与担当、国学与文化、翻译与传播"

的办赛理念,采取灵活多样的形式,将中国典籍与口笔译相结合,或者让学生利用教育信息技术进行中国典籍翻译传播展示,为所有热爱中华传统文化以及翻译传播的同学提供一个相互交流、展示自我的平台。

翻译传播大赛可通过人才跨界合作,立足"中国典籍翻译与传播",邀请国内外国学专家、翻译家、传播学专家、文化企业家作为大赛顾问与评委。翻译大赛设置颁奖会议与会议议题,如中国典籍翻译与海外传播、中国典籍翻译与新媒体推广、中国典籍翻译与文化传承创新、中国典籍翻译传播与国际人才培养、"政校企"联合培养人才的新模式,以进一步推进中华文化经典双语创造性转化、创新性发展与国际化传播。

翻译传播大赛可增强学生对中华传统文化与翻译艺术和现代科技传播的领悟,增进学生对中国典籍的认识,营造传承与传播中国典籍、潜心研究文化翻译的学术氛围,让学生学会讲好中国故事,传播好中国文化,展示好中国形象,推动中华文化"走出去"。翻译传播大赛有助于学生增强对中华文化及其传播的热爱,尤其是对那些致力于传播中华文化的同学来说,翻译传播大赛可促使同学们坚定研究翻译与传播中华传统文化经典的信心,思考通过翻译与传播向世界介绍和推广中华优秀传统文化,在中华文化"走出去"以及世界认知中国的过程中促进中外文明交流互鉴与交流。

简言之,高水平的中国典籍翻译传播大赛及相关会议的成功举办有利于推动中华文化经典双语人才培养,推动中国典籍翻译传播研究,有助于提升国家文化软实力并增强中国典籍在国际的影响力。

(3)翻译传播实践基地。政校企共建文化翻译传播实践基地,有助于构建产学研融合的教学模式,改善教师教学方法与提高翻译实训教学能力。在翻译传播实践基地,教师根据社会需求培养学生的人文素养、专业素养与技术素养,帮助学生将翻译传播理论与具体实践相结合,有效提升学生的翻译传播职业能力。

翻译传播实践基地可以将翻译与传播等专业的语言文化资源及需求同先进的技术及平台优势相结合,辅助学校开展教学、科研、学科建设,实现政校企科研的成果转化,实现科学管理与统计分析简便易行,实现中国典籍翻译传播教学的数字化、可控化,提升教师的教研效果与科研水平。

翻译传播实践基地还可实现中国典籍语料资源的连续更新与建设,进一步提升专业课程体系研发能力以及实现多媒体互动教材的充分利用,有助于提升学生的写作能力与科研创新能力。学生在翻译传播实践基地通过掌握项目管理、语言资产管理、预翻译、团队管理、语料信息检索等当下翻译流程的关键环节,提高学生的核心竞争力,提升学生的专业素养、人文素养与信息化素养,进而提高学生的综合翻译传播能力。

此外,学生还可通过参与一些专注于中华优秀文化翻译传播和经典整理的图书出版机构的实习,熟悉传统文化类图书的译介编辑和创作,熟悉中华传统文化翻译传播的理念及其应用。

由此可见,翻译传播实践基地对于高校的科研探究翻译传播教学以及翻译传播实践都大有裨益。它可以帮助学生高效完成大量相关实习与模拟项目,利用大量丰富的翻译语料库以及翻译技术软件提升学生的翻译传播能力。

总之,在信息化时代,创新教育培养理念与教学路径是实现优质中国典籍翻译传播教学的重要组成部分。政校企协同育人可有力推动中国典籍双语政产学研用创新发展,拓展中国典籍翻译传播人才培养途径,丰富学生的学习活动,助力提升学生的自主学习能力、创新能力以及翻译传播职业能力。

(三) 培养效果评价

良好的培养效果评价有利于促进良好的师生关系,促进教师专业发展,提升学生的学习能力与职业能力。学生培养效果评价应围绕中国典籍翻译传播教学内容,考虑培养目标、参考标准,以及评价所要达到的效果。根据评价实施的功能不同,教学评价可以分为诊断性评价、形成性评价与终结性评价。

1. 诊断性评价

诊断性评价也称教学性评价、准备性评价，是指教师在翻译教学活动开始之前对学生的翻译知识储备、翻译技能掌握以及情感状况等进行的预测。通过这种预测，教师可以了解学生的现有翻译水平以及准备程度，以判断学生是否具备实现翻译教学目标所要求的条件，为实现因材施教提供依据。

诊断性评价一般在课程、学期、学年开始或教学过程中需要的时候实施。诊断性评价旨在帮助教师分析自己的教学挑战，设计可以满足不同起点水平和不同学习风格的学生所需的教学方案，并将学生置于最有益的教学过程中。诊断性测试需要遵循五个原则：(1) 有效使用诊断性评价诊断功能的对象是测试使用者与被测试者。(2) 在诊断目的明确的前提下，测试卷的设计应注意较易运作性、较强针对性、较高效率与较高反馈。(3) 诊断过程应从多角度出发，例如，通过设置问卷了解学生对该课程的认识与自我评价，帮助学生了解自己的现状，设定学习目标、思考未来的自己。例如，通过随堂测试了解学生对所学知识点的掌握情况，有针对性地通过指导，帮助学生分析出现错误的原因，巩固所学知识并提高学习能力。(4) 诊断性测试评价应该包含以下四个步骤：聆听和观察、初步评价、诊断测试与改进对策。(5) 诊断性评价应与形成性评价与终结性评价结合使用。

通过各种诊断性测试，教师可了解其所面临的主要教学挑战，如：(1) 学生的外语语言掌握情况不一样，有些学生的语言功底比较强，而有的比较薄弱，需要长期努力。(2) 学生的翻译传播能力存在差异，有的同学具有较强的中国典籍翻译能力，但是传播能力较弱；有的同学具有较强的跨文化交际能力，但是中国典籍翻译实践能力较弱。(3) 对于工作坊等团队活动，有的学生喜欢团队合作，有的学生则不喜欢，教师需要在教学过程中进行协调。

教师需要结合以上教学挑战，思考该课程能够对学生今后的学习、工作和生活产生怎样的影响。教师可从以下几个方面进行翻译课程设计：(1)核心知识：针对学生在测试中出现的问题，通过因材施教，帮助学生理解并记住关键概念与术语等，掌握英汉语言文化差异，识别并记住中国典籍翻译的重要概念、文体特征、翻译方法等。(2)学以致用：学生通过课堂测试、随堂练习对所学知识检验学习成果，用刚学到的知识解决问题。教师让学生完成测验、报告与反馈等活动，并注重分析学生在社会实习实践中运用所学知识进行翻译实践活动的效果。(3)触类旁通：针对学生的思维能力薄弱等问题，教师结合相关中国典籍翻译传播理论与专题实践热点问题进行头脑风暴训练，培养学生的知识迁移能力，让学生逐步完善知识结构，在翻译过程中结合文化传播学等知识融会贯通运用于中国典籍翻译实践，提高中国典籍翻译传播能力。(4)人性维度：通过观察与调研学生的性格差异，教师让学生在学习过程中通过分工合作，增加对自己与他人的了解教师；让学生在学习过程中通过不断反省，提高善解人意、善于倾听他人意见与乐于沟通等品质。(5)志趣情怀：通过观察调研，了解学生是否关心与所学相关的现象和问题，通过深入思考，让学生更加喜爱中国典籍翻译传播课程以及与这门课程相关的内容，如这门课程的社会价值与现实意义，并通过学生的深入学习潜移默化提升自己的思想高度。(6)学会学习：根据学生特点，通过制定学生量表，让学生有意识地养成有效学习的能力与终身学习的习惯，逐渐掌握中国典籍翻译传播的理念与思路，开展更有效的学习与思考。

综上所述，在中国典籍翻译传播课程的教学过程中，教师通过诊断性评价查找学生在学习中出现问题的原因，再通过层层深入分析找到问题的解决策略。因此，诊断性评价作为中国典籍翻译传播教学的重要启示性工具，对于提升教学质量以及提高学生能力都有着重要的启发意义。

2. 形成性评价

形成性评价主要是指教师在课堂教学过程中对学生学习过程和

学习结果所实施的形成性评价。形成性测评在教学过程中进行,除了给教师反馈教学成效,还提供给学生其自身情况的评估,帮助学生改进与提升自己不足之处。

狭义的形成性评价是指课堂中学生的问答互动、作业提交、课件展示以及课堂点评活动。广义的形成性评价是指教师对学生参与教学互动过程的学习状况的了解、反馈、对策及其个性特征的观察判断,包括各种课堂测验、课外作业、小组讨论、研究展示、研究报告等。形成性评价的目的是"激励学生,帮助学生有效调控自己的学习过程"(肖维青,2012),可使学生在学习评价过程中及时修改或调整学习计划,从被动接受评价转变为评价的主体和积极参与者,多方位体验学习成功。

形成性评价的设计应根据学校的学生培养方案与英语专业教学大纲制定,对教学结果进行价值判断,并为教学决策服务。一般而言,一个设计良好的学习测评,应该具备以下特点(McMillan,2000):(1) 公平且公正;(2) 有利于把学习活动分散到整门课程的实施过程中;(3) 促使学生关注学习效果;(4) 让学生有展示自我成就的机会;(5) 为学生提供进一步学习的机会;(6) 给予学生反馈的机会。下文主要从资料来源、评价形式、评价原则与评价特点等维度进行探讨。

形成性评价的材料来源应该权威、难度适中、循序渐进。低年级同学的材料应注重语言能力培养以及中英语言结构转换,中年级同学应注重中国典籍翻译策略的掌握、语篇翻译以及跨文化能力的培养,高年级同学则注重综合翻译能力与翻译传播能力的培养。学生能从阅读理解中国典籍原文本逐渐过渡到最终能对不同译文进行赏析批评、地道翻译以及对外传播的能力。

形成性评价的形式主要是通过课堂考勤、课外作业、阶段测验、期中考试、讨论发言、课程论文或案例分析等考核项目。评价内容包括语义、句法、语篇、风格、文化、翻译策略与传播策略等,旨在通过课堂观察法、测验法、调查法、案例分析等帮助学生掌握翻译与传播策略。这样,教师通过对学生客观评价、学生小组评价、学生自评/互评等评价以及言语体态等课堂表现评价等对学生学习结果进行综合评价分析,为学生提供教学反馈,促进学生学业进步。

形成性评价应遵循以下原则:第一,激励性原则。教学评价应以促进学生发展为目标,采用积极的、肯定的评价方式,激发学生的学习动机、培养学生的学习兴趣。第二,教育性原则。发挥评价的育人功能,遵循教学规律与学生发展特点,强调对学生的系统化与个性化差异评价,循序渐进,系统有序,培养学生的创新能力。第三,全面性原则。强调对学生的学习评价应涉及以人为本的特点,包括知识与能力、过程与方法、情感与价值等。加强师生对话,构建教师评学生、学生互评、学生评教师的多元课堂评价模式(范敏,2020)。

形成性评价具有以下特点:第一,目的性。对学生作业的价值取向定位,是侧重知识检测还是侧重学以致用,是采用问卷调查还是小组讨论都需要根据学生的学习情况而定。冯光伟(2017)指出:"评价的价值取向不同,所选择的评价内容与评价方式就不一样。"第二,反馈性。教师向学生解释他们的学习表现以及后续学习的建议是形成性测评的必要步骤。形成性测评的关键是向学生及时提供有效反馈,如及时诊断学生的翻译错误,及时纠正问题、发现问题,帮助学生提高翻译能力。此外,学生需要提交自我反思报告,对自我过程进行总结并落实到自我的学习行动过程中。第三,动态性。通过教学评价促进师生互动。学生可通过教师的教学评价改进自己的翻译问题,教师对学生的评价也会随着学生认知能力与解决问题能力的提高随时调整评价策略。

形成性评价测评量规的设计要结合教学大纲,根据具体的学习目标与学习活动,遵循一定的原则,尽量做到科学、公平、明确。翻译测评量规是指一系列定义了完成教学质量的目标和标准,并详细解释了用以评价任务表现和学习成效的标准。形成性翻译测评量规注重解析过程,应该包含以下特征:第一,准确描述教学测评任务和内容。第二,详细并清晰描述用于评估成绩的各项具体任务的标准。第三,具有良好的区分度,能根据学生的表现进行客观的评估。例如,中国典籍翻译传播课程论文的测评量规设计与小组合作测评量规的设计是不同的。虽然两者都可以通过是否在超星学习通准时提交等来判断学生的责任心,而且两者都是一种常见的开放性学习任务,评测都相对主观,但是相对而言,课程论文写作是一种更高层次的测评方法,它要求学生针对某个问题或主题建构自己的答案,展示原创性,并用科学的研究思路与方法进行论证。在测评时,教师需要从观点原创性、写作技能准确性、内容结构逻辑性与思路方法清晰性等标准进行考量;而且评分的标准和量规应该条理、清楚并且合理,以确保学生和评阅人都能认可。小组合作测评量规的设计需要考虑以下因素:是否充分承担小组任务职责、为团队贡献知识观点、乐于帮助小组解决问题、积极完成小组任务目标、具有较高解决问题的能力等。

综上所述,结合教育信息技术,形成性评价有助于教师更多关注学生的学习方法,启发学生主动学习与积极思维,关注学生精神发展、学习兴趣、学习素养与个体差异,提高学生的翻译能力与技术传播技能,帮助学生在不断思考学习的过程中提高中国典籍的翻译传播能力。

3. 终结性评价

终结性评价一般是在学期末或学年末或者某一教学活动结束后,为教师了解教学活动的最终效果而进行的评价。终结性评价是以考试成绩来评定学生学习能力和教学质量,旨在检验学生的学业是否最终达到教学目标的要求,并对整个教学活动的效果作出评定。

终结性评价的学习内容常常是可以量化的,如对翻译知识和翻译传播技能的测试评价。评价结果多以精确的百分制来体现,而且往往是通过闭卷考试进行。一方面,终结性评价的优势是对学生的学习效果进行客观评估,促使学生系统复习巩固所学知识;另一方面,终结性评价会给学生造成紧张压抑感觉,而且会造成学生不注意平时翻译传播知识的学习积累以及自我教育能力的培养。学生的主体地位不能得到充分体现,在某种程度上也会遏制学生的人格培养、学习积极性以及教师教学的积极性,不利于各项教学活动的开展。

因此,终结性评价要与诊断性评价与形成性评价一起使用。需要注意的是,尽管终结性评价的根本目的是评量学生的最终学习效果表现,但是如果测评仅仅聚焦于数字化的成绩和等第,而忽略终结性评价更深层次的目的,如提升学生以后的学习效果,那么终结性评价往往不能发挥更有意义的成效。

综上所述,建立科学合理的多元化的中国典籍翻译传播教学评价体系,可促进教学互动与学生学习积极性,引导学生进行深层次的思考学习,关注学生的全面发展,进而提高学生的职业能力。教师要正确运用评价理论,遵循评价原则,并运用科学的评价方法,尽可能全面、客观、科学和公正地去观察和分析学生的中国典籍翻译传播学习过程与结果。

总之,在教育信息化时代,中国典籍翻译传播的人才培养不仅要注重道德、智力与翻译专业能力,也要注重信息化能力与跨文化传播能力。因此,把素质教育、专业教育与信息技能教育结合是中国典籍翻译传播教学的主要特征。为此,学校联合政校企努力创新人才培养路径,制定科学合理的课程教学规划与考核评价机制,努力培养具有创新意识与较强翻译传播能力的高素质、复合型的中国典籍翻译传播人才。

五、小结

中国典籍的翻译传播是一个动态过程,需要借助译者与国家、政府、高校等合力,通过提高中国典籍文化软实力、增强国外受众跨文化认同、制定中国典籍翻译传播策略、深化中国典籍翻译传播理念、注重中国典籍翻译传播内容、创新中国典籍翻译传播手段、提高中国典籍翻译传播效果、加强中国典籍翻译传播人才培养等措施,促进中华传统文化在海外的传播与接受。其中,译者主体性、文化软实力、翻译传播规律、受众接受、国家政策以及翻译传播教育等因素在中国典籍翻译传播过程中起着重要作用。

第六章 结论与展望

以《论语》为代表的中国典籍的翻译传播是一个复杂、动态、系统的传播过程,不仅理解为翻译传播者、翻译过程、受众与赞助者等所有环节构成的统一体,还应理解为通过翻译传播与社会环境建立某种关联与互动的过程,以及与历史、文化、权力、意识形态和社会生活密切关联的过程。这三个环节相互制约、相互作用,共同决定中国典籍的翻译传播效果。

一、结论

本书通过借助语料库,结合定性分析,对《论语》英译概况以及《论语》及其英译的语篇特征、文化特征、修辞特征、传播历程、传播模式、传播途径、海外接受调查进行了分析探讨,并基于《论语》英译传播研究进而对中国典籍翻译传播的主体多元化、路径创新与人才培养模式创新提出了思考与建议。

从比较文学与跨文化的角度来看,儒家文化的翻译代表了一种"他者"的视角。儒学传统在"中西比较视域下是'一多不分'的哲学体系,具有悠久深厚根源的思想文化传统。在中西比较研究的视野中,儒学传统在宇宙的生成和存在、人生的价值和意义以及社会的实践和发展具有整体性和全息性的共同特征,针对某一哲学问题,儒学传统总会从不断变化的内在关系和始终延续的情势环境出发,展开建构、解构和整体诠释"(安乐哲,2020)。儒家文化要实现与世界文化有效沟通,一个重要的环节就是翻译,"借助翻译,让自己的作品为他国的读者阅读、理解与接受"(许钧和宋学智,2007)。具有鲜明民族特色的儒家经典及其他优秀的中国典籍,只有通过成功的翻译传播,才能在世界文化中找到自己的位置,才能真正融入世界文化。

中国典籍的翻译传播是一种人文关怀的文化交流与接纳。注重文化力的思想认同可以有效提高中国典籍在海外的传播与接受,因此在翻译传播过程中需要注重提高中华优秀传统文化的感召力、吸引力、影响力与接受力。中国典籍中具有普适性的文化如果得到国际社会的有效接受与认可,就会产生更大的吸引力与影响力。这会关涉到中国典籍的海外接受者与译语、译者、源语的多重对话,译者人才培养与素养训练。同时,需要注意的是,受众的接受潜力、文化背景、教育水平、审美情趣、认知能力等都会影响中国典籍的海外接受情况。

第一,注重中国典籍文本的正确字义考查与义理辨析。例如,《论语》成书于春秋战国时期,距今已有2 000多年的历史,从历代《论语》注疏中即可看出,评论家们对《论语》中很多字词的解释多有出入。此外,《论语》蕴含着丰富的哲学思想,"中国先哲之儒道之书,……文虽较简,名辞(词)较少,似易读;而实又非熟玩其言,而前后错综参伍以观之,不能见其义;非循序求之即必可得者……"(唐君毅,2005)。因此,译者需做到对《论语》的正确理解,并具备一定的中西语言文化知识与翻译传播能力,才能准确翻译传播《论语》。

第二,中国典籍的译者风格影响海外接受。译介效果评价多与文化语境和价值评判有关。在当前"文化崛起"语境下,中国典籍中具有国际文化特征的文化内容如要获得外国受众认同与接受,需要发挥译者主体性与创造性。译者既在社会语境中生存,又是社会语境的一部分。译者的价值观、教育背景、译者风格、语篇意识、翻译能力等都会对中国典籍翻译作品产生决定性的影响。译者身兼读者与译者的多重身份,需要考虑时空差异、社会语境、翻译目的与译入语受众的阅读期待和审美距离。

第三,中国典籍的翻译传播内容、文化语境与受众特点影响海外接受。中国典籍翻译传播涉及时空与跨文化交际行为。缺失语境增加了翻译传播内容的复杂性与艰巨性。此外,中西历史文化语境不同会导致意识形态与价值观差异,并影响中国典籍的翻译、传播与接受。此外,由于中西方受众存在认知差异,他们会对中国典籍的文化内容尤其是一些具有深厚历史文化底蕴的典故、习语以及一些特殊的人名与地名等有着不同的理解。因此,翻译传播主体应以文化交流为出发点,客观估计译入语受众的文化接受力,努力实现中华传统文化在异域文化语境中的成功接受。

第四,中国典籍翻译传播过程中的互文因素影响海外接受。翻译传播过程是处于一定的社会语境中的动态过程。翻译传播主体处于动态交际过程的中心地位,协调着文本、受众、赞助人与媒介等外界的互动与交流过程。因此,我们需要注重翻译传播主体与社会环境、语言文化互文、译者与赞助人、受众与文本、受众与媒介等的互动关系,揭示翻译传播活动与权力话语的互动等问题,使中国典籍以更宽阔的研究视角与研究视域面对国际学界,使海外受众真正了解接受中华文化。

第五,中国典籍翻译传播路径与方法影响海外接受。我们应根据译入语文化环境,注重中国典籍翻译传播主体的多元化与传播渠道的多元化传播。在中国典籍翻译传播过程中,充分发挥政府、高校、社会团体等单位合力,采取多种有效措施,拓展中国典籍翻译传播路径并促进其在海外的传播与接受。

综上所述,在当前全球化文化语境下,中国典籍翻译传播需要考虑文本特征、翻译传播主体、翻译传播内容、译入语受众接受、翻译传播语境、翻译传播路径与中国典籍人才培养等各种因素的交互作用。在中国典籍翻译传播过程中,我们一方面要注重提升中华传统文化的自信,以提升国家文化软实力;另一方面要注重创新翻译传播路径与方法,使国外受众容易接受中华传统文化,从而进一步促进中西文化的沟通、对话与融合。这对于中国典籍在海外的传播与接受,促进中西文化对话与交流互鉴,以及提升中国在世界的话语形象都具有重要的参考意义与借鉴价值。

二、展望

本书以《论语》英译与海外接受为个案,对中国典籍海外传播的机制创新进行了探索,并基于对《论语》的翻译、传播和接受三个环节的梳理对当前中国典籍的海外传播的机制创新提出了一些可行性建议。个案英译研究具有代表性,但并不能涵盖中国典籍翻译活动的方方面面。笔者认为,本书还存在一定研究空间,包括中国典籍翻译传播的跨学科与跨文化研究的新路径、中国典籍多语种在线翻译语料库建设与不断完善、中国典籍翻译海外接受的机制创新方法论研究等。

(1) 中国典籍翻译传播的跨学科与跨文化研究的新路径。翻译传播作为一种跨文化交际行为,会受文本、历史、语境等限制因素的影响。中国典籍的文体特征、时空差异以及中西方文化差异增加了中国典籍翻译传播的复杂性。因此,中国典籍翻译传播主体如何处理不同文体类型与社会语境,以及如何实现多语种典籍个案研究的对立与统一,需要结合跨学科与跨文化研究等前沿成果。此外,优秀的中华文化多语种典籍的译者培养创新还有很大的研究空间。

(2) 中国典籍多语种在线翻译语料库的建设与不断完善。研究者可以根据需要,进一步构建与完善中国典籍的多语种翻译语料库,进行样本提取并结合理论深入分析,进一步客观、系统、量化分析与探究中国典籍文化内容及其多语种译本的翻译风格。中国典籍中具有中国特色的翻译表达、儒家哲学思想的深入研究以及通过话语分析诠释文本中深层的文化权力冲突的路径等,可以在中国典籍多语种多译本的翻译语料库研究中作进一步探讨。

（3）中国典籍翻译海外接受的机制创新方法论研究。中国典籍文本中的较强意合性、修辞空灵性与文化典故的抗译性，以及对受众异质性及其认知心理的准确把握仍有较大研究空间。由于文本阅读是一种文化建构，翻译则是通过"他者"构建和文化认同来建构异国形象，而且随着时间的推移，受众的接受程度也有可能发生变化。因此，翻译传播主体需要进一步思考中国典籍翻译海外接受的机制创新路径，使西方受众最大程度接受中华传统文化的内涵。换言之，中国典籍翻译传播的接受度的研究仍有很大研究空间，需要进一步从多元化视角与多元化路径对海外传播接受机制的创新进行探索。

总之，随着全球化与国际化交流的不断推进，中国也以自己的独特的东方文化魅力得到了世界的认可。中国典籍作为蕴含着优秀社会价值观与精神感召力的文化力，也因众多翻译传播主体的努力而以一种新的姿态丰富滋养着世界文化。但是由于中国典籍本身的语言特点以及固有的中西方文化差异，中华文化经典的重新诠释变得愈发重要。因此，翻译传播主体需充分发挥能动性，借助社会各界力量，根据时代特点与受众需求，通过创新翻译传播路径，进一步完善具有全球视野与鲜明特色，并能融通中外、兼容并蓄的中国典籍翻译传播话语体系。

参 考 文 献

[1] 安乐哲.儒家角色伦理学:一套特色伦理学词汇[M].孟巍隆,译.田辰山,校.济南:山东人民出版社,2017.

[2] 安乐哲.和而不同:比较哲学与中西会通[M].北京:北京大学出版社,2002.

[3] 安乐哲.自我的圆成:中西互镜下的古典儒学与道家[M].彭国翔,编译.石家庄:河北人民出版社,2006.

[4] 安乐哲,郝大维.道不远人:比较哲学视域中的《老子》[M].何金俐,译.北京:学苑出版社,2004.

[5] 安乐哲.让中国哲学讲中国话[N].田辰山,译.人民日报,2015-08-10.

[6] 卞俊峰.豁然:一多不分[M].杭州:浙江大学出版社,2019.

[7] 柴明颎.对专业翻译教学建构的思考:现状、问题和对策[J].中国翻译,2010(1):54-56.

[8] 陈安定.英汉比较与翻译[M].北京:中国对外翻译出版公司,1998.

[9] 曹明伦.翻译理论是从哪里来的?——再论翻译理论与翻译实践的关系[J].上海翻译,2019(6):1-7.

[10] 陈兼,陈之宏.孔飞力与《中国现代国家的起源》[J].开放时代,2012(7):140-158.

[11] 陈国明,安然.跨文化传播学关键术语解读[M].北京:中国社会科学出版社,2010.

[12] 陈国兴.论安乐哲《论语》翻译的哲学思想[J].中国比较文学,2010(1):25-26.

[13] 陈梅,文军.中国典籍英译国外阅读市场研究及启示——亚马逊(Amazon)图书网上中国典籍英译本的调查[J].外语教学,2011,32(4):96-100.

[14] 陈望道.修辞学发凡[M].上海:复旦大学出版社,2017.

[15] 陈向红.中国文学在英语世界的译介、传播与接受研究:以杨宪益英译作品为个案[M].上海:上海交通大学出版社,2019.

[16] 程曼丽.国际传播学教程[M].北京:北京大学出版社,2006.

[17] 程树德.论语集释[M].北京:中华书局出版社,1990.

[18] 崔玉军.英国汉学界的《论语》英译:历史与问题[J/OL].http://www.gwz.fudan.edu.cn/Web/Show/1081,2010 02 15.

[19] 戴元光.传播学研究理论与方法[M].2版.上海:复旦大学出版社,2017.

[20] 丁往道.论语(精选)[M].北京:中国对外翻译出版有限公司,2008.

[21] 范敏.计算机辅助翻译研究的语篇观[J].复旦外国语言文学论丛,2018(1):154-161.

[22] 范敏.基于语料库的《论语》五译本文化高频词翻译研究[J].外语教学,2017(6):80-83.

[23] 范敏.教育信息化时代翻译教师信息素养研究[J].翻译季刊,2016(80):63-75.

[24] 范敏.《论语》的文化维度与翻译策略[J].天津外国语大学学报,2015(5):34-39.

[25] 范敏.《论语》五译本译者风格研究——基于语料库的统计与分析[J].北京航空航天大学学报,2016(6):81-88.

[26] 范敏.新时代《论语》翻译策略及其传播路径创新[J].西安外国语大学学报,2019(3):94-98.

[27] 范敏.跨文化认同与《论语》文化翻译[M]//王宏印,朱义华主编.典籍翻译研究(第八辑).北京:外语教学与研究出版社,2017.

[28] 范祥涛.中华典籍外译研究[M].北京:外语教学与研究出版社,2020.

[29] 方梦之.中国译学大辞典[M].上海:上海外语教育出版社,2011.

[30] 冯光伟.课堂教学设计理论与实践[M].北京:科学出版社,2017.

[31] 冯庆华.思维模式下的译文词汇[M].上海:上海外语教育出版社,2012.

[32] 冯天瑜.中华文化辞典[M].武昌:武汉大学出版社,2010.

[33] 傅德岷.论语鉴赏辞典[M].成都:巴蜀书社,2017.

[34] 傅佩荣.傅佩荣的哲学课:先秦儒家哲学[M].北京:北京联合出版公司,2018.

[35] 傅佩荣.论语三百讲(下册)[M].北京:北京联合出版公司,2019.

[36] 高永中.认真学习习近平同志关于中华文化的重要论述以高度的文化自觉深化党史文化研究[J].中党史研究,2014(10):18-27.

[37] 高志强."直译"的政治——论马士曼《孔子的著作》(第一卷)[J].暨南学报(哲学社会科学版),2016(2):1-10,130.

[38] 谷慧娟.《论语》英译与中国文化"走出去"[J].出版发行研究,2019(3):77-81.

[39] 耿强.翻译中的副文本及研究:理论、方法、议题与批评[J].外国语,2016(5):104-112.

[40] 辜鸿铭.辜鸿铭讲论语[M].北京:北京理工大学出版社,2013.

[41] 辜鸿铭.中国人的精神[M].李静,译.天津:天津人民出版社,2016.

[42] 过常宝.《论语》的文体意义[J].清华大学学报(哲学社会科学版),2007(6):29-34.

[43] 郭齐勇.中国儒学之精神[M].上海:复旦大学出版社,2009.

[44] 郭齐勇.中国哲学史[M].北京:高等教育出版社,2006.

[45] 郭晓春.《楚辞》在英语世界的译介与研究[M].北京:中国社会科学出版社,2018.

[46] 哈罗德·拉斯韦尔.社会传播的结构与功能[M].何道宽,译.北京:中国传媒大学出版社,2013.

[47] 海伦·蔼蒂丝·理.汉学家理雅各[M].马清河,译.北京:学苑出版社,2011.

[48] 郝大维,安乐哲.汉哲学思维的文化探源[M].施忠连,译.南京:江苏人民出版社,1999.

[49] 郝大维,安乐哲.孔子哲学思微[M].蒋弋为,李志林,译.南京:江苏人民出版社,2018.

[50] 胡庚申.翻译适应选择论[M].武汉:湖北教育出版社,2004.

[51] 胡庚申.生态翻译学:建构与诠释[M].北京:商务印书馆,2013.

[52] 黄国文.翻译研究的语言学探索[M].上海:上海外语教育出版社,2006.

[53] 黄国文.《论语》的篇章结构及英语翻译的几个问题[J].中国外语,2011(6):88-95.

[54] 黄勇.基于语料库的亚瑟·韦利《论语》译本的翻译风格研究[D].武汉:华中师范大学,2012.

[55] 黄忠廉.变译的七种变通手段[J].外语学刊,2002(1):93-96.

[56] 黄忠廉.变译理论[M].北京:中国对外翻译出版公司,2002.

[57] 霍尔.超越文化[M].居延安,等,译.上海:上海文化出版社,1988.

[58] 吉瑞德.朝觐东方:理雅各评传[M].段怀清,周俐玲,周振鹤,译.桂林:广西师范大学出版社,2011.

[59] 金学勤.《论语》注疏之西方传承:从理雅各到森舸澜[J].四川大学学报,2015(3):58-65.

[60] 鞠玉梅.《论语》英译文语篇评价系统之判断资源的修辞功能[J].当代修辞学,2016(5):37-48.

[61] 孔飞力.中国现代国家的起源[M].陈兼,陈之宏,译.北京:三联书店,2013.

[62] 李钢,李金姝.庞德《论语》英译研究[J].湖南社会科学,2013(1):242-244.

[63] 李海军,等.《聊斋志异》英语译介研究(1842—1948).北京:科学出版社,2019.

[64] 李宁.《大中华文库》国人英译本海外接受状况调查——以《孙子兵法》为例[J].上海翻译,2015(2):77-82.

[65] 李天辰.《论语》英译体会点滴[J].外语教学,1999(2):39-41.

[66] 李伟荣.20世纪以来中国典籍出版走出去的回顾与思考[J].中国出版,2016(23):70-73.

[67] 李伟荣.试析《论语》向西方世界传播过程中的诠释精神[J].江西社会科学,2009(5):235-238.

[68] 李伟荣,等.《论语》在西方的前世今生[J].燕山大学学报,2015(2):1-9.

[69] 李伟荣.中国文化"走出去"的外部路径研究——兼论中国文化国际影响力[J].中国文化研究,2015(3):29-46.

[70] 李文娟.安乐哲儒家哲学研究[M].北京:中国社会科学出版社,2017.

[71] 李运兴.翻译语境描写论纲[M].北京:清华大学出版社,2010.

[72] 李运兴.语篇翻译引论[M].北京:中国对外翻译出版公司,2001.

[73] 李泽厚.论语今读[M].合肥:安徽文艺出版社,1998.

[74] 刘承慧.先秦语体类型及其解释[J].当代修辞学,2018(1):59-73.

[75] 刘殿爵.《论语》英译本[M].香港:香港中文大学出版社,1992.

[76] 刘殿爵.语言与思想之间[M].香港:香港中文大学中国文化研究所吴多泰中国语文研究中心,1993.

[77] 刘禾.跨语际实践:文学、民族文化与被译介的现代性[M].北京:

生活·读书·新知三联书店,2014.

[78] 刘禾.帝国的话语政治:从近代中西冲突看现代秩序的形成[M].北京:生活·读书·新知三联书店,2009.

[79] 刘骥翔.从"再现"到"表征":一种以"副文本为中心"的典籍英译本描述性分析方法——以吴经熊《道德经》英译本为例[J].《中外文化与文论》,2019(1):442-455.

[80] 刘立胜.金安平《论语》英译与海外传播研究[J].民族翻译,2020(5):47.

[81] 刘宓庆.翻译与语言哲学[M].北京:中国对外翻译出版公司,2001.

[82] 刘宓庆.文体与翻译[M].北京:中国对外翻译出版公司,2012.

[83] 刘宓庆.中西翻译思想比较研究[M].北京:中国对外翻译出版公司,2005.

[84] 刘雪芹.《论语》英译语境化探索[D].上海:上海外国语大学,2010.

[85] 刘云虹.中国文学对外译介与翻译历史观[J].外语教学理论与实践,2015(4):1-8.

[86] 刘泽权,等.《红楼梦》四个英译本的译者风格初探[J].中国翻译,2011(1):60-64.

[87] 刘重德.《论语》两个英文译本的对比研究[C]//中国英汉语比较研究会第二次全国学术研讨会论文集,1996:334-356.

[88] 陆雄文.管理学大辞典[M].上海:上海辞书出版社,2013.

[89] 罗选民,杨文地.文化自觉与典籍英译[J].外语与外语教学,2012(5):63-66.

[90] 玛丽埃伦·韦默.以学习者为中心教学[M].洪岗,译.杭州:浙江大学出版社,2006.

[91] 孟健,等.文化顺应理论视阈下的典籍英译——以辜鸿铭《论语》英译为例[J].外语学刊,2012,(3):104-108.

[92] 孟怡村.基于语料库的〈论语〉核心哲学术语翻译研究[D].大连:大连海事大学.

[93] 潘震.论中国文学"走出去"之译介模式[J].小说评论,2015(6):48-52.

[94] 钱宁.《论语》纲要:从道理到定理[M].北京:生活·读书·新知三联书店,2019.

[95] 乔纳森·波特,玛格丽特·韦斯雷尔.话语和社会心理学[M].肖文明,吴新利,等译.北京:中国人民大学出版社,2006.

[96] 裴禾敏.我国传统文化海外传播策略探析[J].中国出版,2016(21):61-63.

[97] 曲慧敏.中华文化走出去战略[M].北京:清华大学出版社,2017.

[98] 区永超.《论语》修辞研究[M].上海:复旦大学出版社,2018.

[99] 儒风.《论语》的文化翻译策略研究[J].中国翻译,2008(5):50-54.

[100] 塞缪尔·亨廷顿.文明的冲突与世界秩序的重建[M].周琪,刘绯,张立平,等译.北京:新华出版社,2010.

[101] 森舸澜.为与无为[M].史国强,译.北京:现代出版社,2018.

[102] 施春宏.语体何以作为语法[J].当代修辞学,2019(6):1-20.

[103] 孙艺风.文化翻译[M].北京:北京大学出版,2016.

[104] 孙迎春.译学大词典[M].北京:中国世界语出版社,1999.

[105] 谭晓丽.和而不同:安乐哲儒学典籍英译研究[M].北京:中央编译出版社,2012.

[106] 唐君毅.中国哲学原论·原性篇[M].北京:中国社会科学出版社,2005.

[107] 唐翼明.论语新诠[M].长沙:岳麓书社,2016.

[108] 陶友兰.《论语》英译海外传播多元化策略[N].中国社会科学报,2018-10-19.

[109] 田辰山.辩证唯物主义在中国的再阐释——一个关于和谐与通

变的话题[J].济南大学学报(社会科学版),2003(2):1-9.

[110] 田辰山.关于"马克思主义与中国传统文化"的思考[J].马克思主义与现实,2008(4):11-15.

[111] 田辰山.要重视中西方传统文化的结构差异[J].中国图书评论,2008(8):14-17.

[112] 田辰山.中国辩证法:从《易经》到马克思主义[M].北京:中国人民大学出版社,2008.

[113] 屠国元,朱献珑.译者主体性:阐释学的阐释[J].中国翻译,2003(6):8-14.

[114] 王东波.辜鸿铭《论语》翻译思想探析:文化翻译的范例[J].孔子研究,2011(2):121-126.

[115] 王东波.理雅各与中国经典的译介[J].齐鲁学刊,2008(2):31-34.

[116] 王东风.文化认同机制假说与外来概念引进[J].中国翻译,2002(4):8-12.

[117] 汪福祥.评《论语》一书的英译问题[J].北京第二外国语学院学报.1996(2):19-25.

[118] 王宏.中国典籍翻译:成绩、问题与对策[J].外语教学理论与实践,2012(03):9-14.

[119] 王宏印.文学翻译批评论稿[M].上海:上海外语教育出版社,2006.

[120] 王宏印.中国传统译论经典诠释:从道安到傅雷[M].武汉:湖北教育出版社,2003.

[121] 王辉.理雅各与《中国经典》[J].中国翻译,2003(2):37-41.

[122] 王京涛.西播《论语》回译——辜鸿铭英译《论语》详释[M].上海:东方出版中心,2013.

[123] 王京涛.辜鸿铭英译经典:论语[M].北京:中华书局,2019.

[124] 王鹏飞.英语世界的《红楼梦》的译介与研究[M].西安:陕西师

范大学出版社,2014.

[125] 汪亚利.认知社会语言学视角下与性别相关的会话举止研究[M].北京:外语教学与研究出版社,2016.

[126] 王琰.汉学视阈中的《论语》英译研究[M].北京:外语教学与研究出版社,2013.

[127] 王义桅.打造国际话语体系的困境与路径[J].对外传播,2014(2):13-15.

[128] 魏倩倩.典籍英译与传播——以《孙子兵法》为例[M].北京:人民出版社,2018.

[129] 温海明.安乐哲比较哲学评论与研究[C].贵州:孔学堂书局,2018.

[130] 温海明.安乐哲比较哲学著作选[C].贵州:孔学堂书局,2018.

[131] 文若愚.论语全解[M].北京:中国华侨出版社,2013.

[132] 习近平.从延续民族文化血脉中开拓前进推进各种文明交流交融互学互鉴——在纪念孔子诞辰2565周年国际学术研讨会暨国际儒学联合会第五届会员大会开幕会上的讲话[J].党建,2014(10):4-7.

[133] 习近平:建设社会主义文化强国 着力提高国家文化软实力[EB/OL].[2023-05-20]. http://www.xinhuanet.com/politics/2013-12/31/c_118788013.htm,20131231.

[134] 习近平.习近平谈治国理政(第二卷)[M].北京:外文出版社,2017.

[135] 夏传才.论语讲座[M].桂林:广西师范大学出版社,2017.

[136] 肖维青.本科翻译专业测试研究[M].北京:人民出版社,2012.

[137] 谢天振.中国文学走出去:问题与实质[J].中国比较文学,2014(1):1-10.

[138] 辛红娟."文化软实力"与《道德经》英译[J].外语与外语教学,2009(11):50-52.

[139] 许多,许钧.中华文化典籍的对外译介与传播——关于《大中华文库》的评价与思考[J].外语教学理论与实践,2015(3):13-17;94.

[140] 许钧,李国平.中国文学译介与传播研究[M].杭州:浙江大学出版社,2018.

[141] 许钧,宋学智.20世纪法国文学在中国的译介与接受[M].武汉:湖北教育出版社,2007.

[142] 许雷,屠国元.《论语》英译中华人译者的孔子形象塑造[J].湘潭大学学报,2014(2):103-107.

[143] 严绍璗.我对Sinology的理解和思考[J].世界汉学,2006(1):6-13.

[144] 杨伯峻.论语译注[M].北京:中华书局,2009.

[145] 杨淳伟.中国"文化软实力"研究现状综述[J].中国文化研究,2011(2):195-203.

[146] 杨朝明.孔子文化奖学术精粹丛书·安乐哲卷[M].北京:华夏出版社,2015.

[147] 杨朝明.论语诠解[M].济南:山东友谊出版社,2013.

[148] 杨柳.中国文化典籍英译趋势[J].中国出版,2016(10):39-41.

[149] 杨平.《论语》核心概念"仁"的英译分析[J].外语与外语教学,2008(2):61-63.

[150] 杨平.中西文化交流视域下的《论语》英译研究[M].北京:光明日报出版社,2012.

[151] 杨义.论语还原[M].北京:中华书局,2016.

[152] 杨自俭,刘学云.翻译新论[M].武汉:湖北教育出版社,1994.

[153] 约翰·比格斯,凯瑟琳·唐.卓越的大学教学:建构教与学的一致性[M].王颖,丁妍,高洁,译.上海:复旦大学出版社,2015.

[154] 查明建,田雨.论译者主体性——从译者文化地位的边缘化谈起[J].中国翻译,2003(1):19-24.

[155] 张德福.汉学家《论语》英译研究[M].北京:中国社会科学出版社,2018.

[156] 张德禄.论语篇连贯[J].外语教学与研究,2000(2):103-109.

[157] 张国良.传播学原理[M].上海:复旦大学出版社,2018.

[158] 张升君,文军.翻译批评中的语料库方法[J].外国语言文学研究,2008(2):16-92.

[159] 张西平.比较文学视野下的海外汉学研究[M]//张西平,顾钧,主编.中国文化的域外解读.上海:华东师范大学出版社,2013.

[160] 张西平.中国文化"走出去"年度研究报告[M].北京:北京大学出版社,2016.

[161] 张晓雪.《论语》英译本海外传播现状与对策探讨——基于亚马逊网上书店以及 GoogleScholar 数据统计分析[J].湘潭大学学报(哲学社会科学版),2018(3):157-160.

[162] 张政,胡文潇.《论语》中"天"的英译探析——兼论其对中国文化核心关键词英译的启示[J].中国翻译,2015(6):92-96.

[163] 赵长江.十九世纪中国文化典籍英译史[M].上海:上海外语教育出版社,2017.

[164] 赵巍.《论语》中的"华夷之辨"及译者文化身份研究[J].孔子研究,2015(6):132-137.

[165] 赵征军.中国戏剧典籍译介研究[M].北京:中国社会科学出版社,2015.

[166] 郑铁生.关于中国文化带倾向的问题思考[M]//文化部对外文化联络局,中国翻译协会.摆渡者:中外文化翻译与传播.北京:中央编译出版社,2016.

[167] 周小玲.基于语料库的译者文体研究[D].长沙:湖南师范大学,2011.

[168] 周晓梅.试论中国文学外译中的认同焦虑问题[J].外语与外语教学,2017(3):12-19.

[169] 中共中央宣传部.习近平总书记系列重要讲话读本[M].北京：学习出版社,2016.

[170] 中国孔子基金会.中国儒学百科全书[M].北京:中国大百科全书出版社,1997.

[171] 钟明国.辜鸿铭《论语》翻译的自我东方化倾向及其对翻译目的的消解[J].外国语文,2009(2):135-139.

[172] 钟岳文.新年开篇话《论语》[J].月读,2014(1):6-13.

[173] 朱熹.论语集注[M].北京:中国社会出版社,2013.

[174] AMES R T, ROSEMONT H. The analects of confucius: a philosophical translation[M]. New York: Ballantine, 1998.

[175] APPIAH K A. Thick translation [C]// VENUTI L. The Translation Studies Reader. New York: Routledge, 2000.

[176] AUSTIN J L. A plea for excuses[C]// URMSON J O, WARNOCK G J. Philosophical Papers. Oxford: The Clarendon Press, 1961.

[177] AUSTIN J L. How to do things with words[M]. Oxford: Clarendon Press, 1975.

[178] BAKER M. Routledge encyclopedia of translation studies[M]. London and New York: Routledge, 1998.

[179] BASSNETT S. Translation studies[M]. 3rd ed. Shanghai: Shanghai Foreign Language Education Press, 2004.

[180] BASSNETT S, LEFEVERE A. Constructing cultures: essays on literary translation [M]. Shanghai: Shanghai Foreign Language Education Press, 2001.

[181] BASSNETT S, LEFEVERE A. Translation history and culture [C]. London and New York: Pinter Publishers, 1990.

[182] BATCHELOR K. Translation and paratexts: translation theories explored[M]. London: Routledge, 2018.

[183] BELL R T. Translation and translating: theory and practice [M]. London: Longman, 1991.

[184] BIBER D, SUSAN C, REPPEN R. Corpus linguistics[M]. Cambridge: Cambridge University Press, 1998.

[185] BIGGS J, TANG C. Teaching for quality learning at university [M]. New York: Open University Press, 2011.

[186] BROOKS E B, BROOKS A T. The original analects: sayings of confucius and his successors[M]. New York: Columbia University, 1998.

[187] BRUNER J. The process of education[M]. Cambridge, MA: Harvard University Press, 1961.

[188] CALZADA Pérez M. Apropos of ideology: translation studies on ideology — ideology in translation studies[M]. Manchester: St. Jerome Publishing, 2003.

[189] CHAN S W, POLLARD D E. An encyclopedia of translation: Chinese-English • English-Chinese [M]. Hong Kong: The Chinese University Press, 1995.

[190] CHANG C Y, LEE O. Confucianism: a modern interpretation [M]. Hangzhou: Zhejiang University Press, 2012.

[191] DAWSON R. Confucius: the analects[M]. Oxford: Oxford University Press, 1993.

[192] DE BEAUGRANDE R, DRESSLER W U. Introduction to Text Linguistics[M]. Harlow: Longman, 1981.

[193] DE FINA A, SCHIFFRIN D, BAMBERG M. Discourse and identity[M]. Cambridge: Cambridge University Press, 2006.

[194] DUBOIS N. A sociocognitive approach to social norms[M]. London and New York: Routledge, 2002.

[195] EGGINS S. An Introduction to systematic functional linguistics

[M]. London: Pinter Publishers, 1994.

[196] EGGINS S, SLADE D. Analyzing casual conversation [M]. London: Cassell, 1997.

[197] ENNAJI M. Multilingualism, cultural identity, and education in Morocco[M]. Springer Science & Business Media, 2005.

[198] FAN M. Cultural issues in Chinese idioms translation[J]. Perspectives: Studies in Translatology, 2007(4): 215-229.

[199] FAN M. Translation of the cultural images in the analects[J]. Genre, 2015(35):126-141.

[200] FAN M. A critical study on translation of the analects: an ideological perspective[J]. International Journal of Translation, Interpretation, and Applied Linguistics, 2021(1):45-54.

[201] FAN M. Understanding and translating confucian philosophy in the analects: a sociosemiotic perspective[J]. Semiotica, 2021(1): 287-306.

[202] FISH S. Interpretive communities[C]// RIVKIN J, RYAN M. M. Literary Theory: An Anthology. MA: Blackwell Publishing Limited, 2004.

[203] GARDNER D K. Zhu Xi's reading of the analects: canon, commentary, and the classical tradition [M]. New York: Columbia University Press, 2003.

[204] GENTZLER E. Contemporary translation theories [M]. London: Routledge, 1993.

[205] GILES L. The sayings of confucius: a new translation of the greater part of the confucian analects [M]. London: John Murray, 1907.

[206] GRICE H P. Logic and conversation [M]// COLE P, MORGAN J L. Syntax and semantics. New York: Academic

Press, 1975.

[207] GUTT E A. Translation and relevance: cognition and context [M]. London: Basil Blackwell Ltd, 1994.

[208] HALL E T. Beyond culture [M]. New York: Anchor Press, 1976.

[209] HALLIDAY M. An introduction to functional grammar[M]. London: Edward Arnold Ltd, 1985.

[210] HALLIDAY M, MCINTOSH A, STREVENS P. The linguistic sciences and language teaching[M]. London: Longman, 1964.

[211] HALLIDAY M, HASAN R. Cohesion in English [M]. London: Longman, 1976.

[212] HALLIDAY M, HASAN R. Language, context and text: a social semiotic perspective[M]. Deakin: Deakin University Press, 1985.

[213] HARZING A W, VAN DER WAL R. Google scholar as a new source for citation analysis [J]. Ethics in Science and Environmental Politics, 2008(1): 62-71.

[214] HATIM B, MASON I. Discourse and the translator [M]. London: Longman, 1990.

[215] HATIM B, MASON I. The translator as communicator[M]. London: Routledge, 1997.

[216] HATIM B, MUNDAY J. Translation: an advanced resource book[M]. London and New York: Routledge, 2004.

[217] HUILING Y. Theological interpretation on the sacred books of China and its political implication: a case study on james Legge's translation[J]. Sino-Christian Studies, 2011(11): 27-44.

[218] HOFSTEDE G. Culture's and organizations: software of the

[218] (continued) mind[M]. 3rd ed. London & Norkfolk: Mcgraw-Hill Book of Company Limited, 2010.

[219] HOLMES J S. The name and nature of translation studies[C]// HOLMES J S. Translated Papers on Literary Translation and Translation Studies. Amsterdam: Rodopi: 1988.

[220] HOLMES J S. Translation theory, translation theories, translation studies, and the translator[C]// HOLMES J S. Translated! Papers on literary translation and translation studies. Amsterdam: Rodopi, 1988.

[221] HUNSTON S. Corpora in applied linguistics[M]. Cambridge: Cambridge University Press, 2002.

[222] JAKOBSON R. On linguistic aspects of translation[C]// JAKOBSON R. Selected Writings. The Hague: Mouton, 1971.

[223] JAUSS H R. Literary history as a challenge to literary theory[C]// Newton K M. Twentieth century literary theory. London: Macmillan Education Ltd. , 1984.

[224] JINBO W. Back-translation in bilingual editions of Chinese classics: creating an original for Hong Lou Meng (*A Dream of Red Mansions/The Story of the Stone*)[J]. Translation & Literature, 2020(3): 355-371.

[225] KELLY D. Training the trainers: towards a description of translator trainer competence and training needs analysis[J]. TTR: Traduction, Terminologie, Redaction, 2008(1):99-125.

[226] KU H M. The discourse and sayings of confucius: a new special translation, illustrated with quotations from Goethe and other writers[M]. Shanghai: Kelly and Walsh limited, 1898.

[227] KU H M. The universal order of confucius, or the conduct of

life[M]. London: John Murray, 1906.

[228] LADO R. Linguistics across cultures[M]. Ann Arbor: The University of Michigan Press, 1957.

[229] LAKOFF G, JOHNSON M. Metaphors we live by[M]. London: The University of Chicago Press, 1980.

[230] LANGACKER R W. Foundations of cognitive grammar: theoretical prerequisites[M]. Stanford and California: Stanford University Press, 1987.

[231] LAU D C. Confucius: the analects[M]. London and New York: Penguine Group, 1979.

[232] LAU D C. Confucius: the analects[M]. HK: The Chinese University Press, 1992.

[233] LAVIOSA S. Core patterns of lexical use in a comparable corpus of English narrative prose[J]. Meta, 1988(4): 557-570.

[234] LEFEVERE A. Translation, rewriting and the manipulation of literary fame[M]. Shanghai: Shanghai Foreign Language Education Press, 2004.

[235] LEGGE J. Confucian analects, the great learning, and the doctrine of the mean[M]. Oxford: Clarendon Press, 1893.

[236] LEVINSON S C. Pragmatics[M]. Cambridge: Cambridge University Press, 1983.

[237] LEYS S. The analects of confucius[M]. New York and London: W. W. Norton & Company, 1997.

[238] LIN Y T. The wisdom of confucius[M]. New York: Random House, 1938.

[239] MALETZKE G. Psychology of mass communication: Theory and Systematics[M]. Hamburg: Hans-Bredow Institute, 1963.

[240] MARIA C P. Apropos of ideology[M]. Manchester, UK and Northampton MA: St, Jerome Publishing, 2003.

[241] MARSHMAN J. The works of confucius, containing the original text, with a translation[M]. Serampore: the Mission Press, 1809.

[242] MARTIN J R, ROSE D. Working with the discourse: meaning beyond the clause [M]. Sydney and Hong Kong: Continuum Press, 2003.

[243] MARTIN J R, WHITE P R. The language of evaluation: appraisal in English [M]. London and New York: Palgrave, 2005.

[244] MATTHEWS P H. Oxford concise dictionary of linguistics [Z]. Shanghai: Shanghai Foreign Language Education Press, 2000.

[245] MENGHAN Q. Penguin classics and the canonization of Chinese literature in English translation[J]. Translation & Literature. 2017(3): 295-316.

[246] MCMILLAN J H. Educational research: fundamentals for the consumer[M]. New York: Addison Wesley Longman Inc. , 2000.

[247] MCQUAIL D. Mass communication theory[M]. London: Sage Publications, 1996.

[248] MUNDAY J. Introducing translation studies: theories and applications[M]. London and New York: Routledge, 2001.

[249] NEUBERT A, SHREVE G M. Translation as text[M]. Kent: the Kent University Press, 1992.

[250] NEWMARK P. A textbook of translation[M]. London and New York: Prentice Hall, 1988.

[251] NEWMARK P. About translation[M]. Clevedon: Multilingual Matters, 1991.

[252] NEWMARK P. Approaches to translation [M]. Oxford: Pergamon, 1981.

[253] NYE J. S. Soft power: the means to success in world politics [M]. New York: Public Affairs, 2004.

[254] NI P M. Understanding the analects of confucius: a new translation of *Lunyu* with annotations[M]. New York: State University of New York Press, 2017.

[255] NIDA E A. Toward a science of translating, with special reference to principles and procedures involved in bible translating [M]. Leiden: Brill, 1964.

[256] NIDA E. Language and culture: contexts in translating [M]. Shanghai: Shanghai Foreign Language Education, 2001.

[257] NIDA E, TABER C R. The theory and practice of translation [M]. Leiden: E. J. Brill, 1969.

[258] NIKKILÄ P. Early confucianism and inherited thought in the light of some key terms of the confucian analects [M]. Helsinki: Finnish Oriental Society, 1992.

[259] NORD C. Translation as a purposeful activity: functional approaches explained[M]. Manchester: St. Jerome Publishing, 1997.

[260] NORD C. Translating as a purposeful activity[M]. Shanghai: Shanghai Foreign Language Education, 2001.

[261] NORD C. Text analysis in translation: theory, methodology, and didactic application of a model for translation-oriented text analysis [M]. 2nd ed. Beijing: Foreign Language Teaching and Research Press, 2006.

[262] OLOHAN M. Introducing corpora in translation studies[M]. London and New York: Routledge, 2004.

[263] PEARSON J. Terms in context [M]. Amsterdam and Philadelphia: John Benjamins Publishing Company, 1998.

[264] PLETT H F. Intertextuality[C]. Berlin: Hildebrand, 1991.

[265] POUND E. Confucius: the great digest, the unwobbling pivot, the analects[M]. New York: New Directions: 1951.

[266] ROBINSON D. Western translation theory: from herodotus to nietzsche[M]. Manchester: St. Jerome. 1997.

[267] REISS K. Translation criticism: the potentials & limitations [M]. Manchester: St. Jerome Publishing Company, 1971.

[268] REISS K. Texttypes, translation types and translation assessment[C]// CHESTERMAN A. Readings in Translation Theory. Finland: Oy Finn Lectura Ab. , 1989.

[269] REISS K. Type, kind and individuality of text: decision — making in translation [C]// VENUTI L. The Translation Studies Reader. London and New York: Routledge, 2000.

[270] SALDANHA G. Translator style: methodological considerations [J]. Translator, 2011, 17(1): 25-50.

[271] SAMOVAR L, RICHARD E P, LARRY A. Stefani. communication between cultures[M]. Belmont and California: Wadsworth Publishing, 1997.

[272] SHELBY T. Ideology, racism, and critical social theory[J]. The Philosophical Forum, 2003(2): 153-188.

[273] SHUTTLEWORTH M, COWIE M. Dictionary of translation studies[M]. Shanghai: Shanghai Foreign Language Education Press, 2004.

[274] SNELL-HORNBY M. Translation studies: an integrated

approach[M]. Amsterdam and Philadelphia: John Benjamins, 1988.

[275] SINCLAIR J. Corpus, concordance, collocation[M]. Oxford: Oxford University Press,1991.

[276] SLINGERLAND E. Confucius analects: with selections from traditional commentaries [M]. Indianapolis and Cambridge: Hackett Publishing Company, 2003.

[277] SNELL B, CRAMPTON P. Types of translations [C]// PICKEN C. The Translator's Handbook. London: Aslib, 1983.

[278] SOOTHILL W E. The analects of confucius[M]. Oxford: Oxford University Press, 1937.

[279] TOURY G. Descriptive translation studies and beyond[M]. Shanghai: Shanghai Foreign Language Education Press, 1995.

[280] TROSBORG A. Register, genre and text type [C]// TROSBORG A. Text Typology and Translation. Amsterdam and Philadelphia: John Benjamins Publishing Company, 1997.

[281] TROSBORG A. Text typology and translation [C]. Amsterdam: Benjamins, 1997.

[282] TSAI C C, BRUYA Brian. The analects: an illustrated edition [M]. Princeton, N J: Princeton University Press, 2018.

[283] TYLOR E. B. Primitive culture [M]. New York: Dover Publications, 1871.

[284] VAN DIJK T. Discourse as social interaction[M]. London: Sage Publications Ltd. , 1997.

[285] VAN DIJK T. Critical discourse analysis[C]// SCHIFFRIN T D, Tannen D, Hamilton H E. The Handbook of Discourse Analysis. Oxford: Blackwell, 2001.

[286] WALEY A. The analects of confucius[M]. London: George Allen & Unwin Ltd., 1938.

[287] WIDDOWSON H. Aspect of language teaching[M]. Oxford: Oxford University Press, 1990.

[288] WILSS W. The science of translation: problems and methods[M]. Shanghai: Shanghai Foreign Language Education Press, 2001.

[289] WRIGHT A F. The confucian persuasion[M]. Stanford and California: Stanford University Press, 1960.

[290] YAO X Z. An introduction to confucianism[M]. New York: Cambridge University Press, 2000.

[291] Ying C. Translation of Chinese classics: theory and practice[J]. Babel, 2016(2): 332-339.

附录 第三章例句英译分析示例

【例1】 子贡问曰:"孔文子何以谓之'文'也?"子曰:"敏而好学,不耻下问,是以谓之'文'也。"(《论语·公冶长》)

Legge: Tsze-kung asked, saying, 'On what ground did Kung-wan get that title of Wan?'

The Master said, "He was of an active nature and yet fond of learning, and he was not ashamed to ask and learn of his inferiors!-On these grounds he has been styled Wan."

Ku: A disciple, speaking of an ancient worthy of the time, enquired of Confucius saying, "How was it that he had the title of 'Beau-clerc' added as an honor to his name after his death?" "He was," answered Confucius, "a man of great industry, who applied himself to self-culture; he was not ashamed to seek for information from others more ignorant than himself. For that reason he has had the title of "Beau-clerc" added as an honor to his name after his death."

Lau: Tzu-kung asked, "Why was K'ung Wen Tzu called 'wen'?" The Master said, "He was quick and eager to learn: he was not ashamed to seek the advice of those who were beneath him in station. That is why he was called 'wen'."①

---

① In the chapter dealing with posthumous titles in the *Yi Chou shu* 逸周書 it is said that "diligence in learning and seeking advice is called 'wen'" (p. 196). It is likely that the Yi Chou shu, though traditionally taken to be earlier, in fact took the Analects as one of its sources.

Ames & Rosemont: Zigong inquired, "Why has Kong Wenzi been given the posthumous title of 'refined (wen 文)'?" The Master replied, "He was diligent and fond of learning, and was not ashamed to ask those of a lower status, this is why he has been called 'refined'."

Slingerland: Zigong asked, "Why was Kong Wenzi accorded the title 'Cultured' (wen 文)?"

The Master replied, "He was diligent and loved learning, and was not ashamed to ask advice from his inferiors. This is why he was accorded the title, 'Cultured.'"

Kong Wenzi ("Cultured Master Kong") is the posthumous title of Kong Yu, minister in the state of Wei (d. ca. 480 b.c.e.). Zigong is puzzled by Kong Yu's flattering posthumous title because Kong was a rather unvirtuous person, known for disloyalty and dissoluteness. Confucius' response probably serves a dual purpose. On the one hand, it serves as a statement about what constitutes the virtue of being cultured; on the other, it tells us that the sage focuses on a person's positive rather than negative qualities. As Xue Xuan observes, "The fact that the Master seizes on his inconspicuous goodness, rather than his obvious badness, illustrates the greatness of the sage's Way and the majesty of the sage's Virtue. Relying solely on the accounts of later people, one would be led to think that Kong Yu was a man unworthy of being discussed, and would thereby miss out on this chance to learn about this inconspicuous goodness."

【例2】 子曰:"温故而知新,可以为师矣。"(《论语·学而》)

Legge: The Master said, "If a man keeps cherishing his old knowledge, so as continually to be acquiring new, he may be a teacher of others."

To be able to teach others one must from his old stores be continually developing teaching new. 温 is expressed in the dictionary by 燖, and, with reference to this very passage, it is said, 'one's old learning being thoroughly mastered, again constantly to practice it, is called 温'. Modern commentators say that the 'new learning is in the old.' The idea probably is that of assimilating old acquisitions and new. Compare 中庸, XXVII. Vi.

Ku: Confucius remarked, "If a man will constantly go over what he has acquired and keep continually adding to it new acquirements, he may become a teacher of men."

Lau: The Master said, "A man is worthy of being a teacher who gets to know what is new by keeping fresh in his mind what he is already familiar with."

Ames&Rosemont: The Master said: "Reviewing the old as a means of realizing the new—such a person can be considered a teacher."

Slingerland: The Master said, "Both keeping past teachings alive and understanding the present—someone able to do this is worthy of being a teacher."

There is commentarial disagreement over whether this passage refers to keeping ancient teachings alive, or to keeping what one has previously learned in a lifetime current in one's mind so that one knows what to expect in the future. The role of the teacher would suggest the former. Li Ao points out, however, that passages such as 1.15 ("Informed as to what has gone before, you know what is to come") seem congruent with the latter interpretation.

【例3】 子曰:"三人行,必有我师焉;择其善者而从之,其不善者而改之。"(《论语·述而》)

Legge: The Master said, "When I walk along with two others, they may serve me as my teachers. I will select their good qualities and follow them, their bad qualities and avoid them."

Ku: Confucius remarked, "When three men meet together, one of them who is anxious to learn can always learn something of the other two. He can profit by the good example of the one and avoid the bad example of the other."

Lau: The Master said, "Even when walking in the company of two other men, I am bound to be able to learn from them. The good points of the one I copy; the bad points of the other I correct in myself.

Ames & Rosemont: The Master said, "In strolling in the company of just two other persons, I am bound to find a teacher. Identifying their strengths, I follow them, and identifying their weaknesses, I reform myself accordingly."

Slingerland: The Master said, "When walking with two other people, I will always find a teacher among them. I focus on those who are good and seek to emulate them, and focus on those who are bad in order to be reminded of what needs to be changed in myself."

> Alternately, Confucius may be referring to discrete qualities in his companions rather than their overall characters: in any person he can find both virtues to emulate and vices to avoid. Model emulation is the primary method of moral education for Confucius, and the implication here is that the process of education is never completed: even the Master always has something to learn. Cf. 4.17, 16.11.

【例4】 子曰:"巧言令色,鲜矣仁!"(《论语·学而》)

Legge: The Master said, "Fine words and an insinuating

appearance are seldom associated with true virtue."

Ku: Confucius remarked, "With plausible speech and fine manners will seldom be found moral character."

Lau: The Master said, "It is rare, indeed, for a man with cunning words and an ingratiating countenance to be benevolent."

Ames & Rosemont: The Master said: "it is a rare thing for glib speech and an insinuating appearance to accompany authoritative conduct (ren 仁)."

Slingerland: The Master said, "A clever tongue and fine appearance are rarely signs of Goodness."

This suspicion of glib speech and superficial appearance is found throughout *the Analects*. This saying is repeated in 17.7 below (cf. 5.5, 11.25, 12.3, 16.4), and in 15.11 the danger presented by "glib people" (*ningren* 佞人) is compared to the derangement of morals brought about by the music of Zheng. David Nivison (1999: 751) has made a very interesting observation that may explain Confucius' hatred for these clever, ingratiating people: in archaic Chinese, *ning* was pronounced *nieng*① and is actually a graphic modification of its cognate *ren* 仁(AC *nien*). The original meaning of *ren* was something like "noble in form," and it would appear that *ning* was its counterpart in the verbal realm: "attractive or noble in speech." In giving *ning* a negative meaning in *the Analects*, Confucius drives a wedge between the two qualities: *ren* now becomes "true" (i.e., inner) nobleness or Virtue, whereas *ning* represents the false, external counterfeit of *ren*. This is no doubt the sentiment behind such passages as 12.3, "The Good person is sparing of speech," and 13.27, "reticence is close to Goodness," as well as Confucius' general suspicion of

---

① Generally the modern Mandarin pronunciation of Chinese characters will be given, the Mandarin dialect being the standard form of modern spoken Chinese. When relevant, however, the postulated archaic pronunciation—reconstructed indirectly by historians of phonetics, and denoted with an asterisks—will also be provided.

language and outward show.

【例 5】 定公问:"君使臣,臣事君,如之何?"孔子对曰:"君使臣以礼,臣事君以忠。"(《论语·八佾》)

Legge: The Duke Ting asked how a prince should employ his ministers, and how ministers should serve their prince. Confucius replied, "A prince should employ his minister according to the rules of propriety; ministers should serve their prince with faithfulness."

Ku: The reigning prince of Confucius' native State asked Confucius how a prince should treat his public servant and how a public servant should behave to his prince. "Let the prince," answered Confucius, "treat his public servant with honor. The public servant must serve the prince, his master, with loyalty."

Lau: Duke Ting asked, "How should the ruler employ the services of his subjects? And how should a subject serve his ruler?" Confucius answered, "The ruler should employ the services of his subjects in accordance with the rites. A subject should serve his ruler by doing his utmost."

Ames & Rosemont: Duke Ding of Lu inquired: "How should rulers employ their ministers, and how should the ministers serve their lord?" Confucius replied, "Rulers should employ their ministers by observing ritual propriety (li 礼), and ministers should serve their lord by doing their utmost (zhong 忠)."

Slingerland: Duke Ding asked, "How should a lord employ his ministers? How should a minister serve his lord?"

Confucius replied, "A lord should employ his ministers with ritual, and ministers should serve their lord with dutifulness."

Again we have a general observation about ritual and virtue that probably has a more specific target as well. As Jiao Hong explains, "In *the Annals of Master Yan* we read, 'Only by means of ritual can one govern a state.' Ritual is the tool employed by the Former Kings when they considered titles and social distinctions and thereby eliminated the seeds of disorder. Duke Ding was the kind of ruler who 'held the blade of the sword and offered the handle to his enemies,'① and therefore Confucius wants him to protect himself by means of ritual. The Three Families were the type of ministers of whom one might say, 'the tail is too big to wag,'② and therefore Confucius wishes to instruct them in the ways of dutifulness."

【例6】 子曰:"出则事公卿,入则事父兄,丧事不敢不勉,不为酒困,何有于我哉?"(《论语·子罕》)

Legge: The Master said, "Abroad, to serve the high ministers and nobles; at home, to serve one's father and elder brothers; in all duties to the dead, not to dare not to exert one's self; and not to be overcome of wine: which one of these things do I attain to?"

Ku: Confucius remarked, "In public life to do one's duty to the nobles and princes whom one serves under; in private life to do one's duty to the members of one's family; in performing the last offices to the dead, to spare no pains lest anything should be neglected; and in using wine, to be able to resist the temptation of taking it to excess;—which one of there things can I say that I have been able to do?"

---

① A colloquial saying (literally 'to hold *tai-a* 太阿 [a famously sharp sword] backward') meaning essentially "to give someone the stick with which to beat you." The phrase first appeared in the *History of the Han*.

② That is, those in a normally inferior position have grown more powerful than those in a normally superior position—not too far in general meaning from the English saying, "The tail wagging the dog." The original reference is to the *Zuo Commentary* (Legge 1994d: 635).

Lau: The Master said, "To serve high officials when abroad, and my own elders when at home, in arranging funerals not to dare to spare myself, and to be able to hold my drink—For me, there is nothing to these at all."

Ames & Rosemont: The Master said, "To serve the Duke and his ministers at court, and to serve my elders at home, in funerary matters not to presume to give less than my best efforts, and not to be overcome by drink—how could such things give me any trouble at all?"

Slingerland: The Master said, "When in public, serving the Duke and his ministers; when at home, serving my father and elders; not daring to not exert myself to the utmost in performing funerary tasks; and not allowing myself to be befuddled by wine—these sorts of things present me with no trouble."

> This is a somewhat opaque passage. Perhaps the most sensible interpretation of it is that of Zhang Zhentao, who see it as a rebuke of those among Confucius' contemporaries who "though humble, were not willing to serve those who were noble; though young, were not willing to serve those who were elder; and who moreover were perfunctory and sloppy in their funeral arrangements and often besotted with wine."

【例7】 孔子于乡党,恂恂如也,似不能言者。其在宗庙朝廷,便便言,唯谨尔。(《论语·乡党》)

Legge: Confucius, in his village, looked simple and sincere, and as if he were not able to speak. When he was in the prince's ancestral temple, or in the court, he spoke minutely on every point, but cautiously.

Ku: Confucius in his life at home was shy and diffident, as if he were not a good speaker. In public life, however, in courts and councils, he spoke readily, but with deliberation.

Lau: In the local community, Confucius was submissive and seemed to be inarticulate. In the ancestral temple and at court, though fluent, he did not speak lightly.

Ames & Rosemont: In Confucius' home village, he was most deferential, as though at a loss for words, and yet in the ancestral temple and at court, he spoke articulately, though with deliberation.

Slingerland: In his village community, Confucius was respectful and circumspect, seeming to be at a loss for words. When in the ancestral temples or at court, however, he spoke eloquently, though always with caution and restraint.

As Zhu Xi understands it, this passage describes how Confucius' manner of speaking changed to accord with the social context:

> Seeming to be at a loss for words is a way to express humility and acquiescence, to avoid putting oneself above others by displaying one's sagely knowledge. In Confucius' home village, his elders and ancestors were present, and therefore when he was dwelling there his countenance was deferential. On the other hand, the ancestral temples are where ritual standards are preserved, and the court is where governmental affairs are decided, and therefore Confucius could not but be clear and particular in his speech: in such situations, it is necessary to inquire in detail and discuss at length, while at the same time always remaining cautious and not speaking carelessly.

Confucius' lack of eloquence at home, then, is an expression of reverence for his elders: even if he knew better than they did, he would acquiesce out of respect. In public life, however, a greater degree of forthrightness is called for. Cf. 3.15, 10.21.

【例8】 有子曰:"信近于义,言可复也。恭近于礼,远耻辱也。因不失其亲,亦可宗也。"(《论语·学而》)

Legge: The philosopher Yu said, "When agreements are made according to what is right, what is spoken can be made good. When respect is shown according to what is proper, one keeps far from shame and disgrace. When the parties upon whom a man leans are proper persons to be intimate with, he can make them his guides and masters."

Ku: A disciple of Confucius remarked, "If you make promises within the bounds of what is right, you will be able to keep your word. If you confine earnestness within the bounds of judgment and good taste, you will keep out of discomfiture and insult. If you make friends of those with whom you ought to, you will be able to depend upon them."

Lau: Yu Tzu said, 'To be trustworthy in word is close to being moral in that it enables one's words to be repeated.① To be respectful is to being observant of the rites in that it enables to stay clear of disgrace and insult. If, in promoting good relationship with relatives by marriage, a man manages not to lose the good will of his own kinsmen, he is worthy of being looked up to as the head of the clan.'②

Ames & Rosemont: Master You said: "That making good on one's word (*xin* 信) gets one close to being appropriate (*yi* 义) is because then what one says will bear repeating. That being deferential gets one close to observing ritual propriety (*li* 礼) is because it keeps

---

① For a discussion of the interpretation of this sentence see D. C. Lau, 'On the expression *fu yen*'.

② The sense of this last sentence is rather obscure. The present translation, though tentative, is based on a comment of Cheng Hsuan's on the word yin in the *Chou li* (*Chou li chu shu*, 10. 24b).

disgrace and insult at a distance. Those who are accommodating and do not lose those with whom they are close are deserving of esteem."

Slingerland: Master You said, "Trustworthiness comes close to rightness, in that your word can be counted upon. Reverence comes close to ritual propriety, in that it allows you to keep shame and public disgrace at a distance. Simply following these virtues, never letting them out of your sight-one cannot deny that this is worthy of respect."

Described here are secondary virtues that allow one to live a respectable life, but that lack the flexibility and subtlety of the primary virtues. In explaining why trustworthiness (xin) is only "close" to rightness, Liu Baonan cites Mencius 4: B: 11 "The great person is not always necessarily true to his word (xin), because he is concerned only with rightness," explaining that "trustworthiness must always be practiced with an eye toward what is right." Huang Kan illustrates the potential tension between trustworthiness and rightness with the story of the legendary paragon of trustworthiness, Wei Sheng, who once promised to meet a girl under a river bridge, come hell or high water. Unfortunately there was a great storm the next day, and the high water did come: the girl stayed at home, but Wei Sheng obstinately refused to abandon the appointed meeting place and so was drowned. "This is an example of trustworthiness not according with what is appropriate to the situation (yi 宜), where in fact it would be best if one did not keep one's word," Huang Kan concludes. Similarly, the feeling of reverence-although the root of ritual propriety-can in its raw form motivate actions that do not accord with the subtly-tuned dictates of ritual propriety.

【例9】 子曰:"能以礼让为国乎,何有! 不能以礼让为国,如礼何?"(《论语·里仁》)

Legge: The Master said, "If a prince is able to govern his kingdom with the complaisance proper to the rules of propriety, what difficulty will he have? If he cannot govern it with that complaisance, what has he to do with the rules of propriety?"

Ku: Confucius remarked, He who can rule a country by real courtesy and good manners that are in him, will find no difficulty in doing it. But a ruler who has no real courtesy and good manners in him, what can the mere rules of etiquette and formality avail him."

Lau: The Master said, 'If a man is able to govern a state by observing the rites and showing deference, what difficulties will he have in public life? If he is unable to govern a state by observing the rites and showing deference, what good are the rites to him?'

Ames & Rosemont: The Master said, "If rulers are able to effect order in the state through the combination of observing ritual propriety (*li* 礼) and deferring to others (*rang* 让), what more is needed? But if they are unable to accomplish this, what have they to do with observing ritual propriety?"

Slingerland: The Master said, "If a person is able to govern the state by means of ritual propriety and deference, what difficulties will he encounter? If, on the other hand, a person is not able to govern the state through ritual propriety and deference, of what use are the rites to him?"

Here we see two themes emphasized. The first concerns the efficacy of Virtue-based government, as opposed to government by force or reward and punishment, and is related to the distaste for contention and considerations of profit expressed throughout this Book. A passage from the *Zuo Commentary* describes the importance of ritual and deference for the functioning of the state:

Deference is the mainstay of ritual propriety. In an ordered age, gentlemen honor ability and defer to those below them, while the common people attend to their agricultural labors in order to serve those above them. In this way, both above and below ritual prevail, and slan- derers and evil men are dismissed and ostracized. All of this arises from a lack of contention, and is referred to as "excellent Virtue." Once an age declines into disorder, gentlemen strut about announcing their achievements in order to lord over the common people, and the common people boast of their skills in order to encroach upon the gentlemen. Both above and below there is a lack of ritual, giving birth simultaneously to disorder and cruelty. All of this arises from people contending over excellence, and is referred to as "darkened Virtue."

It is a constant principle that the collapse of the state will inevitably result from such a situation.

The second theme is related to the sort of anti-Ivory-Tower attitude expressed in 13.5: traditional practices are meant to be applied to the real world, not merely studied theoretically.

【例10】 子曰:"管仲之器小哉。"或曰:"管仲俭乎?"曰:"管氏有三归,官事不摄,焉得俭?""然则管仲知礼乎?"曰:"邦君树塞门,管氏亦树塞门。邦君为两君之好,有反坫,管氏亦有反坫。管氏而知礼,孰不知礼?"(《论语•八佾》)

Legge: The Master said, "Small indeed was the capacity[①] of Kwan Chung!" Someone said, "Was Kwan Chung parsimonious?" "Kwan," was the reply, "had the San Kwei, and his officers performed no double duties; how can he be considered parsimonious?" "Then, did Kwan Chung know the rules of propriety?" The Master said, "The princes of States have a screen intercepting the view at their gates. Kwan had likewise a screen at his gate. The princes of

---

① 器 see II. xii, but its significance here is different, and ＝our *measure* or *capacity*.

States on any friendly meeting between two of them, had a stand on which to place their inverted cups. Kwan had also such a stand. If Kwan Zhong knew the rules of propriety, who does not know them?"

Ku: Confucius, speaking of a famous statesman (the Bismarck of the time), remarked, "Kuan Chung was by no means a great-minded man!" "But," said somebody, "Kuan Chung was simple in his life: was he not?" "Why," replied Confucius, "Kuan Chung had that magnificent Sansouci Pleasaunce of his. Besides, he had a special officer appointed to every function in his household. How can one say that he was simple in his life?" "Well," rejoined the enquirer, "but still, Kuan Chung was a man of taste who observed the correct forms; was he not?" "No," answered Confucius, "The reigning princes have walls built before their palace gates. Kuan Chung also had a wall built before his door. When two reigning princes meet, each has a special buffet. Kuan Chung also had his special buffet. If you say Kuan Chung was a man of taste①, who is not a man of taste?"

Lau: The Master said, "Kuan Chung was, indeed, a vessel of small capacity." Someone remarked, "Was Kuan Chung frugal, then?"

"Kuan Chung kept three separate establishments, each complete with its own staff. How can he be called frugal?' 'In that case, did Kuan Chung understand the rites?"

"Rulers of states erect gate-screens; Kuan Chung erected such a screen as well. The ruler of a state, when entertaining the ruler of another state, has a stand for inverted cups; Kuan Chung had such a

---

① It is curious that kuan Chung, the Bismarck of ancient China, adopted the same motto in politics as that famous motto of the modern Founder of the German Empire—Do, ut des—*in Chinese* 欲取之故与之.

stand as well. If even Kuan Chung understood the rites, who does not understand them?"

Ames & Rosemont: The Master said: "Guanzhong was lacking in capacity." Someone asked: "Do you mean that Guanzhong was frugal?" The Master replied: "Guanzhong had three residences and each member of his staff had only one responsibility. Where's the frugality?" "This being so, did Guanzhong understand the observance of ritual propriety (*li* 礼)?" he was asked. The Master replied: "The ruler of the state set up ornamental stone blinds before his gates, and Guanzhong did the same; for entertaining other rulers the ruler of the state had a stand for inverting drinking vessels, and Guanzhong had the same. If we say that Guanzhong understood the observance of ritual propriety, then who doesn't?"

Slingerland: The Master said, "Guan Zhong's vessel was of small capacity." Someone asked, "Do you mean that he was frugal?"

The Master replied, "Guan maintained three separate residences and had a separate staff member for each duty. How could he be called frugal?"

"Well, then, do you mean to say that Guan Zhong understood ritual?

The Master replied, "The lord of a state erects a wall in front of his gate, and Guan did the same. The lord of a state, when entertaining other lords, has a stand upon which to place the drinking cups after the toast, and Guan also had one of these. If Guan understood ritual, who does not understand it?"

Qi 器 refers literally to a ritual vessel, and Confucius' helpfully obtuse questioner is apparently taking his statement at face value: perhaps Confucius means that Guan Zhong was frugal and used small, unelaborated ritual implements, or perhaps that he used small ritual vessels because this is what was ritually proper to do. Both questions give Confucius an opportunity to remark upon Guan Zhong's moral failings, and to make it clear that he means *qi* in the metaphorical sense we saw in 2.12: a person who is a narrow specialist or technician. Guan Zhong was a seventh century b.c.e. statesman who encouraged Duke Huan of *Qi* to dispense with the traditional Zhou feudal state structure and helped him reorganize *Qi* along more technocratic, efficient lines. This caused *Qi* to become quite powerful economically and militarily, allowing Duke Huan to officially subordinate other Zhou states under his rule and thus become the first of the officially recognized hegemons (*ba* 霸). Although Confucius expresses admiration for Guan Zhong in 14.16 and 14.17 (and perhaps in 14.9), at a deeper level he disapproves of his narrowly pragmatic approach and flouting of traditional norms and institutions.

【例 11】 子曰:"君子喻于义,小人喻于利"。(《论语•里仁》)

Legge: The Master said, "The mind of the superior man is conversant with righteousness; the mind of the mean man is conversant with gain."

Ku: Confucius remarked, "A wise man sees what is right in a question; a fool, what is advantageous to himself."

Lau: The Master said, "The gentleman is versed in what is moral. The small man is versed in what is profitable."

Ames & Rosemont: The Master said, "Exemplary persons (*junzi* 君子) understand what is appropriate (*yi* 义); petty persons understand what is of personal advantage (*li* 利)."

Slingerland: The Master said, "The gentleman understands rightness, whereas the petty person understands profit."

Again, the gentleman is motivated by the inner goods of Confucian practice rather than the promise of external goods. Cf. 4.2, 4.5, 4.9, 4.11, and 4.12. Some commentators argue that the distinction between the gentleman and the petty person (*xiaoren*) should be understood in terms of social class, because *xiaoren* is often used in Han texts to indicate simply the "common people." It is clear, though, that Confucius felt anyone from any social class could potentially become a gentleman (6.6, 7.7) and that social status did not necessarily correspond to actual moral worth. It is apparent that—in the *Analects* at least—the gentleman/*xiaoren* distinction refers to moral character rather than social status.

【例12】 孔子谓季氏,"八佾舞于庭,是可忍也,孰不可忍也。"(《论语·八佾》)

Legge: Confucius said of the head of the Chi family, who had eight rows of pantomimes in his area, "If he can bear to do this, what may he not bear to do?"

Note: 季氏, by contraction for 季孙氏; see on IL. V. 氏 and 姓 are now used without distinction, meaning "surname," only that the 氏 of a woman is always spoken of, and not her 姓. Originally the 氏 appears to have been used to denote the branch families of one surname. 季氏, "The Chi family," with special reference to its head, "The Chi," as we should say. 佾, "a row of dancers," or pantomimes rather, who kept time in the temple services, in the 庭, the front space before the rasied portion in the principal hall, moving or brandishing feathers, flags, or other articles. In his ancestral temple, the king had eight rows, each row consisting of eight men, a duke or prince had six, and a great officer only four. For the Chi, therefore, to use eight rows was a usurpation, for though it may be argued, that to the ducal family of Lu royal rites were conceded, and that the offshoots of it (LI. V) might use the same, still great officers were confined to the ordinances proper to their rank. 谓 is used here, as frequently, in the sense — to speak of. Confucius's remark may also be translated, "If this be endured, what may not be translated?"

Ku: The head of a powerful family of nobles in Confucius' native State employed eight sets of choristers [an Imperial prerogative] in their family chapel. Confucius, remarking on this, was heard to say, "If this is allowed to pass, what may not be allowed?"

Lau: Confucius said of the Chi family, "They use eight rows of eight dancers each① to perform in their courtyard. If this can be tolerated, what cannot be tolerated?"

Ames & Rosemont: Confucius remarked on the Ji clan: "If the Ji clan's use of the imperial eight rows of eight dancers in the courtyard of their estate can be condoned, what cannot be?"

Slingerland: Confucius said of the Ji Family, "They have eight rows of dancers performing in their courtyard. If they can condone this, what are they not capable of?"

According to later ritual texts, different ranks in society were allowed different numbers of dancers to perform outside the ancestral hall during ceremonial occasions: the Son of Heaven allowed eight rows of eight dancers, feudal lords six rows, ministers four rows, and official two rows. Although he was de facto ruler of Lu, the head of the Ji Family officially held only the position of minister, and his use of eight dancers thus represented an outrageous usurpation of the ritual prerogatives of the Zhou king.

【例 13】 子曰:"三军可夺帅也,匹夫不可夺志也。"(《论语·子罕》)

Legge: The Master said, "The commander of the forces of a large

---

① A prerogative of the Emperor.

state may be carried off, but the will of even a common man cannot be taken from him."

Ku: Confucius remarked, "The general of an army may be carried off, but a man of the common people cannot be robbed of his free will."

Lau: The Master said, "The Three Armies can be deprived of their commander, but there is no way a common man can be deprived of his purpose."

Ames & Rosemont: The Master said, "The Combined Armies can be deprived of their commander, but common peasants cannot be deprived of their purposes."

Slingerland: The Master said, "The three armies① can have their general taken from them by force, but even a commoner cannot be deprived of his will in this fashion."

As Kong Anguo comments, "Although the three armies are numerous, people's hearts are not unified, and therefore you can forcibly deprive such a group of their general and thereby take them. Although a common person is negligible, if he manages to hold firmly to his will, one will not be able to take it from him." For a similar metaphor of the will as military "general" in charge of guiding the rest of the self, see Mencius 2: A:2. Hu Bingwen relates 9.26 to the passages that precede it by arguing that it has to do with dedication to learning:

The ten passages from 9.17 to 9.26 all have to do with encouraging people and urging them on in the task of learning. When it comes to learning, there is nothing more crucial than "setting your heart [will] upon it."② If you have set

---

① I. e., the combined forces of an entire state; cf. 7.11.
② A reference to 2.4, where *lizhi* 立志(more literally "establishing one's will [with regard to]") was translated as "setting one's heart [upon]."

your heart upon learning you can move forward [9.19], which must necessarily be unremitting like the flow of the river toward the sea [9.17]. Without such a will you will stop short, which will necessarily leave the mountain uncompleted [9.19]. Thus, those who engage in learning but who are in the end taken by some external object are simply lacking in willpower.

Part of the point of this passage is thus that all people possess their own, self-determined will, which means that there is simply no excuse for not directing it toward self-cultivation. Cf. 6.12, 9.31.

【例14】 有子曰:"礼之用,和为贵。先王之道,斯为美;小大由之。有所不行,知和而和,不以礼节之,亦不可行也。"(《论语·学而》)

Legge: The philosopher Yu said, "In practicing the rules of propriety, a natural ease is to be prized. In the ways prescribed by the ancient kings, this is the excellent quality, and in things small and great we follow them. "Yet it is not to be observed in all cases. If one, knowing how such ease should be prized, manifests it, without regulating it by the rules of propriety, this likewise is not to be done."

Note: In ceremonies a natural ease is is to be realized, and yet to be subordinate to the end of ceremonies,—the reverential observance of propriety. 1. 礼 is not easily rendered in another language. There underlies it the idea of what is proper. It is 事之宜, "the fitness of things," what reason calls for in the performance of duties towards superior beings, and between man and man. Our term "ceremonies" comes near its meaning here. 道 is here a name for 礼, as indicating the courses or ways to be trodden by men. In 小大由之, the antecedent to 之 is not 和, but 礼 or 道. 2. Observe the force of the 亦, "also", in the last clause, and how it affirms the general principle enunciated in the first paragraph.

Ku: A disciple of Confucius remarked, "In the practice of art,① what is valuable is natural spontaneity. According to the rules of art held by the ancient kings it was this quality in a work of art which constituted its excellence; in great as well as in small things they were guided by this principle. But in being natural there is something not permitted. To know that it is necessary to be natural without restraining the impulse to be natural by the strict principle of art— that is something not permitted."

The English word "art", if we mistake not, is used in various senses to express: 1st, a work of art; 2nd, the practice of art; 3rd, artificial as opposed to natural; 4th, the principle of art as opposed to the principle of nature; 5th, the strict principle of art. In this last sense of the use of the Englsih word "art" lies, as DR. LEGGE says of the Chinese word mentioned above, "the idea of what is proper " and fit, ΤΟπΡ´επΟV, in all *relations* of things.

For those who may be interested in the subject, we may here mention that the modern Japanese invention, *bijutsu* 美术 (beautiful legerdemain) for "art" is not a happy one. The proper term in Chinese for a workd of art would be 文物; for the practice of art, 艺. In fact, the Japanese word Geisha. 艺师 means literally an artiste. As for the use of the term "art" in the sense of "artficial" as opposed to something "natural", the philosopher Chuang TZ uses 人 (human) and 天 (divine).

Then "the principle of art", not taken by itself, but as opposed to the principle pf nature, would be in Chinese 文 for "art" and 质 for "nature". Such a sentence as that of GOETHE, for instance, "Art is called Art, because it is not Nature," would be rendered into Chinese or Japanese thus: 文之所以谓之文

---

① Dr. Legge says of the Chinese word 礼, which we have here translated "art", that it is a word not easily rendered in another language. On the other hand, Mr. B. H. CHAMBERLAIN, in his book *Things Japanese*, remarks that the Japanese language [China and Japan have the same written language] has no genuine native word for "art".

为非质也. Chinese are critics also speaks of 化工 creative art and 画工 initiative art. Finally, we may as well add, the Chinese term for mechanical art or the practice of it is 技艺.

Lau: Yu Tzu said, 'Of the things brought about by the rites, harmony is the most valuable. Of the ways of the Former Kings, this is the most beautiful, and is followed alike in matters great and small, yet this will not always work: to aim always at harmony without regulating it by the rites simply because one knows only about harmony will not, in fact, work.'

Ames & Rosemont: Master You said: "Achieving harmony (*he* 和) is the most valuable function of observing ritual propriety (*li* 礼). In the ways of the Former Kings, this achievement of harmony made them elegant, and was a guiding standard in all things large and small. But when things are not going well, to realize harmony just for its own sake without regulating the situation through observing ritual propriety will not work."

Slingerland: Master You said, "When it comes to the practice of ritual, it is harmonious ease (he) that is to be valued. It is precisely such harmony that makes the Way of the Former Kings so beautiful. If you merely stick rigidly to ritual in all matters, great and small, there will remain that which you cannot accomplish. Yet if you know enough to value harmonious ease but try to attain it without being regulated by the rites, this will not work either."

What it means to practice ritual with "harmonious ease" (i.e., in an wu-wei fashion) is illustrated in the description of Confucius' ritual behavior in Book Ten. Ritual behavior must be accompanied by such easy joy and harmony if it is to be truly valued. On the other hand, such "ease" involves more than simply indulging one's innate emotions: the innate emotions must be properly shaped by ritual forms before they can become truly "harmonious." The message here is related to the theme of possessing both "native substance" (*zhi* 质) and "cultural refinement" (*wen* 文) in their proper balance (cf. 3.8, 6.18).

【例15】 子曰:"人而不仁,如礼何? 人而不仁,如乐何?"(《论语·八佾》)

Legge: The Master said, "If a man be without the virtues proper to humanity, what has he to do with the rites of propriety? If a man be without the virtues proper to humanity, what has he to do with music?"

Ku: Confucius remarked, "If a man is without moral character, what good can the use of the fine arts do him? If a man is without moral character, what good can the use of music do him?"

Lau: The Master said, 'What can a man do with the rites who is not benevolent? What can a man do with music who is not benevolent?'

Ames & Rosemont: The Master said: "What has a person who is not authoritative (ren 仁) got to do with observing ritual propriety (li 礼)? What has a person who is not authoritative got to do with the playing of music (yue 乐)?"

Slingerland: The Master said, "A man who is not Good-what has he to do with ritual? A man who is not Good-what has he to do with music?"

Although it serves as a general statement concerning the relationship of internal disposition to Confucian practice (cf. 3.12 and 17.11), this comment is probably more specifically directed at the head of the Ji Family and the other leading families of Lu criticized in 3.1 and 3.2. A passage in the History of the

Han, after quoting this line, explains,

> The point is that a person who is not Good does not have the means to apply himself … not having the means to apply himself, he is unable to practice ritual and music. Even if he has many other talents, they will only be used to do no good. During the Master's age, ritual and music were under attack by the ministers [of Lu], who greedily usurped the prerogatives of the king and mutually followed the established habits of corruption, and practiced wrongness so that it triumphed over what was right.

【例16】 父在观其志,父没观其行,三年无改于父之道,可谓孝矣。(《论语·学而》)

Legge: The Master said, "While a man's father is alive, look at the bent of his will; when his father is dead, look at his conduct. If for three years he does not alter from the way of his father, he may be called filial."

Ku: Confucius remarked, "When a man's father is living the son should have regard to what his father would have him do; when the father is dead, to what his father has done. A son who for three years after his father's death does not in his own life change his father's principles, may be said to be a good son."

Lau: The Master said, "Observe what a man has in mind to do when his father is living, and then observe what he does when his father is dead. If, for three years, he makes no changes to his father's ways, he can be said to be a good son."

Ames & Rosemont: The Master said: "While a person's father is still alive, observe what he intends; when his father dies, observe what he does. A person who for three years refrains from reforming the ways (*dao* 道) of his late father can be called a filial son (*xiao* 孝)."

Slingerland: The Master said, "When someone's father is still alive, observe his intentions; after his father has passed away, observe his conduct. If for three years he does not alter the ways of his father, he may be called a filial son."

Three years (usually understood as into the third year, or twenty five months) is the standard mourning period for a parent. As Kong Anguo explains, "When his father is still alive, the son is not able to act as he wants [because he must obey the father's commands], so one can only observe his intentions in order to judge his character. It is only once his father has passed away that the son can learn about his character by observing his own actions. As long as the filial son is in mourning, his sorrow and longing is such that it is as if the father were still present, and this is why he does not alter the ways of his father." Yin Tun clarifies, "If the ways of his father are in accor- dance with the Way, it would be perfectly acceptable to go his entire life without changing them. If they are not in accordance with the Way, though, why does he wait three years to change them? Even in the latter case, the filial son goes three years without making any changes because his heart is blocked by a certain reluctance." In this passage, we see hints of the priority given to familial affection and loyalty over considerations of what is more abstractly "right" that is expressed more starkly in 13.18.

【例17】 子曰:"学而时习之,不亦说乎? 有朋自远方来,不亦乐乎? 人不知而不愠,不亦君子乎?"(《论语·学而》)

Legge: The Master said "Is it not pleasant to learn with a constant perseverance and application? "Is it not delightful to have friends coming from distant quarters? "Is he not a man of complete virtue, who feels no discomposure though men may take no note of him?"

Note: The word 学, "learn", rightly occupies the forfront in the studies of a nation, of which its education system has so long been the distinction and glory.

君子: I translate here—a man of complete virtue. Literally, it is—"a pincely man." See on 子, above. It is a technical term in Chinese moral writers, for which there is no exact correspondency in English, and which cannot be rendered always in the same way. See Morrison's Dictionary.

Ku: Confucius remarked, "It is indeed a pleasure to acquire knowledge and, as you go on acquiring, to put into practice what you have acquired. A greater pleasure still it is when friends of congenial minds come from afar to seek you because of your attainments. But he is truly a wise and good man who feels no discomposure even when he is not noticed of men."

Lau: The Master said, "Is it not a pleasure, having learned something, to try it out at due intervals? Is it not a joy to have like-minded friends come from afar? Is it not gentlemanly not to take offence when others fail to appreciate your abilities?"

Ames & Rosemont: The Master said: "Having studied[1], to then repeatedly apply what you have learned—is this not a source of pleasure? To have friends come from distant quarters—is this not a source of enjoyment? To go unacknowledged by others without harboring frustration—is this not the mark of an exemplary person (*junzi* 君子).

Gilbert Ryle (1949) makes a distinction between "task" or "process" words such as "study", and "achievement" or "success" words such as "learn." Given the priority of process and change over form and stasis as the natural condition of things in classical Chinese cosmology, the language tends to favor the former. See Hall and Ames(1998): 229-30 and Hall and Ames(1995):183-97.

(Ames & Rosemont, 1998:230)

Slingerland: The Master said, "To learn and then have occasion to practice what you have learned—is this not satisfying? To have friends arrive from afar—is this not a joy? To be patient even when others do not understand—is this not the mark of the gentleman?"

As Cheng Shude (following Mao Qiling) notes, "People today think of 'learning' as the pursuit of knowledge, whereas the ancients thought of 'learning' as cultivating the self." For evidence, he points to 6.3, where Confucius cites Yan Hui as the only one of his disciples that truly loved learning because he "never misdirected his anger and never repeated a mistake twice," and 2.18, where learning is described in terms of seldom erring in one's speech and seldom having cause for regret in one's behavior. This is an important point: we will see throughout the text that the sort of learning Confucius is interested in is a practical kind of "know-how" rather than abstract theoretical knowledge (see 1.7). Li Chong explains that the three activities mentioned in 1.1 refer to the stages of learning: mastering the basics, discussing them with fellow students and working hard at mastering them, and finally becoming a teacher of others.

【例 18】 子曰:"由,诲女知之乎! 知之为知之,不知为不知,是知也。"(《论语·为政》)

Legge: The Master said, "Yu, shall I teach you what knowledge is? When you know a thing, to hold that you know it; and when you do not know a thing, to allow that you do not know it; this is knowledge."

Ku: Confucius said to a disciple, "shall I teach you what is understanding? To know what it is that you know, and to know what it is that you do not know, — that is understanding."

Lau: The Master said, "Yu, shall I tell you what it is to know. To say you know when you know, and to say you do not when you do not, that is knowledge."

Ames & Rosemont: The Master said: "Zilu, shall I teach you what wisdom (*zhi* 知) means?" To know (*zhi* 知) what you know and know what you do not know—this then is wisdom."

Slingerland: The Master said, "Zilu, remark well what I am about to teach you! This is wisdom: to recognize what you know as what you know, and recognize what you do not know as what you do not know."

An elaborated version of this story, which also links it to 2.18 below, is found in the Xunzi. Zilu appears to Confucius dressed in what the Master deems to be a pretentious manner, and is therefore scolded. After hurrying out to change into more humble clothing, Zilu reappears and is lectured to by the Master:

"Remark well what I am about to tell you. One who is not careful about his words becomes pompous, and one who is not careful about his behavior becomes a show-off. One who puts on the appearance of knowledge and ability is a petty person. Therefore, when the gentleman knows something, he says, 'I know it,' and when he doesn't know something, he says, 'I do not know it.' This is the essence of speech. When the gentleman is able to do something, he says, 'I am able to do it,' and when he is not able to do something, he says, 'I am not able to do it.' This is the perfection of behavior."

We also read in the Xunzi the helpful comment, "Knowing when it is appropriate to speak is wisdom; knowing when it is appropriate to remain silent is also wisdom."

【例 19】 子曰:"《诗》三百,一言以蔽之,曰:'思无邪。'"(《论语·为政》)

Legge: The Master said, "In *the Book of Poetry* are three hundred pieces, but the design of them all may be embraced in one sentence 'Having no depraved thoughts.'"

Note: The pure design of the design or *the book or poetry*. The number of compositions in the Shih-ching is rather more than the round number here given. 思无邪, see Shih-ching, IV. ii. 1. st. 4. The sentence there is indicative, and, in praise of the duke Hal, who had no depraved thoughts. The sage would seem to have been intending the design in compiling the Shih. A few individual pieces are calculated to have a different effect.

Ku: Confucius remarked, "*The Book of Ballads, Songs and Psalms* contains three hundred pieces. The moral of them all may be summed up in one sentence: 'Have no evil thoughts.'"

Lau: The Master said, "*The Odes* are three hundred in number. They can be summed up in one phrase: 'Swerving not from the right path'①.

Ames & Rosemont: The Master said: "Although *the Songs* are three hundred in number, they can be covered in one expression: 'Go vigorously without swerving.'"

Slingerland: The Master said, "*The Odes* number several hundred, and yet can be judged with a single phrase: 'Oh, they will not lead you astray.'"

The quoted phrase is from *Ode* 297. The original reference is to powerful

---

① This line is from *Ode* 297 where it describes a team of horses going straight ahead without swerving to left or right.

war horses bred to pull chariots and trained not to swerve from the desired path. The metaphorical meaning is that one committed through study to *the Odes*—"yoked" to them, as it were—will not be lead astray from the Confucian Way.

【例20】 子曰:"兴于《诗》,立于礼,成于乐。"(《论语·泰伯》)

Legge: The Master said, "It is by *the Odes* that the mind is aroused. "It is by the Rules of Propriety that the character is established. "It is from Music that the finish is received."

Note: The terms 诗, 礼, 乐 have all specific references to the Books so called.

Ku: Confucius remarked, "In education sentiment is called out by the study of poetry; judgment is formed by the study of the arts; and education of the character is completed by the study of music."

Lau: The Master said, 'Be stimulated by *the Odes*, take your stand on the rites and be perfected by music.'

Ames & Rosemont: The Master said, "I find inspiration by intoning the songs, I learn where to stand from observing ritual propriety (*li* 礼), and I find fulfillment in playing music."

Slingerland: The Master said, "Find inspiration in *the Odes*, take your place through ritual, and achieve perfection with music."

Here we have a more succinct version of the course of Confucian self-cultivation described in 2.4. The translation of the first phrase follows Jiang Xi's interpretation of *xing* 兴 as "to inspire, stimulate": "Gazing upon the intentions of the ancients can give inspiration to one's own intention." Bao Xian takes *xing* to mean, more prosaically, "to begin": "The point is that the cultivation of the self should start with study of *the Odes*." "Taking one's place" through ritual involves, as discussed in 2. 4, taking up one's role as an adult among other adults in society, something that requires a mastery of the rituals governing social interactions. Steps one and two thus represent, respectively, cognitive shaping through learning and behavioral shaping through ritual training. Finally, the joy inspired by the powerfully moving music of the ancients brings the cognitive and behavioral together into the unselfconscious, effortless perfection that is wu-wei. *Mencius* 4: A: 27, which invokes the metaphor of dance, represents perhaps the best commentary on this passage:

The substance of benevolence (*ren*) is the serving of one's parents; the substance of rightness is obeying one's elders; the substance of wisdom is to understand benevolence and rightness and to not let them go; the substance of ritual propriety is the regulation and adornment of benevolence and rightness; and the substance of music is the joy one takes in benevolence and rightness. Once such joy is born, it cannot be stopped. Once it cannot be stopped, then one begins unconsciously to dance it with one's feet and wave one's arms in time with it.

Some commentators take all three nouns in the passage as titles of classical texts- "Take inspiration from *the Book of Odes*, take your place with *the Book of Ritual*, and perfect yourself with *the Book of Music*"-but it is unlikely that such books existed in Confucius' time.

【例21】 子贡曰:"贫而无谄,富而无骄,何如?"子曰:"可也;未若贫而乐,富而好礼者也。"子贡曰:"《诗》云:'如切如磋,如琢如磨',其斯之谓与?"子曰:"赐也,始可与言《诗》已矣,告诸往而知来者。"(《论语·学而》)

Legge: Tsze-kung said, "What do you pronounce concerning the poor man who yet does not flatter, and the rich man who is not proud?" The Master replied, "They will do; but they are not equal to him, who, though poor, is yet cheerful, and to him, who, though rich, loves the rules of propriety." Tsze-kung replied, "It is said in the Book of Poetry, 'As you cut and then file, as you carve and then polish.'-The meaning is the same, I apprehend, as that which you have just expressed." The Master said, "With one like Ts'ze, I can begin to talk about *the Odes*. I told him one point, and he knew its proper sequence."

Ku: A disciple of Confucius said to him, "To be poor and yet not to be servile; to be rich and yet not to be proud, what do you say to that?" "It is good." replied Confucius, "but better still it is to be poor and yet contented; to be rich and yet know how to be courteous." "I understand," answered the disciple "'we must cut, we must file, must chisel and must grind.' That is what you mean, is it not?" "My friend," replied Confucius, "now I can begin to speak of poetry to you. I see you understand how to apply the moral."

Lau: Tzu-kung said, '"Poor without being obsequious, wealthy without being arrogant.' What do you think of this saying?'"

The Master said, 'That will do, but better still "Poor yet delighting in the Way, wealthy yet observant of the rites."'

Tzu-kung said, '*The Odes* say, Like bone cut, like horn polished, Like jade carved, like stone ground. Is not what you have said a case in point?' The Master said, 'Ssu①, only with a man like you can one discuss the Odes. Tell such a man something and he can see its relevance to what he has not been told.'

Ames & Rosemont: Zigong said: "What do you think of the saying: 'Poor but not inferior; rich but not superior'?" The Master replied: "Not bad, but not as good as: 'Poor but enjoying the way (*li* 道); rich but loving ritual propriety (*li* 礼).'" Zigong said:

---

① Tuan-mu Ssu, Tzu-kung.

"*The Book of Songs* states: 'Like bone carved and polished, like jade cut and ground.' Is this not what you have in mind?" The Master said: "Zigong, it is only with the likes of you then that I can discuss the Songs! On the basis of what has been said, you know what is yet to come."

Slingerland: Zigong said, "Poor without being obsequious, rich without being arrogant-what would you say about someone like that?"

The Master answered, "That is acceptable, but it is still not as good as being poor and yet joyful, rich and yet loving ritual."

Zigong said, "An ode says, 'As if cut, as if polished; As if carved, as if ground. Is this not what you have in mind?"

The Master said, "Zigong, you are precisely the kind of person with whom one can begin to discuss *the Odes*. Informed as to what has gone before, you know what is to come."

"Cutting and polishing" refer to the working of bone and ivory, while "carving and grinding" refer to jade work: cutting and carving being the initial rough stages, and polishing and grinding the finishing touches. Here the task of self-cultivation is understood metaphorically in terms of the arduous process of roughly shaping and then laboriously finishing recalcitrant materials. Zigong's quotation of this ode shows that he has instantly grasped Confucius' point, explained quite nicely by Zhu Xi:

Ordinary people become mired in poverty or wealth, not knowing how to be self-possessed in such circumstances, necessarily leading to the two faults of obsequiousness or arrogance. A person who is able to be free of both knows how to be self-possessed, but has still not reached the point of completely transcending poverty and wealth ... When a person is joyful he is relaxed in his mind and physically at ease, and therefore forgets about poverty; when he loves ritual, he is at peace wherever he goes and follows principles in a cheerful, good-natured fashion, being equally unconscious of wealth. Zigong was a businessman, probably starting out poor and then becoming rich, and therefore had to exert effort to remain self-possessed. This is why he asked this particular question. The Master's answer was probably intended to acknowledge what Zigong had already achieved while at the same time encouraging him to continue striving after that which he had yet to attain.

Zhu Xi also notes that Zigong's quotation reveals not only that he has grasped Confucius' specific point-that he, Zigong, still has quite a bit of "finishing" work to do-but also serves as a general statement of the Confucian view of self-cultivation: that one "should not be so satisfied with small achievements that one fails to urge oneself on" (5.8). This instant grasping of the larger point to be taught is an excellent example of a student "being given three corners of a square and coming up with the fourth" (7.8).

【例 22】 尧曰:"咨!尔舜。天之历数在尔躬,允执其中。四海困穷,天禄永终。"舜亦以命禹。曰:"予小子履,敢用玄牡,敢昭告于皇皇后帝:有罪不敢赦。帝臣不蔽,简在帝心。朕躬有罪,无以万方;万方有罪,罪在朕躬。"周有大赉,善人是富。"虽有周亲,不如仁人。百姓有过,在予一人。"谨权量,审法度,修废官,四方之政行焉。兴灭国,继绝世,举逸民,天下之民归心焉。所重:民、食、丧、祭。宽则得众,信则民任焉,敏则有功,公则说。(《论语·尧曰》)

Legge: Yao said, "Oh! You, Shun, the Heaven-determined order of succession now rests in your person. Sincerely hold fast the due Mean. If there shall be distress and want within the four seas, the Heavenly revenue will come to a perpetual end."

Shun also used the same language in giving charge to Yu. T'ang said, "I the child Li, presume to use a dark-colored victim, and presume to announce to Thee, O most great and sovereign God, that the sinner I dare not pardon, and thy ministers, O God, I do not keep in obscurity. The examination of them is by thy mind, O God. If, in my person, I commit offenses, they are not to be attributed to you, the people of the myriad regions. If you in the myriad regions commit offenses, these offenses must rest on my person."

Chau conferred great gifts, and the good were enriched. "Although he has his near relatives, they are not equal to my virtuous men. The people are throwing blame upon me, the One man."

He carefully attended to the weights and measures, examined the body of the laws, restored the discarded officers, and the good government of the kingdom took its course. He revived states that had been extinguished, restored families whose line of succession had been broken, and called to office those who had retired into obscurity, so that throughout the kingdom the hearts of the people turned towards him. What he attached chief importance to were the food of the people, the duties of mourning, and sacrifices. By his generosity, he won all. By his sincerity, he made the people repose trust in him. By his earnest activity, his achievements were great. By his justice, all were delighted.

Ku: The ancient Emperor Yao, when in his old age he abdicated the throne in favour of his successor, Shun, thus gave him charge: "Hail to thee, O Shun! The God-ordained order of succession now rests upon thy person. Hold fast with thy heart and soul to the true middle course of right. If there shall be distress and what among the people within the Empire, the title and honour which God has given to thee will be taken away from thee for ever." Afterwards the Emperor Shun, when he abdicated in favour of his successor, the great Yü, used the same language in giving him charge. The Emperor T'ang, when he ascended the Imperial throne, thus offered up his prayer to God:

"I, Li, who am one of thy children, do here take upon me to offer up to thee in sacrifice this black heifer, and to announce to Thee, O supreme and sovereign God, that sinners I shall not dare to pardon; and, in the choice of Thy servants, I pray Thee, O God, that thou wilt let me know Thy will and pleasure. If I do sin against Thee, let not the people suffer for my sin. But if the people shall sin against Thee, let me alone bear the penalty of their iniquities." With the inauguration of the Chou dynasty, the country was greatly prosperous; but only the good were rich. The Emperors guided themselves by the principle contained in these words: "Although there are men attached and related to our person, yet we do not consider them equal in value to men of moral character. If the people fail in their conduct, it is we alone who are to blame." The Emperors set themselves to adjust and enforce uniformity in the use of weights and measures; to organize the administration and laws; to re-establish disused offices in this way the administration throughout the Empire was welt carried out. They restored extinct families of nobles; called to office retired men of virtue and learning: thus the people throughout the Empire gladly acknowledged their authority. What they paid serious attention to were food for the people, rituals and mourning for the dead, and religious services. By considerateness, they won the heart of the people; by good faith, they caused the people to have confidence in them; by diligence in business, what they undertook prospered; by their fair and impartial dealing, the people were contented.

Lau: Yao said, "oh, Shun, the succession, ordained by Heaven, has fallen on thy person. Holdst thou truly to the middle way. If the Empire should be reduced to dire straits, the honours bestowed on thee by Heaven will be terminated for ever. Shun commanded Yü in like manner. [T'ang] said, "I, Lü, the little one, dare to offer a black bull and to make this declaration before the great Lord. I dare not pardon those who have transgressed. I shall present thy servants as they are so that the choice rests with Thee alone. If I transgress, let not the ten thousand states suffer because of me; but if the ten thousand states transgress, the guilt is mine alone." The Chou handed out great gifts and good men alone were enriched. I may have close relatives, but better for me to have benevolent men. If the people transgress Let my person be punished. ① Decide on standard weights and measures after careful consideration, and re-establish official posts fallen into disuse, and government measures will be enforced everywhere. Restore states that have been annexed, revive lines that have become extinct, raise men who have withdrawn from society and the hearts of all the common people in the Empire will turn to you. What was considered of importance: the common people, food, mourning and sacrifice. If a man is tolerant, he will win the multitude. If he is trustworthy in word, the common people will entrust him with responsibility. If he is quick he will achieve results. ② If he is impartial the common people will be pleased. ③

---

① It has been suggested that these are the words used by King Wu in enfeoffing feudal lords, and may have been used, in particular, in the enfeoffment of T'ai Kung of Ch'i.

This whole passage consists of advice to kings or declarations by them. These kings all founded new dynasties. Shun founded the Yü 虞, Yü 禹 founded the Hsia 夏, T'ang 湯 founded the Yin 殷, and King Wu founded the Chou. It must have been taken from the Book of History, although only the saying of T'ang is found quoted in ancient works. (See Ch'en Meng-chia, Shang shu t'ung lun, p. 23, and n. 4 on p. 25.) This kind of material was probably used for teaching purposes in the Confucian school.

② The paragraph up to this point is also found in XVII. 6 where instead of min (common people) the text reads jen (fellow men).

③ This passage is not attributed to any speaker. It seems to consist of a number of unconnected parts on various aspects of government. Although one of these parts, as we have just pointed out, is, indeed, attributed to Confucius in XVII. 6, it would be rash to infer from this that Confucius must have been responsible for everything else as well.

Ames & Rosemont: Yao said, "Oh you Siun! The line of succession conferred by tian 天 rests on your person. Grasp it sincerdy and without deviation. If all within the four seas sink into dire straits, Tian's charge will be severed utterly." In just this manner, Shun in due course ceded his throne to Yu. [Tang] said, "I, Lu, dare to humbly offer in sacrifice a black bull, and dare to call upon the August High Ancestor. Those who do wrong will not be pardoned. I will not shield your subjects from your sight, but will let all decisions rest with you. If I, your subject, personally do wrong, let not the many states be implicated; if any of the many states do wrong, the guilt lies with me personally." The House of Zhou made great gifts, and truly efficacious (*shan* 善) persons were enriched therefrom. I certainly have my immediate relatives, But better to have authoritative persons (*renren* 仁人). Where the people go astray, Let the blame rest with me alone. Carefully calibrate the scales and measures, review the laws and statutes, and revive those offices that have fallen into disuse, and government policies will be carried out everywhere. Restore those states that have been destroyed, continue those lineages that have been broken, lift up those subjects whose talents have been lost to the people, and you will win over the hearts-and-minds of the common people throughout the land. Priorities: the common people, sufficient food, mourning practices, and the sacrifices. Those who are tolerant will win over the many; if they make good on their word (*xin* 信), others will rely upon them; if diligent, they will get results; if impartial, the people will be happy.

Slingerland: Yao said, "Oh, you Shun! The orderly succession of Heaven now rests upon your shoulders. Hold faithfully to the mean. If those within the Four Seas should fall into hardship and poverty,

Heaven's emoluments will be cut off from you forever."

The occasion of this remark is Yao's passing on of the throne to Shun. This address of Yao's does not appear in Chapter 1 ("The Canon of Yao") of the current Book of Documents, but pieces of it can be found in the probably spurious Chapter 3 ("The Counsels of the Great Yu"), where they are presented as Shun's words to Yu. The translation of the second half of the passage follows Zhu Xi, who understands it as a warning to Shun: if Shun should fail to care for and protect the people, Heaven's favor will be withdrawn from him. Bao Xian takes it somewhat differently: "If you can faithfully hold to the mean, you will be able to exhaustively extend [your rule] throughout the Four Seas, and Heaven's emoluments will last forever." Huang Kan follows Bao Xian, elaborating: "If Shun is able to internally hold fast to the Way of the correct mean, then his Virtuous instructive influence will externally cover the Four Seas, so that everyone will submit and be transformed, and there will be nowhere that this influence does not reach." Zhu Xi's reading seems preferable, however, better fitting the context in which these lines appear in the received version of the Documents, and allowing a less forced reading of the text.

Shun charged Yu with the same words.

Here we have the transition from Shun's rule to first founder of the Xia Dynasty, Yu. When Shun passed the throne on, he made the same pronouncement that Yao had made to him.

[Tang] said, "I, your little child Lü, dare to offer up a black bull in sacrifice, and make so bold as to plainly declare to you, my Most August Sovereign Lord, that I do not dare to pardon those who have committed offenses. Your servant, Lord, conceals nothing; examine my actions with your mind, oh Lord. If I should personally commit an offense, let not the punishment be visited upon the inhabitants of the myriad regions; if the inhabitants of the myriad regions commit offenses, let the punishment be visited upon me personally."

The personal name Lü in this declaration marks it as the words of Tang, the supposed founder of the Shang Dynasty, who—unlike Yu and Shun before him—had to take his throne by force of arms. Again, the passage does not correspond exactly to anything in the received *Documents*, but fragments of it are scattered throughout Chapter 12 ("The Announcement of Tang"). Kong Anguo believes this to be the declaration made by Tang to Heaven before he launched his punitive attack on the last of the Xia kings, the infamous Jie. Although the color of the Shang was to be white, Kong explains that Tang offers a black bull—black being the color of the Xia—because he does not yet dare to alter the Xia rituals. Understood this way, this declaration serves as Tang's excuse for having to resort to force, the point being that, in attacking the Xia, he is merely doing Heaven's will, serving as the instrument of Heaven's wrath in punishing the evil Jie. The request, "examine my actions with your mind, oh Lord" (lit. "let the review-inspection lie in the Lord's mind"), is a declaration of sincerity: Tang has nothing to hide, and his motivations are pure.

The Zhou were generously endowed, rich in excellent men.

We have now moved on to the transition to the Zhou. The translation follows He Yan in reading this first sentence together with 8.20: the Zhou had ten worthy ministers. It might alternately be rendered, "The Zhou gave generous gifts, and excellent men were enriched thereby," presumably referring to the enfeofment of those who aided in the Zhou conquest of the Shang. This latter reading is supported by a fragment, "[King Wu] gave generous gifts to all within the Four Seas, and the myriad people joyfully submitted," in the received *Book of Documents*.

[King Wu said,] "Though I may have many close kinsmen, it is better to employ Good men. If any of the Hundred Clans commit a transgression, let the punishment be visited upon me alone."

The quoted words are presumed by most commentators to be the words of King Wu after he had conquered the Shang, and they are in fact attributed to him in an alternate version of this account found in the *Mozi*. The first half of King Wu's statement appears in the received version of the *Documents*, and Kong Anguo's interpretation of it is as follows: "King Wu would punish even a close relative who was not dutiful or worthy—his punishment of prince of Guan and the prince of Cai are examples of this. By 'Good men' he means people like the Master of Ji and Master of Wei. If they came, he would employ them." An alternate rendering of this line is suggested in a commentary to the Documents falsely attributed to Kong Anguo—"the point is that, although King Zhow has many close relatives around him, they are not the equal of the many Good men of the Zhou family"—and this reading is adopted by Zhu Xi.

He was scrupulous about weights and measures, carefully examined models and regulations, restored neglected official posts, and the administration of the four quarters was thereby carried out.

In *the History of the Han*, this section is presented as an injunction from the mouth of Confucius, rather than a description of the actual behavior of King Wu. In the absence of a marker such as, "The Master said," however, it seems best to take it and the following sections as accounts of King Wu's rule.

He restored destroyed states, re-established interrupted lines of succession, raised lost people back into prominence, and the hearts and minds of all the people in the world turned to him.

> According to *the Exoteric Commentary*, "restoring destroyed states" refers to returning land to the blameless descendents of those whose states were confiscated for wrong-doing, and "re-establishing severed lines of succession" refers to allowing worthy individuals from side-branches of a family to take over the succession, rather than allowing a line to die out. "Lost people" probably refers to virtuous men who had gone into reclusion to avoid immoral rulers.

He gave weight to the people, food, mourning, and sacrifice.

> As Kong Anguo comments, "The common people are important because they are the basis of the state; food is important because it is the livelihood of the people. Mourning is important because it is the means by which one gives full expression to grief, and sacrifice is important because it is the means by which one fully expresses respect."

Generous, he won over the masses. Trustworthy, the people put their faith in him. Diligent, he was successful. Just, [the people] were pleased.

> Kong Anguo concludes, "This sums up the means by which the two Lords and three Kings established order, and is recorded in order to serve as a message to later generations."

【例23】 太宰问于子贡曰:"夫子圣者与? 何其多能也?"子贡曰:"固天纵之将圣,又多能也。"子闻之,曰:"太宰知我乎? 吾少也贱,故多能鄙事。君子多乎哉? 不多也。"(《论语·子罕》)

Legge: A high officer asked Tsze-kung, saying, "May we not say that your Master is a sage? How various is his ability!" Tsze-kung said, "Certainly Heaven has endowed him unlimitedly. He is about a sage. And, moreover, his ability is various." The Master heard of the conversation and said, "Does the high officer know me? When I was young, my condition was low, and I acquired my ability in many things, but they were mean matters. Must the superior man have such variety of ability? He does not need variety of ability.

Ku: A minister of a certain State asked a disciple of Confucius, saying: "Your teacher—he is a holy man, is he not? What a variety of acquirements he seems to possess." The disciple replied, "God has certainly been bountiful to him to make him a holy man. Besides he has himself acquired knowledge in many things."

When Confucius afterwards heard of the conversation, he remarked, "Does the minister know me? When I was young, I was in a low position in life: therefore I had to acquire knowledge in many things; but they were merely ordinary matters of routine. You think a wise and good man requires much knowledge to make him so: no, he does not require much."

Lau: The t'ai tsai① asked Tzu-kung, "Surely the Master is a sage, is he not? Otherwise why is it he is skilled in so many things?" Tzu-kung said, "It is true, Heaven set him on the path to sagehood. However, he is, in addition, skilled in many things."

The Master, on hearing of this, said, "How well the t'ai tsai knows me! I was of humble station when young. That is why I am

---

① This is the title of a high office. It is not clear who the person referred to was or even from which state he came.

skilled in many menial things. Should a gentleman be skilled in many things? No, not at all."

Ames & Rosemont: Grand Minister asked Zigong, "Your Master is a sage, is he not? Then how is it he is skilled in so many things?" Zigong replied, "*Tian* 天 definitely set him on course to become a sage (*sheng* 圣), but he also has many skill." On hearing of this, the Master said, "The Grand Minister certainly knows me! We were poor when I was young, so I learned many a menial skill. Does an exemplary person (*junzi* 君子) have these skills? I think not."

Slingerland: The Prime Minister asked Zigong, "Your Master is a sage, is he not? How is it, then, that he is skilled at so many menial tasks?"

Zigong replied, "Surely Heaven not only not intends him for sagehood, but also gave him many other talents."

When the Master heard of this, he remarked, "How well the Prime Minister knows me! In my youth, I was of humble status, so I became proficient in many menial tasks. Is the gentleman broadly skilled in trivial matters? No, he is not."

> There is a great deal of commentarial debate over the identity of the Prime Minister mentioned here, but none of the arguments offered are entirely convincing. The Prime Minister was presumably familiar with Confucius' many technical abilities, and apparently has trouble reconciling this with Confucius' own teaching that "the gentleman is not a vessel" (2.12). Zigong attempts to finesse the issue, but Confucius has no patience for this: his technical skills are the result of his humble background rather than being desiderata for an aspiring gentleman (cf. 9.2, 19.4, 19.7). Although—as implied in the elaboration 9.7—technical skills might come in handy for one who has yet to be properly employed.

【例 24】 子曰:"予欲无言。"子贡曰:"子如不言,则小子何述焉?"子曰:"天何言哉? 四时行焉,百物生焉,天何言哉?"(《论语•阳货》)

Leggge: The Master said, "I would prefer not speaking." Tsze-kung said, "If you, Master, do not speak, what shall we, your disciples, have to record?"

The Master said, "Does Heaven speak? The four seasons pursue their courses, and all things are continually being produced, but does Heaven say anything?"

Ku: Confucius was once heard to say, "I would rather not speak at all." "But if you do not speak, sir," asked a disciple, "What shall we, your disciples learn from you to be taught to others?" "Look at the Heaven there," answered Confucius, "Does it speak? And yet the seasons run their appointed courses and all things in nature grow up in their time. Look at the Heaven there: does it speak?"

Lau: The Master said, "I am thinking of giving up speech." Tzu-kung said, "If you did not speak, what would there be for us, your juniors, to transmit?" The Master said, "What does Heaven ever say? Yet there are the four seasons going round and there are the hundred things coming into being. What does Heaven ever say?"

Ames & Rosemont: The Master said, "I think I will leave off speaking." "If you do not speak," Zigong replied, "how will we your followers find the proper way?" The Master responded, "Does *tian* 天 speak? And yet the four seasons turn and the myriad things are born and grow within it. Dose *tian* speak?"

Slingerland: The Master sighed, "Would that I did not have to speak!"

Zigong said, "If the Master did not speak, then how would we little ones receive guidance from you?"

The Master replied, "What does Heaven ever say? Yet the four seasons are put in motion by it, and the myriad creatures receive their life from it. What does Heaven ever say?"

Reading this passage together with the ones that precede it, the theme is related to the suspicion of glibness and hypocrisy: whenever there is speech, there is the danger of a discrepancy between speech and action, which is why Confucius elsewhere has been led to declare that "the Good person is sparing of speech" (12.3) and "reticence is close to Goodness" (13.27). We see here again the metaphor of Heaven as ruler: Heaven governs the natural world in an effortless fashion, without having to issue orders, and the counterpart to Heaven in the social world is the sage-king of old, someone like Shun, "who ruled by means of wu-wei" (15.5). We have already seen the analogy between the wu-wei manner of ordering the human world and the spon- taneous harmony effected by Heaven in the natural realm in 2.1, where one who rules by means of virtue is compared to the Pole Star. Like the natural world, then, a properly ordered human society functions silently, inevitably and unselfconsciously. Confucius' somewhat exasperated remark here is therefore inspired by the contrast between the natural, silent, and true order that prevailed in ancient times and the garrulous, self-righteous, hypocritical disorder that characterizes his own age.

【例 25】 孔子曰:"君子有三畏:畏天命,畏大人,畏圣人之言。小人不知天命而不畏也,狎大人,侮圣人之言。"(《论语·季氏》)

Legge: Confucius said, "There are three things of which the superior man stands in awe. He stands in awe of the ordinances of Heaven. He stands in awe of great men. He stands in awe of the words of sages. "The mean man does not know the ordinances of Heaven, and consequently does not stand in awe of them. He is disrespectful to great men. He makes sport of the words of sages."

> Note: 天命, according to Chu Hal, means the moral nature of man, conferred by Heaven. High above the nature of other creatures, it lays him under great responsibility to cherish and cultivate himself. The old interpreters take the phrase to indicate Heaven's moral administration by rewards and puninhments. The 'great men' are men high in position and great in wisdom and virtue, the royal instructors, who have been raised up by Heaven for the training and ruling of mankind. So the commentators; but the 狎 suggests at once a more general and a lower view of the phrase.

Ku: Confucius remarked, "There are three things which a wise and good man holds in awe. He holds in awe the Laws of God, persons in authority, and the words of wisdom of holy men. A fool, on the other hand, does not know that there are Laws of God①; he, therefore, has no reverence for them; he is disrespectful to persons in authority, and contemns the words of wisdom of holy men."

> "Oh that my lot might lead me in the path of holy pureness of thought and deed, the path which august laws ordain, laws which in the brightest heaven had their birth; ... *the power of God is mighty in them and growth not old.*"

Lau: Confucius said, "The gentleman stands in awe of three things. He is in awe of the Decree of Heaven. He is in awe of great

---

① literally, "Commandments of God." In other places we have translated these words as Religion; for that — not the laws of Moses, Lycurgus, Christ or Confucius, which are merely interpretations of the Laws of God, —is, we believe, what is called Religion in Europe. The Laws of God comprises all, from the simple law that two and two make four; That ginger is hot for the mouth; the laws that guide the courses of sun, moon and stars, to, finally, the highest Law of Right and Wrong in the heart of man.

men. He is in awe of the words of the sages. The small man, being ignorant of the Decree of Heaven, does not stand in awe of it. He treats great men with familiarity and the words of the sages with insolence."

Ames & Rosemont: Confucius said, "Exemplary persons (*junzi* 君子) hold three things in awe: the propensities of tian (*tianming* 天命), persons in high station, and the words of the sages (*shengren* 圣人). Petty persons, knowing nothing of the propensities of tian, does not hold it in awe; they are unduly familiar with persons in high station, and ridicules the words of the sages."

Slingerland: The Master said, "The gentleman stands in awe of three things: the Mandate of Heaven, great men, and the teachings of the sages. The petty person does not understand the Mandate of Heaven, and thus does not regard it with awe; he shows disrespect to great men, and ridicules the teachings of the sages."

This parallel to 16.7 can perhaps be compared to 2.4, where recognizing or understanding (*zhi* 知) the Mandate of Heaven is presented as an essential step in comprehending the Way and achieving wu-wei perfection. Two views on how to understand "great men" can be traced back to He Yan and Zheng Xuan, with He Yan arguing that it refers simply to morally great people, such as the sages, and Zheng Xuan arguing that it refers specifically to socio-political superiors. Either interpretation is plausible, but the metaphorical structure of the concept of the "Mandate of Heaven" supports the latter, suggesting a parallel between submitting to fate and showing due deference to a political superior. Things that are beyond the immediate control of the individual (wealth, fame, health, lifespan) are metaphorically "commanded" or "mandated" by the Heavenly ruler, and thus the true gentleman—understood in the metaphor as a loyal minister—submits to these "decisions" without anxiety or complaint. The petty person, on the other hand, has no respect for rank, does not know his place, and is always scrambling to get ahead. Cf. 11.19, where the disciple Zigong, who has been engaging in business speculation and trying to get ahead economically, is criticized for "not recognizing fate-Mandate," as well as 12.4 and 12.5.

【例26】 子贡曰:"夫子之文章,可得而闻也;夫子之言性与天道,不可得而闻也。"(《论语·公冶长》)

Legge: Tsze-kung said, "The Master's personal displays of his principles and ordinary descriptions of them may be heard. His discourses about man's nature, and the way of Heaven, cannot be heard."

Ku: A disciple of Confucius remarked, "You will often hear the master speak on the subjects of art and literature, but you will never hear him speak on the subjects of metaphysics or theology."

Lau: Tzu-kung said, "One can get to hear about the Master's accomplishments, but one cannot get to hear his views on human nature and the Way of Heaven."

Ames & Rosemont: Zigong said, "We can learn from the Master's cultural refinements, but do not hear him discourse on subjects such as our 'natural disposition (*xing* 性)' and 'the way of tian (*tiandao* 天道)'."

Slingerland: Zigong said, "The Master's cultural brilliance is something that is readily heard about, whereas one does not get to hear the Master expounding upon the subjects of human nature or the Way of Heaven."

This passage has presented something of a puzzle to some interpreters, seeing that we can find one mention of human nature (*xing* 性) (17.2) in the

Analects, and that— although the term "Way of Heaven" (*tiandao* 天道) appears nowhere else in the text— we do find quite a few mentions of the Mandate of Heaven or other topics having to do with Heaven's will. 17.2 might be dismissed as a late addition, and even if we include it with all the various mentions of Heaven, it remains true that Confucius focuses primarily on "this world"—that is, the human world of learning and self-cultivation. Thus, one way to understand this passage is that Confucius did not concern himself much with such theoretical, esoteric subjects as human nature or the Way of Heaven, but rather tried to focus his disciples' attention on the task at hand: acquiring the cultural refinement necessary to become gentlemen (cf. 6.22, 7.20, 11.12). A related interpretation is suggested by commentators who argue that "human nature" refers to the variable endowment one receives at birth (rather than to some theoretical stance about human nature as we see in *the Mencius and Xunzi*), and that, in classical texts, the "Way of Heaven" often refers simply to what we might call luck" or "fate." Understood this way, "human nature" and the "Way of Heaven" collectively refer to the range of things that are beyond human control, and the point is that the Master focused on what was within human control: commitment to learning and the Confucian Way. This harmonizes well with Confucius' comment in 7.20 that he was not born knowing it, but simply loves learning—you cannot control your inborn qualities or your external luck, but you can decide whether or not to set your mind on learning and take your stand with ritual. It also harmonizes well with other statements concerning fate (*ming*) in the text (4.14, 6.10, 7.3, 7.19, 11.18, 14.36, 12.4-5, 20.3).2

【例27】 孔子曰:"天下有道,则礼乐征伐自天子出;天下无道,则礼乐征伐自诸侯出。自诸侯出,盖十世希不失矣;自大夫出,五世希不失矣;陪臣执国命,三世希不失矣。天下有道,则政不在大夫。天下有道,则庶人不议。"(《论语·季氏》)

Legge: Confucius said, "When good government prevails in the empire, ceremonies, music, and punitive military expeditions proceed from the son of Heaven. When bad government prevails in the empire, ceremonies, music, and punitive military expeditions proceed from the princes. When these things proceed from the princes, as a rule, the cases will be few in which they do not lose their power in ten generations. When they proceed from the great officers of the princes, as a rule, the case will be few in which they do not lose their power in five generations. When the subsidiary ministers of the great officers hold in their grasp the orders of the state, as a rule the cases will be few in which they do not lose their power in three generations. "When right principles prevail in the kingdom, government will not be in the hands of the great officers. "When right principles prevail in the kingdom, there will be no discussions among the common people. "

Ku: Confucius remarked, "In the normal state of the government of an empire, the initiative and final decision in matters of religion, education, and declaration of war form the supreme prerogative of the emperor. During abnormal conditions in the government of the empire, that prerogative passes into the hands of the princes of the empire: in which case it is seldom that ten generations pass before they lose it. Should that prerogative pass into the hands of the nobility of the empire, it has rarely happened that they have retained it for five generations. When subordinate officers have the power of government in their hands they generally lose their authority in the course of three generations. "When there are order and justice in the government of a country, the supreme power of government will not be in the hands of the nobility or of a ruling class. When there are justice and order in the government of a country, the common people will not meddle with

the government."①

Lau: Confucius said, 'When the Way prevails in the Empire, the rites and music and punitive expeditions are initiated by the Emperor. When the Way does not prevail in the Empire, they are initiated by the feudal lords. When they are initiated by the feudal lords, it is surprising if power does no pass from the Emperor within ten generations. When they are initiated by the Counsellors, it is surprising if power does not pass from the feudal lords within five generations. When the prerogative to command in a state is in the hands of officials of the Counsellors it is surprising if power does not pass from the Counsellors within three generations. When the Way prevails in the Empire, policy does not rest with the Counsellors. When the Way prevails in the Empire, the Commoners do not express critical views.'

Ames & Rosemont: Confucius said, "When the way (*dao* 道) prevails in the world, ritual propriety (*li* 礼), music (*yue* 乐), and punitive campaigns are initiated by the emperor. If the way does not prevail in the world, then they are initiated by the various nobles. When they are initiated by the various nobles, it is unlikely that the state will survive beyond ten generations. When they are initiated by the ministers, it is unlikely that the state will survive beyond five generations. When the household stewards of the ministers seize command of the state, it is unlikely that the state will survive beyond three generations. When the way prevails in the world, governing

---

① Confucius meant by the first what is called in Europe "an oligarchy," and by the second "democracy": both of which, according to the passage here, can never be the true normal permanent state of government in a country. The ruling class or nobility in ancient China corresponds to what Mr. RUSKIN called or country gentlemen of England.

does not lie in the hands of the ministers; when the way prevails in the world, the common people do not debate affairs of state."

Slingerland: Confucius said, "When the Way prevails in the world, rituals, music, punitive expeditions, and attacks against foreign powers issue from the Son of Heaven. When the Way does not prevail in the world, these things issue from the feudal lords. When they issue from the feudal lords, it is seldom more than ten generations before the lords lose control of them. When they issue from ministers, it is seldom more than five generations before the ministers lose control of them, and once household ministers seize control of state commands, it is seldom more than three generations before they lose control of them."

> This passage may form a pair with 16.1, serving as a bleak assessment of the state of the world when the head of the Ji Family, officially only a minister, can take it upon himself to initiate a military campaign. Many commentators take Confucius' comment here literally, and a great deal of ink has been spilled culling through Chinese historical records, tracing the precise time intervals mentioned in order to document the truth of the Master's claim. Kong Anguo's comment on this passage is representative, if more concise than most:
>
> > After King You of the Zhou was killed by the Quan Rong barbarians, King Ping moved the capital to the east, and this is when the Zhou began to decline. It was beginning in the reign of Duke Yin that the feudal lords began creating new ritual and music, and taking the initiative in launching punitive military expeditions. Ten generations later, during the reign of Duke Zhao, the government of Lu was lost, and Duke Zhao died in Qian Hou. Once Ji Wenzi first took over control of the government, it was five generations later, during the reign of Ji Hengzi, that the Ji Family head was imprisoned by Yang Huo.
>
> Ma Rong then finishes out the account: "Three generations after Yang Huo became the family minister of the Ji Family, he was forced to flee to Qi." It is

more likely, however, that the numbers mentioned by Confucius are meant to be taken as expressions of relative magnitude rather than literally, which would explain why they do not match the numbers presented in the actual case-example given in 16.3.

"When the Way prevails in the world, control of the government does not reside with the ministers. When the Way prevails in the world, commoners do not debate matters of government."

The former statement is probably also meant as a criticism of the current situation in Lu, while the latter reflects a traditional ideal of Chinese government that is still very much alive today: political debate among the common people is a sign of disorder, because in a properly run state, the people will be busy and content, and will have no cause to form or express opinions about how the state is being run. Alternately, *yi* 議 ("express opinion, debate") could be taken in a more negative sense ("criticize, critique"), in which case there might be room for positive expressions among the commoners. This is how Huang Kan takes it: "When the lord possesses the Way, sounds of praise will fill the streets, and the sentiments of a harmonious age will prevail. This being so, common people and inferiors will not gather in streets and alleyways to critique and debate the achievements and failures of [those governing] the four quarters of the world."

【例28】 孔子曰:"见善如不及,见不善如探汤。吾见其人矣,吾闻其语矣。隐居以求其志,行义以达其道。吾闻其语矣,未见其人也。"(《论语·季氏》)

Legge: Confucius said, "Contemplating good, and pursuing it, as if they could not reach it; contemplating evil! And shrinking from it, as they would from thrusting the hand into boiling water:-I have seen such men, as I have heard such words. "Living in retirement to study their aims, and practicing righteousness to carry out their principles: I have heard these words, but I have not seen such men."

Ku Hungming: Confucius remarked, "Men who, when they see what is good and honest, try to act up to it, and when they see what is bad and dishonest try to avoid it as if avoiding scalding water: such men I have known and the expressions of such principles I have heard. But men who live in retirement in order to study their aims and who practice righteousness in order to carry out their principles: the expression of such principles I have heard, but I have not seen such men."

Lau: Confucius said, " 'Seeing what is good I act as if I risked failing to catch up with it; seeing what is not good I act as if I were testing hot water.' I have met such a man; I have heard such a claim.

" 'I live in retirement in order to attain my purpose and practise what is right in order to realize my way.' I have heard such a claim, but I have yet to meet such a man."

Ames & Rosemont: Confucius said, " 'On seeing ability (*shan* 善), I go after it as though I cannot catch up to it; On seeing a lack of ability, I recoil from it as though testing boiling water. I have heard such words, and have even seen such persons. 'I dwell in seclusion to pursue my ends, And act on my sense of what is appropriate (*yi* 义) to extend my way (*dao* 道).' I have heard such words, but I have yet to see such persons."

Slingerland: Confucius said, " 'Seeing goodness, and striving for it urgently, as if never able catch up; seeing badness, and recoiling as if scalded by hot water'—I have seen such people, and have heard such words."

"'Dwelling in seclusion in order to pursue one's aspirations, practicing rightness in order to realize the Way'—I have heard such words, but have yet to see such a person."

The quoted phrases are probably proverbial sayings. The first half of the first saying is similar to 8.17. The second half of the passage may be a critique of the principled recluses we have seen before, and will see again in Book Eighteen: they claim a noble motivation for their actions, but the Master remains dubious. The point, of course, is that words do not always match actions, and therefore one must examine both closely; cf. 5.10.

【例29】 定公问:"一言而可以兴邦,有诸?"孔子对曰:"言不可以若是其几也。人之言曰:'为君难,为臣不易。'如知为君之难也,不几乎一言而兴邦乎?"曰:"一言而丧邦,有诸?"孔子对曰:"言不可以若是其几也。人之言曰:'予无乐乎为君,唯其言而莫予违也。'如其善而莫之违也,不亦善乎? 如不善而莫之违也,不几乎一言而丧邦乎?"(《论语·子路》)

Legge: The Duke Ting asked whether there was a single sentence which could make a country prosperous. Confucius replied, "Such an effect cannot be expected from one sentence. "There is a saying, however, which people have -'To be a prince is difficult; to be a minister is not easy.' "If a ruler knows this,-the difficulty of being a prince,-may there not be expected from this one sentence the prosperity of his country?"

The duke then said, "Is there a single sentence which can ruin a country?"

Confucius replied, "Such an effect as that cannot be expected from one sentence. There is, however, the saying which people have-'I have no pleasure in being a prince, but only in that no one can offer any opposition to what I say!' "If a ruler's words be good, is it not also good that no one oppose them? But if they are not good, and no one opposes them, may there not be expected from this one sentence the ruin of his country?"

Ku: The reigning prince of Confucius' native State enquired if the principle to make a country prosperous could be expressed in one single sentence. Confucius answered, "One cannot expect so much meaning from a single sentence. There is, however, a saying which the people have, 'To be a ruler of men is difficult and to be public servant is not easy.' Now if one only knew that it a difficult to be a ruler of men, would not that alone almost make a country prosperous?" The prince then asked if the principle to ruin a country could be expressed in one single sentence. Confucius answered, "So much meaning is not to be expected from one single sentence. There is, however, a saying among the people; 'I find on pleasure in being a ruler of men, except in that whatsoever I order no man shall oppose.' Now if what is ordered is right, it is well and good that on one oppose it; but if what is ordered is not right and no one opposes it, —is not that alone enough to ruin a country?"

Lau: Duke Ting asked, "Is there such a thing as a single saying that can make a state prosper?"

Confucius answered, "A saying cannot quite do that. There is a saying amongst men: 'It is difficult to be a ruler, and it is not easy to be a subject either.' If the ruler understands the difficulty of being a ruler, then is this not almost a case of a saying making a state prosper?"

"Is there such a thing as a saying that can ruin a state?"

Confucius answered, "A saying cannot quite do that. There is a saying amongst men: 'I do not at all enjoy being a ruler, except for the fact that there is no one to go against what I say.' If what he says is good and no one goes against him, good. But if what he says is not good and no one goes against him, then is this not almost a case of a saying ruining a state?"

Ames & Rosemont: Duke Ding inquired, "Is there any one saying that can make a state prosper?" "A saying itself cannot have such effect," said the Master, "but there is the saying, 'Ruling is difficult, and ministering is not easy either.' If the ruler really does understand the difficulty of ruling, is this not close to a saying making a state prosper?" "Is there any one saying that can ruin a state?" Duck Ding asked. " A saying itself cannot have such effect," replied Confucius, "but there is the saying, ' I find little pleasure in ruling, save that no one will take exception to what I say.' If what one has to say is efficacious (*shan* 善) and no one takes exception, fine indeed. But if what one has to say is not efficacious and no one takes exception, is this not close to a saying ruining a state?"

Slingerland: Duke Ding asked, "A single saying that can cause a state to flourish—is there such a thing as this?"

Confucius replied, "There is no saying that can have that sort of effect. There is, however, something close. People have a saying, 'Being a ruler is difficult, and being a minister is not easy.' If this saying helps you to understand that being a ruler is difficult, does it not come close to being a single saying that can cause a state to flourish?"

The proverbial saying quoted here is similar to lines from Ode 236 ("It is difficult to trust Heaven/It is not easy to be a king") and from *the Book of Documents* ("If the sovereign can realize the difficulty of being a sovereign, and the minister realize the dif- ficulty of being a minister, then the government will be well ordered, and the common people will strive diligently after Virtue"). ① The point is that, as Zhu Xi explains, "If, as a result of this saying, one could understand the difficulty of being a ruler, then one will necessarily be 'fearful and cautious/as if skirting the edge of a deep abyss/as if treading upon thin ice' [8.3], and as a result one would not dare to handle casually even a single affair."

Duke Ding asked, "A single saying that can cause a state to perish—is there such a thing as this?"

Confucius replied, "There is no saying that can have that sort of effect. There is, however, something close. People have a saying, 'I take no joy in being a ruler, except that no one dares to oppose what I say.' If what the ruler says is good, and no one opposes him, is this not good? On the other hand, if what he says is not good, and no one opposes him, does this not come close to being a single saying that can cause a state to perish?"

In a passage from the Hanfeizi, this saying is attributed to Duke Ping of Jin:

> Duke Ping of Jin was drinking wine with his assembled ministers. Drinking to his heart's content, the Duke loudly sighed to his ministers, "I find no joy in being a ruler, except that no one dares to oppose what I say." [The blind] Music Master Guang was in attendance before him. Taking hold of his zither, he threw it at the Duke. Gathering up his robe, the Duke dodged and managed to avoid it, and it instead hit the wall, creating a hole. The Duke said, "At whom did the Music Master throw his zither?" The Music Master said, "Just now, some petty person was sounding off at my side; I was aiming my zither at

---

① Chapter 3 ("The Counsels of the Great Yu"); Legge 1991b: 53.

him." The Duke replied, "That person was I." "Alas!" the Music Master sighed, "Those are not the words of a gentleman!" The attendants asked permission to repair the wall, but the Duke said to them, "Leave it. It will serve as a constant admonition to me."

One of the duties of a loyal minister is to remonstrate with his lord when he has done or said something wrong. As Fan Ziyu comments, "If what the ruler says is not good and no one opposes it, then dutiful advice will never reach his ears. When the ruler is daily growing more arrogant and the ministers are daily growing more obsequious, there has never been a case when the state was not lost." Brooks and Brooks also observe that "this is one of several Analects passages defining the idea of the censo-rate, an institutionalized internal criticism that is the most recognizably Confucian of Imperial government forms" (1998: 101).

【例30】 季康子问政于孔子曰:"如杀无道,以就有道,何如?"孔子对曰:"子为政,焉用杀?子欲善而民善矣。君子之德风,小人之德草。草上之风必偃。"(《论语·颜渊》)

Legge: Chi K'ang asked Confucius about government, saying, "What do you say to killing the unprincipled for the good of the principled?"

Confucius replied, "Sir, in carrying on your government, why should you use killing at all? Let your evinced desires be for what is good, and the people will be good. The relation between superiors and inferiors is like that between the wind and the grass. The grass must bend, when the wind blows across it."

Ku Hungming: The same noble again asked about government, saying, "What do you say to putting to death the wicked in the interests of the good?"

"In your government," answered Confucius, "why should you

think it necessary to depend upon capital punishments? Wish for honesty, and the people will be honest. The moral power of the rulers is as the wind, and that of the people is as the grass. Whithersoever the wind blows, the grass is sure to bend. "

Lau: K'ang Tzu asked Confucius about government, saying, "What would you think if, in order to move closer to those who possess the Way, I were to kill those who do not follow the Way?" Confucius answered, "In administering your government, what need is there for you to kill? Just desire the good yourself and the common people will be good. By nature the gentleman is like wind and the small man like grass. Let the wind sweep over the grass and it is sure to bend. "①

Ames & Rosemont: Ji Kangzi asked Confucius about governing effectively (*zheng* 政), saying, "What if I kill those who have abandoned the way (*dao* 道) to attract those who are on it?" "If you govern effectively," Confucius replied, "what need is there for killing? If you want to be truly adept (*shan* 善), the people will also be adept. The excellence (*de* 德) of the exemplary person (*junzi* 君子) is the wind, while that of the petty person is the grass. As the wind blows, the grass is sure to bend. "

Slingerland: Ji Kangzi asked Confucius about governing, saying, "If I were to execute those who lacked the Way in order to advance those who possessed the Way, how would that be?"

Confucius responded, "In your governing, Sir, what need is there for executions? If you desire goodness, then the common people will be good. The Virtue of a gentleman is like the wind, and the Virtue of

---

① This saying is quoted in the Mencius, III. A. 2.

a petty person is like the grass—when the wind moves over the grass, the grass is sure to bend."

An alternate version of this story is found in the Exoteric Commentary:
The state of Lu had a case of a father and son filing civil complaints against each other, and Ji Kangzi wanted to have them executed. Confucius said, "You cannot execute them ... When the common people do something that is not right, it is only because their superiors have lost the Way ... If the superiors make manifest their teachings and then take the lead in obeying these teachings, the common people will then follow as if being impelled by a wind."①

We also find this wind metaphor for the virtuous influence of the ruler② in a passage from *the Garden of Persuasions*—"Those below are transformed by those above like grass bending in the wind ... the direction from which the wind is blowing will determine the direction in which the grass bends. This is why the ruler of men must be very careful about his behavior"—and it also appears in a warning to a ruler in a portion of the Book of Documents: "You are the wind, and the people below are the grass."③ In this passage, we see again a suspicion of recourse to legal means and reliance on punishment—wide- spread disorder among the common people is a sign of immorality among the ruling class, and in such a situation it is actually cruel and unfair to punish the people for their transgressions. Throughout traditional Chinese texts on rulership the common people are portrayed as childlike and easily influenced by their superiors, and therefore not totally accountable for their behavior. Some modern scholars of Confucianism present passages such as *Analects* 12.17-12.19 as examples of how traditional China had something like the modern Western liberal-democratic ideal of governmental accountability, but it is important not to lose sight of how distinct from modern liberal ideals the early Confucian conception

---

① Chapter 3.22; Hightower 1952: 100-101; see also 3.24: 105-106.
② Cf. the "press-frame" metaphor in 2.19 and 12.22.
③ Book 21 ("Jun Chen"); Legge 1991a: 539. Most scholars believe that this book is a forgery dating to the fourth century b.c.e. Also cf. the quotation of 12.19 in Mencius 3: A:2.

actually was.

【例31】 子路从而后，遇丈人，以杖荷蓧。子路问曰："子见夫子乎？"丈人曰："四体不勤，五谷不分，孰为夫子？"植其杖而芸。子路拱而立。止子路宿，杀鸡为黍而食之，见其二子焉。明日，子路行以告。子曰："隐者也。"使子路反见之。至，则行矣。子路曰："不仕无义。长幼之节，不可废也；君臣之义，如之何其废之？欲洁其身，而乱大伦。君子之仕也，行其义也。道之不行，已知之矣。"(《论语·微子》)

Legge: Tsze-lu, following the Master, happened to fall behind, when he met an old man, carrying across his shoulder on a staff a basket for weeds. Tsze-lu said to him, "Have you seen my master, sir?"

The old man replied, "Your four limbs are unaccustomed to toil; you cannot distinguish the five kinds of grain: who is your master?"

With this, he planted his staff in the ground, and proceeded to weed. Tsze-lu joined his hands across his breast, and stood before him. The old man kept Tsze-lu to pass the night in his house, killed a fowl, prepared millet, and feasted him. He also introduced to him his two sons. Next day, Tsze-lu went on his way, and reported his adventure.

The Master said, "He is a recluse," and sent Tsze-lu back to see him again, but when he got to the place, the old man was gone. Tsze-lu then said to the family, "Not to take office is not righteous. If the relations between old and young may not be neglected, how is it that he sets aside the duties that should be observed between sovereign and minister? Wishing to maintain his personal purity, he allows that great relation to come to confusion. A superior man takes office, and performs the righteous duties belonging to it. As to the failure of right principles to make progress, he is aware of that."

Ku: On another occasion when Confucius was on his travels, a disciple, the intrepid Chung Yu, got separated from the party. Chung Yu met an old man carrying across his shoulders, on a staff, a basket for weeds. Chung Yu said to him, "Have you seen the Teacher Sir?" The old man looked at him and replied gruffly, "Your body has never known toil and you cannot tell the difference between the five kinds of grain: who is your Teacher?" With that, the old man planted his staff on he ground and fell to his work, weeding the ground. Chung Yu, however, laid his hands across his breast and respectfully waited. Afterwards, the old man took Chung Yu to his home and made him pass a night in his house, killing a fowl and making millet pudding for him to eat. The old man also presented his two sons to Chung Yu. The next day Chung Yu went on his way and, on rejoining Confucius, reported his adventure. "He is a hermit," said Confucius, and sent Chung Yu back to see him, but when Chung Yu got to the place the old man was nowhere to be found. When Chung Yu again returned, Confucius said, "It is not right to refuse to enter the public service. For if it is wrong to ignore the duties arising out of the relations between the members of a family, how is it right to ignore the duties a man owes to his sovereign and country. A man who withdraws himself from the world for no other reason than to show his personal purity of motive, is one who breaks up one of the greatest ties in the foundation of society. A good and wise man, on the other hand, who enters the public service, tries to carry out what he thinks to be right. As to the failure of right principles to make progress, he is well aware of that."

Lau: Tzu-lu, when travelling with [Confucius], fell behind. He met an old man, carrying a basket on a staff over his shoulder. Tzu-lu asked, "Have you seen my Master?" The old man said, "You seem neither to have toiled with your limbs nor to be able to tell one kind of grain from another. Who may your Master be?" He planted his staff in the ground and started weeding. Tzu-lu stood, cupping one hand respectfully in the other. The old man invited Tzu-lu to stay for the night. He killed a chicken and prepared some millet for his guest to eat, and presented his two sons to him. The next day, Tzu-lu resumed his journey and reported this conversation. The Master said, "He must be a recluse." He sent Tzu-lu back to see him again. When he arrived, the old man had departed. Tzu-lu commented, "Not to enter public life is to ignore one's duty. Even the proper regulation of old and young cannot be set aside. How, then, can the duty between ruler and subject be set aside? This is to cause confusion in the most important of human relationships simply because one desired to keep unsullied one's character. The gentleman takes office in order to do his duty. As for putting the Way into practice, he knows all along that it is hopeless."

Ames & Rosemont: Zilu was accompanying the Master when he fell behind. He came across an old man using his staff to tote his baskets on his shoulder. "Have you seen my Master?" asked Zilu. The old man replied, "You—'a person who does no work And who can't tell one grain from another—'" "who would your Master be?" He then stuck his staff in the ground and continued his weeding. Zilu stood by him with his hands cupped respectfully in a salute. The old man invited Zilu to spend the night. He killed a chicken and prepared some special millet for the occasion, and presented his two sons to his guest. On the following day, Zilu tock his leave, and reported the event to Confucius. "He is a recluse." said the Master, and sent Zilu back to see him again. On Zilu's arrival, he discovered the old man had already left. Zilu remarked, "To refuse office is to fail to do what is important and appropriate (*yi* 义). If the differentiation between young and old cannot be abandoned, how could one think of abandoning what is appropriate between ruler and subject? This is to throw the most important relationships into turmoil in one's efforts to remain personally untarnished. The opportunity of the exemplary person (*junzi* 君子) to serve in office is the occasion to effect what is judged to be important and appropriate. That the way (*dao* 道) does not prevail—this is known already."

Slingerland: Zilu was traveling with Confucius, but had fallen behind. He encountered an old man carrying a wicker basket suspended from his staff. Zilu asked, "Have you seen my Master?"

The old man answered,

" 'Won't soil his dainty hands

Can't tell millet from corn.'

Who, then, might your master be?"

He then planted his staff in the ground and began weeding.

[Not knowing how to reply], Zilu simply remained standing with his hands clasped as a sign of respect.

The old man's comment is a rhyming verse in the Chinese—an indication that again we are not dealing with an ordinary, illiterate farmer. Its target is both Zilu and Confucius: in his scholar-official dress and with his unsoiled hands, Zilu is clearly not suited to manual labor in the fields. The farmer is gently mocking both Zilu's uselessness and the sort of education that produced it. Zilu does not respond to this rather rude remark, probably out of respect for the old farmer's age, and his quiet, dignified demeanor apparently wins the old man over.

The old man subsequently invited Zilu back to his house to stay the night. After killing a chicken and preparing some millet for Zilu to eat, he presented his two sons to him. The next day, Zilu caught up to Confucius and told him what had happened.

"He must be a scholar recluse," the Master said. He sent Zilu back to the old farmer's house to meet with him again, but by the time Zilu got there the man had already disappeared. Zilu then remarked, "To avoid public service is to be without a sense of what is right. Proper relations between elders and juniors cannot be discarded—how, then, can one discard the rightness that obtains between ruler and minister? To do so is to wish to keep one's hands from getting dirty at the expense of throwing the great social order into chaos. The gentle- man takes office in order to do what is right, even though he already knows that the Way will not be realized."

  Commentators believe that Zilu's final remarks are delivered to the old farmer's two sons, presumably to be passed on when he returns. The point is that the old recluse clearly recognizes the first set of relationships (between elders and juniors) in requiting Zilu's formal hand clasping—an expression of respect by a younger man for an elder—by providing Zilu with proper hospitality and formally presenting his sons, but he ignores the second (between ruler and minister) by living in reclusion and avoiding any sort of official contact. Cf. the account of a similar encounter between Confucius, Zilu, and a recluse in the *Zhuangzi*.

【例32】 子曰:"为政以德,譬如北辰,居其所而众星共之。"(《论语·为政》)

Legge: The Master said, "He who exercises government by means of his virtue may be compared to the north polar star, which keeps its place and all the stars turn towards it."

Ku Hungming: Confucius remarked, "He who rules the people, depending upon the moral sentiment, is like the Pole-star, which keeps its place while all the other stars revolve round it."

Lau: The Master said, "The rule of virtue can be compared to the Pole Star which commands the homage of the multitude of stars simply by remaining in its place."

Ames & Rosemont: The Master said: "Governing with excellence (*de* 德) can be compared to being the North Star: the North Star dwells in its place, and the multitude of stars pay it tribute."

Slingerland: The Master said, "One who rules through the power of Virtue is analogous to the Pole Star: it simply remains in its place and receives the homage of the myriad lesser stars."

The point of this passage is that the spontaneous harmony brought about by Heaven in the natural world is to be a model for the human ruler, who—in a wu-wei fashion— will bring the world to order silently, inevitably, and unselfconsciously through the power of his perfected moral Virtue. As Bao Xian notes, "One who possesses Virtue is wu-wei, and—like the Pole Star—does not move yet receives the homage of the myriad lesser stars." Cf. 2.3, 2.21, 12.17, 12.19, and especially 15.5.

【例33】 子曰:"譬如为山,未成一篑,止,吾止也。譬如平地,虽覆一篑,进,吾往也。"(《论语·子罕》)

Legge: The Master said, "The prosecution of learning may be compared to what may happen in raising a mound. If there want but one basket of earth to complete the work, and I stop, the stopping is my own work. It may be compared to throwing down the earth on the level ground. Though but one basketful is thrown at a time, the advancing with it my own going forward."

Ku Hungming: Confucius remarked, "Suppose a man wants to raise a mound" and, just as it wants only one basket more of earth to complete the work, suppose he were suddenly to stop: the stopping depends entirely upon himself. Suppose again a man wants to level a road, although he has just thrown over it only one basket of earth; to proceed with the work also depends entirely upon himself."

Lau: The Master said, "As in the case of making a mound, if, before the very last basketful, I stop, then I shall have stopped. As in the case of levelling the ground, if, though tipping only one basketful, I am going forward, then I shall be making progress."

Ames & Rosemont: The Master said, "As in piling up earth to erect a mountain, if, only one basketful short of completion, I stop, I have stopped. As in filling a ditch to level the ground, if, having dumped in only one basketful, I continue, I am progressing."

Slingerland: The Master said, "[The task of self-cultivation] might be compared to the task of building up a mountain: if I stop even one basketful of earth short of completion, then I have stopped completely. It might also be compared to the task of leveling ground: even if I have only dumped a single basketful of earth, at least I am moving forward."

The first half of this passage echoes 1.15, 8.7, and 9.17 in emphasizing the need for constant effort and indefatigable determination if one is to completely walk the long and arduous Confucian Way. As Zhu Xi puts it, "If the student is able to steel himself and not desist, then his accumulated small efforts will result in great success. If, on the other hand, he stops halfway down the road, then he has thrown away everything he has already achieved." The second half provides some encouragement, somewhat balancing out Yan Hui's lament in 9.11: the Way is long, but with every step one is making progress. An ancillary point is that, when it comes to self-cultivation, it is the internal decisions of the individual that determine success or failure; as Zhu Xi explains, "The decision to stop or move forward lies entirely within me, and is not determined by others" (cf. 12.1). 9.20 and 9.21 seem to flesh this passage out by providing a model of one who never grew tired or stopped in his forward progress: the perfect disciple Yan Hui.

【例34】 仪封人请见，曰："君子之至于斯也，吾未尝不得见也。"从者见之。出曰："二三子何患于丧乎？天将以夫子为木铎。"(《论语·八佾》)

Legge: The followers of the sage introduced him, and when he came out from the interview, he said, "My friends, why are you distressed by your master's loss of office? The kingdom has long been without the principles of truth and right; Heaven is going to use your master as a bell with its wooden tongue."

Ku: An officer in command of a certain Pass on the frontier where Confucius on his travels was passing, asked for the permission to be presented to him, saying, "Whenever a wise man passes this way, I have always had the honor to wait upon him." Confucius' disciples accordingly presented him. When the officer came out of the interview he said to the disciples, "Gentlemen, why should you be concerned at your present want of official position! The world has long been without the order and justice of good government; now God is going to make use of your Teacher as a tocsin to awaken the world."

Lau: The border official of Yi requested an audience, saying, "I have never been denied an audience by any gentleman who has come to this place." The followers presented him. When he came out, he said, "What worry have you, gentlemen, about the loss of office? The Empire has long been without the Way. Heaven is about to use your Master as the wooden tongue for a bell."①

Ames & Rosemont: A border official at Yi asked for an interview with the Master, saying: "I have always been accorded an interview with those distinguished persons who have made their way here." Confucius' followers presented him. On taking his leave, he said: "Why worry over the loss of office, my friends? All under *tian* 天 have long since lost their way (*dao* 道), and *tian* is going to use your Master as a wooden bell — clapper."

Slingerland: A border official from the town of Yi② requested an audience with the Master, saying, "I have never failed to obtain an audience with the gentlemen who have passed this way." Confucius' followers thereupon presented him.

After emerging from the audience, the border official remarked, "You disciples, why should you be concerned about your Master's loss of office? The world has been without the Way for a long time now, and Heaven intends to use your Master like the wooden clapper for a bell."

Most commentators take this as a reference to Confucius' loss of the office

---

① to rouse the Empire.
② In the state of Wei, on the border with Lu.

of Criminal Judge in the state of Lu; this is presumably the reason that Confucius and his disciples are leaving the state. The ability of the border official to see Confucius' true mission is taken by many commentators as an indication that he is a sage in hiding: a virtuous man who has taken a lowly position in order to protect himself in chaotic and unvirtuous times. The bell referred to is (depending on which source one consults) the kind used either by itinerant collectors and transmitters of folk songs or functionaries who circulated around the countryside promulgating official announcements. In either case, the border official's point is thus that Heaven has deliberately caused Confucius to lose his official position so that he might wander throughout the realm, spreading the teachings of the Way and waking up the fallen world.

【例 35】 子贡问曰:"赐也何如?"子曰:"女,器也。"曰:"何器也?"曰:"瑚琏也。"(《论语·公冶长》)

Legge: Tsze-kung asked, "What do you say of me, Ts'ze!"
The Master said, "You are a utensil."
"What utensil?"
"A gemmed sacrificial utensil."

Note: The 瑚琏 were vessels richly adorned, used to contain grain-offerings in the royal ancestral temples. Under the Haia dynasty they were called 琏, and 瑚 under the Yin. See the Li Chi, XII. ii. While the sage did not grant to Ts'ze that he was a Chun-tsze (II. Xii), he made him "a vessel of honour," valuable and fit for use on high occasions.

Ku Hungming: Another disciple who heard the above remarks said then to Confucius, "And I, what do you say of me?" "You are," answered Confucius, "a work of art." "What work of art?" asked the other. "A rich jewelled work of art," was the reply.

Lau: Tzu-kung asked, "What do you think of me?"

The Master said, "You are a vessel."

"What kind of vessel?"

"A sacrificial vessel."①

Ames & Rosemont: Zigong inquired, "And what do you think of me?" The Master replied, "You are a vessel." Zigong asked, "What kind of a vessel?" The Master replied, "You are a most precious and sacred kind of vessel."

Slingerland: Zigong asked, "What do you think of me?" The Master replied, "You are a vessel." "What sort of vessel?"

"A *hu* 瑚 or *lian* 琏 vessel."

Of course, "the gentleman is not a vessel" (2.12)—i. e., the true gentleman is more than a mere specialist. According to commentators, the hu and lian were precious jade food-offering vessels that were the most important ritual vessels in the ancestral temples of the Xia and Shang dynasties, respectively. Commentators point out that Confucius' elaboration is double-edged: comforting, in that Zigong is no ordinary vessel, but perhaps even more critical because the hu and lian vessels were both archaic curiosities (no longer used in the Zhou rites) and extremely specialized (thus seldom used even during Xia and Shang times). Zigong was a highly accomplished statesman, skillful speaker (11.3), and successful businessman (11.18), but Confucius seems to have felt that he lacked the flexibility and sympathy toward others characteristic of Goodness. This is perhaps why Confucius uses Zigong as his audience for his teaching about understanding in 6.30 and singles out Zigong for his message that "be understanding" is the one teaching that can serve as a life-long guide in 15.24. Zigong seems to be the disciple designated throughout the Analects to illustrate the shortcomings of dutifulness uninformed by understanding. Here,

---

① made of jade.

his fastidious adherence to the rites leads Confucius to dub him a "sacrificial vessel" of limited capacity; in 5.11, his claim to be understanding is sharply dismissed by the Master; in 5.18, a person he presumably admires is dismissed as being dutiful but not Good; and in 14.29, he is criticized by Confucius for being too strict with others (i.e., for not moderating his duty-based demands on others with understanding). See also 9.6, 9.13, 11.13, 13.20, 14.17, 17.19.

【例 36】 子曰:"君子不器。"(《论语·为政》)

Legge: The Master said, "The accomplished scholar is not a utensil."

Ku: Confucius remarked, "A wise man will not make himself into a mere machine fit only to do one kind of work."

Lau: The Master said, "The gentleman is no vessel."①

Ames & Rosemont: The Master said: "Exemplary persons (*junzi* 君子) are not mere vessels."

Slingerland: The Master said, "The gentleman is not a vessel."

Qi 器, literally a ritual vessel or implement designed to serve a particular function, is also used metaphorically to refer to people who are specialized in one particular task. Although some commentators take this passage to mean that the gentleman is universally—rather than narrowly—skilled, the point seems rather that the gentleman is not a specialist (cf. 6.13, 9.2, 9.6, 13.4 and 19.7). As Li Guangdi explains,

> We call a "vessel" someone who establishes a name for himself on the basis of a single ability. Consider Zilu's ability to collect taxes, Ran You's ability to serve as a steward, Gong Xihua's ability to regulate the etiquette of host and

---

① i.e., he is no specialist, as every vessel is designed for a specific purpose.

guest [5.8], and even Zigong's ability to serve as a "precious jade vessel" [5.4]—these are all cases of being a "vessel" in this sense. The learning of the gentleman emphasizes the perfection of Virtue over attainment in the arts, and perfection in behavior over the mere accomplishment of tasks. Somewhere in Yan Hui's manner of seeing and hearing, speaking and moving, or Zengzi's appearance, attitude, and demeanor ... we can discern the working of Virtue—this is what it means to "not serve as a vessel." Taking this passage to mean that there is nothing the gentleman does not know or nothing that he cannot do is simply to fall back into the trap of "vessel"-thinking.

【例37】 叔孙武叔语大夫于朝,曰:"子贡贤于仲尼。"子服景伯以告子贡。子贡曰:"譬之宫墙,赐之墙也及肩,窥见室家之好。夫子之墙数仞,不得其门而入,不见宗庙之美,百官之富。得其门者或寡矣。夫子之云,不亦宜乎!"(《论语·子张》)

Legge: Shu-sun Wu-shu observed to the great officers in the court, saying, "Tsze-kung is superior to Chung-ni."

Tsze-fu Ching-po reported the observation to Tsze-kung, who said, "Let me use the comparison of a house and its encompassing wall. My wall only reaches to the shoulders. One may peep over it, and see whatever is valuable in the apartments. "The wall of my Master is several fathoms high. If one do not find the door and enter by it, he cannot see the ancestral temple with its beauties, nor all the officers in their rich array. "But I may assume that they are few who find the door. Was not the observation of the chief only what might have been expected?"

Ku Hungming: An officer of the Court in Confucius' native State, expressing admiration for a disciple of Confucius, remarked in presence of the other Court officers: "In my opinion this disciple of Confucius is superior to Confucius himself." Afterwards, when somebody reported what the officer had said to the disciple above referred to, the latter said: "Let me use the comparison of two buildings. The wall of my building only reaches to the shoulders; one has only to look over and he can see all that is valuable in the apartments. But the wall of the Master's building is hundreds of feet high. If one does not find the door to enter by, he can never see the treasures of art and the glory of the men that are in the holy temple. Perhaps, however, there are few men who have found the door. I do not therefore wonder that the officer spoke as he did."

Lau: Shu-sun Wu-shu said to the Counsellors at court, "Tzu-kung is superior to Chung-ni." This was reported to Tzu-kung by Tzu-fu Ching-po. Tzu-kung said, "Let us take outer walls as an analogy. My walls are shoulder high so that it is possible to peer over them and see the beauty of the house. But the Master's walls are twenty or thirty feet high so that, unless one gains admittance through the gate, one cannot see the magnificence of the ancestral temples or the sumptuousness of the official buildings. Since those who gain admittance through the gate are, shall we say, few, is it any wonder that the gentleman should have spoken as he did?"

Ames & Rosemont: Shusun Wushu said to the other ministers at court, "Zigong is a better man than Confucius." Zifu Jingbo reported this to Zigong. Zigong replied, "Let us take a perimeter wall as an analogy. My wall is shoulder high, so one can catch a glimpse of the charm of the buildings inside. The Master's wall, on the other hand, is massive, rising some twenty or thirty feet in the air. Without gaining entry through the gate, one cannot see the magnificence of the ancestral temple or the lavishness of the estate inside. Since those who gain entry are few, is it surprising that the minister speaks as he does?"

Slingerland: Shusun Wushu remarked to his ministers at court, "Zigong is an even greater worthy than Confucius." Zifu Jingbo reported this to Zigong.

> Shusun Wushu was a high minister in the state of Lu, a member of the Shu Family. Zifu Jingbo was one of lower ministers in his court; cf. 14.36 for his friendly attitude toward Confucius.

Zigong replied, "Let us use the analogy of a residence surrounded by a wall. The walls around my residence are only shoulder-high, so people can look over them and see the beauty of the chambers and apartments within. The walls of the Master's residence, on the other hand, are fifteen feet high. This means that, unless one is able to enter through the gate, one cannot see the fineness of the ancestral temples or the luxuriousness of the various offices. Those who have been able to enter through the gate are rather few, so it is not at all surprising that your master spoke as he did."

> We see here the beginning of the myth of Confucius as a mysteriously transcendent and incomprehensibly profound being that became the basis of his deification in the Han. Zigong was one of the more successful of Confucius' disciples, eventually serving as a high minister in the states of both Lu and Wei—a much higher position than Confucius ever obtained—which is probably why he is singled out for praise by third parties here and in 19.25.

【例38】 子曰:"夏礼,吾能言之,杞不足征也;殷礼,吾能言之,宋不足征也。文献不足故也,足则吾能征之矣。"(《论语·八佾》)

Legge: The Master said, "I could describe the ceremonies of the

Hsia dynasty, but Chi cannot sufficiently attest my words. I could describe the ceremonies of the Yin dynasty, but Sung cannot sufficiently attest my words. (*They cannot do so*) because of the insufficiency of their records and wise men. If those were sufficient, I could adduce them in support of my words."

Ku: Confucius remarked to a disciple, I can tell you of the state of the arts and civilization during the Hsia dynasty [say the Greek civilization]①; but the modern State of Ts'i [say modern Greece] cannot furnish sufficient evidence to prove what I say. I can tell you of the state of the arts and civilization during the Yin dynasty [say Roman civilization]; but the modern state of Sung [say Italy] cannot furnish sufficient evidence to prove what I say. The reason is because the literary monuments extant are too meager, — otherwise I could prove to you what I say."

Lau: The Master said, I am able to discourse on the rites of the Hsia, but the state of Ch'i② does not furnish sufficient supporting evidence; I am able to discourse on the rites of the Yin, but the state of Sung does not furnish sufficient supporting evidence. This is because there are not enough records and men of erudition. Otherwise I would be able to support what I say with evidence.

Ames & Rosemont: The Master said: "I am able to speak on ritual propriety (*li* 礼) during the Xia dynasty, but its descendent state, *Qi*, *does* not provide adequate evidence. I am able to speak on the ritual propriety during the Yin dynasty, but its descendent state, Song, docs not provide adequate evidence. It is because these states

---

① see Note, Chapter II, section 23.
② After the overthrow of the two dynasties, the descendants of the Hsia were enfeoffed in the state of Ch'i while those of the Yin were enfeoffed in the state of Sung.

have inadequate documentation and few men of letters. If they were adequate in these respects, I would be able to give the evidence for what I say."

Slingerland: The Master said, "As for the rites of the Xia Dynasty, I can speak of them, but there is little remaining in the state of Qii to document them. As for the rites of the Shang Dynasty, I can speak of them, but there is little remaining in the state of Song to document them. This is because there is not much in the way of culture or moral worthies left in either state. If there were something there, then I would be able to document them."

Qii was a minor state in which the remnants of the Xia royal line were enfeoffed after their defeat by the Shang, and Song was the state where the remnants of the Shang were enfeoffed after their defeat by the Zhou. Neither of these states was successful in preserving their cultural traditions, unlike the state of Lu—the home of the Zhou cultural tradition—where the essence of Zhou culture could still be found. The most cogent interpretation of this passage is that of Zheng Ruxie, who explains:

> Qii and Song had lost the ritual practices of the Xia and Shang, as evidenced by the fact that there was no remaining culture or moral worthies left in these states that could document these cultures. Lu, on the other hand, was not like this: with regard to culture, it still possessed the classic documents, and with regard to worthiness, it possessed the Master. How is it that none of the rulers and ministers of Lu saw fit to examine this evidence? Thus, in making this comment the Master did not really have Qii or Song in mind, but was instead using the examples of Qii and Song to express his opinion, for it is in fact particularly with regard to Lu that the subtle point of his words are directed.

Here again, we have a rebuke of the Lu leadership for its neglect or flouting of its cultural heritage. Also compare this passage with a later, slightly elaborated version in *the Record of Ritual*.

【例39】 子曰:"苗而不秀者有矣夫! 秀而不实者有矣夫!"(《论语·子罕》)

Legge: The Master said, "There are cases in which the blade springs, but the plant does not go on to flower! There are cases where it flowers but fruit is not subsequently produced!"

Ku Hungming: Confucius once, speaking of the career of his many disciples, remarked: "Some only sprout up, but do not flower; some only flower, but do not ripen into fruit."

Lau: The Master said, "There are, are there not, young plants that fail to produce blossoms, and blossoms that fail to produce fruit?"

Ames & Rosemont: The Master said, "There are indeed seedlings that do not flower, and there are flowers that do not fruit."

Slingerland: The Master said, "Surely there are some sprouts that fail to flower, just as surely as there are some flowers that fail to bear fruit!"

Commentators from the Han to the Tang take this passage together with 9.20 and 9.21 as specifically referring to Yan Hui's untimely death. Zhu Xi, on the other hand, takes it together with 9.17 and 9.19 as a general comment on self-cultivation: "Learning that is not completed is like this, which is why the gentleman values self-motivation." As Huan Maoyong notes, an argument in favor of this latter interpretation is that it also makes 9.22 fit well with 9.23. Both interpretations are plausible.

【例40】 子曰:"鲁卫之政,兄弟也。"(《论语·子路》)

Legge: The Master said, "The governments of Lu and Wei are brothers."

Ku: Confucius remarked of the state of government of his own State and that of another State in his time: "The one is about the same as the other."

Lau: The Master said, "In their government the states of Lu and Wei are as alike as brothers."

Ames & Rosemont: The Master remarked, "The governments of Lu and Wei are elder and younger brother respectively."

Slingerland: The Master said, "In their forms of government, the states of Lu and Wei are like elder and younger brother."

One interpretation of this cryptic remark is that of Bao Xian, who notes that Lu was given as a fiefdom to the descendents of the Duke of Zhou, and Wei was given to the descendents of Kang Shu—the fourth and seventh sons, respectively, of King Wen. The two states were thus founded by brothers, and presumably had similarly virtuous governments as a result. Su Shi, on the other hand, takes it as a negative comment on current affairs:

This comment was made in Year 7 of Duke Ai of Lu's reign (489 b. c. e.), which corresponds to Year 5 of Duke Chu of Wei's reign. In the government of Wei at this time, fathers were not behaving as true fathers and sons were not behaving as true sons, 7 and in the government of Lu, the lord was not acting like a true lord, and the ministers were not acting like true ministers. 8 In the end, Duke Ai fled to Zhu and ended up dying in Yue, and Duke Chu escaped to Song and also ended up dying in Yue. Thus, their situations were not so different.

Most likely, both senses of Lu and Wei being "like brothers" is meant, and this is how Zhu Xi takes it: "Lu was the fiefdom of the descendents of Duke Zhou, and Wei of the descendents of Kang Shu, and thus, the two state were originally founded by brothers. In Confucius' age, moreover, both had declined and become disordered to the point that their governments resembled one another, and this is why the Master voices this lament."

【例 41】 哀公问社于宰我。宰我对曰:"夏后氏以松,殷人以柏,周人以栗,曰,使民战栗。"子闻之,曰:"成事不说,遂事不谏,既往不咎。"(《论语·八佾》)

Legge: The Duke Ai asked Tsai Wo about the altars of the spirits of the land. Tsai Wo replied, "The Hsia sovereign planted the pine tree about them; the men of the Yin planted the cypress; and the men of the Chau planted the chestnut tree, meaning thereby to cause the people to bein awe."

When the Master heard it, he said, "Things that are done, it is needless to speak about; things that have had their course, it is needless to remonstrate about; things that arepast, it is needless to blame."

Note:哀公, see Ⅱ. xix. Tsai Wo, by name 予, and styled 子我, was an eloquent disciple of the sage, a native of Lu. His place is the second west among the wise ons. 社, from 示(ch'i), 'spirit or spirits of the earth,' and 土 means 土地神主, "the resting-place or altars of the spirits of the land or ground Wo simply tells the duke that the founders of the several dynasties planted much and such trees about those altars. The reason was that the soil suited such trees; but as 栗, "the chestnut tree,' the tree of the existing dynasty, is used in the sense of li 慄 to be afraid,'. he suggested a reason for its planting which might lead the duke to severe measures against his people to be carried into effect at the altars. 其他如夏后氏、殷人、周人的注解略(作者)。

Ku: The reigning prince of Confucius' native State asked a disciple of Confucius about the emblems used on the altars to the Titular Genius of the land.

The disciple answered, "The sovereigns of the House of Hsia planted the pine tree; the people of the Yin dynasty adopted the cypress; and the people of the present Chou dynasty has chosen the *li* (chestnut) tree as a symbol of awe (*li*) to the population."

When Confucius afterwards heard of what the disciple said, he remarked, "It is useless to speak of a thing that is done; to change a course that is begun; or to blame what is past and gone.

Lau: Duke Ai asked Tsai Wo about the altar to the god of earth. Tsai Wo replied, "The Hsia used the pine, the Yin used the cedar, and the men of Chou used the chestnut (*li*), saying that it made the common people tremble (*li*)."

The Master, on hearing of this reply, commented, "One does not explain away what is already done, one does not advise against what is already accomplished, and one does not condemn what has already gone by."

Ames & Rosemont: Duke Ai asked Zaiwo about the altar pole to the god of the soil. Zaiwo replied: "The Xia clans used wood of the pine (*song* 松), the Yin peoples used the cypress (*bai* 柏), and the Zhou peoples used the chestnut (*li* 栗). It is said that they wanted to make the people fearful (*zhanli* 战栗)." When the Master heard of this, he said: "You don't discuss what is finished and done with; you don't remonstrate over what happens as a matter of course; you don't level blame against what is long gone."

Slingerland: Duke Ai asked Zai Wo about the altar to the soil①. Zai Wo replied, "The clans of the Xia sovereigns used the pine tree,

---

① The altar of the soil, one of the most important religious sites in a state, was marked with a sacred tree.

the Shang people used the cypress tree, and the Zhou people used the chestnut tree (*li*). It is said that they wanted to instill fear (*li* 栗) in the people."

Having been informed of this, the Master remarked, "One does not try to explain what is over and done with, one does not try to criticize what is already gone, and one does not try to censure that which is already past."

The *Annals* tells us that the altar to the soil in the state of Lu was destroyed by fire during the fourth year of the reign of Duke Ai (Legge 1994d: 804). This is probably the reason for his questioning of Zai Wo, who at the time was apparently being employed by the Duke as a ritual specialist. In his answer, Zai Wo is playing upon a graphic pun between *li* 栗 "chestnut" and *li* 栗 "fear, awe" (later distinguished with the heart radical, *li* 栗)①. There are many ways to understand this passage. Perhaps the simplest interpretation is that of Kong Anguo and others, who see it as a rebuke of Zai Wo's reckless speculation: different states used different trees to mark their altars because of variations in local growing conditions; to derive significance from a pun as Zai Wo does is both foolish and insulting to the ancients. Alternately, Confucius saw Zai Wo's comment as being critical of the Zhou, and thus a violation of ritual propriety—especially when speaking to one of the Zhou's direct descendents, Duke Ai. Perhaps more interesting are interpretations that see this exchange as a coded reference to current affairs. In addition to their sacrificial function, altars to the soil doubled as sites of public executions. Some commentators see the Duke's question as an oblique way of suggesting that he use force against those in the state who oppose him, and Zai Wo's answer ("it is said they wanted

---

① It is possible that the other tree names had similar double meanings as the result of puns: "pine" (*song* 松 being graphically similar to *rong* 容 ("accommodating") and having the phonetic *gong* 公 ("just, public"; "lord") and "cypress" (*bo* 柏) being similar to *po* 迫 ("to press") or *pa* 怕 ("quiet, still"; "to fear").

to instill fear in the people") as an implicit approval of this strategy. There is some variation in which commentators identify as the specific players in this drama, but the explanation of Liu Baonan is representative:

It seems to me that "that which is already past" refers to the actions of Ji Pingzi①. Pingzi did not act as a minister should, even going so far as to force Duke Zhao from power. No doubt Duke Ai saw this "past action" of Pingzi's as the root of his current troubles, and wished to announce his crime in order to bring punishment down upon his descendents. This is an example of "trying to censure what is already past." However, the loss of favor experienced by the Ducal House and the devolvement of real power into the hands of the ministers was not brought about in a single day. Duke Ai does not yet realize that "one should employ one's ministers in accordance with ritual" (3.19), and furthermore he was not yet capable of employing Confucius. Instead, he impatiently wants to make a show of power in order to vent his anger, and thinks he can rely upon this to recapture his lost power and influence. This, of course, will not work at all, and this is why the Master tries to restrain him with his comment.

---

① The Ji Family head who is the probable target of 3.1 and who, with the help of the other infamous Three Families, attacked his lord, Duke Zhao, and forced him from office.

后　记

　　时光荏苒。我要衷心感谢所有在我的学术路上给予我支持关照的学校、导师、专家、同仁、编辑以及我的家人。

　　第一，我要感谢在牛津大学访学期间，该校老师们拓宽了我的学术视野。海外访学经历使我体会到中西文化的差异以及西方受众对中国文化接受的复杂性，使我认识到提高中国文化自信与坚定中西文化融通体系建构的重要性。而《论语》作为中国儒家文化的代表作，既是经典的，又是世界的。因此，《论语》翻译传播的重要性也不言而喻。

　　第二，我要感谢山东大学、香港浸会大学与香港中文大学以及上海外国语大学在我求学研究期间提供的学术平台。我要衷心感谢博士导师孙迎春教授、联合培养博士生导师张佩瑶和陈善伟教授以及合作博士后导师冯庆华教授。导师们渊博的知识、严谨的治学态度、敏锐的科学思维以及谦虚的作风让我敬佩不已。

　　第三，我要感谢在上海立信会计金融学院工作期间，"立信"文化带给我的启迪与力量。"立信"之名源于《论语》中"民无信不立"之意，学校的起源可追溯到由著名教育家、会计学家、"中国现代会计之父"潘序伦先生于1928年创办的立信教育事业。学校恪守"立信"校训，秉持"立诚明德、经世致用"的大学精神，坚持把科研创新作为兴校之源，重视中华传统文化对外传播，并在丹麦设有孔子学院。这也是为什么我对中国儒家经典《论语》翻译传播一直特别重视的原因之一。

　　第四，我要感谢各位专家、同仁以及家人的大力支持。本课题在研期间，我潜心向学，不畏艰难，克服各种科研工作与教学工作压力，在各位专家、同仁以及家人的帮助鼓励下终于得以完成这部专著。

第五,我要感谢立信会计出版社对本书的大力支持,尤其是彭秋龙编辑,对本书进行多次修订与完善。他的严谨的学术态度与求真务实的工作精神令我非常敬佩。

路漫漫其修远兮,吾将上下而求索。我会在追求学术的道路上不断探索,勇敢前行。

由于学术能力有限,书中难免会有疏漏之处,敬请专家学者给予批评指正。

范敏

2023 年 7 月于上海